With my best wishes for
peace on Earth among all peoples

Jeo Rempel
5-15-2015

Letters of a Mennonite couple
Nicolai and Katharina Rempel
Russia: War and Revolution
1914-1917

Letters Edited by Teodor Rempel

Translated by Teodor Rempel
with Agatha Klassen

CENTER FOR
MENNONITE BRETHREN STUDIES
2014

Letters of a Mennonite couple
Nicolai and Katharina Rempel
Russia: War and Revolution
1914-1917

© Copyright 2014 by Teodor Rempel

Center for Mennonite Brethren Studies
1717 S. Chestnut Avenue
Fresno, California
USA 93702

ISBN: 978-1-877941-16-0

Library of Congress Cataloging-in-Publication Data
has been ordered.

All rights reserved. With the exception of brief excerpts for reviews, no part of this book may be reproduced, stored in a retrieval system or transmitted in whole or in part, in any form, by any means, electronic, mechanical, photocopying, recording or otherwise without prior permission of the publisher.

Cover Design by Cooperative Effort

Printed in the United States by Print Source Direct

Dedicated To
Nicolai and Katharina Rempel
and their Descendants

Wedding Katharina and Nicolai Rempel July 20, 1909

CONTENTS

Acknowledgement vii
Preface ix
Introduction xv
Nicolai's Diary Entry xxii
Letters
Part One: Rempel Letters 1914 1
Part Two: Rempel Letters 1915 31
Part Three: Rempel Letters 1916 121
Part Four: Rempel Letters 1917 161
Epilogue 219
Family Heritage Bible 240
Bibliography 245

ACKNOWLEGMENTS

According to Sam Sacks, "self-promotion runs like a viral strain throughout every acknowledgments page."[1] This page may be infected with that strain against which, I am afraid, there is little safeguard other than caution.

These letters of Nicolai and Katharina Rempel are published and archived largely at the encouragement and guidance of Professor Paul Toews, historian and archivist at Fresno Pacific University. He has scoured the manuscript of errors and added valuable historic information. His contributions and my debt to him are spelled out more fully in the Preface. I am indebted to Agatha Klassen for her assistance in translating the letters from German. To decipher the old German script that harkens back to the sixteenth century is essentially a lost skill. Thanks to Olga Shmakina for her help with the Russian.

I am indebted to James Urry, Professor Emeritus at Victoria University of Wellington, New Zealand, who has been most helpful and encouraging. He wrote his PhD dissertation at Oxford on Mennonites. He is not "one of us" or, as the Mennonites would say in Plautdietsch, "*Hee es nijh eena fonn oons*," and as an outsider, he brings a special perspective and understanding, a more cosmopolitan picture of the Mennonites that is reflected in his extensive publications. Professor Urry went through the manuscript line by line, suggesting emendations, correcting errors in historical facts, recommending other historical sources. Many of the explanatory footnotes were provided by him. I owe him a special debt of gratitude.

Thanks to Professor John B. Toews, Regent College, Vancouver, British Columbia, (*Hee es eena fonn oons*) whose encouragement to publish the letters and whose scholarly writings on Mennonite history were an invaluable resource to me. I would be remiss if I did not acknowledge my debt to the late Professor David G. Rempel whose knowledge of the Russian Mennonite story through personal experience and extensive scholarly work places him at the vanguard of Mennonite historians.

Thanks to my brother, Bernard, who has spent years faithfully archiving family photos, drawing up genealogies, and keeping other family records. The few photos herein do not begin to reflect the help and encouragement he so generously supplied. And thanks for those silent but nevertheless substantial contributions of my late brother John, an ethnic Mennonite, who took one of the first Mennonite bus tours in the late 1980's to our ancestral home in Ukraine. He brought back from that tour, guided by John B. Toews, a renewed interest in the social values of our Mennonite ancestors and tried to kindle them in Nicolai and Tina's decedents.

I thank all those from whose comments and support I have benefited, especially

---

[1] Sacks, Sam, "Endorsements," *The New Yorker* (August 24, 2012), p. 63

to Martin Lind, Chuck Pennington, my son David Rempel, and to other family members.

And to my wife, Doris, if the measure of her love and support in this project alone were taken, she would stand front and center in my life. But to factor in the more than six decades that she has with grace and quietude borne my foibles, even as my dear mother, Tina, put up with those of my father, Nicolai, then I have to reach for the words of the poet to express my gratitude, "and, if God choose, I shall but love thee better after death."[2]

---

[2] Browning, Elizabeth Barrett, "Sonnets from the Portuguese 43: How do I love thee?" *The Norton Anthology of English Literature* Vol. 2, (New York: W. W. Norton & Company, 1968), p. 1148.

PREFACE

    The letters in this volume are from the correspondence of my parents, Nicolai and Katharina (Tina) Rempel, written while Nicolai served as a medic in World War One in Russia, caring for wounded soldiers as they were being carried from the front to receiving hospitals. These and other letters came into my possession unexpectedly in April 1956. I had been home six months earlier when my mother died, and now I had been granted another leave from my teaching position in California to return to my father's bedside in Canada. I spent ten days with him. Although bedridden and very weak, he was still able to recount the family history in lucid and, I presume, reasonably accurate detail: the story of our ancestors' migration from Prussia to New Russia (Ukraine) early in the nineteenth century and a brief biographical sketch of his seven brothers and two sisters. Some of the talk was difficult for both of us. It was an attempt to become reconciled, to try to understand what had happened between us and why I had become so alienated from my Mennonite roots.

    The day before I left, my father told me that he had something for me. He asked me to get the two bundles of letters that lay in a drawer in his desk among other papers. Each of the bundles was held together with twine, probably the same twine that bound them when my parents brought them from the Soviet Union to Canada in 1925. He told me that he was placing these letters in my trust because I seemed to show much interest in the family history.

    "These letters are what is left of the correspondence Mother and I had while I was away in the forestry service for two years and then away again in the war. I am giving these letters to you. Take from them what you see as worth preserving for the family history and then burn them. They have some matters that are rather private." I had seen these two packages several times in my childhood but had no idea of their significance. There were some 350 letters.

    When I returned to California, I put the letters into a trunk where they lay for three-and-a-half decades, my conscience pricking me now and then, reminding me of my father's request. Only once during those decades were they opened. When my sisters, Alice, Hilda and Selma, mentioned frequently in those letters, came to visit my wife, Doris, and me in 1980, I asked them if they would like to read some of the letters. They began going through them carefully, reading in silence, then reading portions out loud, reminding each other of certain incidents, laughing and shaking their heads. But for whatever reason, they left most of them unread and turned their attention back to knitting, to gossiping about people they knew and to church matters. After they left, I read some of the letters before returning them to the trunk, finding myself somehow uncomfortable looking at my parents' past at such close quarters.

    In 2007, my wife and I joined the Mennonite Heritage Cruise in Ukraine down the Dnieper River from Kiev to Odessa, stopping along the way to visit what was left of ancestral Mennonite villages. The cruise included lectures on Mennonite history given primarily by Professor Paul Toews, historian and archivist at Fresno Pacific University. In one of his lectures, he touched on events in Moscow in 1917, events in which my father had participated and had described in one of the half dozen of my parents' letters that I had brought along on the cruise. I gave them to Paul to peruse and he then suggested to me that the letters might be of some historic value and should be archived and perhaps published. So it is largely at Professor Toews's encouragement that I took on the task of translating and editing my parents' letters, going some distance beyond what my father had asked me to do. I am greatly indebted to Paul Toews for his encouragement, for guiding me through the steps to publication, for reviewing the manuscript and putting right historical facts and perspectives, and for archiving the original letters in the Mennonite Library and Archives, Fresno Pacific University.

Most of the letters were written in German, and because Russia was at war with Germany, correspondence in that language was suspect. Some government restrictions were placed on the use of German, especially in personal correspondence; however, these regulations were poorly enforced except in a few regions. The reason that the letters were written in German is explained below in greater detail; suffice it to say for now that my parents, as mentioned already, were Mennonites whose ancestors had emigrated to South Russia (Ukraine) from Prussia early in the nineteenth century and who continued to cling to German, their mother tongue, decades after they had settled in Russia.

Even though I consider myself fluent in German, the translations proved somewhat problematic for me. First, because the German spoken by the Mennonites when these letters were written a century ago was even then rather antiquated vis-à-vis that spoken in Germany. Translating that parlance into contemporary English was a challenge. Secondly, my mother's (Tina) letters were written in an antiquated German cursive, known variously as *Frakturschrift* or Gothic script[3]—a script that can be read today only by few older persons, even in Germany. I have no problem with the Gothic print or the so-called Roman script used by my father, Nicolai, but I am unable to read Gothic cursive with any measure of fluency. Fortunately, Agatha Klassen, a Canadian Mennonite lady who had command of Gothic script, translated them for me. I am greatly beholden to her for her help. I edited the letters to fit more appropriately into the context and contemporary idiom of what I felt the letters were saying. The most difficult of all translations, except poetry, is letters with their nuances and idioms. To find the right words to convey a nuance or to translate into current English what was written in German 100 years ago and to avoid transliteration, called for much more patience, more time and energy than I had anticipated. To revisit parents long after they are gone is a privilege few people have. However, it was not an easy confrontation.

---

[3] *Fracturschrift* or *Gothic* script, as it is variously known, originated in the sixteenth century. In 1911 the Berlin graphic artist, Ludwig Sütterlin, at the behest of the Prussian Ministry of Culture, refined and standardization *Frakturschrift*, known after that as *Sütterlin Schreibschrift* (cursive) The latter was taught in German schools from 1935 until 1941. The script used by Tina predates Sütterlin by some centuries. Nicolai uses contemporary script much like English.

I alluded above to the attempt at reconciliation with my father. That issue deserves some explanation as it may shed some light onto the strongly held religious views expressed in these letters. I was born in 1929, the tenth of twelve children of a Russian Mennonite family that had immigrated to Canada in 1925. My parents and five siblings left behind them in the Soviet Union a decade of war, revolution, starvation and two graves of little children who had died of malnutrition shortly before the family emigrated. They brought with them a few of their personal belongings, some photos, the letters included in this volume and a debt to the Canadian government[4] for steerage. They also carried with them a fundamental faith that knew no distinction between religion and the Mennonite culture. That culture, although narrow, was rich within its confines. It included among other assets the knowledge of three languages: German, Plautdietsch and Russian. In our home German was the official language. Plautdietsch[5] was the parlance of our Mennonite friends and neighbors. Our parents often spoke Russian with each other and with their older friends. We siblings spoke English with each other as soon as we learned that language. It was the practice in our home to read the Bible daily: the New Testament at morning devotions and the Old Testament at evening devotions, of course, always in German, as were the prayers we children had to recite. Church services were also conducted in German, and so German became the language of God. Furthermore, my father was the minister in our little Mennonite Brethren church and knew my every move as he delivered the Word from the pulpit. My childhood knew no clear distinction between religion and culture. We were taught God created the world in perfect order, and that that order had been shattered by Satan, and I could be redeemed to God's holy order only by acceding to the demands of the Mennonite Brethren Church. The attitude of this denomination toward the world was not only fundamentalist,[6] curbed by a Russian Mennonite ethnicity, it attempted to establish a church community whose members were to live a life of personal godliness. It was essentially exclusionary.

When I gained my post-pubescent consciousness, however, I saw this concept of my place in the universe as quite out of step with the world order around me. The demands that the older Russian Mennonite generation placed on their Canadian-born children precipitated in many a rebellion born of an anti-authoritarian skepticism against the church and its community. The departure of my generation from the Mennonite (church) community was a loss to the older generation as well as to those of us who left, some in bitter disappointment. That

---

[4] Immigrants were brought to Canada by the Canadian Pacific Railway, remuneration for steerage guaranteed by the Canadian government if not paid by the passengers within a specified time. My parents were able to submit their final payment in 1942. See Ted Regehr, "The Economic Transformation of Canadian Mennonite Brethren," in Paul Toews, ed., *Bridging Troubled Waters: Mennonite Brethren at Mid-Century* (Winnipeg: Kindred Productions, 1995), p. 99.

[5] *Plautdietsch*: Also known as Low German, its origin is Flemish and lowland German with some Polish, Russian and Ukrainian thrown into the mix. It is one of the numerous dialects of Low German.

[6] Fundamentalism is essentially exclusionary, requiring strict and literal adherence to its set code. Although usually ascribed to religious groups, any ideology can fall prey to it, be it atheism, communism, even some groups functioning under the guise of liberalism. Fundamentalism in any form is dangerous because in its extreme form will abide no view but its own and has been known to burn people at the stake for differing with its belief. I once referred to the Mennonite Brethren in Yarrow and Coaldale as Christian El Qaida and was promptly upbraided.

schism somehow diminished the integrity of both. We were no longer integrated—"No longer at ease here, in the old dispensation."[7] So in our attempt to leave that identity behind, we turned to the secular community trying to find a place there to fill the vacuum, to calm the spiritual unrest, but often found ourselves ill at ease there also with its social behavior and code. The yearning for that residual Mennonite culture—its naiveté, its blunt trustfulness, its surface openness, its concerns for others, its inside jokes, its zwieback—but without the yoke of its religiosity.

Saul Bellow, to whom I am indebted for some of the reflections above, said in his Nobel Laureate speech that "to turn away from my [Jewish] origins, has always seemed to me an utter impossibility....One may be tempted to ... invent something better, to attempt to reenter life at a more advantageous point. In America this is common, we have all seen it done, but the thought of such an attempt never entered my mind. Thus I may have been archaic, but I escaped the horrors of an identity crisis." I, like many other Canadian Mennonite youth, was not so fortunate. Turning away from my origins, as did some of my siblings, caused my parents and me much grief. They could not accept the "way of the world" that I had taken, nor could I accept their way. Consequently clashes arose during those years. In my files there is a letter that my father handed me when I, a teenager, came home from a party after two o'clock one morning. It stated that he would have to resign his position as "bishop" of the church because of my conduct.

But as my parents aged they became more accepting of their wider community, less exclusionary. They had welcomed into our family four non-Mennonite daughters-in-law. On occasion my father exchanged pulpits with other denominations, he worked with the Red Cross, Alcoholics Anonymous and with other community organizations. I, too, had changed. Now I was sitting at my dying father's bedside, both of us negotiating some kind of truce, as it were. Before he gave me the bundles of correspondence, he asked me to forgive him for the wrongs he had done me. Was placing the letters in my trust his way of forgiving me for the pain I had caused him? Was that trust a reaching out to embrace a prodigal son?

J.B. Toews, in the introduction to his *Pilgrimage of Faith*, says, "The word 'remember' serves as a continuous exhortation to review the past so we can understand the present...interrelationship of the present with both the past and the future receives marginal attention today." And he is right, the problem of identity, or should I say the loss of it in this age, plagues the modern thinking person. Perhaps the current trend to trace genealogies speaks to the void of identity.

The Bible admonishes us to honor (i.e., to respect) our parents. The word *respect* derives from Latin the verb *respicere* 'look back at,' that is, to give our parents a second look. Rabbi Shimon bar Yochai said, "The most difficult of all the mitzvot is to honor your father and mother (Tachuma, Ekev 2). There is no limit to the honor that is due to them, and often obedience to this commandment is taxing."

---

[7] Eliot, T.S., "*Journey of the Magi*" in *The Complete Poems and Plays, 1909-1950* (New York: Harcourt, Brace and Company, 1958), p, 68.

> Moskauden 9 Mai 1916.
>
> Mein innigstgeliebtes Weib & Kinder!
> Aus den letzten Zeilen meines vorigen Briefs
> siehst Du das ich nicht mehr im Hospital bin,
> sondern in der Kanzelei arbeite. Schrieb
> damals den Brief vor mittag, hatte ihn
> aber weder durchgesehen noch ein kowertet.
> Ging denn aufwaschen, & wie ich das hatte, da
> legte ich mich hin um ein Mittagschläfchen
> zuhalten, nichts von einer Veränderung

Nicolai's letter in German script Deutsche Normalschrift

Tina's letter in Frakturschrift

INTRODUCTION

Background to Correspondence of
Nicolai and Katharina Rempel in Russia During WWI

As mentioned in the Preface, the letters in this book are some of the correspondence of my parents, Nicolai and Katharina (Tina) Rempel, an exchange of letters that occurred while he was in the service of the All Russian Zemstvo Union from September 1, 1914, until November 1917, in World War I. Nicolai and Katharina were Mennonites. Their forefathers had migrated from Prussia/Poland to New Russia—today Ukraine—beginning in the 1780s. Mennonites were among the wave of foreign immigrants who came to settle the new lands that Tsarina Catharine had taken from the Ottoman Empire. They came because of generous inducements the Russian state offered—land and various economic benefits, relative cultural isolation where traditional culture and language could be perpetuated, and freedom to practice their distinctive religious traditions and exemption from military conscription.

The first Mennonites arrived in New Russia in 1789, and settled in what became known as the Khortitsa settlement (or colony). Nicolai and Katharina's forebears came later to the Molochna settlement, established in 1804. Katharina (Tina) was born in Berdiansk, Sea of Azov, but grew up in the Schoenfeld settlement, a smaller cluster of farms and landed estates just north of the Molochna colony. Nicolai grew up in Mariental, a village some thirty kilometers (versts) north of the Sea of Azov in the Molochna settlement.

Mennonites, because of their religious beliefs, were a nonresistant Christian people who refused to bear arms, insisting on and receiving exemption from military service before emigrating from Prussia in 1788. That "eternal exemption" was codified by the charter (Privilegium) received from the Russian state. During the great reforms of Tsar Alexander II, following Russia's defeat in the Crimean War in 1856, that exemption was threatened. Legislation requiring universal military service took effect on January 1, 1874. During the next six years Mennonites negotiated a compromise whereby forestry service would be an acceptable alternative. Thus their eligible young men were assigned to work at forest care and tree planting. Mennonites and the Russian government jointly funded the camps in which they were housed. The system remained in place through the intervening years and during World War I. An added form of service during the Great War was working on hospital trains run by the Red Cross under the auspices of the All Russian Zemstvo Union. Between the onset of the war July 1914, and the Russian withdrawal from the war in the spring of 1918, some 7,000 of Mennonite young men, roughly 50 percent, met their military obligation by working as medics (Sanitäter) on these hospital trains.[8]

Nicolai entered the service about a month after Germany declared war on Russia on July 24, 1914. This was his second tour of duty. He had already completed an obligatory service in forestry (Försteidienst) from 1910 until 1912. Now only two years later, he had to leave his family again.[9] After very brief basic training as a medic in a Red Cross hospital in Ekaterinoslav (Ukraine), he found himself heading to Moscow with hundreds of other medics. There he became part of the staff on Royal Red Cross Hospital Evacuation train No. 10/160 that carried wounded soldiers from the battlefield and transported them to military hospitals in Minsk, Moscow, Kiev, St. Petersburg and other receiving stations.

These letters tell the story of Nicolai and Tina, two insignificant players in the "theater of war." A few of their letters are carefully honed, but most are dashed off in haste by husband and wife reaching out to each other, trying to maintain a marriage that was challenged by their physical separation and the demands of daily struggles during war. There are no letters extant from Katharina (Tina) in 1914, although we know she had written Nicolai because his letters suggest an exchange. Whether these were not saved or simply lost is unclear. Some of their letters during the four years of their correspondence were lost due to the failing of the Russian mail system and Nicolai's frequent change of address, at least from 1914 until 1916, after which he was stationed in Moscow.

The first letter of record was written on September 10, 1914, while Nicolai was waiting to be shipped out to Moscow, where he boarded a train that would essentially be his home for the next year and a half. His mood in this letter was upbeat, and like most Mennonite servicemen who were doing alternate service as conscientious objectors (CO's) in Russia at the onset of WWI, he was very patriotic. He expressed his patriotism in a few lines he entered in the little notebook he carried with him.[10] He was not prepared, however, for the horror that met him when he arrived at the battlefield at Brest-Litovsk.

What Nicolai experienced and recorded in his letters when his train arrived at the battlefront in early October fleshes out the report that M. V. Rodzianko, chairman of the Russian Duma, (Parliament) sent to Tsar Nicholas II. Upon hearing accounts about the lack of proper medical care for the wounded, Rodzianko visited the battlefield that led to the following report:

---

[8] The historical perspective by Professor Paul Toews.

[9] Technically Mennonites are not pacifists but non-resistant Christians opposed to violence, war and serving in the military. Mennonites only had to perform alternative service in Forestry camps according to the agreement made in the 1870s. During the Russo-Japanese War (1905/06), some young men elected to perform their service as medical orderlies. This set a precedent for WW1. Even so, Mennonites could not be forced into this kind of service; they had to volunteer (although I suspect not all understood this). When war broke out, there were differences in opinion about what should be done. Khortitsa wanted to serve the state through the agencies being set-up by the Zemstva organizations – rural and urban. Although the debate tended more to the conservative, it eventually they followed Khortitsa although the Forestry camps continued. (This historical perspective by Professor James Urry).

[10] *"How good it is that the father of this land, Nicholas II, has such loyal subjects. And I am pleased that I too can contribute something to the welfare of this our Fatherland, but I fear that I am not up to the task yet because this is the first time I am on my way to the battlefield to help the wounded soldiers"* (Nicolai's Diary).

After the first battles, reports began to come from the front about the disturbing state of sanitary affairs in respect to the movement of the wounded.... The confusion was complete. Freight trains came to Moscow, in which the wounded lay without straw, often without clothing, badly bandaged, and unfed for several days. At that time my wife, supervisor of the Elizabeth Society, received reports . . . that such trains were passing by their detachments and even were standing at the stations, and the nurses were not admitted to the trains and remained idle....

Worst of all was the rendering of first aid by the military: there were neither wagons nor horses, nor first aid supplies, and moreover, other organizations were not allowed to go to the forward areas....

Soon after my arrival at Warsaw in 1914, Vyrebov . . . came to me and proposed that we visit the Warsaw-Vienna station, where there were about 17,000 men wounded in the battles at Lodz and Berezina. At the station we found a terrible scene: on the platforms in dirt, filth and cold, in the rain, on the ground, even without straw, an unbelievable quantity of wounded, who filled the air with heartrending cries, dolefully asked: "For God's sake, order them to dress our wounds, for five days we have not been attended to." It must be said that after the bloody battles these wounded had been hauled in complete disorder in freight cars and abandoned at the Warsaw-Vienna station without aid. The only medical forces that attended these unfortunates were Warsaw doctors, aided by volunteer nurses...[11]

That is the scene that met Nicolai when he arrived at Ivangorod on October 8, 1914, at the front (battlefield). Because Russia did not have enough hospital trains at the beginning of the war, some of the wounded were transported in freight cars fitted with roughly constructed wooden benches that served as beds. In a few instances freight cars that had just carried horses to the front were hastily swept clean of the manure, straw was strewn on the floor and the wounded were laid down on the straw.

Nicolai worked as a medic caring for the wounded until early 1916, when, quite burned out and after many requests for transfer, he was assigned to the Administrative Headquarters of the Zemstvo in Moscow. He was in Moscow in March 1917, when Tsar Nicholas II abdicated and the Provisional Government collapsed, and at the onset of the Bolshevik Revolution in late 1917.

Most of the time during those years, Tina was living with her parents on the Peters' estate in Schoenfeld, caring for her three little daughters and doing all she could to earn her keep in that household. Other sisters were often there, too, with their children while their husbands were away in the service. As a result the atmosphere became stressful, especially between the daughters and their mother. When the stress became too great, Tina went to live with her mother-in-law, Sara Rempel, in Mariental, a quieter setting a day's journey away.

The letters reveal a story that has been experienced by countless couples separated by war. It is unique in that it records the day-to-day struggles of Nicolai and Tina as they try to hold their marriage together. They write intimately of their feelings for each other, and about their three little daughters, Alice, Hilda and Selma,

---

[11] *Excerpt from report of* M. V. Rodzianko, "Krushenie Imperii," *Arkhiv Russkoi Revoliutsii* (Berlin, 1926), XVII, 82-85, translated by J. S. Curtiss, in *The Russian Revolutions of 1917* (New York: Van Nostrand, 1957).

as Tina tries to raise them. At times he becomes so exasperated at their situation that he censures her harshly, but in his next letter he begs her forgiveness and declares his deep love and affection for her. They talk about their parents, their siblings and friends, and gossip about those who make up their daily life. The letters stitch together a mosaic of a married couple, a mosaic that shows how difficult such a separation can be, severely stressing a marriage where problems can be worked out mainly on paper. This stress has shattered many marriages. But Tina and Nicolai's marriage was solid, lasting until her death in 1955.

These letters, however, tell a story of more than that. They are a record not only of the brutality of war that Nicolai witnesses, but also the desperate longing for family and the boredom and numbing of the spirit. Nicolai writes about the horrific scenes he experiences at the fringe of the battlefield near Brest-Litovsk; the terrible suffering of the wounded and the dying as they are transported from the battlefield, loaded into the medical evacuation trains and carried to one of the 1,600 receiving hospitals. His early letters describe the terrible scenes, and he expresses outrage at the savagery the soldiers suffer. He turns to his religious faith for support against the pain and confusion that grow with his exposure to the conveyer-belt of broken bodies. Suffering must mean something. It must have a purpose: "…if God wants, He can stop this carnage…" Nicolai writes to Tina. It is inconceivable for him to see God as an absence or as a meaningless void and so he reaches for meaning to an immediate and personal God. One might be dismissive of Nicolai's "simplistic" answer to suffering. Viktor Frankl insists that life holds a potential meaning under any condition, even the most miserable ones but how we hold that meaning is a personal choice.[12] As the war wears on, Nicolai seems to become somewhat inured to the suffering and his religious convictions seem to be tempered, but he never abandons his personal God—a God who is in control.

While the cost of these experiences followed him throughout the days of his life, he was able to harvest from them slowly through the years what J. J. R. Tolkien called an eucatastrophe—to bring the impact of catastrophe to a favorable resolution. But that mitigation in Nicolai and Tina's life is not explicit in these letters. Only their correspondence from the beginning of the Great War in 1914 to the collapse in late 1917 when Nicolai returned home to his family is recorded here, and one must draw from the letters what I hope will help each to work for peace on this earth.

When Nicolai was transferred to the United Council of Nobility headquarters in Moscow, it was a welcome relief from the continuous exposure to suffering and death. But as Russia experienced defeat after defeat, her armies retreating, soldiers deserting and returning to their homes and to Moscow, many with their weapons, he recorded the gradual decline of civility in that city as it moved into chaos and revolution. There are moments of hope for a better life, however. On May Day, 1917, he and many of his fellow Mennonite medics joined thousands of soldiers, factory workers, common laborers, and a mass of other Russian citizens to march in great joy to the Palace of Labor where thousands gathered to celebrate the New Revolution—the dawning of a new freedom for the common man and equity for

---

[12] See Frankl, Viktor *Man's Search for Meaning* (New York: Simon and Schuster, 1984), Preface.

all, where officers march arm in arm with common soldiers to the *Marseillaise*. Nicolai joined that march to the new freedom and espoused Democratic Socialism. He writes home an account of this "great day" and asks Tina if the home front has joined in the revolution. Nevertheless, at the sunset of that joyous day in Moscow, gray clouds are beginning to gather over this city and soon he sends home reports of increasing food shortages, and escalating civil disorder and violence.

Nicolai and Tina came from the confines of Mennonite communities that had for years been somewhat sequestered from the larger Russian culture. Furthermore, the Mennonite communities had, beginning in the 1860s, undergone a religious revival that had precipitated a schism within many communities. Generally, the well-established, wealthier landed gentry were content with the established church and less inclined to the pietism that began to take hold through preachers coming from Germany and America, calling for spiritual reform and the need for a "personal conversion experience" to gain salvation. The emotional pietistic movement appealed largely to the less well educated and the poor, especially the landless, whose numbers in the Mennonite communities had increased in proportion to their population over the years as land became scarcer and wealth shifted to those at the top of the socio-economic ladder. The Rempel family, although among the landed and better educated, experienced the schism. Most of Nicolai's six brothers had completed high school (*Oberrealschule*) and three were teachers. Two had studied at the Teachers Academy in St. Petersburg. Some remained in the established Mennonite church while others, like Nicolai, his brother Hermann, his sister Tina and their mother were caught up in the spirit of revival and broke away to the more pious Mennonite Brethren church.

Tina and Nicolai's religious faith sustained them during their years of separation that were followed by revolution, anarchy, famine and disease that swept through South Russia, especially in Mennonite settlements. At one time brigands broke into their home, lined them up with their children against a wall at gunpoint and took what they wanted. On his deathbed my father told me once more how his life had been saved when a Makhno[i] bandit forced him at gunpoint against a tree to execute him. A brigand who knew my father intervened to save his life. Was that an angel sent by God as my father claimed? In spite of their personal harrowing experiences, they were fortunate. In many Mennonite villages, especially on large estates, the owners were murdered, their women raped, homes sacked and their possessions carried off by the bandits in the wagons of owners.

The anarchy of 1918 and 1919 was followed in the 1920s by a semblance of order as the Soviet government began establishing itself in South Russia, but the reordering of the political system was accompanied by economic mismanagement. The transformation from the ordered agricultural structure that had existed before 1914 to a system, which worked effectively only on paper, was administered largely by inexperienced bureaucrats. The redistribution of land to inexperienced peasants, the lack of farm equipment and seed grain, and the demand for quotas of grain to be delivered to government facilities, along with severe drought, resulted in starvation that took hundreds of thousands. Starvation claimed two of Nicolai and Tina's six children, Irma and Eduard. A letter written by Nicolai in June of 1923 (see Epilogue) gives us a glimpse into starvation and hope, an anomaly that I, who have never hungered, cannot fathom. In the letter their little daughter, Irma, talks to her Papa about her hunger and hope that food will arrive from America. Food does arrive but it is too late for little Irma. "In these our most trying hours we found comfort in the words of our Lord and Master," Nicolai writes. That faith sustained them through the rest of their lives.

The story told in these letters is not singular. It has been told since time immemorial, not recorded perhaps as Nicolai and Tina have done. The story continues today as soldiers return home from the battlefield and millions starve.

Teo Rempel

PRELUDE

"You must never write history until you can hear the people speak." Arthur Hebbert

The Emperor

Emperor Franz Joseph, even on this day at age 84, had risen before dawn and after having said his prayers on his knees, was at his desk by five o'clock as usual, behavior he had been following most of the sixty-six years as sovereign of the Austro-Hungarian Empire. He would on this day, July 13, 1914, sign a document—an ultimatum to Serbia—that would touch off World War I.

Although always averse to entering war, the old Emperor now was too exhausted to stand up against his ministers to avoid the conflict with the rebellious Serbs, who were seeking to break away from Austrian control. Only days before, on June 28, the Emperor's nephew, Francis Ferdinand, Archduke of Austria, and his wife had been assassinated in the Serbian capital, Sarajevo. Two of the Emperor's ministers had taken the opportunity of the assassination to draft a list of ultimatums they knew Serbia would not agree to, thus giving Austria an excuse to subdue Serbia through military action. The Emperor had resisted signing the document. Under pressure and lies concocted by his ministers, however, he had given in and with hands shaking so severely that his signature was scarcely legible, Emperor Franz Joseph had issued the ultimatum to Serbia that would lead to World War I. With that signature he had signed the death warrant of millions of people. It would draw all of the great nations of Europe into the conflict and toward the end the United States, also.[13]

On July 28, 1914, exactly one month after the assassination, Austria-Hungary officially declared war on Serbia. She had secured the backing of Kaiser Wilhelm II of Germany. Russia, having a treaty with Serbia, had entered the war in support of Serbia, but Russia had treaties also with France and Britain. So by August 6, 1914, all major countries of Europe found themselves moving their troops into the carnage that would last until November 11, 1918. In the Great War, as it came to be known, some 10 million soldiers and millions of civilians died.

The Recruit

On September 1, 1914, one month after the start of the war, 26-year-old Nicolai Abram Rempel, husband of Katharina (Tina) and father of three little girls—Alice, Hilda and Selma—found himself on the way to war. He had risen before 2:00 a.m., and by 3:00 a.m. he left his village, Marienthal, in South Russia where he had grown up and was on his way by droshky[14] to a railway station some thirty verst (kilometers) away. There he would join 329 other Mennonite inductees being

---

[13] G. J. Meyer, *A World Undone: The Story of the Great War, 1914 to 1918* (New York: Delacorte Press, 2006), p. 26.

[14] Droshky: A horse-drawn coach. The driver of a Reitdroshky rides one of the horses.

mobilized into the Russian military as medics. They would care for wounded Russian soldiers being transported from the battlefield in evacuation trains to hospitals in Moscow, St. Petersburg, Kiev and other cities.

During the first few months of his service, Nicolai carried a small notebook in his pocket, a diary of sorts, in which he made entries whenever he had time. Information in the diary entries sometimes formed a basis for his letters, but usually in greater detail. In the first entry below, i.e. of September 1, 1914, he relates his experience on the day he leaves for the war. Some of the other entries are included in the Epilogue. Tina wrote many letters in 1914 also but none of hers have survived.

From Nicolai's Diary
Entry September 1, 1914

It was still early in the morning when we arrived at the Stulnevo railway station [Nicolai uses the German name Waldheim; the Russian is Stulnevo] at Gnadenfeld where the reservists from the Gnadenfeld Volost (District) who had been notified to report for basic medical training in Ekaterinoslav had gathered. Ten railway freight cars fitted with wooden benches were waiting for us when we arrived. Some 330 of us recruits were leaving for the war and at least as many family members and friends had come along to the station to bid us farewell.

My wife, my sister Tina, and my brother Heinrich had driven me to the station. It was three o'clock in the morning, a beautiful full moon night, when we left my home in Mariental to cover the thirty versts to the Waldheim station where a train was waiting for us. My dear wife pressed close to me as I to her. All was silent except for the muttering of wheels of the droshky and the thumping of the horse's hooves as it trotted along the dirt road carrying us to our destination. Neither of us said a word, although both understood what the other wanted to say. But beneath the calm façade, a storm was raging wildly in each of us. What will happen? Will we even see each other again? Perhaps we are sitting so close to each other for the last time. And what will happen to our little ones, our three little girls, if I am killed at the front in the battlefield, by a shot that will erase everything. These thoughts pushed my heart into my throat as they stormed through my mind.

War! How horrible, how horrible! "But you Lord will take care of everything. You have assured us that not a hair will fall off our head without your willing it."

When we arrived at the railway station on the east end of Waldheim, we joined the rest of the milling crowd that had already gathered to bid farewell. We were standing by our loved ones among the gathered crowd, some silent, others chatting quietly, a few weeping, when the commanding officer asked the mayors (Schulze) from each region if all of their recruits were present, and then we were marched to the row of railway cars waiting for us, and after each of us had found our carriage and loaded our gear, we looked out at our loved ones in a final auf Wiedersehen. Only a few wives had come to the station and most of them were now weeping bitterly; however, my dear wife, Tina, stood like a hero in stoic silence. She did not cry. No one would have thought that she was taking leave of her husband who was heading into war. She did not want to make this separation, this terrible moment, more difficult than it was. But most could not contain their feelings, tears streaming down cheeks as the train slowly began to move out of the station.

For one last moment our eyes met—my wife's and mine—and then we were carried away from the waving hands and diminishing cries of "auf Wiedersehen" drowned out by the train's whistle as it, too, bade farewell while it carried us to the next station and into the unknown.

But our attitudes soon turned upbeat as we greeted friends and acquaintances, and in short time the train came to a halt in Halbstadt. Here again a huge crowd had gathered to confusing excitement and anguish. I stepped out of the carriage immediately to look for my brother Aron. I had pushed only short distance into the crowd when I came upon the Wilmsen family, his in-laws, standing there pressed together and weeping, so I assumed that Aron must be there also. But just at that moment, Aron shouted to me quite joyously from the window of the carriage assigned to Halbstadt inductees. Other friends and acquaintances also waved greetings to me—Hermann Hamm and John Adrian, among others. I turned briefly to say good-bye to the Wilmsen family before going to the carriage to greet those men.

The stop here was only ten minutes, so the farewells were brief before the train shuffled out of the station away from the families bidding farewells to the recruits with shouts of auf Wiedersehen, some waving handkerchiefs, some weeping, some few standing silently. That was the last we saw of them as Halbstadt disappeared behind and we moved on to Lichtenau. Along the railway line stood many inquisitive people who had been unable to come to Halbstadt. They waved to us sadly as we passed by in the mourning train (Trauerzug) as it was called by some of the recruits.

When we arrived at Lichtenau, the whole station again was full of Mennists (Mennonites). As at the other stops, here the scene was similar—the sad farewells, some embracing, some waving their handkerchiefs. And there was weeping here, also. This was our final stop. "Auf Wiedersehen! Auf Wiedersehen!" came the cry from all quarters, and then we were away from our loved ones and our homes. Many a longing look was cast as we passed other Mennonite villages along the way, and all was silent except for some sighing and the rumbling of the railway carriages. Silent turmoil—what would happen to us? What would the future bring us? When would we return to our homes, if at all? Would we ever see our homeland again? Thus we sat silently almost to Ekaterinoslav as we rocked back and forth on our benches until someone said, "Hey, you can see Ekaterinoslav," and we were all stirred out of our reveries to look out of our railway carriages at our future.

THE LETTERS
PART ONE

Letters of Nicolai and Katharina Rempel 1914

Sketch by Doris Rempel

The letters of 1914 include only those written by Nicolai. We know that Tina wrote to him because he acknowledges having received some letters from her, but none of hers have survived, apparently lost. The first letter of record (September 10) is from Nicolai just after he had competed some brief basic training as a medic [Sanitär] in Ekaterinoslav, South Russia [Ukriane]. He was waiting to be shipped out to one of the 136 Tsar's Red Cross Evacuation Hospital trains that carried wounded soldiers from the front to military receiving hospitals in Moscow, St. Petersburg, Kiev and other cities.

From Nicolai
Ekaterinoslav, September 10, 1914

My dearest wife and children!

You will probably realize why I haven't written so long because we discussed it when I last saw you. I, with 800 other men, am waiting every day to be shipped out from Ekaterinoslav to what we think will be Moscow, but because nothing has happened so far, I will try to explain to you how we are spending our time here.

I have to pause briefly because just now a soldier came to announce that all of us are to appear before the military commander without delay because we may be moving out immanently.

I'm back again. Nothing has happened with our moving out today, so who knows when it will be. However, we are having a great time here. Two thousand men have already been moved out, some here and some there. Brother Julius transferred out, too, on Monday [to another branch of service]. I guess he didn't want to be a medic. We asked him many times to stay on with us so that we four brothers could be together, but he wasn't willing to do that. Every day we have to appear at Headquarters and stand there for several hours at times, and then we are sent back to our barracks again. If we want to leave, we have to get special permission from Jakob Dick, Manja's husband, who is chief medical officer over 100 of us.

Willy [Tina's brother] visited us yesterday. He is very happy that he doesn't have to leave for Moscow. One of the medics is lying in the hospital with typhoid fever. Another one received a telegram yesterday that his wife had died. A third one received a message that his child had died. So happiness and sadness are mixed together here, too. Mennonites from all of European Russia are gathered here, and there are many happy meetings but also, soon after, sad farewells. Many, probably most of them, have been sent away already. Our superiors are very good to us and we have nothing to complain about. The room in the barrack in which I live with three other men is very practical. We have a kitchen, a washroom with running water, and water heating. I share a nice room with an Ivan Ivanovich Dyck and a Berg from the Crimea. In the evening, devotions (singing hymns, Bible reading, prayer) are held in the second or third stories because they have large meeting rooms there, whereas the rooms in the ground floor are not big enough.

I will close for today but will write more frequently from now on. Please continue to send your letters but write at top of the envelope, "If address cannot be located, return letter to sender." We often gossip about our wives here what good and wonderful persons you are and that you make life so comfortable for us. Thank you for everything that you sent along with me, even those things I thought I didn't want; it turns out they are really quite helpful to me. Don't forget to pray for me. Be faithful and courageous.

With heartfelt kisses and hugs I am, Your Nicolai.

And greet everyone, parents, grandparents, siblings, uncles and aunts

From Nicolai
Ekaterinoslav, September 12, 1914

My dear Tienchen,

I will quickly write a letter and send it to you with Peter Heidebrecht,[15] who is here right at the moment. Just moved out of our clean and comfortable barracks into a dreadful rat- and lice- infested hole. We all regret the move, but the barracks we occupied in the last while are to be converted into a hospital, so this puts us into our third residence since I came here. There's still no word about our being moved to Moscow. Yesterday, seventy-five of our men were hired by the city to do various menial moonlighting jobs, and they will likely stay on here. Last night, fifteen men

---

[15] Peter Kornelius Heidebrecht (1868-1941), a minister and supervisor of a Forestry camp (see Aron A. Toews, *Mennonite Martyrs: People who suffered for their Faith*, edited and translated by John B. Toews, (Winnipeg: Kindred Press, 1990), pp. 100-07 (Note by Urry).

were sent to work in a hospital in Kherson, and it could happen that we will be shipped out on short notice. If the people in Schoenfeld were sensible, they would establish a hospital there for wounded soldiers, and it is possible that we would be sent there to nurse them. They would have to begin the process of organizing this project right away, however. I was told that if each household were to take in two wounded soldiers to care for, we could be assigned to assist with their care. Well, there's much babbling going on here also, and you have to sift through what you hear pretty carefully in order to get to any truth.

Today for the first time I ate a good meal here in the city. Until now I have been eating the borscht that has been our endless diet here to the point of nausea and the tables and dishes are so filthy—you just can't imagine. We have put out many a kopek for food, whether we want to or not because we get only one meal a day, so we have to buy the rest ourselves.[16] I borrowed a small box of coffee from Schroeder. Will you replace it, please?

When you write, use this address: City Ekaterinaslav, N. A. Rempel, to General Delivery.

Ask Papa to write this address for you; he knows how it is written. Many greetings and kisses, from your Nicolai.

From Nicolai
Ekaterinoslav, September 16, 1914

Dear Tina!

There is an opportunity to send mail to Schoenfeld with Aron Rempel, who apparently is here now and I hope to find him. This will be my last letter from Ekaterinoslav. Tomorrow at 8:00 a.m., 400 of us men are being sent to Petrograd. Because this is a congenial group of men, our trip should go well. I don't know how everything else will go, but time will tell. I'll keep you informed of where we are and how our trip is going. You could write as soon as you receive this letter so that there will be a letter waiting for me when I arrive at our new posting.

Thank you so very much for your last letter, the cookies, the apples and the coffee. And thanks also for the handkerchiefs; I didn't have very many left. You are so loving and kind to think of everything, even wanting to do extra sewing for pocket money. I have enough money now to buy food to last me for some time. We

---

[16] Immediately after Germany declared war on Russia in July 1914, the Mennonite elders urged their young men to volunteer as medics. They authorized funds to support these servicemen and their families and thus demonstrated their patriotism in their support of the war effort both financially and with volunteers. This action was an attempt to underscore their loyalty to Russia, their Fatherland, and to Tsar Nicholas II, their commander in chief. Because of their Prussian (German) heritage, the Mennonites were under suspicion as to their patriotism and came under attack in some newspapers questioning their loyalty. This patriotism was quite evident in Nicolai's family. All seven brothers rendered service to Mother Russia in one form or another but mainly as Red Cross medics. According to conversations with my father, Nicolai, the four Rempel brothers—Hermann, Aron, Nicolai and Julius—left home for basic medical training (medics) on the same train or at least within a few days of each other. Nicolai's brother Hermann served on the same train with him for a year and a half before he died of typhus (Note letter June 4, 1915).

have to buy food if we want to stay alive, and I try to be very frugal, but don't worry about me.

Your attitude regarding your sister Truda, encouraging her not to be so hypersensitive, is to be commended. Sometimes you may be overcome by jealousy when you see that she can visit her husband Schroeder [who had a desk job in Ekaterinoslav] and can even live with him for longer periods of time. So, my dear, be on guard and overcome evil with good. Whenever possible, be helpful and friendly toward her. I don't think I will be getting a furlough soon, but the greater will be our joy when I do get one or return home for good. But if God has another plan for us, we will see each other in heaven. Just hold your head high and don't lose courage.

There's little to write about from here, but the transfer to the new posting will provide more things to write about. Have to rush to the military chief and roll call now. If there is an opportunity to have my fur coat sent from Mariental [his family home] to Schoenfeld, please see to that. I won't need it unless it becomes very cold in Petrograd [St. Petersburg]. In that case it would be more convenient for you to send it from Schoenfeld. I'm almost rid of my cold and cough. Otherwise I am in good health. But I must hurry and finish because the others have already left.

Warmest greetings and kisses to all of you from your loving Nicolai.

P.S. Have you seen brother Hans? Greet the parents, grandparents, siblings, uncles and aunts. My address is: Petrograd, Nevski Bookstore, Raduga[17]—Forward to N. A. Rempel

From Nicolai
Evacuation Station
Medical Train No. 10/160
Moscow, September 29, 1914

My dear Tienchen,

We arrived here in Moscow today at 4 a.m. On arrival, 150 men were taken by the Zemski Union and the Red Cross, and 250 of us stayed on at the station for several hours. Then we were given an address and were marched off to that place, expecting a reception similar to the one we got at St. Petersburg. However, to our surprise we were received with a friendly welcome. The general, who met us right at the door, was very friendly, gave his assistant some money for us and told us that we should first go and enjoy a cup of tea and then go to our quarters. We were taken to a teahouse, enjoyed some tea and then wandered off to our living quarters.

Here each went to his room where everything was already prepared for us. Each was assigned a cot on which lay a sack filled with straw, a felt blanket as thick as a thumb that then served as a mattress, also a pillow with a white pillowcase, a clean white sheet and a blanket. Everything looked very clean. It seemed beautiful after sleeping in lice-infected barracks for a month. It was certainly the best a soldier could wish for. Our supervisor is very friendly. If this continues, our time here will

---

[17] Petrograd address is the publishing house associated with the Mennonite Brethren, Raduga (Rainbow), in Halbstadt that printed and distributed evangelical literature. (Urry)

be a pleasant experience. The food is clean and tasty. Everyone gets his own bowl of borscht.

Tomorrow, thirteen of our group will go to Lvov for a week to prepare for the wounded soldiers, and from there, after loading some wounded, we will probably leave to take them to various places in Russia. One thing will be somewhat troublesome, which is that I won't receive your letters easily because I'll be traveling a lot. Nevertheless, you should continue to write. I will give you this address and all mail will be forwarded from here. I would so like to see you and the children, but there is no possible chance for that. If at all possible, have a photo taken of you and the children by a skilled photographer and send it to me. Be joyful and courageous at all times and be a light in your surroundings.

Many thousands of greetings from your Nicolai

From Nicolai
Evacuation Station
Medical Train No. 10/160
Lvov, October 4, 1914

Dear Tina!

Things are going slowly—making little progress. That's the way it is on this trip, the train moving slowly closer to the war zone. We are sitting in Lvov for the third day, unable to proceed because of the over-burdened railways. We could get to Skorinsk, but we want to go further so that it doesn't matter where we are halted. We were just informed by telegram that our train must definitely leave tomorrow afternoon for Skorinsk. When we arrive there, we will be near the war zone—more accurately said—*in* the war zone. At the moment, our train is standing approximately one kilometer from the station—a Polish village on one side and Lvov on the other side.

When we arrive at the front, we will take at most forty-five wounded in each fourth-class carriage. This means there will be 135 wounded soldiers for every two medics. If the need is not so urgent, then we'll take in only twenty wounded per car. Our general says that it is better anyway for the wounded soldiers to be moved out of the war zone even if into these uncomfortable railway [freight] cars—it is much better than lying in the wet, cold trenches. Of course, it is clear to all of us what is best for the wounded men. Our decision will be determined when we see how many wounded there are and how many rail carriages will be available there.[18]

I will probably not help a great deal on this trip, as I was quite sick for a few days. [Cause of injury explained in next letter.] Now I have almost recovered. Our doctor came to my compartment frequently and did what he could to help me. The medical officers were also all around me showing their concern. Hermann Enns sat with me a lot and applied cold compresses. In other words, I was well cared for. But,

---

[18] Russia's attacks on Germany at the start of the War had ended in military disaster as fictionalized in Aleksandr Solzhenitsyn's *August 1914*. But Russian attacks on the Polish fronts in Galicia against Austro-Hungarian troops proved more successful, and it was to this area that Nicolai was sent to deal with the casualties from the extensive fighting. (Urry)

Eastern Front 1914

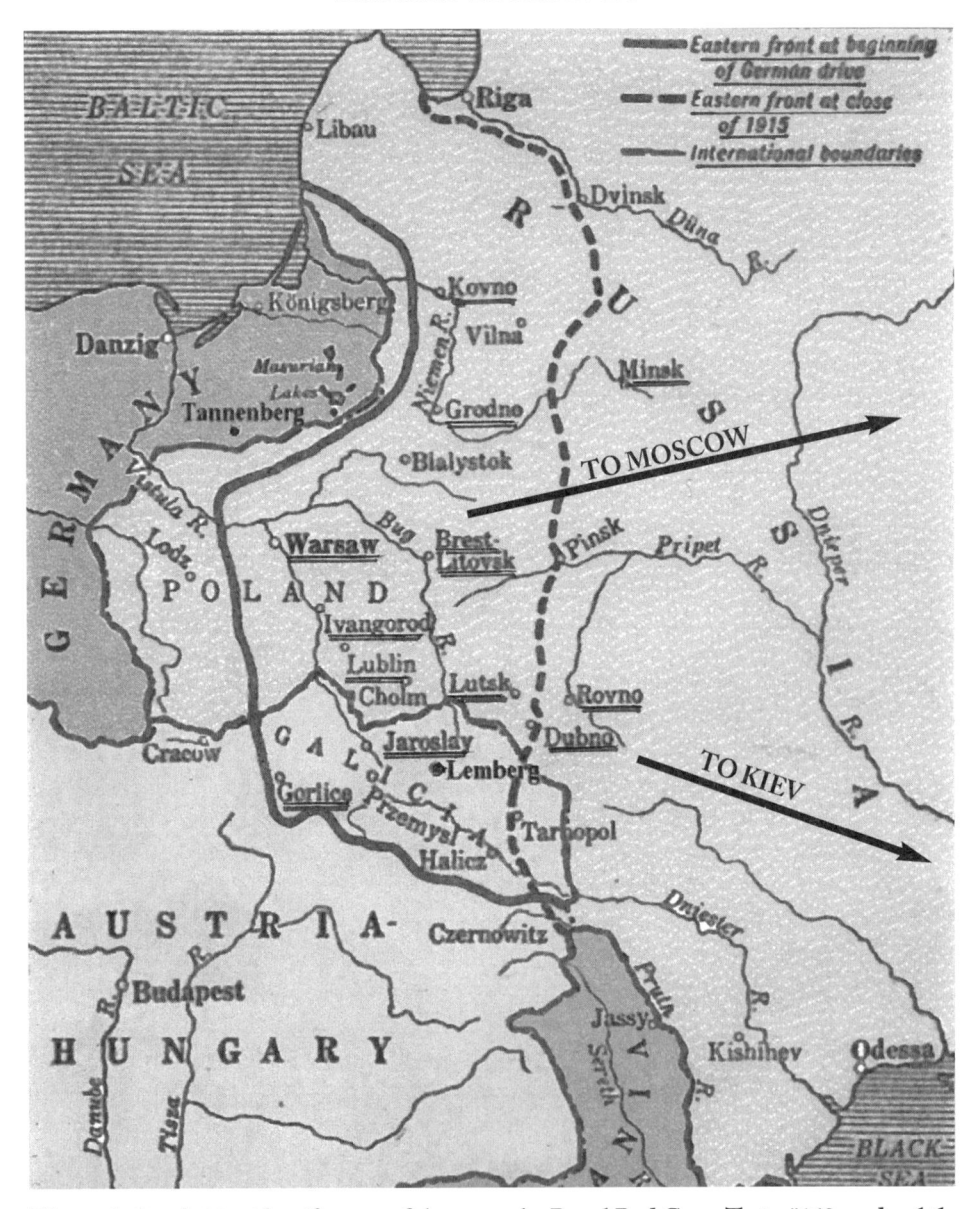

The underlined cities identify most of the stops the Royal Red Cross Train #160 made while Nicolai served on it as a medic. From these points on the front the wounded were transported to St. Petersburg, Moscow, Kiev and some 160 receiving hospitals away from the front. *Courtesy of the United States Military Academy Department of History.*

how good I would have felt if you had been my nurse. Your care can be compared to nothing else.

You must excuse me if this letter is brief and lacks content. I am healthy but very weak. In two or three days I will have recuperated completely because I am eating normally again. If you meet brother Heinrich, ask him if he has taken in any

Southern Russia 1914

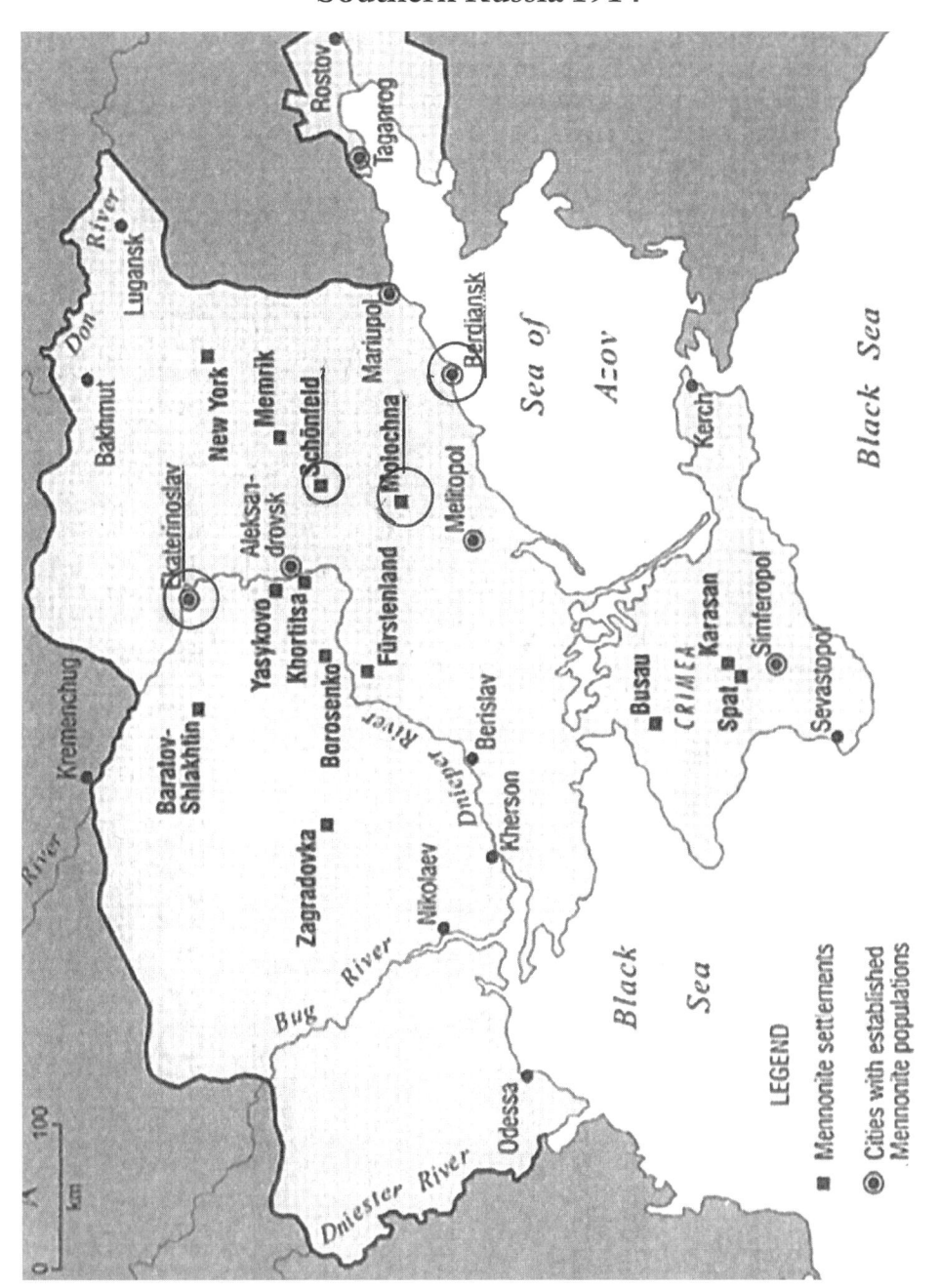

Map shows Mennonite colonies in Ukraine. Some 60 miles apart, Schoenfeld was Tina's home, while Mariental in the Molochna Colony was Nicolai's family home. Map is courtesy of James Urry, *Mennonite Politics and Peoplehood: Europe-Russia-Canada, 1525-1980* (Winnipeg: University of Manitoba Press, 2006), p 112).

money and tell him that he should definitely send me a few rubles. I will close for today.

Many greetings and kisses from your Nicolai.

From Nicolai
Evacuation Station
Medical Train No. 10/160
Borisovy, October 5, 1914

My dear wife and children,

As you could tell from the card I sent, I am no longer in Moscow but on the way to the battlefield. All is going well so far; everyone is cheerful and happy except Hermann Enns, who is suffering from a bad toothache. In Moscow I had some bad luck, too. I went to the sauna with the two Fast brothers and Jakob Enns. There Isaak Fast dumped some cold water on me and I wanted to do the same to him, but I slipped and fell backwards, ending up with a two-inch cut in the back of my head. When I fell I thought I had smashed my head into pieces, but I was lucky that only the skin was broken. I went to see the doctor right away, who bandaged it, and now I am fine, thank God.

Our train is moving out again. At the stations where the train stops, we usually have work to do, and we are glad when there is a change of pace. Boxes and bundles carrying various bandages and medical supplies have to be sorted, the water in the kitchen has to be replenished, etc. People always greet us very friendly when we arrive and tell us not to do the dirty work. But we know quite well that in order to keep an honest peace, we can't hold back from the work. There is always plenty to do, clean up the linen closets, etc. I showed one of the doctors the linen closets and asked if the closets always looked like that. "Unfortunately most of them are like that," was his answer. "I am afraid that the medical personnel here before you usually left things looking like that when they left. We are so happy that we now have eight men on duty who like order." Dirty laundry lay mixed with the clean, the dirty dishes from the previous tour remain unwashed, and in many carriages the latrines from the last trip are still full of night soil.

I didn't finish writing this letter yesterday. It is night and all around me people are asleep, except me and a man from a monastery. It is our turn to stand watch. Our carriages are not locked, so at each station we alternate making rounds, checking to see if everything is in order. It is a pleasant hour when we can be alone with God and our loved ones at home, even if only in Spirit. I am so blessed whenever I have the opportunity to sing those wonderful Christian songs that our Mennonites sing. It all seems so beautiful so my dear Tina sing a lot of those hymns. All of the recollections seems so precious to me now. That we are separated from each other once again may even be good for us.[19]

It is Sunday and in seven hours you will be going to church, but we will not celebrate a real Sunday. We are three stations away from Brest-Litovsk and then

---

[19] They had been separated for two years while Nicolai did his alternate service in forestry (See Introduction).

we must prepare everything again for the wounded. All the linens have to be washed, the beds made, the dishes cleaned, and meat and bread bought. Our Commander says that the people will come running to our train to beg for any piece of bread that we would consider stale and uneatable. And there will be plenty of the acrid smell of gunpowder for us, too. We will probably be back in Moscow in fourteen days or longer or perhaps in only one week.

Please address all letters as I told you, and please excuse my poor writing, but it is hard to write when the train is moving so fast. A thousand greetings and kisses from your Nicolai.

From Nicolai
Evacuation Station
Medical Train No. 10/160
Ivangorod, October 8, 1914

My Beloved Tina!

We arrived here in Ivangorod this morning but will probably move on during the night. There is much, so much, to see when one is so close to the battlefield. Here in Ivangorod a terrible war was raging only few weeks ago, but now only the distant thunder of the cannons is heard off and on as the enemy retreats. The Prussians have been driven back and drubbed quite thoroughly.

This morning our general took us out to have a look at that battleground—the fortifications, the trenches, the wasted fields and forests—where the battle had raged. We crossed the Vistula River and saw a great deal more of the ravages of the war. Well, words cannot describe at all as it actually is, but sometimes I feel it's regrettable that you, too, can't see all of this. It is quite remarkable how far the thunder of the cannon reaches as it shoots; its reach is especially far when it rolls down the course of the river. My description of this war scene is quite inadequate—words just cannot draw such a fascinatingly, horrible picture. [20]

Sometimes it seems to me that writing is quite useless because I don't know whether you have received any message from me. Your last letter is from October 13 [he means September 13] and I've received no letter from you since then. If you received a letter from me, there must surely be a letter on its return trip from you, too, or one waiting for me in Brest. I wrote you a card asking you to address letters to Brest now. Did you get it?

Here in Ivangorod everything is terribly expensive. We can hardly pay for our food. We did buy enough bread in Zemstvo and also a lot of meat, which, incidentally, we've already salted down. The bread was quite old and so dry that it has difficulty sliding down without butter. Well, we won't be getting to Moscow where the butter we asked you to send us should be waiting for us. Our coffee has also run out. Here it costs 1.40 kopeks per pound. I will burden you once more with a request. If it is possible, please send me by post, packed in a tin container, some

---

[20] Ivangorod was one of a number of Russian fortresses built along the Vistula and was the scene of fierce fighting with German and Austro-Hungarian troops in September and October 1914. See Norman Stone, *The Eastern Front,* 1914-1917 (New York: Scribner, 1976), Chapter 5. (Urry)

butter and coffee. Send it to Brest. Phone Frau Enns and ask her to send something for her husband, Hermann, to bring here on his return trip, or the two of you could put a package of things together for us. And tell the wives of Gerhard and Kornelius Fast to send half of the side of their recently butchered pig; this is Isaak Fast's request.

I just received a letter from Willy [Tina's brother] that was brought to me from Brest. I wrote him recently, gave him my address, and already have an answer. That seems fast to me. The poor fellow has now also volunteered as a medic. Well, I think he will be very disappointed if he gets it, although I wish him all the best.

According to yesterday's news, the Prussians are supposed to have suffered the loss of two military regiments and another one has been taken captive. Five more are totally surrounded and will soon be out of combat, too. So our Russians have taken eight military regiments in the last days—that is 36,000 men. If that's true, then there will soon be peace. Well, may God grant us peace very soon.

A thousand greetings from your dear Nicolai

From Nicolai
Evacuation Station
Medical Train No. 10/160
Brest-Litovsk, October 12, 1914

My dear Tinchen!

The 12th of October has slipped us by on the calendar once more, a day that will never leave my memory, nor yours either, I should think. We are at work very early today and things are being thoroughly scrubbed and brushed in our carriage. They say it is Sunday, but generally speaking it never seems like Sunday since our work goes on as usual whether Sunday or workday. This is our second time here in Brest-Litovsk and now our second day waiting for orders. Last time we were here for three days before taking on 450 wounded soldiers, transporting them to Moscow, unloading them, and then returning here to Brest-Litovsk. Yesterday our supervisor told us that we were going to Lvov to pick up wounded, but one never knows where we are going until just before departure. We asked our commander to request that the wounded we will be picking up now be transported to Berdiansk. That would make all of us soldiers very happy because you could all come to Berdiansk then. At the present time we all are terribly homesick for our wives and children, and I am probably not the least among the homesick.

I must give you a bit of an overview of how we transport these wounded men. I told you once before how our train is organized. In the middle of all the carriages are two for medics, surgeons, nurses, etc. Then next to our carriage is a carriage (second class) for wounded officers, and after that a carriage (third class) for seriously wounded soldiers. When we get to the place where we take on the wounded, we all stand in a group, i.e. line up in receiving order, the regimental surgeon, the surgeons, medics, nurses, etc.—near the carriage second class.

When the wounded are brought to us one gurney after the other, each carried by four men—a **gruesome** sight—on each gurney lies a man so seriously wounded that you can scarcely hold back tears. We are then instructed where to stand in order to receive our charges. Very slowly and carefully the gurney is set down and then we place the man on our arms and lift him into the carriage. It is most difficult, almost impossible, to carry or even to touch these fellows without causing them great pain. I have carried many by myself because it is usually easier if only one person handles him, but that is often not possible.

On our first trip (our introductory one) to the front, we took on about twelve very seriously wounded; the others could walk on unassisted because their injuries were primarily to hands, backs or arms, though serious nevertheless. Each of us medics is responsible for two carriages, twelve men in each for a total of twenty-four men. So we do a lot of running back and forth, bringing bread, tea, hot and cold water, and chopping wood to keep the stoves burning. Some of the less seriously wounded take over the heating of their stoves themselves and even fetch their own water. Sometimes we help these men write letters to their loved ones. At night we take turns keeping watch and answering their calls for any needs they may have. Everything moves at a fast pace, always something to repair or to clean, definitely no one stands around with hands in their pockets.

Usually we get along with the wounded men very well; however, we are in tight quarters and occasionally there are wounded who are quite dangerous. Recently one went berserk and chopped mightily into blocks of wood with an ax, believing them to be Prussians. Kornelius Fast wanted to help him, unaware of the condition of this man, and so he almost had an ax driven into his head. One has to be cautious. I thank God when we complete the day unharmed. However, such situations should not hold us back from our work because our brothers out in the trenches are in much greater danger. Secondly, we are never out of the sight of our Lord.

I had not finished this letter when word came that each of us was to load wood into his carriage, enough for several days. I split mine, loaded it, and finished my lunch. Yesterday we prepared our carriages from top to bottom because we were told that Prince Oldenburg was going to inspect our train, so everyone had to dig in once more; even those who usually stand around with their hands in their pockets had to help make everything spic and span. I had almost completed cleaning my two carriages when I received the message that the Prince would be arriving toward evening. I had worked very hard from early morning on to get my two carriages in order. It took a whole day to do this, but the carriages are spic and span ready for inspection: the beds made, sheets and pillow slips changed, dishes washed until shiny and bright, blankets and pillows fluffed up, wood split and stacked for the heaters.

Of course, after every trip a general cleaning has to be done. Each carriage is disinfected thoroughly to prevent contagious diseases from spreading. One has to deal not only with the wounds but also with many communicable diseases. The spread of all kinds of contagion is a constant threat, especially in a city like Brest, the biggest receiving station in these parts. There is also a very large fortress here and a flight field with many airplanes that fly around every day, but one's curiosity about them soon diminishes.

Just now we received the notice that we are being sent to Brody to get wounded (near the Austrian border). We are leaving in a couple of hours, and it will take at least three days to get there. Who knows when we will reach Moscow again to receive mail from you. We will bring this train full of wounded to Kiev, and from there we will go somewhere else again but we don't know where.

Jakov Ivanovich sends greetings. Well, the page is full and so my letter is completed. Many greetings from your Nicolai

From Nicolai
Evacuation Station
Medical Train No. 10/160
Rovno, October 15, 1914

My dear, dear Tina and children!

I wrote my last letter from Brest. Now, as you see, we have moved on a bit further to Brody. Left Brest Sunday night and arrived here in Rovno Monday the 13th at noon. Because it appeared that we would be sitting here at this station for a long time, our physician left right away for Brody in order to clear the way for our train so that we wouldn't have to wait so long. But it all seems hopeless because we have been here already for the third day with no prospect of moving on any time soon. The physician telegraphed from Brody that the railway was over-burdened with sidetracked trains. In Brody alone there are forty-five trains with soldiers [Could it be that these trains are loaded with soldiers destined for the front?] so no route through can be found.

We see quite a few German locomotives and freight cars that our Russians have captured from the Prussians. These are then loaded on to our flatbed railway cars and taken to the interior of Russia because our tracks have a wider gauge than the German tracks. We hear from reliable sources that the Prussians are taking a really good thrashing even though the newspapers don't report that any big battles are taking place. Perhaps Russia wants to inform us about our victories in one big announcement so that it will be a welcome surprise for all citizens.

The day before yesterday, we all walked into town. Yes, Rovno is a town! As we trundled through the streets, we were astonished at the unimaginable filth and squalor visible everywhere. Well, after all, it is a Jewish town. Essentially only Jews live here—of course, with some few Russians and probably quite a few Poles.

Must hurry because the Assistant Commander-in-Chief came just now to tell us that we would take on wounded soldiers here again and transport them to Kiev. So there is a lot of work ahead of us now because all the bedding and mattresses, etc., were placed into one empty carriage to be de-. However, the things were all put into storage without disinfecting them, so all the work was useless.

It is raining and night has set in long ago, but it sounds as if we will be loading the wounded yet today, and that means hard work and no sleep for anyone tonight, that's certain. Well, everything is in turmoil but things will eventually settle down. As far as I can tell, we will certainly have to go back to Moscow from Kiev because we have no more clean laundry for the next trip. We all hope to be in Moscow within one week so that we can finally receive letters from our wives.

Kornelius Fast wrote to his wife about butter. I will be getting some of that butter, too, so please settle with Mrs. Fast for my share. How are things going at home? What are you and the children doing? Is Selma talking already? I can't imagine what she looks like. Would it be possible to send a photograph of you with our children? Tina, I would like to tell you my dreams. Our first night in Moscow I dreamt that I was at home with you, but you didn't want to have anything to do with me, and as soon as you saw me you ran away. The next night I dreamt the same thing. Of course, this dream was totally foolish. The opposite will happen when I arrive home. Please write to me often.

Many greetings and kisses from your loving Nicolai.

From Nicolai
Evacuation Station
Medical Train No. 10/160
Brest-Litovsk, October 21, 1914

Beloved Tina!

Yesterday was a very pleasant day for us. We unexpectedly received letters from our wives. I received yours of October 7th and 13th and for that I thank you many times. Our previous commander was transferred and the general from Moscow who replaced him brought us the letters here to our train that is standing in Brest currently. We could have kissed this old General for delivering our mail. You ask if I need anything and I can tell you in a good conscience that I have managed well until now. I have money and our meals are provided for us now, as well as stamps for our letters, so you don't need to about me. I have been very frugal until now and will continue to be so.

I miss you and the little ones terribly and would give anything to be with you. Don't send the fur coat I requested because I can't use it here anyway. All of us bought leather jackets so that we don't have to be worried about the rain or the lice so much. Brother Aron wanted to stay with our train but he was in the city just at the time of our departure from Moscow and so, as I heard yesterday, he is still there.

By now you have received my letter from Rovno. I wrote you that we would not go to Goroge, but instead had to take wounded from Rovno to Kiev. On October 15 we took on 680 wounded soldiers at Rovno and brought them to Kiev. It was a very difficult trip that took two nights and a day, and there was no time to eat or sleep, so to speak. You get really tired working thirty hours without rest. But on the other hand, we do make up for that when we return to the front with our carriages empty. Well, we have to sweat a bit while preparing the carriages for our next assignment, like today when I scrubbed the floors in my two carriages very thoroughly. Now we're waiting for orders to move on from here. We don't know when this will happen.

On our last trip with wounded charges, I met the young Bayanov from Kharkov from whom we used to buy those caps. He lay among the other wounded and I would never have believed it was he had he not told me himself. The train was so terribly overcrowded that I had to care for thirty-five men. Here in Brest there are eight to ten Red Cross Evacuation Medical Trains waiting, but none are permitted to leave Brest. It appears that we will stay here for a whole week, and we will bring the wounded we take on then to Moscow. I have just had a thorough bath in my compartment that I had heated well. Here you have to be very careful not to become infected with lice. If you have a chance, please send me some underwear to Moscow. I still have enough of everything, but the first thing I would need is clothing if the situation changes.

We [he and his brother Hermann] received a letter from Mama [their mother] who wrote that our heifer died. She also mentions that they have not received a letter from you. I hope you will make up what you have may neglected. Please send me Schroeder's address. It seems to me that you are jealous of Trudchen because she is together with "her Schroeder" and you have to be without your Nicolai. Be careful that jealousy does not consume you. Remember that Satan uses every possible device to deceive. And, my dearest Tina, pray that the war might soon end, and teach our dear little ones that war wreaks terrible things. And pray for me that I don't lose my faith and will continue to serve my patients with joy, humility, and endurance.

And what's the situation with Selma? Are her pockmarks very prominent? Be very careful that she doesn't get a cold during this time. Have you weaned Selma because of her age or was there another reason? Please write me everything that is happening there. According to reports we will be here in Brest another week before we take the wounded to Moscow. And our butter should be there by then. Please greet the parents and siblings. Have they not received my letter?

Heartfelt greeting to you and the dear children and many kisses, Your Nicolai

From Nicolai's niece Sarah
Mariental[21]
October 22, 1914
Dear Uncles Hermann and Nicolai! [22]

Since Aunt Tina [Nicolai's sister] is writing you a letter, I have to write, too, as I promised. All of us are well and until now have always attended school. Karl

---

[21] Nicolai was born in Ogustobe in the Crimean Peninsula, but when he was 4 or 5 his family moved to the village of Mariental in the Molochna Mennonite Colony where he grew up and considered this his parental home. Nicolai's mother, widowed in 1906, who owned a half farm, thirty-seven dessatines (99.8 acres) needed help on her farm. Heinrich was the youngest of the seven sons. All of them except Heinrich and Hermann were married. Hermann was a teacher who had been assisting his mother financially before his entering the Red Cross Service as a Sanitäter. The Mennonite servicemen did not receive a government stipend. They were to receive financial support for food and clothing through a special fund set up by the Mennonite elders and ministers, very loosely structured initially but was soon folded into the All-Russian Zemstvo Union, an organization to render aid to sick and wounded soldiers. This agency "ultimately provided the framework in which hundreds of Mennonites worked as medical orderlies on Red Cross trains bringing the wounded from the front line." See John B. Toews, *Czars, Soviets and Mennonites* (Newton, KS: Faith and Life Press, 1982), p. 67.

[22] The four persons named above were the children of Nicolai Rempel's oldest sister, Anna, who shortly after her marriage to Abram Neufeld moved to the Kuban where she died of typhus while their four children were quite young. Neufeld remarried but because his second wife didn't want the children, they were sent to live with their grandmother, Sarah Rempel, in Mariental. Abram came to Canada with my family in 1925. He died in 1933 of a concussion resulting from a kick to his head by a horse.

Schmidt visited us today. My brothers Abrahm and Gerhard are removing seeds from pumpkins, and aunt Tina, Mika and I are washing the seeds. We've already had heavy frost for several days so that the windows were frosted right up to the top. Our teacher, David Koehn, died a short time ago. The funeral service took place in the school. This teacher did things in this way: if a student had not been reprimanded for half a week, he was rewarded with a picture. Now I must close because I have nothing else to write about.

Greetings from your niece, Sarah. P. S. Mika, Abram and Gerhard send greetings.

From Nicolai's sister Tina
Mariental, October 22, 1914

Dear brothers, Hermann and Nicolai!

I want to try once more to send you a letter, but if you don't get this letter, I'll stop writing. How often we have written and you have received none of our letters. On Monday, October 20, Heinrich left for Moscow to train as a medical orderly. Before that he had been in Chernegovka trying to get a deferment, but of course there was no thought of being freed from military duty. So now we are alone here but at least we have the children [the four Neufeld's children: Abram, Gerhard, Sarah and Mika] so it doesn't seem so lonely. Otherwise everything is as it was when you left. I would like to write something about our farm, but I have sent so many volumes of letters where we described everything. Because you didn't receive any of them, I won't waste any more paper and ink.

All of us are well. The schools are closed for a whole week on account of illness. The boys, Abram and Gerhard, don't know what to do in the evenings. Gerhard is using this time while I'm writing to fill my ears with perpetual whining about this and that. I will close for now.

Your sister, Tina

From Nicolai
Evacuation Station
Medical Train No. 10/160
Brest-Litovsk, October 26, 1914

My dear wife!

It is Sunday night and that is usually the darkest hour for us, especially on evenings like this when the stars and the moon smile down on us from the clear sky. That's when homesickness strikes hardest, knowing that that same moon and stars are shining down on my loved ones. It seems to me that the moon is gloating impishly [*schadenfroh*] as if to say, "I can see your Tinchen and your little daughters whom you so much would love to see, too." That moon that knows no misery, no farewells, no war, is to be envied. When we look up at the heavens, at that magnificent starry sky spread before our eyes, we are reminded of that great sacrifice of love we were given through Christ's suffering and death. When we quietly observe all of this grandeur, we can only thank him, the Creator of all things, it is a small matter to protect us in war from the rain of bullets, and that this Creator can also bring an end to the war. However, if he lets this war rage on, then it is meant for our own good to suffer longer, but he can and will give us the strength to patiently endure these hardships and draw us closer to Himself. …We have to admit that we deserve punishment for our lack of faithfulness to our God, who draws us to himself with gentleness and love. And even in the present situation, we can do nothing but give thanks for his beneficence. Naturally, there are times when we desperately need strength in order to perform our duties to others quietly and faithfully. We might have difficulty performing tasks that we see as futile, yet must do them regardless if for no other reason than to be an example to others or simply to avoid strife.

We have been standing here eight days already and still we have no idea when we will move on. During this time our train is slowly undergoing renovations. We have set up our kitchen in the 4th class carriage and the officials' dining room is being increased in size. The freight cars that have served as transport for the wounded until now are being exchanged with fourth-class passenger carriages. These carriages are much more convenient to care for the wounded. We can now feed them while traveling since we can walk directly through carriages to the kitchen to fetch the soup and then return with the food. Our carriages have all been washed thoroughly, that is, we washed them ourselves, including carriages for ten other units. Tomorrow we will get even more to sanitize and prepare completely before turning them over to the crew who will use them.

At noon we were served meatballs [*Katletten*] for the first time, and the prospect of getting roast beef several times a week is promising. We were certain that we would receive letters from Moscow today because our general sent a telegraph requesting that our mail be forwarded to Brest-Litovsk. Perhaps the letters will arrive tomorrow morning and that will be a great joy for us! None of us knows when we are going to Moscow. Jakob Ubanobur sends greetings to you and the parents, siblings and grandparents, and please give all of them greetings from me, too.

Kiss our children for me and many kisses and greetings to you, my dearest. Your Nicolai.

From Nicolai
Evacuation Station
Medical Train No. 10/160
Brest-Litovsk, October 30, 1914

My most beloved Tienchen!

A most difficult week will soon be behind us. Much, much work but all was totally senseless; bad enough to want to desert, to abandon the place. Everything's in chaos! We really have no idea why this mess exists.

Here's an example. All the red freight cars[23] that we'd made cleaned thoroughly,

---
[23] Initially freight cars were used to transport the wounded. Note Introduction.

completely ready for service, were without explanation called out of service. We scrubbed the floors and washed everything, made up the beds; simply stated, they were completely ready. Then suddenly, six fourth-class carriages were made available. So that night the contents of ten freight cars had to be taken from them and transferred into a single freight car and a warehouse first, because those fourth-class carriages, now available, had not been sanitized yet. So the next day those fourth-class carriages were washed and the things that had been stored during the night in the one freight car were transferred into them. And the things from the warehouse were also placed into carriages, but with neither rhyme nor reason, regarding what was to go where: unloading, reloading, cleaning, washing, everything pell-mell, until some official recognized the stupidity of it all and everything was put in a supposed proper place.

The following day, more fourth-class carriages were made available and the whole procedure was repeated. So we had to scrub these new carriages down at night, and that's the way things went until we had only fourth-class carriages. But the anticipation of moving about within the carriages freely while in transit, which was not possible in the red freight cars, was worth the labor and perhaps reduced the absurdity of the whole thing.

But today while working hard, putting the final touches on our train so that we could take on wounded soldiers, horrors of horrors, word came down that we were to give up four of our carriages in exchange for six of those red freight cars. So tomorrow or even tonight, we go at it again, washing, sanitizing and dragging things around. The carriages we gave up were, of course, clean and ready to go. In addition to all this craziness, we have to put up with these miserable attendants who think their duty is to push us around. Well, today when one of them became so obnoxious, yelling at us, demanding that we perform tasks that were quite out of his range of authority, I couldn't take it any longer. I jumped up and was about to give this jerk a sound thrashing when, thank God, I was able to restrain myself at the last moment and tell him he'd better leave [take a hike] immediately. Gerhard Fast went and complained to the authorities who gave the scoundrel a thorough dressing down.

Well, you can see how one is often tempted to behave inappropriately for a Christian; something you and I have often talked about, i.e., we really can't do much without honest prayer for guidance and patience. Without prayer we stray from God. It's like Peter's answer to Jesus (John 6:67) when Jesus asked his disciples if they too wanted to leave him, "Lord, where shall we go…."

It seems that we are leaving tomorrow for Radomich to pick up wounded soldiers and take them to Moscow. Who knows where our letters are languishing now? I received only your letter from the 13th of the month. Please let me know the dates of the letters you received from me. Maybe it would be better to write our letters in Russian, although there are no secrets in them. Have you written to Mariental?

Waiting anxiously for an answer, I remain your loving Nicolai.

From Nicolai
Evacuation Station
Medical Train No. 10/160
Borodino,[24] November 15, 1914

Dear Tina!

We arrived in Moscow yesterday morning, delivered our wounded servicemen, and worked until midnight preparing everything just in time for our train to move out again. We thought we would be staying in Moscow for several days, but because we had to leave so quickly, some of our things had to be left in there. But our general permitted Enns and Fast to stay behind to sort out all of our missing baggage and deliver it to us on a later train. The butter was probably sold at auction because it was sent some time ago.

Well, I received two letters from you, one from October 27th and one from the 2nd of this month. How happy I was to finally hold a letter from you in my hands. Thank you very much for always writing to me in spite of the fact that I hardly ever seem to get them. But this fractured correspondence will change if you continue to send letters to the Brest address. Tomorrow or the next day we should arrive in Brest, and there should be something from you. Do you intend to send me some underwear or have you already sent them? Did you send some items along with Fast's things? Does some of the butter and coffee in Fast's baggage belong to me? We thought we'd be staying in Moscow longer but instead moved out to Brest right away. In order to get the butter, the money and the letters that are waiting in Moscow for us, we gave Herman Enns and Gerhard Fast power of attorney to get permission from our general in Moscow to stay on there and retrieve those things that actually belonged in this train. Who knows whether the butter was sold already because it's been there a long time.

But back to our last trip. We arrived in Ivangorod [some eighty miles southwest of Warsaw] on the 8th in the morning and went, as I already wrote you, to walk around the fortifications to look at everything. We remained in Ivangorod a second day and while on the second day, many of our fellow countrymen from, Minsk guberniamente and other districts arrived. Farmers who had been pressed into service together with their horses and wagons were now carrying from the station in Ivangorod to the frontline a constant supply of provisions to the warriors [Krieger] there. Many were quite scantily dressed, and as the weather was turning cold, these poor men will suffer miserably.

In the evening of the 9th, we were notified that our train would be leaving for Kelvshch within the hour. This message had no sooner reached us when another order came down that all medics were to come out of the train immediately and feed the wounded some bread. There before our eyes lay a terribly tragic scene. A freight train had just pulled up next to ours with approximately 1,000 wounded soldiers, who lay in filthy freight cars terribly over-crowded. Where we would ordinarily have only twelve men, now lay forty-five, fifty and up to fifty-five men.

---

[24] Borodino is a rail station before Moscow, close to the site of the major battle between Russian and French sources under Napoleon in 1812 so vividly described by Tolstoy in his *War & Peace* (Urry).

There were no heaters in these freight cars and it was cold. The wounded men had built fires directly on the floors, never mind the smoke that filled car. These poor fellows just wanted to be warm. There were no bedsteads; the floors were covered with horse manure (still there from the horses that had been freighted to the front in these cars). For four days they had eaten nothing. When we gave them the bread, they devoured it as ravenously as wild animals. You simply can't even imagine it.

Now our general was asked to accommodate these wounded men in our train and evacuate them to the receiving military hospitals where they were supposed to be going. He resisted for quite a while but finally agreed to take on 667 of the wounded soldiers. As soon as we had finished loading them, we left. Our carriages were warm and the beds had been newly made, so it was not long after we took them in and helped them to their beds that they were asleep. When on my watch, that required me to walk through the carriages to look to the men's needs, I was met with such horrible stench that you simply couldn't imagine. In the past I have marveled at how women could change children's diapers without feeling nauseated. Now I have to perform tasks that are unimaginably worse than changing any diapers.

You ask if the problem with lice is as severe as Hermann Enns described it. Well, if you could see these poor soldiers, you would not doubt for a moment what Hermann related. These soldiers are thick with lice and we take extreme caution by wearing leather jackets so that the lice can't crawl on us so easily. Often all the clothes of the wounded—underwear, shirts, pants, etc.—are tossed out because we don't know how to get rid of this vermin. Otherwise this trip was quite satisfactory in a strange sort of way, but we are very happy that we are now traveling empty, as it were. Yesterday at one of the stations I met Bergen from Schardau. He could scarcely believe his eyes as he recognized that it was me who was standing in front of him.

Well, my dearest treasure, I must close. This was written while traveling and the pen doesn't always do what I want it to do. Warmest greetings and kisses from your Nicolai.

P.S. Greetings to the parents and siblings.

From Nicolai
Evacuation Station
Medical Train No. 10/160
Baranovichi,[25] November 22, 1914

My dearest Tinchen,

It seems that I don't get enough time anymore to write a letter when the train stops at a station, so you will have to be satisfied with these scribbled lines as we are on the move. When we arrived at Brest I went to the post office immediately,

---

[25] "Baranovichi, the major rail junction between Warsaw and Moscow, was chosen as headquarters town because of the universal idea that headquarters would have to be mobile. It lay on railway lines to north and south, east and west…though not much more than a collection of huts and railway-carriages, [it] became headquarters of the Russian army for the next year of war" Stone, *Eastern Front*, pp. 52-53 (Urry).

convinced that there would be a letter for me, but there was nothing. I was very unhappy with you and decided to give you a good piece of my mind. However, the next day I did receive your little letter and I thank you much. I had no reason to be angry with you, but now and then one becomes impatient and annoyed with everything.

Just now we left the St. Golodmnvo station where we finally found Hermann Enns and Gerhard Fast who had stayed behind in Moscow to pick up our parcels and letters. And I also received your letter along with the baggage. I regret that you didn't send the letter the way I had requested, i.e., to Pogodino Fort here in Brest. Believe me, Tinchen, it is much more practical for me if you send everything, correspondence and other things, to Brest. In the future, could you please do what I request even if you think it is better another way. Actually, why didn't you put things in with Mrs. Fast's—the two of you could have send things together. All I can do now is watch the others enjoy their fresh butter and coffee. Of course, they always invite me to join them, but I feel too embarrassed to take handouts. I will not receive the baggage that recently went to Moscow very soon, and who knows when we will go there again. I know that your intentions are the best, but why send me more warm shirts when I haven't used the ones I took along from the last time I was home? I beg you not to send me anything in the future until I make a request, and use the address I ask you to use. Our situation has improved so much that we can get socks, shirts, underwear, handkerchiefs, pillowslips, slippers, pajamas—everything we need, we get. Of these items we have thousands. I wear my underwear until they are dirty and then exchange them for clean ones.

Today is the 24th of November, and our train has been standing here in Brest since the night before last. Last time when we came from Moscow to Brest, we took on some 500 wounded men and brought them to Minsk. Now we're waiting to be sent off again. Yesterday, Sunday, we worked hard preparing our carriages and also had our photos taken. As soon as the photographs are ready, I'll send them to you. I suppose you won't send yours very soon. If you send me one, choose one showing you in profile, tear off the bottom half, take the top half and peal the photo from the cardboard, wrap it in paper, place it in an envelope and send that to me. Then at least I'll have your photo; otherwise I'll forget what you all look like.[26] And with the children, you must often or perhaps always speak Russian so that our little ones learn the language of their country well from infancy. We are Russians and our children must absolutely speak Russian from infancy even though our ancestry is from Holland.

A short while ago David Hamm came to see me. His train, No. 14, was standing next to ours since last night but now they have left. Apparently brother Aron is in the Austria. Eleven of our trains of the Old Nobility Organization are working there.

Enough for today. Hugs and kisses from your loving Nicolai.

---

[26] One can assume that he is making this request to expedite getting a photo or perhaps he is mocking her failure to fulfill a former request.

From Nicolai
Evacuation Station
Medical Train No. 10/160
Lukov, November 26, 1914

Dear Tina!

We are in Lukov once more where we sat for five days last time. You may need a map to locate us. Our intentions are ambitious, but whether we will accomplish as much as we want to is questionable. Our destination is Andreyev, not far from Krakow, where the fighting is very severe. It takes four days to go from Ivangorod to Andreyev because all stations between have been destroyed. Everything is lying in ruins, so the trains move very, very slowly. One could cover at least as much in a day by walking.

Will take a break because our *kascha* [buckwheat] is ready. I have become so used to *kascha* that I am beginning to like it. Well, nothing came of finishing this letter after supper last night, so I am back at it now, the 27th. Our train is still here in Lukov but is to move out soon to get wounded. In queue ahead of us are two other medical evacuation trains, neither has any wounded either. And so at every station you see hospital trains, some empty, some loaded, one leaving the war zone, others moving into it. You would be dumbfounded at this rail traffic transport in human beings in and out of the war zone. Anyone seeing this has to ask, "How terribly many human beings are being shunted west into this battlefield!" When you see all of these soldiers being sent to this frontier, you would think that we would soon be done with these Prussian scoundrels. Well, I hope it will happen and that we can soon have peace. The soldiers at least are fortunate to have mild weather; otherwise these poor fellows would be lying in the trenches in frost and muck.

Today I saw a Pole plowing, so you see that the weather is still quite mild and, of course, such conditions make our work less unpleasant. However, nothing could be better than you and I working together, enjoying our family life once more.[27] Recently I dreamt that I had come home and that the children came rushing toward me; Alice and Hilda knew me quite well. How happy I felt to have all of you around me. Sadly it was only a dream, but hopefully it will become a reality someday. How are the little angels doing? And Selma, can she talk already or does she still run around mute? What about Alice and Hilda, do they scrap frequently? Aren't you weary of these little scoundrels?

How are things in general? Are you getting along with your siblings and parents? Are you sometimes helping out in the store? Did father buy a lot of Christmas merchandise, or are sales not heavy enough for it to be worthwhile? Why don't any of them write me? Surely they could find enough time. Have you been to Marientral lately? There they had to butcher our cow because she aborted repeatedly and the heifer croaked [*krepiert*], too. We have really had bad luck with our cattle.

Who knows how we will celebrate this Christmas—everyone will miss

---

[27] Apparently they had a plot of land in Marientral, perhaps part of or adjoining his mother's farm where animals and machinery were kept.

someone. We here will miss our wives and children, and you wives will miss your husbands. But in spite of it all, we will celebrate this greatest of festivals—the birth of the Savior.

Many greetings from your Nicolai.

From Nicolai
Evacuation Station
Medical Train No. 2
Vloschtschovo, December 1, 1914

My dear Tienchen!

We arrived here in Vloschtschovo early yesterday. A terribly sad sight greeted us! The railway station lies in ruins. The station agents are living in freight cars. From early till late you hear the distant thunder of canons. Everywhere soldiers are lying under the open skies beside fires that burn day and night, trying to protect themselves against the cold. An endless line of horse-drawn wagons carries provisions to the soldiers in the battlefield. These provisions include bread, canned goods, flour, oats and hay for the horses, bombs, shrapnel, shells—all needed to feed this war machine, and everything is carried by horse-drawn wagons from the end railway station to the field of slaughter (*Schlachtfeld*)—wagon upon wagon from early till late. And then these self-same vehicles return laden with wounded soldiers.[28]

Yesterday we loaded wounded into our hospital train late into the night into train No. 2. Our carriage took on thirty-six soldiers last night, and we are now waiting for the arrival of more wagons with the wounded to fill the rest of our train. It is heart wrenching to sees these poor men in the rain, wet and cold, lying in the filthy straw in these carts—I almost said "in this death-train,"—many deathly ill, some dying even when they have been carried this far. You can hear them begging, crying out in terrible pain, asking someone to relieve them of the horrible suffering. I simply can't describe the horror of it all.

Had to stop here yesterday because they brought us more wounded. Perhaps if more of our Mennonites—young and old—were to witness the misery of war, see the plight of these desperate soldiers, I am sure they would storm the throne of our heavenly Father, pleading to bring an end to this carnage.

Today is the 7th of December. We just arrived back in Brest, and as I have a bit of time now, I'll go back to where I stopped writing on December 1 and try to describe a little better our work with the wounded soldiers and their delivery to Gomel.

At approximately eleven in the morning (on the 1st), we were all sent to our medical carriages because the wounded soldiers had just arrived. Soon each of us was ready at his station waiting for patients. The wounded are triaged immediately into three categories: the seriously wounded, the less seriously wounded who can

---

[28] For information about the eastern front from September 1914 through September 1916 go to: http://www.westpoint.edu/history/SitePages/WWI.aspx

walk on, and the sick. My carriage is the second from the end, so I could see each patient very well as he was carried by. I could hear the moaning and rattling in throats and I could see in each face the terrible pain. As a backdrop to this terrible scene, the thunder of the cannons never stopped—a constant reminder that at every moment, men were being mutilated and slaughtered.

As gently as possible we carried these poor fellows into the carriages. Of course this could not be done without some groaning and screaming. The first one we loaded had lost his left leg to the knee—the flesh of his rear on one side had been torn away and a large piece of flesh was missing from the other side also. The next one was similarly missing a leg, plus a terrible wound in his side and one of his arms was seriously injured. The next two men were unconscious; then came one who screamed constantly, begging for his wife to come to him. After a while he simply screamed in terrible pain. If anyone walked near him, he grabbed their apron and said, "Tama, my wife, don't you know me? Why don't you come to me?" The last two wounded we had with us only a day and a half. They never regained consciousness so we unloaded them at Keubyb. They had severe head wounds and are probably both dead by now. Very many similarly wounded. One with a large side-wound, begged us, while we were carrying him in, to really turn up the heat. He was severely frostbitten. Well, I covered this poor man well with warm blankets and when I looked down at him, he was shivering severely and crying bitterly. This scene I shall never forget! By the time we arrived in Ivanovadch, he had died. We unloaded him there—no fanfare.

This was, shall I say, a most difficult journey! One could often not get the bedpan in place under the patient and the stench wounds, awful. One of my patients was an Austrian, who had lost both legs and had ghastly wounds in his side and back. He asked me to place the bedpan under him. Another medic standing nearby grabbed the bedpan and told me to lift the man while he placed it under him, but he screamed so excruciatingly that it was impossible. He cried out in pain for an hour until the doctor came and redressed his wounds. We were tremendously relieved when we finally arrived at our destination, Gomel to hand over to others our wounded soldiers. We will stay here for a few days, disinfect our train, and then move on again.

Today I met brother Aron, who was here on his medical evacuation train. But he complained that their administrators are not as good as ours and he would like to be transferred to our train.

I received your dear letter that you had written on the 24th of last month. I am surprised that you always seem to write to me in the evening when you are already tired. Your hands are probably tired from washing Trudchen's clothes. I can imagine Lady Trudchen coming home and having you do her delicate laundry. You know quite well, my dear Tina, that I am not pleased when I can have you only at the end of the day when you are tired and have no desire to write. So from now on, please set aside some time to write your husband during the day and edit it carefully, otherwise I might draw the conclusion that to you, your husband is merely secondary in your life.

Concerning the butter, I guess I didn't explain myself very clearly. I suggested that Mrs. Fast was to send a case of butter with her husband for all of us and then you other wives were to replace the butter or pay her for it. But now all the women added butter into the container except you. But it doesn't really matter as I always get a share of butter from the rest. I still don't have the things you sent to Moscow. I am so glad that you soldier wives stick together so well. Someone told me that Mrs. Enns, Manja, you and the Fast wives stick together closely. I appreciate that you often meet with each other and discuss matters. Let's not get too worried about my coming home for Christmas. We shouldn't even think about it.

Pray for peace. Kisses and greetings from your loving Nicolai

From Nicolai
Evacuation Station
Medical Train No. 10/160
Brest-Litovsk, December 10, 1914

Dear Tina and children!

Yesterday quite unexpectedly I received the parcel you sent. How wonderful everything you sent tasted and I thank you for everything, everything! You wrote, "I don't know if I've met your needs, what you wanted, this time." Of course, you sent the right things, and I have no complaints knowing that you always do the best. If it weren't that way I would let you know. When I might simply make a suggestion that doesn't mean that I'm scolding. Don't worry about the money and don't write requesting any from Mariental as little has come in there and whatever has been taken in has been spoken for.

We don't know whether we will spend Christmas in Brest or in Moscow, but probably here in Brest. Hermann Hamm has already written his wife that she send his Christmas package here. Butter and other perishables should not be sent to Brest because they are sold at auction right at the station if they aren't picked up within two days of arrival. Well, Papa knows all about this so just ask him. Notify Mrs. Enns and Manja when you are sending me a package so that they can then include something for their husbands also. Another fifteen pounds could have been added without any extra cost to the last package; the first pud [thirty-six pounds] has to be paid in full anyway.

Esau, my service colleague, brother Aron and Peter Wilms visited me and praised your wonderful *pfeffernuesse* and send you greetings. Esau told Aron, "Nicolai has a better wife than you; she sends him things often." Aron told him that his wife sent him things, too, but to Moscow, to which Esau countered, "Nicolai's wife sent a package here to Brest and to Moscow." See, my dear, even the Crimean people praise you here. Yesterday we were sent three more Mennonite medical personnel. You know them: N. Driediger, W. Heidebrecht, and I. Klassen. Other Schoenfelders are here, too: P. Neufeld is in train No. 1 and Dyck, Matthies, from Schoenbrunn in train No. 19. We are here for four days already and still don't know when we will be leaving. It seems almost as if a ceasefire has been initiated since so many medical trains are waiting here.

If we celebrate Christmas the day after tomorrow with the Poles (according to the Old Calendar) we will celebrate it twice this year. Yesterday we did a thorough cleaning of all the coaches and now we are ready to leave. Winter has set in these last days and everything is blanketed in snow. A wind is blowing and we are having frost. My thoughts are often with the poor soldiers lying out there in those wet, cold trenches. Our last transport carried some who had frostbitten feet. Who knows how many will be brought in this time? Here everyone is also in danger of contracting communicable diseases, and thank God we haven't contracted cholera or some other diseases we haven't even heard of.

Teach our children to pray for the many suffering soldiers. Many thanks for everything you have sent me. Nicolai

P. S. Why doesn't anyone write to me? Surely, Anna, Susa or Mika could write.

Please greet parents, siblings, uncles and aunties. Ask brother Hans if he has received my letter. From now on I will number my letters so that we know how many are lost. N. R.

From Nicolai
Evacuation Station
Medical Train No. 10/160
Brest-Litovsk, December 16, 1914

My dear, dear wife!

As we will soon, i.e., today, be taking in wounded soldiers again, I will write a brief note so that you won't have to wait as long as last time. We have been able to rest up and recover from our last difficult journey, now standing here the tenth day since returning to Brest-Litovsk. Here one day is almost like the next day—doing a bit of work, writing letters, reading newspapers or visiting neighbors. Next to ours is a train from the Provincial Union where I often visit some of my service brothers, like that Epp from the Old Colony I told you about who was in Germany as a prisoner of war for nine weeks. Well, he tells some interesting stories about how dastardly the prisoners were treated by the Prussians, etc. He and his wife escaped by bribing a doctor who gave him a certificate stating that he had tuberculosis. On his way back, the poor fellow had a stopover in Stockholm, where his wife gave birth to a son. It must have been quite a complicated trip. He considers himself fortunate to be back in Russia again.

According to what I just read in the newspaper, *Russ-Slovo*, all eligible Mennonite men will be drafted, so Jakob Wiens, Kornelius Peters and many others like them will have to serve, too. It will be good for many of them if they get away from home for a while. In any case, they won't be inducted before Christmas, so they can enjoy the Christmas holidays with their loved ones. I would also love to be home for a few days at Christmas, but it's better not even to talk about it lest I begin feeling sorry for myself.

But even so we will probably experience the real joy of Christmas here, also. May the dear Lord fill our hearts with joy even if we can't together celebrate Christmas. Let's remember the thousands who have lost a loved one during this war. It has made many widows and orphans, and yet we are still here and quite healthy. Just think, my dear Tina, if we look at all the misery and awful suffering the war has brought on, we have every reason to be grateful to Him who has protected us. Some medical officers here have died of typhoid fever, as we know, and many of those who were sent directly into the battlefield may have died. It is the only by the grace of God that I have not contracted a communicable disease. Sister Tina writes that in Mariental a group of her girls get together to pray for those who are in the war. Do keep praying together with our children. It is not possible that He would deny the prayers of these innocent children. I pray for you every day and am convinced that God hears my requests.

I wish you and the children a joyous Christmas and don't be sad because there is nothing to be sad about. Forgive me that I can't send you any gifts for Christmas other than my most heartfelt greetings and kisses.

From Nicolai
Evacuation Station
Medical Train No. 10/160
Okarjmsko, December 22, 1914

My dear Tienchen and children,

I had not planned to write to you again before Christmas, but as I have an opportunity to send a letter with a colleague, you would be hurt if didn't write, having spoiled you by writing almost twice a week. You have not spoiled me like that. Is it possible that you are still sick, my dear, and thus can't write? Of course, as Gerhard Fast is leaving soon for Schoenfeld to see his newborn son, he can tell you everything that we are doing. But you must definitely go to visit him and give him a full account of how things are going so that he can relate it all to me.

We will celebrate Christmas in peace and quiet here in Okarsmsko, where we arrived this morning and thought we'd move on right away to Ostrovetz to take on some wounded soldiers and then return immediately. In fact we planned to be in Brest for Christmas, but it isn't going to happen because we will be sitting here another five days.

Today we bought some Christmas decorations and will put up a tree, if possible, and look at it, all the while thinking of you at home. Again, we wish you all happy holidays. So be joyful as if no one is missing from your midst. Please send the *Heimatklaenge*[29] and a book of chorales with Fast, otherwise I will forget all the beautiful hymns and songs. I am ashamed that I can't send you anything for Christmas, but you understand.

---

[29] *Heimatklaenge* is a published collection of Mennonite Brethren of religious songs. See Heinrich Braun & Isaac M. Born, *Heimatklaenge: eine Sammlung auserwählter, geistlicher lieblicher Lieder* (Neu-Halbstadt, Ukraine: H. J. Braun, 1905).

Please greet our parents, siblings, grandparents, uncles and aunts.

Many greetings are sent to you from the far West, Your Nicolai.

From Nicolai
Evacuation Station
Medical Train No. 10/160
Ostrovets, Christmas Day, December 25, 1914

My dear Tinchen and my dear children!

The first day of Christmas is nearly past. You have been much in my thoughts even though I was very busy and I know that you, too, at least in your spirit, have been in fellowship with me. And you, my little darlings, have certainly talked about your Papa today. How I would love to have brought you a special Christmas surprise, hugged you and kissed you.

Last night we celebrated a lovely Christmas Eve. Our train was still standing in Ekarjesko at eleven at night where no wounded could be seen. We had fetched a little Christmas tree from the woods nearby, and decorated it with a several candles and some confectionary so that it looked quite festive. Toward evening we tried to find a church to attend but it was so overfilled that there wasn't even standing room. We stood outside for a while, listened to the singing and then went back to our carriage where we felt quite at home by now. Then we lit the candles, sang many Christmas songs, Hermann [Nicolai's brother] read the Christmas story from Luke, then said a prayer and we sang a few more Christmas songs. Thus ended our Christmas Eve service.

We had scarcely completed the service when our train quite unexpectedly began to move and we were on our way to Ostrovetz, arriving here early in the morning. We thought we would have to take on wounded soldiers right away but that didn't happen. Our former and also our current commanding officer entered our carriage to wish us the best for Christmas. I probably I haven't written you that in Okajmsko we got a new commanding officer, our third. We could have wept when the second one, a sterling person, left our train. We didn't mind losing our first commanding officer, but then we lost the chief medical officer also who went on furlough and didn't return and that was another great loss for us. But when our top administrator [the second CO], a general, was elevated to honorary marshal and wrote to tell us that he would not be returning, well, that was a real blow. His assistant, a professor, took his place—again, a very good person, but he also has been transferred out, so now we feel like orphans even though we have a new commanding officer and a new chief medical officer. This new CMO is thoroughly disliked because he is terribly lazy and seems to be a know-it-all. But we medical personnel can't complain about him yet.

Well, you must excuse my digression from the account of our Christmas to a talk about our administrators. Here we woke up here in Ostrovetz Christmas morning to the whistles of factories calling their people to work. This place is an industrial city with many factories and mills and it looked like anything other than a Christmas celebration. Of course, we were very busy but were shocked, nevertheless, when we looked up from our work and asked ourselves if this was really Christmas day. To which we had to answer, "Yes, it is Christmas, but Christians don't have time to celebrate the birth of Christ. They are busy fighting, murdering, spilling blood—driving themselves to destruction." We, for whom Christ died, have no time for Him. Christ tells us to love our neighbor as ourselves, but how many prayers are sent up to God, by those who call themselves Christians, requesting that He help us kill our neighbor— to prosecute war. Is it not an outrage—a shame—that we Christians are not striving for peace, making every effort to live in peace with everyone…?

I was just beginning to write this letter when the train left Ostrovetz, but now we are back in Brest again. I have received two of your letters, the *raisenstritzel* and the *pfeffernusse*, and have devoured all of it already. What is most important, we have reached the end of year. Only an hour and fifty minutes and we will be writing 1915. May God grant that this war will stop raging on. For the New Year, I wish us all a new heart full of love, kindness, gentleness and patience. It is difficult to imagine that I cannot come home for the holidays. That's of course obvious. But in spite of it all, we cannot complain.

But let me try to answer your questions. First, I have heard nothing from Heinrich, i.e., he has not written so far. Second, why don't you go and visit Truda for fourteen days. Third, if the horses haven't been sold yet, it's all right to sell them because we won't have peace for some time yet. Anyway, I told Matthies to sell them. Fourth, our pigs have been butchered; at least I asked them to do it. Fifth, do whatever you would like with the hams.

And now, my love, warmest greetings and many thanks for the package you sent me. Greetings also from brother Hermann and all the others. Jakov Ivanovich greets you and your parents and requests that you find out why his wife, Manja, is not writing anymore.

Once more, a happy new year and kisses from Nicolai.

May God bring Peace on Earth!

Courtesy of Canan Tolon
Untitled (polyptych) 1996, Oilstick on mylar, mounted on canvas. 49 x 36 inches
This painting was inspired by the bombing of Kosovo 1996

The only thing worse than assuming you could get the better of suffering is imagining you could do nothing in its wake. You could be strong enough to witness suffering, and yet human enough not to pretend to be master of it. Sometimes it's those things we least understand that deserve our deepest trust. Pico Iyer, From "The Value of Suffering"

PART TWO

Letters of Nicolai and Katharina Rempel 1915

Russia began to suffer serious setbacks in 1915 in spite of her much larger armies than her enemies'. The cause was mainly shortages of war materials and poor supply lines. Nicolai was appalled at the shear masses of soldiers, "… one trainload of soldiers after another is dispatched to the front. When I hear the whistle blowing for departure, it sounds to me like music from hell luring a whole stream of healthy, young men … to [their] death. It is gruesome." In one night 12,000 flimsily dressed soldiers "froze to death when the temperature plunged over night."[30]

The homefront was beginning feel the strain of the war also. The Peters' household in the Schoenfeld settlement, something a compound, now often housed their three married daughters, Greta, Tina and Truda, with their children while their husbands were away in the service. Some of the employees who helped in the household and in the Peters' business lived there, also. The family business (a dry goods store, agricultural machinery sales, woodwork shop for furniture construction, etc.) was thriving until 1914, but now in 1915 they began to feel the pinch of the war economy. Shortages were beginning to be felt as food, material goods and farm animals were shifted to support the war. The Mennonite communities had to support their own servicemen either financially or by supplying them with food and clothing.

With the increased shortages of goods, reduced income and the many mouths to feed, tensions began to rise. Tina's mother became testy at times, complaining of having to support her children and grandchildren, but her father was able to meet the exigencies with greater equanimity. Tina and her sisters did not only take care of their children, but worked hard in the household and in the business, also. As the stress mounted, however, Tina asked for Nicolai's approval to go to live with his mother in Mariental. She and Nicolai had been living there, setting up a small farm of their own, when the war broke into their plans. Eventually, because of the financial demands, they begin to sell some of the equipment they had purchased to establish their farm: wagon, harvester and their horses. Nicolai, too, was increasingly frustrated and anxious because he is unable to do much about Tina's lack of place other than consent to move in with his mother.

But the most severe blow to Nicolai and his family was the death of his brother, Hermann. He and Nicolai had been serving as medics on the same train since their

---
[30] G. J. Meyer, *A World Undone*, p. 402.

induction. Hermann had acted as the head of the family after their father died in 1906, supporting his mother and sister. Before the war he had been a teacher and principal in Gnadenfeld high school. Being a deeply religious man, exacting great discipline of himself, he impacted the family with a strong pietism. According to Nicolai, Hermann got up at 4:00 a.m. for ten years straight, practiced his religious exercises, prepared for his day's work and "carried his Christian faith in his daily life as no one else" he knew. Hermann had great influence on Nicolai. The letter from Nicolai to the family describing that death and the memorial service for his brother Hermann in Brest-Lietovsk is deeply moving. The letters that follow the memorial service show Nicolai in the depths of grief and depression, leading to his request to be transferred from the service on the Red Cross Evacuation train to some other department of the Zemstvo.

From Nicolai
Evacuation Station
Medical Train No. 10/160
Brest-Litovsk, January 2, 1915

My dearest Tinchen and children,

How long it's been since I wrote the last letter, I can't even recall, but it must be at least eight days, so must try to redeem the neglected and write you. Had we not been so terribly busy, I would surely have dropped you some lines; however, it was impossible under these conditions. But I'll move on to other matters.

Just returned here from another trip, not a long one, transporting wounded soldiers from Brest to Gomel. When we returned here from Gomel, Gerhard Fast had already come back from Schoenfeld with all the parcels from you. My most heartfelt thanks for everything you've sent me. Who sewed the Red Cross armbands and the two shirts? But of course, you had written that you were making them. Both fit very well, except the sleeves were a bit too long so I hemmed them up and now they fit very well.

You ask if I have received the Christmas packages. Let me describe everything I have received. At the beginning of December, the package with the coffee, the butter and the *pfeffernuesse* [small round, hard cookies flavored with spices] arrived, and at Christmas, a package with *raisinen stritzel* [raisin], more coffee and the two blouses, four Red Cross armbands, the *Heimatklaenge* [folksongs], and the book of hymns got here. Yesterday brother Aron brought me the box of clothes from Moscow that you had sent in November. So I have received four packages for Christmas from you. The box with confectionaries, cookies and nuts were meant for Enns, right? All the Schoenfelder here have received sausages and the spareribs, so now we are eating just as we did at home, and I must say that we have almost too much of a good thing. Brother Aron has just come from Moscow and is visiting here in my carriage at the moment because his train is not ready yet to transport the wounded out. He also received butter, coffee and various other Christmas gifts. He even got a scarf from Tante Minna for Christmas. But enough about gifts.

You ask about my furlough—whether it is true that we medics can go home, taking furloughs alternately. We really know nothing about going home, and, in any case, I would not be able to come home even if I were given a furlough because I don't have the money for the fare. So let's be patient and set our heart's compass on October, because I believe the war will soon be over, i.e., by that time, around October. Should I, however, be able to get a free round-trip ticket, I would be tempted to come home to spend a few days in your midst.

You write so little about our children. What they are up to, what kind of gifts have they made, and what you gave them for Christmas? I am interested in everything, but sadly you write so little about them. Why is that?

Nothing new with the transporting of the wounded; everything is continuing down the same path. I'm sure you are familiar with the nature of my work here. I believe I described everything about it. However, a nasty bit of work is now developing with the wounded. Recently we have had outbreaks of typhoid, cholera and scarlet fever among the soldiers that have been brought in from the battlefield. In order to prevent these diseases from spreading, every train has to sit in quarantine for five days outside of Brest, and during that time medics may not leave the train. Soldiers with rifles stationed around everywhere make sure of that. You can well imagine how it feels having to sit as though incarcerated in the train for five days, especially with all these seriously wounded soldiers.

[End missing]

From Nicolai
Evacuation Station
Medical Train No. 10/160
Brest-Litovsk, January 6, 1915

My dear Tina and children!

If things went as you planned, you are probably in Mariental now, and, in my mind's eye, I feel as though I am walking around our little estate with you, trying to decide what work is most important and how we will organize things. Unfortunately we are very far apart, and there are still no prospects that we will be surveying our little plot of land [in Mariental] soon, and who knows whether anything will come of those plans at all.

According to the newspapers yesterday, all Germans who live in the Crimea are supposed to be evacuated because no Germans may live closer than 100 versts [one verst = 0.606 mile] from the Black Sea and the Sea of Azov. [To wit, the Japanese in WWII in the USA] If this applies to the Mennonites, then we too will have to leave Mariental because it is only thirty versts from the Sea of Azov.[31]

---

[31] The Mennonites during WWI came under increasing attack by some Russian newspapers, questioning their loyalty, their citizenship and even suggesting that their land be redistributed to the peasant class. To prove their loyalty, the Mennonites supported (as conscientious objectors) the war, pledging loyalty to the Tsar, and volunteered in large numbers (10,000 of a Mennonite population of some 110,000). They insisted that they were of Dutch heritage. Nicolai makes that point emphatically in a letter. They tried hard not to be identified with the Prussians (Germans) who were at war with Russia. There is evidence even today in the surviving buildings constructed by the Mennonites before WWI in Ukraine that reflect a strong heritage of Dutch Renaissance architecture. See Rudy Friesen, *Building on the Past Mennonite Architecture, Landscape and Settlements in Russia/Ukraine* (Winnipeg: Raduga Publications, 2004).

Actually, this can hardly apply to the Mennonites because they are not at all German. Well, all things must happen according to God's will. There is no other way, even though thousands or millions "conspire against us, they will not prevail if the Lord is with us." After having thought hard about this question, I found Psalm 91[32] and it made me very happy last night. No doubt God led me to this Psalm that has been a comfort to me frequently in the past. We can only apply this to ourselves if we belong to those of whom the Psalmist speaks in Verse 14. Let's read this Psalm frequently because it contains many comforting words.

And what are our dear children doing? Have they forgotten me? Do Alice and Hilda recognize me in the photograph? Do they talk about their Papa often? Can Selma prattle a few words already? How are things going in general with our little champions? If they quarrel heatedly at play, what do you do, or do the three get along well? Please write me all about the children: what kind of progress they are making, how they converse with each other, etc. I think the children would be very happy if you would help them to write little letters to their Papa. Last night I went to the post office hoping there would be a letter for me, but I was disappointed. Only the others from Schoenfeld received letters. It seems to me that you often don't know what to write, and finally you actually believe that you have nothing to write about. May I suggest, first of all, that your husband is interested in everything: what you are doing, how everyone is getting along. Rightfully you should write four times a week while I write once a week. Although I am familiar with everything that's going on generally, I would like to know more details. Secondly, don't treat writing to your husband as though it is some minor matter. Writing to me should be second only to prayer and meditation, don't you think?

Warmest greetings, your Nicolai

From Nicolai
Evacuation Station
Medical Train No. 10/160
Brest-Litovsk, January 17, 1915

Dear Tina!

We have just returned to Brest-Litovsk from Minsk where we had taken our wounded. When we were leaving Brest with the wounded, I received your letter of the 8th of this month in which you expressed yourself in a rather remarkable way about the fact that I allowed our pigs to be slaughtered. The fact is there was no grain left to feed them, and you are sitting right there and aren't even aware how matters look at our farm. You've never really cared a wit about our chickens and pigs in Mariental, nor have you ever had any desire to live there, but now you are castigating me for having done something without your approval.

You write much about Mariental but as no one answers the letters you write to them, you have no desire to go there. First of all, you know quite well that only Russian may be written in that area and that few German letters arrive at their

---

[32] Psalm 91:14. "Because he loves me," says the LORD, "I will rescue him; I will protect him, for he acknowledges my name. 15 He will call upon me, and I will answer him; I will be with him in trouble, I will deliver him and honor him. With long life will I satisfy him and show him my salvation."

destined address from there. Then it takes several months before you write to Marienthal at all and only after I have urged you several times to do so. You, however, demand an immediate response from them to your letters. It has always been that way; where I wanted to go, you were hesitant go. You've never been drawn to my siblings. In short, you are most comfortable in Schoenfeld where you never, or rarely, have to have contact with the Rempels. Well, it makes a difference now that you have little children, otherwise you would prefer still to be called Miss Peters [her maiden name]. You must really be longing for that! Your letters seem quite cold as though you write to me merely to fulfill your duty as a wife. Mrs. Dueck has already written seven letters after Christmas and how many has Mrs. Rempel written? Two!

I think it is better that we stop writing altogether. Surely you would agree to that, right? The Zemstvo Union has already sent 700 Mennonite medics into the battlefield, and the All Nobility Organization wants to send some of its Mennonites there also. David Hamm has already enlisted for duty at the front. I will probably do the same and that will be the end of it. A decision has to be taken for better or worse.

Your Nicolai

From Nicolai
Evacuation Station
Medical Train No. 10/160
Brest-Lietovsk
January 25, 1915

My dear Tina,

After waiting patiently I finally received your dear letter the 18th of the month. Oh, how I would caress you and hug you if you were here for such a beautiful letter as this one. This time you have described everything the children are doing, how things are going with them, etc. The only thing missing is that such letters don't come frequently enough, something I always hope for. And you, my dearest Tina, will think that I am worried that this hope will not be dashed, right? You will probably already have received my last letter, and you will most likely not have been very happy with it. But nothing can be done now. I sent it and you got it and for your good, I believe. If, however, it is too harsh, I apologize. You, my dearest, know that I am often a bit nervous (irritable) and then in the heat of the situation express myself too rudely. To discuss a matter and to express my opinion about it, I never regret, but never to do it rudely.

If you were here now, you would be convinced that we love our wives more and more, and if we complain sometimes, that is merely a type of jealousy. None of us wants to admit that other wives love their husbands more than he is loved by his. For example, if it appears that Hermann Enns is loved more by his old lady (Mrs. Enns) than you love me, I don't want to admit that and then it can happen that I scold you because I get fewer letters than he gets. I brag a lot about how much you, my dearest, love me and what kind of a sweet, long letter you have written. Enns, on the other hand, got no letter today. It seems to me that a competition like ours must please you, and you should not be miffed even though we are a bit gruff at times. And I am sure that I can swear that you will never complain to anyone when I overreach and scold you once in a while. One of the soldatkas (wife of a soldier) there has complained to strangers about her husband that he scolds her. Please tell me truthfully, have you complained to any one about me?

I am really very, very sorry that you have had such a rough time with the children during their illness. How gladly I would have helped you nurse the dear little dears. Well, wherever I can help, I will. First, to thank God that they are well again and even though I can't help you raise (nurture) them, I can at lest pray that the Lord will always give you strength and council. My plan to come home on furlough has come to naught; otherwise I would now in your midst. And Hermann Enns is still here in our carriage and will probably not be going on furlough soon either. We've been standing here in Brest-Lietovsk eight days, waiting to be sent out from here. We will probably be here until the train is fully renovated.

They are currently putting in side-doors so that the most seriously wounded can be loaded into the carriages more easily. So that is a problem with the windows. And every carriage in hospital trains is having a red cross painted on the roof that stretches across the full width of the roof, and the red cross is enclosed in a white circle so it can be spotted easily. They're adding these red crosses because the airplanes of the enemy have shelled so many hospital trains. Fortunately we don't have to paint these red crosses. That would be no fun in this cold.

But now to answer your questions. You ask why it is that the others have so much spare time, I don't. Let me explain. Each of the other medics takes care of the wounded in his carriage, but since January I have been in the surgery where the wounded are bandaged. Although perhaps not as hard, but I have much more work that is really time consuming. And my work consists first of all in keeping everything clean: floors, buckets, glasses, bottles, surgical tools, etc, and all water has to be replenished that has been used, set up the borax-sublimation equipment, and filter them, to cut bandages and prepare them, and the like, and much, much more, even when the train has no wounded on board. However, when we have wounded, I have to assist with the bandaging. i.e., remove the old dressing, wash out the wound, clean it and help to put on the new dressing. Now, however, I am supposed to do what a nurse did until now, that is, she stood by at one end of the bandaging room (surgery) while a wound was being dressed. Had everything at hand that was needed for cutting, bandaging, etc., and ready to hand with a pair of tongs whatever was demanded and simultaneously boiling everything, i.e., all instruments that come near the wound. And that's what keeps me so busy. When I have to stand so long in one place, then I too become quite tired. If I don't like it here in the surgery I can, of course, go back where I worked formerly and reclaim my carriage (ward). Till now I have enjoyed working here so at least for the time being I'll stay.

Last Sunday the Aron Rempels were my guests. It came as quite a surprise when these old folks suddenly appeared in our carriage. Actually we all were quite happy for this visit and I think the Rempels also enjoyed it. Well, I won't tell you much about how and where the Rempels lived while with us here. You have to go over to them and ask them about everything because old ladies can tell everything much better than we men can. She owes you a kiss from me, so go over and cash in. She gave each of us a kiss when she left with the understanding that she would deliver one to each of our wives. Nothing would please me more than if your were to go and visit all those who live in Schoenfeld because it is high time that all of the Mennonites became more trusting of each other and would love each other earnestly as our Lord taught us. This command of our Lord—to love one another— is very, very important, but followed so poorly. And the result of our failure to obey this command we can see in this war. Were there more love among people, this war that is causing so much misery and tears would not exist.

It is not good that you always sit at home, rarely making contact with others. Why don't you go and visit others more? You probably have not dropped in at Hermann Enns's in Wiesenfeld all the while, have you? Have you distributed all of the photographs? And do you see Manja very often. Since yesterday her husband (—-) is my neighbor because one of the medic was sent to Moscow because of a heart problem, a Hübert from Einlage. Three of us are now in one room: Ub. W. Heidebrecht and I. Peter Neufeld is also in our train. This luck is incomprehensible. Old lady Rempel has no idea how fortunate she was while she was here. Peter moved into our train the same day the Rempels left and the train he left was sent off that evening. It seems that Peter is quite happy about this trade.

Do convey greetings to your parents and siblings and the grandparents and the Aron Rempels when you go there. And so I'll close in sending you the most affectionate greetings and kisses, Your ever loving, Nicolai

From Nicolai
Evacuation Station
Medical Train No. 10/160
Brest-Litovsk, Sunday, February 8, 1915

My dearest Tinchen,

Tomorrow is your birthday and until last night I thought you would celebrate it in Marienthal, but after I received your dear letter written the first of the month, I realized that you changed your plan and decided to celebrate it in Schoenfeld. Yesterday's letter from you gave me indescribable joy. Even though I sent you a letter the day before yesterday, I am writing another today. You will surely not be annoyed when you get two letters the same day. I am quite surprised that you did not yet receive my letters of the 26th and the 31st. Well, it happens here also that letters go astray. However, letters are delivered even without stamps so it must be the changes of address. If you will omit from the address the station, they should not be meandering around so long.

I'm afraid my birthday letter will reach your hand belatedly as it was addressed to Marientha, but that doesn't really matter because I see that God has granted us our birthday wishes, and that is what made me so happy when I read your letter yesterday. He has opened our eyes to our sinfulness and punished us duly for our spiritual sloth, but when we truly recognize our sins, that is already a penance and he reaches out to us with his loving hand, showing us his unspeakable love.

Everything seems so festive today, something that I have not experienced on a Sunday forenoon since I have been in the service. Why this is so I don't really don't know, but it is for me a real Sunday morning. Perhaps I can attribute much of this to the fact that we have no work this morning, which happens rarely, although there may be some work this afternoon, one never knows. My thoughts are constantly with you today—what an important day it is! You are concluding the 25th year of your life this day. May God grant you a true birthday in that he will make us his faithful followers.

Couldn't finish this letter yesterday but I must add a line now, the 9th of February, for your birthday. I feel as though I must go to you, congratulate you and give you a most affectionate kiss. Unfortunately, we know that we will have to go on without that, but I am with you in spirit, hug you and kiss you today especially and wish you all the best, much happiness, God's blessing, strength and patience to guide our dear children on the right path. I sent you a little lamp for your birthday. You have to pour a little benzene into it, but be careful.

A hospital train with Mennonite medics on it was taken captive day before yesterday. We are still sitting here since the 17th of January. Most affectionate greetings and kisses to you and the dear children, Nicolai.

From Nicolai
Evacuation Station
Medical Train No. 10/160
Meshirjetsche, February 12, 1915

Dearest wife and children,

As you see by the name of this place, we are away from Brest-Litovsk, now on our way to Warsaw. I started this letter just as we were leaving Mesurefechze but had to stop since work beckoned. We are halted seventeen verst from Warsaw, so I can continue—But no, the train is moving again, so I'll stop.

Have just arrived in Warsaw but don't know yet if we will take on wounded here or if we will be sent on down the line. Things here in Warsaw are as they were, I almost said, but since this is my first time here, I can't really say what it once looked like. It is interesting to travel an area that one hasn't covered before, as we did today. Here, too, as in the rest of Poland the landscape is sandy and swampy with some beautiful forests. Except for these sad times, one could be more enthusiastic about the beautiful regions we travel through. Now, however, wherever we go, we see poor soldiers loitering about and one trainload of soldiers after another is dispatched to the front. When I hear the whistle blowing for departure, it sounds to me like music from hell that is enticing a whole stream of healthy, young men along behind it, only to deliver them to death. It is gruesome. We are not grateful enough that God has protected us from all possible sickness and the pierce of a fiendish bullet.

Will begin to describe a bit of what's been happening. When we awoke yesterday, the train was no longer in Brest-Litovsk where it seemed we had taken root. During today's travel we all busied ourselves, each medic making sure everything was clean and in order. I worked all day at my first aid post. Despite our sitting idly in Brest so long and cleaning everything frequently, it was still quite necessary to give it another thorough going over. I had no guilt pangs about carelessly soiling things at home that you had just laundered. When I return home to you again, I shall make greater efforts to be more helpful to you and keep everything nice and clean and not to stomp across the freshly washed floor with muddy boots. It happens here frequently that just after I have cleaned up, someone stomps in and messes everything up again. But truthfully, I must say most persons do try not to make extra work for me. As for my part, we can take on wounded tomorrow morning. I am ready.

Before we left Brest yesterday the others got letters from their wives, only I didn't get one from my wife. My last letter from you was from the first of the month and it will probably be a long time before I will receive another. Fast even got a photograph of his wife and children that Aron Thiessen had taken. I certainly would be very happy to receive a photograph of my family. Maybe Thiessen will consider taking a photo of you and the children, if you have money.

>My heartfelt greetings to you and the dear children,
>Your loving Nicolai

From Nicolai
Evacuation Station
Medical Train No. 10/160
Moscow, February 20, 1915

My much loved Tina and children,

It is eight days since I sent my last letter to you from Warsaw and now we are in Moscow; however, we will probably leave today again for Brest-Litovsk or Warsaw. It was a good thing that we did not know what lay ahead of us eight days ago or we would have gone to work with great anxiety. We have made very difficult trips before, but the last one surpassed all others. From Warsaw we traveled on further to Nowy Dvor and Nowy Georgievskaia. There we took on 627 wounded men, almost all very seriously, and with these we moved back to Warsaw and then from Warsaw finally to Moscow. This transport took five days, from the 13th to the 18th, and during these five days and nights we worked essentially without rest. For three days I worked a twenty-one- to twenty-two-hour schedule but then on the fourth day, my work stopped on its own—I was simply finished. I worked only till 1:00 a.m., and then I said, "I can't do it any more, excuse me but I am going to rest"—which I did. But on the fifth day I was energetic and strong again after that much needed rest.

Here in Moscow we have had two very busy days like today. I ate only breakfast and now it's nine in the evening and I am having a cup coffee. Can't write sensibly at all, I'm so tired and our train is moving and you can't write while it is in motion.

K. Fast is going home today, so you should at least be getting something from me. Are you quite well, everything normal? Let Fast tell you everything about the scene here. Please send some coffee and butter with him. If he cannot take it, send it to me by mail, but if I have to pay three rubles extra here for the baggage, well, I can't afford that. It would be a good idea if you war wives got together and discussed it all [the matter of sending food] with Fast.

I'll close now with many greetings and kisses for you and the children. Your Nicolai

From Nicolai
Evacuation Station
Medical Train No. 10/160
Warsaw, February 25, 1915

My dear Tina,

It is almost shameful of me, my dearest wife, that I have not written to you for so long, but I could not write, though I desperately wanted to. Now I have stolen away from my work so that I could answer your dear letters, one from the 13th, one from the 15th, and one from the 5th that you sent from Mariental. For all of them, thank you heartily. I had not heard anything from you for some time and am now so much the happier for your letters.

How our last trip with the wounded went, Fast will have told you, and that's the way it has gone for us till now. We have taken on some 700 wounded men today, but fortunately not severely wounded ones. We were really not given time to prepare our medical evacuation carriages; everything had to be done on the run while we were traveling. Today I was given an assistant in the admitting department, so that I don't have to do all the dirty work. Even though I was very busy, things went quite well. All were very understanding and kind to me, that is, the doctors and nurses. I can now more or less do as I please in every situation. If only I could have a little more time. Well, the time will come again when we will get more rest, but that will wait until after the 40,000 wounded have been evacuated from Warsaw.

Please send me with Fast two knives that have the English IXL stamp on them. We can't get them here. We are about to get underway to Moscow and I must I get to work. Please forgive me that I write such a short letter, but even by my best efforts I can't do more. I am quite healthy, happy and in good spirits. Wishing all of you many blessings and health. Many kisses and greetings,

Yours, Nicolai

From Nicolai
Evacuation Station
Medical Train No. 10/160
Moscow, March 1, 1915

My dear wife and children!

We have just transferred our wounded soldiers to a receiving hospital here in Moscow, and I have given my bandage room a surface cleaning. I want to take the first spare moments to chat with you. All of us are happy now that we handed off all of our patients even though this trip was easier than the last one. All of them could, albeit with difficulty, walk on by themselves, whereas the time before almost all of them simply lay there without being able to move. How terribly difficult it was to load all of those broken and severely maimed soldiers. There were, for example, many who had been shot through the leg so that you could see right through the limb. Just imagine bandaging a shattered leg like that. You have to hold it in such a way that the leg lies straight and flat so that the bones don't pinch or pierce the flesh. To support the leg and hold it steady is usually my task because the others can really not bear up under the stress of holding it steady. It is very difficult to hold a leg in that position for any length of time. And then there are some wounds that are putrid and festering, emitting a terrible stench.

By now I have become accustomed to everything, but when I first started, when I had to hold a leg like that with its large open wound where the bones and sinews were exposed and the surgeon began to cut, to pull out the splinters of bone, when the stench rose up into my nostrils and the puss ran over my hands, then, then I could hardly stand it and sometimes became light headed. On this trip we again had many with fractured arms and wounds, the stench so vile that even our surgeon could hardly endure it. We now have a very fine surgeon whose assignment here, unfortunately, is temporary. In spite of the fact that we are very busy and the conditions awful, the atmosphere is sometimes jovial. Even the seriously wounded enjoy a bit of joking now and then, seem to forget for the moment their wounds. If only the top brass were a man with a brain, things could and would go better.

Recently the meals leave, to say the least, something to be desired. Sometimes we've had no noon meal at all and boiled macaroni for supper. We often just drink tea during the day. In other words, there's sometimes almost nothing to eat. Recently while I was cleaning up quite late in the surgery, the doctor came with the broom and threatened to sweep me out so I would stop working. He said to me, "You are quite exhausted and get some rest, otherwise you will not hold up to the end of the trip." I liked that and said, "Oh, I could hold up OK if only I got something to eat. When you work hard all day and get only tea at meal time—then naturally I won't hold out to the end of the trip, just like the other medics, who won't either." He stared at me with alarm and said, "What? Aren't you given anything to eat?"

"No," I said, "We have had only tea to drink today." He was quite disgusted that we were not fed better and assured me that things were going to change. "I'll see that!" The nurse then brought me a nice supper: sausage, coffee, meatballs, and so forth, and urged me to eat. Naturally I didn't do that and told them that I was not the only hungry one and that the others were hungry, also. If they were not going to eat, then I wouldn't either. In the meantime, things have improved. But I wonder why the people at home look so down cast, as you write, that there are but few happy faces. Here we are usually quite cheerful; sometimes we're simply boisterous and on occasion things break out into gallows humor.

Now I want to answer your questions. Those miracles like getting two letters from me on the same day rarely happen; well, that is your own fault. Whenever I have had time, I would write twice a week. But you have time; you can take as much time as you want to write to me. But you don't write even when I have begged you to write and to write with greater joy. Today again all the Schoenfelder received letters from home but not I. And that's how it has been going. Everyone gets news of what's going on before I do. I know now that you have no time to write to your husband. But I don't want to force you to write, because I want to learn to accommodate you in all ways, even though it is very painful that you won't exercise a bit of self-denial to write to your husband. According to your letter to me, two of my letters have gone lost, namely from January 29 and February 2nd. That you were unable to see Mrs. Enns in the last six months is hardly possible, and those are only excuses. But it doesn't matter. I won't let it bother me too much. In these matters I was unable achieve anything with you even when I was still at home.

In my opinion a child of God should forget what is in the past, to forgive everything and try not to live only for ourselves, but also to enjoy others and to be with other good people and to try to see the good in one's fellow man. It has always been my strong desire that you would care for and communicate with our friends.

The lamp I sent to you I bought in Brest, and it cost 150 rubles. The train wants to leave right away, and so I had better close so that it will be mailed from Moscow. We are going to Warsaw again. Many greetings and kisses from your loving Nicolai.

From Nicolai
Evacuation Station
Medical Train No. 10/160
Brest-Litovsk, March 4, 1915

My dearest beloved Tina,

We just arrived here in Brest and that was just by chance. I have finally received all of your dear letters. Your letter from the second of March arrived as well as letters from the 24th and the 27th of February. Am somewhat at a loss because I get so little news from Schoenfeld, but I seem to be adjusting to the situation, have got accustomed to this. The last time we were sitting here in Brest was the eleventh of February, and we won't be here again soon because our train doesn't belong to this front anymore.[33] Even now we are parked here for only a couple of hours and then we are off to Warsaw once more.

Our train is in such chaos it can't be described. The new commander of this train is a total dunderhead with whom you can discuss nothing. He runs about as though he's possessed and yells at each person who happens to cross his path. You can never do anything right for him or satisfy him. He has the poor chiefs running back and forth like wild animals. For example, we are provided with kindling for our carriage and for the heated freight cars, but this new commander objects to wood being stored in our carriages and screams at the workers: "Even if you have to carry the wood on your heads, it's not going to be stored in the carriage." The poor medical personnel are sometimes at wits end trying to figure out what to do. The carriages are supposed to be heated, yet he insists that the wood should not be stored in them. If there is a shortage of any supplies, that's too bad, he will not allot any more money to replace what is missing. Fortunately I am not directly under his 'sovereignty.' No doubt I would have got a thorough dressing down many times if I were but now the doctor is the first in line to scold me if I do something wrong.

---

[33] Their unit has been assigned to the Austrian front.

I didn't finish this letter yesterday so I will try again now. We arrived here in Siedletz this morning at 11 a.m. and will be here till evening since they are installing a different kitchen and exchanging a few carriages, so we'll have a bit of a break to rest from a hectic schedule. Until now everyone has been unbelievably busy, chased about like a herd of wild beasts, that's how we have had to work.

We just had a visitor who inspected our train, and everything we medics had done was found to in be good order. Only our *Zemskii* [Zemstvo representative] was called on a number of failures—things he had neglected to do. Well, when it comes right down to it, a loud mouth like our big cheese can be cut down to size quite easily, and so he just stands there like a rooster in the pouring rain and doesn't know up from down.

Last night I received a letter from Mama. She writes that Suderman bought my horses for 450 rubles. I sent part of the money to Sawatsky in Lichtfeld and sent 200 rubles to Matthies. He had borrowed that amount for me from the bank in Halbstadt. I am really sorry about our dapple-grays, but what else can one do? Debts have to be paid and just to go on feeding them, well, that doesn't make sense either. Heinrich sent me a postcard from Chaplino.[34] He has a month's furlough but apparently is not really well.

Just now we heard the news that we are being sent to Ostrolechaplika.[35] Who knows what we can expect from this trip? Another two Red Cross hospital trains have been captured, one from the army and the other from Zemstvo Union. Which number they are I don't know. Other than that there's nothing important to report.

Heartfelt greetings and kisses to you and the little ones,
Your Nicolai.

From Nicolai
Evacuation Station
Medical Train No. 10/160
Dwencky, March 11, 1915

My treasured Tinchen,

While I am able for a few moments to tear myself from my work, I will quickly answer your dear letter that I received in Vilna. One is from February and one from the 2nd of March. Thank you very much for both of them. I always carry the letters in my pocket for a time, and then, when there is a free moment, I take them out quickly and read them again and again. It seems so comical to me, for example, that Selma is running around and chatters away about everything, as you have written. When I left she was still this mute, helpless little creature and now suddenly all of that has changed. I really can't imagine how everything looks and what is going on out there with you. Please write me in detail all of such things that you may think are not of interest to me.

---

[34] Chaplino is a rail station on the line from Ekaterinoslav to Berdiansk. Heinrich was Nicolai's youngest brother who never emigrated. In 1937 he was arrested while teaching, taken away and never heard from again. (See Epilogue).

[35] Seventy miles northeast of Warsaw.

That you didn't send the things with K. Fast is very good. First of all, he already had so many things for others, and to send it by mail is actually much cheaper. My packages as well as the things that Fast brought along are still lying in Brest. Who knows when we will get there. One does not really know where one should have his correspondence sent since that hasn't been clearly determined yet.

How is it that you are always the last to go see one of the husbands who is home on furlough? The other wives seem to get there sooner than you. You seem to go only at the last minute when that person is ready to leave and is tired of making conversation. Are not you interested enough in your husband to go there right away to inquire after me? I am really surprised. You know very well what pleases me and sometimes you seem to do just the opposite.

Why haven't you had a photograph taken with the children in Gulaipole by Lejtman? Mrs. Enns had him make photos of her with her little lads, or perhaps Mrs. Enns went to Gulaipole. That, of course, would be a different matter. I long to see just what you all look like now. I really regret that I have so little time to chat with you, but there is such a rat race around here now so that one can hardly come to one's senses. You will have to excuse me if I don't write as often as the others do; they really do have more time. My rat race here allows me little time.

We have made three long runs this month: the first from Nowy-Georgievsk to Moscow, then from Warsaw again to Moscow, then from Ostroleka to Riga. In all, we have evacuated about 1,800 wounded men in one month. We made 4,000 bandages, so you can imagine how we worked to prepare all those things, i.e., to cut the cotton batten as well as to the gauze, then to fold it and finally to sterilize it all. Well, that is a huge amount of work. But enough of this.

How is it going with our dear little ones? Are they more obedient now? I don't want my children to be punished under any circumstance except by you and Papa [their grandfather Peters' punishments were rarely corporal]. No one except you two should dare to lay a hand on them. I understand very well how difficult it is for you with the children. But please don't ever forget that it is your sacred and primary duty to nurture and to train the children, and you must allow yourself much time for them. Teach them that God gives strength for all good things. Do you always pray with the children in the morning? Please do that and pray much for me. I really miss fellowshipping with children of God; that is, I miss the freedom as it was before the war, to go to church, to sing and pray, and especially to talk with you about the sacred matters.

Many greetings and kisses to all of you from your Nicolai.

From Tina [Nicolai had been home on furlough.]
Schoenfeld, April 5, 1915

Dear Nicolai,

Finally, finally, a long difficult week has ended for me and also for you, I should think. How quickly time flew by when you were home with us and how good that was. Do come home again soon! Come home to stay! I thought surely I would hear from you yesterday but no news. We received a telegram from Hermann and two postcards that were addressed to you. I wanted to wait until I heard more from you before writing. Perhaps you have miss-addressed your letter. But I can't wait any longer; I need to write now so I can send the letter with Schroeder as he is leaving this evening. His furlough has ended, and he has to leave even though he hasn't finished all he wanted to do here. Well, he may feel worse than you and me.

Yesterday the Ratniks brothers left and brother Johannes finally had to go, too. Just why do all of these people have to be taken into the service, I don't understand. Unfortunately, we can't know what God is doing with us. Perhaps it's because He has not been able to draw us close to Him so He must be using these means to do that. The children always ask, "Why does Papa stay so long in Mariental. He could surely come home by now?" In this world there is only goodbye—Auf Wiedersehen! When will this finally end?

In a neighboring colony, they have taken into the service five wagons with horses and drivers from each village. People are afraid that this will happen here, too, especially Franz Rempel, who said that if this happened, he would be the first to be affected and that he would then definitely leave. All of your mother's seven sons are in the service now. Until recently only five of you were servicing, but now all seven of you? What would your father[36] have said to all of this if he were still living? Well, it's better for him now than for us. No one can hurt him now. Be very careful that you don't fall a victim of any diseases or other dangers. You would be leaving behind a wife and three children. If it's God's will, nothing will happen to you.

Now you will likely get more medical workers in each train because 1,000 medics are supposed to be added to the medical corps, some transferred from the Forestry Service. That's what Aron Rempel said. He came from Gnadenfeld yesterday on a one-horse buggy; had gone there for seed grain. The children are playing ball in our yard. Schroeder in their midst. But enough for this time. I'll wait now until I hear from you. You wanted to write while you were underway. The children and I are well. I hope the food you took along was good.

Once more many greetings and kisses from your loving, Tina and children.

From Nicolai
Evacuation Station
Medical Train No. 10/160
Moscow, April 19, 1915

Dearest Tina!

Have just arrived in Moscow and as I have a break now, I'll quickly drop you a line. You are probably unhappy with me, and rightfully so, because I haven't written sooner. I could at least have sent you a few cards, but I comfort myself with the assurance that you are so good to me and always ready to forgive me. As Enns has already told you, we were sent with the wounded from Moscow to Kiev and then returned, bringing the wounded back with us here to Moscow where we will be

---
[36] Nicolai's father died in 1906, leaving his widow, Sara (nee Lange) with seven sons and two daughters in Mariental, Molochna Mennonite colony.

sitting for two days. I have quite adjusted again to caring for the wounded, but I need to, or better said, we all now have to get used to this new doctor who joined us in here Moscow. He seems like a very fine fellow, although rather strict. He is Polish and a sincere Catholic, who doffs his hat every time he passes a picture of a Saint. I am very pleased when persons honors their faith and are not ashamed of it, whoever they may be, whether Mennonites, True Believers,[37] Jews or Mohammedans.

We Mennonites are much too unfaithful and lax in our faith, and as a result I believe we will have to experience some stormy times. We can see it quite clearly even now as we get one blow after another, God's small punishments as warnings, and we can expect these to continue. From childhood we have heard the gospel preached and generally have not heeded it and so the punishment will come. Until now we have got only minor punishments, one after another, as warnings. Our situation is similar to the time when God sent a messenger to Pharaoh telling him to let the people of Israel go. "Woe to us if we harden our hearts" like Pharaoh; plagues will come to us, also. I believe there is already much grief among Mennonites even now that so many of the young men are being inducted and also those who have had to take their horses and wagons into the war theater. Well, it is our duty to do something to help the poor wounded, wherever that may be, whether on the field of slaughter (*Schlachtfeld*), in the trains or in military hospitals. It is our Christian responsibility to help everyone.

Only yesterday I was told that L. Toews has also been conscripted; however, I can't believe it, but soon we will get more uncomfortable news, as our Schoenfelder in Moscow will probably have the latest information from home. I have heard nothing from you because we have not been in Brest yet. In the meanwhile you can address all letters to: Kiev Railway Station, Medical Train No. 10/160 of the All-Nobility Organization, N Rempel

We were supposed to be coming to Ekaterinoslav next and, of course, and then we would probably be very homesick. Unfortunately, we will have to forget about that for now and will simply have to wait the war out. May God grant that it will end very, very soon. If Enns wants to bring something back here for me, give him a long letter, nothing else. It is very uncomfortable to drag around so much baggage when one is trying to catch a train.

During the last trip (with the wounded) nothing special happened; everything followed the same old path. The Old Man was more or less decent, only once did he do something very stupid. He has to stick his nose into everything, so once when he gawked into a compartment where the wounded lay, he saw that the bandage of one soldier was soaked through. Immediately he raced to the dining room where the doctors and nurses were having lunch and began to yell, "In one of my compartments someone is bleeding and you sit here." Naturally they all ran to

---

[37] The Old Believers seceded from the Russian Orthodox Church because of church reforms introduced by Patriarch Nikon in 1666, and continued to follow the liturgies of the Greek Orthodox Church. Their religious activities were quite restricted because of being classified as a sect by the Russian government. The Mennonites were initially not classified as a sect and were given full freedom to practice their faith except that they were not allowed to proselytize. But in 1870 the threat of being reclassified as a sect caused them some concern especially because their freedom from duty was threatened. Urry, *Mennonites, Politics and Peoplehood*, p. 120.

staunch the bleeding, as every moment is precious. When they came there, they saw that the problem was minor and so the Old Man was crestfallen and returned to his carriage somewhat ashamed.

Again my letter is not finished. There is always something that keeps one from writing. Today is April the 22nd and we are ready to move on. Yesterday ten new recruits from Schoenfeld spent the night here. Two of them were Heidebrechts, two were Cornelsons, a Thiessen, a Rogalski, a Penner and others. It was really quite nice to visit with Schoenfelder again. Peter Heidebrecht had not imagined how difficult it would be to say goodbye to his family. He still can't adjust to the idea.

Today we gave our carriage a thorough scrubbing from stem to stern, but it still looks quite unsettled as things are scattered about, not yet in their proper places.

And now be hugged and kissed by your Nicolai.

From Tina
Schoenfeld, April 19, 1915

Dear, dear Nikolai,

As everyone has gone out and it's quiet here, I must chat a little with you. I am sitting and listening to see if Truda needs anything. This is her sixth day in bed after delivery [Their first child]. She is doing very well. Schroeder came on the 14th and is leaving tomorrow. It is very good that he is here because Truda has to be carried from one bed to the other. They named the little girl Margareta. But enough of that.

Hermann Enns came home this morning. I was really happy for Mrs. Enns but was a bit disappointed that I didn't receive a letter from you. I had counted on it. Well, you probably didn't have time to write. Enns conveyed your greetings and that all is well. I hope to see him before he returns. You will already know that your brother Johannes has been assigned to the Red Cross Military hospital in Berdiansk. He was home for four days but he became ill again just before he left. He looked quite strained.

I am waiting for a telephone call from you telling me to come to Ekaterinoslav. I think all the women will come for a visit [with their husbands] and so will I, even if it costs seven rubles. To see you again is priceless. If only the War would end, surely we would be able to make our living as long as we remain healthy. We have someone in whom we can put our trust and He will not forsake us. Our garden is beautiful as are the fields. The trees are in full bloom and it is magnificent to see God in all of nature. I feel that the war will not last much longer. What a happy celebration that will be for all of Russia. Perhaps after that there will be peace forever in the whole world. It says in Scripture: "Repent, for the Kingdom of Heaven is near." The Lord showers us with so many blessings, but so often we fail to obey Him. We see his love and kindness that He showers on us in good health or in the fact that you can come home to us and, if need be, I can come to see you.

I have been quite busy looking after the sick for a week and tomorrow I'll start with the laundry. That's a week's work but that too shall pass. On the 22nd the inspectors will come to check all of the scales here. They have already inspected them in many businesses. The weather is fine today but a few days ago it was quite cold and the children were wearing their coats playing outside. Are you very busy now? We hear so little about the war. Will you be going to Brest again? I sent two letters there. I thought you had forgotten about Alice's birthday. Did you receive any of the letters I wrote after Easter? I will close mine for now, but I'll add a few lines later. It will be sent tomorrow.

This is how far I wrote yesterday and today I will add a little. [End missing]

From Tina
Schoenfeld, April 24, 1915

My dear Nicolai,

The day before yesterday I received your letter of April 16th and a card from April 12th. How happy a letter from you makes me. From your card I see you are not well. Are you experiencing the same sickness again? I'm sorry that you don't get more rest. If only you could get out of that hole. You write that you received a parcel, but I sent two. Did you receive only one? Do write me what kind of food you get. Friesen is lucky again. He was sent by his commander on a time of "refreshing" [R & R] and that will certainly please him! The new recruits were supposed to leave from here by April 25, but now they will stay till May 19. Gerhard has to leave earlier.

I must inform you of the death of Jacob Klassen's daughter. She was alert to the end and then she just fell asleep blissfully. I hope to go that way when I am called. I will not close this letter because I may think of something else to write later.

Aron Rempel's children are going to Gnadenfeld soon with the wagon. If they will take me along, I will go with them to fetch some spare parts if they are available there. Yesterday I received 1,200 rubles from Mantler for your machinery and he gave Mother 300 rubles. I gave him a receipt for the money. We had the voluntary mobilization again for horses and wagons the 22nd and 23rd. Naturally it was muddy again. They paid from twenty-two up to forty-two rubles for a horse and more, a fairly good price.

I have managed to hide in order to continue writing so no one will find me. I am sitting on the floor of my room where it's quiet. It is Sunday so most of the family went to church, but they are coming home from church already. However, I don't let that disturb me because my week to cook has ended. I think I am answering most your questions but I do forget many things. We are not busy in the store. We have bolts of cloth, as well as tobacco, paraffin, matches, syrup, rice, cereal and a few incidentals in good supply.

We don't have a servant at the moment, so Gerhard has to do the chores in the barn. Reinhold has been busy all week assembling and taking care of the machinery [in that sales department.] If all things go as they are now, we women will have work enough to keep us busy all summer. In addition, we have agreed to look after the Toews' garden. Because the fruit harvest looks good, we'll have a lot to dehydrate. I am hopeful that you will come home for the summer and hope does not disappoint. Well, God does provide everything in His good time for us. Most important is that you stay healthy, and, if you should become ill, you could come home to recover. Don't be concerned about the children; they are well. Hilda is an unruly child. She bruises her big toes every day and then she comes to me and wants them bandaged.

You have time away from your work only once a week? Please write me if you have to wear your own clothes or if they are supplied. What would you say if I were to come to Moscow like some of the other women? Well, perhaps it is better for me not to come. Let me know what you think.

Well, another Sunday is past. It was one of those cloudy Sundays. Lena Wiebe from Berdiansk was here for lunch. I have to stop and leave something for next time.

Greetings and kisses from your loving Tina and children

From Nicolai
Evacuation Station
Medical Train No. 10/160
April 27, 1915
Trip from Kiev to Sokal[38]

My deeply loved Tinchen,

Yesterday when we were coming to Kiev, I received three letters from you. They refreshed my spirits a lot and I thank you heartily. It really is wonderful that we can communicate at least in this manner and one learns to appreciate this especially when one has not got any message in long time. It was almost a month that I last heard from you and now three letters from you in a one day. I am quite overjoyed, really animated to receive these letters. I am sorry that you and all the others have had such a difficult time of it recently. Take care of your sister Truda tenderly and patiently as long as she needs help and remember how good it felt when you were taken care of so well. God will reward you. I know that I don't have to encourage you in this because you are always ready to serve without a reminder. Please don't take it the wrong way. I always feel as though I should be helping you take care of Truda and as I can't, you have to take care of everything by yourself. Poor Truda had to suffer so much giving birth to little Margareta, but the now her happiness for the little darling will be the greater because of the pain she had to endure.

Your father, who really couldn't handle such matters well, now has to live through such hardships with his children. I can image how dreadfully hard it was for him and his pain will not have been less than Truda's. Thank God that everything turned out quite well, as you have written. If she has a restless child to care for, then she won't have so much time to feel homesick for her Gerhardt. I guess that fellow will come home more often now.

As for our coming to Ekaterinoslav, that won't happen this time. As you can see from the address, we are on our way to Sokal where we will take on some wounded but where we will take them is not known. We think we may go to Kiev.

---
[38] Sokal was an area of the Austro-Hungarian Empire captured by Russian troops in August 1914.

The Old Man wants to go to the Prussian front, but it is not clear yet if it will happen. At the moment, the young people in our train are quite upbeat. They are singing, "You, you are near to my heart," (*Du, du, liegst mir am Herzen*) and so on. Aron Thiessen brought some photos back that he had taken of the gatherings back home. All of the girls from Gorkoe and Hanovkoe seem to be on the photos, and so these fellows as they look at them are moved to sing these heart-rending songs.

At times we feel terribly homesick for our loved ones and our homes and all that they represent. Especially now in this beautiful springtime, we feel the tug of home. When we sit in our carriages and look out through the windows onto all those lovely green fields and forests, especially now when the fir trees are at their most beautiful, then we feel like caged birds. But when will all this misery of the war finally end? I am so happy that you have not lost courage yet and even think that we will have our livelihood after this war. Well, if God will continue to grant us the health that we have had till now, I will not fear anything. What would you think about our moving to America or to some other country? It is quite possible that this could happen. Here we talk about emigrating quite often. I have recently received another helper in the emergency room, and she is under my supervision. The nurse who has been here till now has been relieved of her position and I have replaced her. What all of my responsibilities will be, I don't know yet but time will tell.

But to your questions. Brother Hermann had been ill while I was home but is well again. Our workload has been somewhat reduced recently because we are stopping frequently for an hour or two at smaller stations. I have ample provisions at this time but thanks for the offer. And you needn't send me any money as I still have some. Those poor children who in their innocence ask you, for example, why I am staying so long in Mariental, etc. How is Alice? Is she still so pale? If at all possible, do take her to Halbstadt or Orloff and have her examined to see if she still has that little clasp in her that she swallowed. And how do you feel? Is your stomach pain gone or is something else amiss? Please keep me informed of everything and continue to be as courageous as you have been till now and trust God with all your heart for He will never forsake you. Pray for me and teach the children to pray for me.

Your Nicolai, who loves you intimately and holds you always in his thoughts, sends you these greeting and kisses.

Please also greet the parents, siblings, grandparents, uncles and aunts. What is Hermann Enns up to? Do visit Sara often because time will be slow for her.

From Nicolai
Evacuation Station
Medical Train No. 10/160
Kiev, May 3, 1915

My dear, dear Tinchen!

Everything is restful and quiet in my carriage, no patients, very conducive to writing letters so I'll take advantage of this moment to chat with you. The other medical personnel who are dead tired have gone for an afternoon nap.

Well, this is how far I got with my writing in Kiev when there was suddenly a rush to work –all men on deck to pitch in and I had to suspend that attempt to write. Now I can return to writing here in Soval on May 5. It appears we will be here several days because five trains have arrived ahead of us also waiting to be sent on down the line to Sokal to load wounded. This is a single tract railway line, so the whole process is moving ahead very slowly again. Our last evacuation of wounded from Sokal to Kiev was terribly difficult because there were some horribly mutilated soldiers among them so that we scarcely knew how we would manage. We finally arrived in Kiev dead tired, and then were told that the wounded men would not be accepted there, that we would have to go on to Kharkov. We simply stood there dumb founded, not knowing what to do. But then suddenly the situation changed, and we were able leave our wounded in Kiev after all. By 2:00 a.m. we had finished unloading our wounded and then went to bed, but were back up at 6:00 a.m. to begin our work again. We are finished and it is now 8:00 P.M. so now I can sit down to answer your letters that I received the night before last, one through Hermann Enns and the other by mail.

Again my writing was disrupted and had to postpone it till noon when I wanted to finish. However, by then I was so tired that I lay down after lunch for an hour's rest, intending to continue then, but unfortunately I slept far beyond that hour. They tried to wake me at suppertime, but I didn't get up and slept through till eight this morning. However, there were many others who also took seventeen-hour afternoon naps. But then it was back to work with a rush to complete preparing our train on time since it was now moving back to the front as though pursued by devils, rushing without stopping. So we have worked hard all day and are pretty well caught up and might even get enough rest to generate strength for the trip that lies ahead of us.

In Kiev we were told that we should probably be prepared to go from Sokal to Kharkov. Sokal belonged to Austria before the war, but now the city belongs to Russia. It is a Jewish settlement, the likes of which I have never seen before. Even the youngest boys have long ringlets hanging down the front of their ears. Jews can generally be recognized here at a distance. The other people also wear peculiar garb. Actually, this is a very lovely region where nature is glowing wonderfully now. In winter we envied those who could stay home and did not have to serve because of the freedom they enjoyed. When I think that you can always enjoy fresh air and can walk about freely in the garden, the fields, and the forests, I can't describe my feelings. [End page missing]

From Nicolai
Evacuation Station
Medical Train No. 10/160
Kiev, May 10, 1915

My dear, dear Tinchen!

Soon we will be at our destination, Kiev, with our wounded wards, and if we are fortunate, we will arrive at the station in half an hour. [The skyline of Kiev with its golden domed churches is inordinately beautiful.] How happy we all will be when we have unloaded every one of the wounded men. This time we took on board such severely wounded soldiers in Sokel as we have not had in all of these months. In fact our doctor protested strongly against having to take on such a heavy load, but he received a curt answer, "Our responsibility is to see that the wounded are evacuated from here. Your responsibility is to have enough medical officers." Our doctor protested that there were too few medical officers to take so many wounded on board and that the medic's work is extremely hard and some were totally exhausted. During this trip here I could not work much but just lay around because I was quite ill.

In the meantime evening has set in and we have arrived at the evacuation station, so now we will have to begin transferring the wounded. That will take at least four hours, and by four o'clock in the morning the disinfection is to start, and so we medics will again have no time to rest. In the morning we will most likely be leaving for Sokel again, a place we're quite anxious about because we will take on only heavily wounded soldiers there. The lightly wounded, as I have written you already, are carried in ordinary freight cars back here to Russia. They have to get along without the help of medics. On our last trip we had a wounded colonel who cursed the attendants so fiercely because of their disorderliness that they all feared him. One evening he sent the attendant to fetch our chief officer, probably wanting to curse him as well. But the officer was apparently too afraid to go there and sent the attendant back with the message that he was already asleep.

I thought that I would surely get a letter from you, but I was disappointed. Am certain that you wrote and the letter is somewhere on the way. Only Kornelius Fast received two letters, but none of the rest of us received mail. You probably celebrated Pentecost today and I wish you restful and blessed Pentecost days. With us, of course, there is no trace of a holiday here, and we have no prospect of any rest soon. But our distress is nothing, nothing compared with these poor soldiers who moan and cry out for some relief from their suffering, and some die in their terrible agony. Two persons have died and one officer almost bled to death. He received an injection of about five tea glasses of a certain solution that was to replace the blood loss. He lay unconscious all night and is still very weak.

I wish all people could witness just once a scene like this when these wounded men are brought here from the battlefield—how terribly injured they are. It is really dumbfounding, unconscionable that people cannot come to their senses and see how totally senseless this whole war is and bring it to a halt. It brings nothing but misery and destruction. There is not one iota of good in it!

What about Manja? I suppose she is still waiting for her Jash [Jacob]? I believe he won't be coming home very soon because he has become the recording secretary in the government office and it is difficult to get time off there. He sends greetings to you. I received a letter from home lately in which Mama writes, among other things, that Mary Janzen is engaged to her brother-in-law Peters. She also writes that she sold our old cow for fifty-five rubles. You probably have not written home for a long time. And what about small pox, has it spread any further? Have you all been inoculated? Definitely do so. I'm closing with heartfelt kisses and greetings. Your Nicolai who loves you dearly.

From Nicolai (Post Card)
Sokal, May 12, 1915

To: Katharina Borisovna Rempel, Village: Krasnopol

Dear Katja,[39]

We have just received an order to go to Lublin and I beg you to send me even one letter to Lublin. The address is: Station Lublin, Evacuation Station, Medical Train, N101160, NAR. [Nikolai Abramovich Rempel]

Nothing has changed in our lives here. We work, work, work and have no time to think of anything else. You have all kinds of celebrations, but we don't even have time to give a nod to celebrations, not Easter or any other holidays. But our time to celebrate will come!

Bowing to you and kissing you, your Nikolai.

From Nicolai
Evacuation Station
Medical Train No. 10/160
Lublin, May 13, 1915

My treasured Tinchen and my dear children,

Hardly a moment passes that I don't think of you. I think of you constantly of the happy time I had the good fortune to be in your midst. The time was so beautiful and wonderful. You were always so good and loving to me. I didn't value all that enough and didn't thank the God adequately for it. For this reason God probably allowed our separation for a time, because I did not value our time enough while you and the children surrounded me. Now I understand Mama and my siblings better, who at times made bitter accusations that I often had so little time for you and my children. It is true I should have paid a lot more attention to you than I did. I am deeply embarrassed when I think back to the evenings when I was out and about till late at night and you had to be alone with the children. When I came home you were frequently lying in bed fully dressed. I could see that you had been waiting for me. You had very often prepared something to eat for me. You are really a good wife to the very core. If you were here now how I would kiss and hug you.[40]

Well, I don't want to have another time of such a busy life as I've had in these two years since entering the Service. That kind of life is so unnatural, having to neglect the family and owing the family so much. Training the children is also my task, not only yours. As things have gone up to this point, our children can scarcely come to know their father. When I am always away traveling and then come home, I am quite nervous and tired, and under such conditions the family has to suffer.

---

[39] Names change according to custom and mood. *Tina* is a shorten version of Katharina. Tinchen (pronounced 'Teenchen') a form of endearment. Katja is the Russian equivalent of Tina. Throughout the letters Nicolai varies the salutation for his wife. Sometimes he addresses her as 'mein Weib', i.e. my wife. That too was at that time a form of endearment. In current German such use of the word "Weib" when addressing ones wife or any woman is quite unacceptable. Kolja is short for Nicolai.

[40] Nicolai is recalling his last furlough and, like so many soldiers who return home even today, his conduct is uneven.

Fearful worries and anxiety bring us nothing but harm. Until now we have lacked nothing, even though we had very little. God will continue to provide for us because his Word says that not a hair falls from one's head that he doesn't know about. How I regret my impatience, my lack of faith and love.

About half an hour ago we arrived at Vonvolestja (Wolyskii?) and are now in the midst of taking on wounded, but not many, about 300. We heard that we are going to Minsk from here. Yesterday I wrote you a card in which I asked you to send a letter to Lublin. Yes, first send me a letter here to Lublin and the others to Brest again. Do it this way until I advise you of a change of address. I am quite healthy again, except that I am still coughing. I wanted to start to work today but the doctor said that I should stay inside since I could easily catch cold.

Yes, I almost forgot, I was told that Tante Sanchen has married Mr. Enns. Is that true? What about Marie Wall, has she visited you with her bridegroom and what kind of a fellow is he? I am at the end of my page so I have to close. I send you and my family a thousand greetings and kisses. Your Nicolai

P.S. Anna, Susie and Mika were going to write. I wonder where those letters are?

From Tina
Schoenfeld, May 15, 1915

Dear, dear Nicolai,

There is much talk here that Hermann may have died, and I want so much to receive some accurate news about his death if that is true, but have got nothing. I said if it were true then you would definitely have sent me a message. I have been wondering how many of you seven brothers will return home. How dreadful if you should not return home to us again? I don't even want to allow myself the thought finding myself in that position. Yet we don't want to complain against God even if He allowed it to happen and it could happen. Since I heard that Hermann has died, I'm afraid that I might soon hear of others who have died.

Are you still using the old calendar[41] in your train? Someone said that you are out of the Bandaging Unit. Is that right? I received a letter from Mariental the day before yesterday in which Mama writes that I should come and get Popbja. I want to go soon with all three girls for a few weeks. I will send a letter or a card the day I leave so that you can address your correspondence to Mariental, OK? Today we were notified that food packages could no longer be sent by mail or by freight because the mail trains are so slow and the food would spoil. It will be too bad, however, if you don't get the box with the butter.

My mouth has not quite healed from the extractions of my teeth. I go to the dentist every day to have him check my mouth. I am so happy to be rid of all those bad teeth. Many people here have very bad teeth but don't get them extracted because of the cost. I spent a good portion of the day sorting all the clothes in the closet again. Too bad you are so far away otherwise I would send you cherries more

---

[41] Russia was still on the Julian calendar whereas most of Europe was on the Gregorian calendar. Russia adopted the latter officially in 1918.

often. We have them in abundance in our orchard this year and many of them are already ripe. The children sit in the garden all day eating cherries and driving the birds away. If I go to Mariental, Gerhard will come along so that he can bring the parts for the wagons back here. People need the repair parts and so we can sell them readily as well as the complete coaches. Gerhard would also gladly take your motorcycle, but he did not know if you would approve of that. Please write me what you want done.

Alice is sitting with me, asking what I am writing! "Do you think of something or does Papa tell you what you should write?" Strange questions? I am losing weight and I don't know why. I guess it may be because I am worrying so often about the future, what it will bring. Well, I would deny myself the good things if only I could have you back. That is my greatest wish. The children are all quite well and so am I. I wish you the best of health. Grandpa's health is deteriorating from day to day.

The new law states that no letters should be written in German. I will try it out and see if you will receive this letter. I'll mark a cross in this letter to identify it. Many, many greetings and kisses from your Tina with everlasting love.

From Nicolai
Evacuation Station
Medical Train No. 10/160
Brest-Litovsk, May 19, 1915

My dearest Tienchen and my children!

It doesn't happen very often but this is what happened yesterday. At two o'clock at night I received the letter you had written May 12th. I had long been waiting for a letter from you, but the waiting seemed in vain, no letter came. That you would not write for so long I simply found hard to believe. Sixteen days had passed since I got your last letter, the one that you sent with H. Enns. So you can imagine with what longing I waited for news from you, my loved ones. I was so happy when I finally received this letter that I couldn't fall asleep for a long time.

As you can see, we have finally reached Brest again, an arrival we had been looking forward to. We've been here two days and will probably stay a few more days. Then we'll be underway steadily for some 26 days before we can finally get a thorough rest from this work. I myself am not that much in need of rest because, as I wrote you, I had rested for nine days before this trip, but the other medics are in much greater need of rest. Koop from Orenburg became quite ill and had to be hospitalized in the military hospital here in Brest. In addition to that he was quite badly jaundiced, the result of the lack of sleep. The frequent interruptions of sleep, of course, happen here a lot. Brother n is sick now also, down with a fever. Willy Heidebrecht is not quite well, although he's up today, but last night there was much moaning because of terribly bad stomach ailments. However, these sicknesses are nothing compared to the terrible wounds suffered out there on the battlefield. How many thousands are lying out there now in horrible agony calling for relief from their suffering, and how many are probably being wounded at this very moment because of the horrible slaughter raging there.

However, the greatest abominations are the many traitors here. Just in the last few days, another gang of these traitors, who were ready to sell out a city for money, was caught.[42] No wonder the Government has to impose such strict rules; they really can't do anything else. Traitors like this are quite without feelings, quite oblivious to the innocent blood they spill through their treachery; they are looking only to line their own pockets. Well, God punishes such miscreants and severely. Witness Judas who sold Jesus for thirty pieces of silver and for that betrayal later hung himself. May God spare us from such vile, shameful deeds. According to what an Austrian soldier who was recently taken prisoner reports that severe unrest is beginning to stir in Germany and the public is beginning to oppose the war. Well, it won't be long until Germany will have its full measure and will suffer a thorough defeat, which will actually be of great benefit for the German people. May the time be here soon when we can call out, "PEACE!" How we all are now longing for peace, something we never cherished enough! When I think about how wonderful it will be when we will be on our way home and won't have to go back to war, I want even now just to scream for joy!

And how is Hilda's foot? Is it better already? Please be very careful that she doesn't get an infection in it. What about Alice? Is she still so pale and weak? Does she seem to be getting a little stronger? And has Selma suffered anything as a result of her fall? What about you, Tienchen? Have you experienced any change? Was Gerhard called up to the induction lottery yet?[43] What about the parents and the other siblings? What is everyone doing? Please write much. I want to know what everyone is doing. I received a card from brother Abraham. He writes that he is working in a sawmill in Memrik but secretly is hoping to be sent up as a medic.

Sending you and the children most heartfelt love and greetings,

Your loving and praying Nicolai.

From Nicolai
Evacuation Station
Medical Train No. 10/160
Baranovichi, May 25, 1915

My dearest Tinchen!

Have once again completed a run from Baranovichi to Gomel. It was quite easy this time because we had only lightly wounded soldiers. What a great difference it makes for us if we care for lightly wounded vis-à-vis seriously wounded ones. Now

---

[42] In March 1915 a Russian officer was executed in Warsaw on charges of treason and this led to an outbreak of "spy mania" in Russia. Jews and also German Russians, including Mennonites, were often singled-out and persecuted.

[43] The agreement with the Russian state in the 1870's was that the Mennonite community assumed responsibility for a large part of the costs of the alternative service system. It was entirely outside the military system apart from the fact that recruitment into the service followed the system of military recruitment. Young men, reaching a certain age, reported to a designated center and drew a ball from a bag. If they drew a certain ball they were enlisted. But like the military system they served their time and were released as reservists (hence the reference to reservists) just like those conscripted. So in time of War, just as soldiers were recalled to service in age cohorts, so Mennonites were liable to recall. This obviously is what happened to Nicolai. He was recalled to service but not to the military. (Urry)

we are on the way to Lublin and from there we usually move on further up the line. If matters continue in our train as they are now with sick staff, our train will not be going to Asodum very often any more.

As I wrote you last time, we had two very seriously sick medics on our train. One was Koop and the other was brother Hermann. We admitted them both at that time to the military hospital in Brest. One day after Hermann had been admitted to hospital, I visited him. He was so weak then that he could scarcely move his arms. There was not the slightest possibility of his getting up or walking. Often he couldn't understand when he was asked a question nor even recognize persons right away. Such periods when he seemed unaware lasted only five to ten minutes. In one word, he looked very, very sick. If God doesn't help, then we might lose our brother. Tinchen, let's pray earnestly and maybe God will hear our plea and restore our dear Hermann back to health. Many of the medical staff are feeling ill. A nurse and the assistant commanding officer are also very sick, as are the other nurse and the youngest doctor, but not so seriously. What the problem is, I don't really know, but it probably stems from the stress and exhaustion we have had from heavy workload that leaves one quite vulnerable to illness.

Tomorrow we are returning to Brest, and if at all possible I want to try to visit Hermann then. Yesterday I suddenly felt very ill with stomach cramps, diarrhea and vomiting. I became quite anxious, so I took a good dose of opium right away and by evening it was all over. Now I feel completely well. Thank God for those eight or nine days of rest I had; they were very good for me. If all could get a thorough rest, the situation here would be quite different, too. Living such irregular schedules can't be good. And with the meals it's the same. Sometimes we eat lunch twelve o'clock, sometimes at three or four o'clock. And sometimes we simply do not have time at all during the day to eat. And our sleeping pattern is similar. However, nothing can be done about it and with God's help we will make it through.

Elven the Zemstvo representative is the same as always. There is no end to his ranting once he gets into that state and woe to anyone whom he encounters while he's in a bad mood. I have always been fortunate, have always avoided him by the skin of my teeth. But poor Enns, I feel sorry for him. He invariably seems to get caught. Well, we hope the war will end soon and then everything will change. How are things going at home? Are all of you well, my dear ones? How is Hilda's foot? Is she feeling better? As we are going to pass through Brest, I ask you, my dearest Tina, to send a few pounds of butter by mail. Dry bread slides down reluctantly without butter.

In closing my letter I send you warmest greetings and kisses,

Your Nicolai

From Tina
Schoenfeld, May 26, 1915

Dear Nicolai,

On May 21, I sent my last letter to you to Lublin and this evening I received your letter of May 13 in which you write that I should address my letters to Brest. You will probably wonder why I have not written. You may think it was because I have been so busy washing floors, but that's not the case. In fact we, Anna, Papa and I went by wagon to Mary Wall's wedding. We had hired some horses for the trip. On the way, we stopped at Heinrich Loewens, had a cup of coffee and then I went on to Willmsens where Lenchen [Wife of Nicolai's brother, Aron] is staying now. You can imagine how surprised she was when I suddenly appeared at her door. I met Willie Fast there, who was home on furlough for one month. We stayed there one night, and the next day, after breakfast, we went on to Lichtfelde, got there at noon. That was on Saturday, May 23, and on Sunday we attended the wedding. There I met a number of people I knew and met some others I didn't know. Even Anna Friesen, the teacher's daughter from Mariental, was there.

Then on Sunday afternoon Anna and I went to Halbstadt, stayed the night, but Papa went along with the Balzers to Schardau, and then on Monday early, he went with the Schardauers to Chernigovka, where the lottery for the military service was held. He wanted to see if Gerhard would be released from service. We'll find out today or tomorrow. Well, the trip home with Loewen Monday morning early was not very easy. First of all, two of the harness traces broke, so we were delayed about an hour, and from Burakov to Schoenbrun, it rained so we got soaked. Well, I'm happy to be home again. Mariechen Wall's husband is a fine chap, a fellow named Penner. He's from the Old Colony.[44] They did not visit us as a bridal couple. And what you write about Aunt Sara is an imagined story. There is no substance to it at all.

Had another tooth pulled yesterday. Now I have lost four roots and one tooth with four more to go. Today when he extracted a tooth, it bled very much because the tooth broke off. That's why it was quite difficult. When the tooth had finally been extracted, I trembled all over. I wanted him to finish the extractions but he postponed them till tomorrow. Well, at this rate I will probably lose all my bad teeth, which of course will make you very happy. But I'll wait with getting dentures till next year. The cost is too high. Imagine such an expensive mouth during this war year? I am writing so much about this that you will be bored reading it. I heard from Manja that there are a number of people ill in your train. How is the state of your health? [Last page missing.]

From Tina
Schoenfeld, May 31, 1915

Dear Nicolai,

Yesterday I received another dear letter from you. If you had been home, I would have spoken very little to you this week because my mouth is so sore, but now I am rid of all my bad teeth, something I intended to do for a long time, but I was afraid to have them pulled. Don't be concerned that my cheeks will look hollow. They look as they always did.

You wrote that Herman is very ill. If only he were home, mother would give him the best care. Oh, if only I could come to Brest, I would care for you both but that of course is impossible. If we pray earnestly, God will surely help.

---
[44] The Old Colony (Khortitsa) was the first settlement in New Russia (Ukraine) of Mennonites who migrated from Prussia in the late 1700's. See Introduction.

Why didn't you write sooner concerning the butter? I would have sent it to you long ago if only I had known where to send it. When I think that you are eating one meal a day and we eat more than twice as many, well then I'm ashamed. You must be out of coffee already. If you're sick, coffee will perk you up. I will send you butter at the earliest opportunity. Manja went to Berdiansk to visit her parents, for how long I don't know. Hans Wilms is here at our place now. He has an infection in his heel. It finally came to a head after fourteen days, so I lanced it with a razor. He suffered a lot in these two weeks and looked very ill. Hilda's foot is completely better. The three girls are very healthy and into everything.

Now the roses are blooming beautifully, and the girls knock them over as they bend down to smell them. They pick apples or uproot beets; everything in their path they pull out. Otto has left the store because he wants to spend the rest of his furlough at home. He leaves back to service on the 29th. We don't know anything about Gerhard's military situation yet. When he reported, they merely weighed him and told him he could go home. We don't know if he will have to begin to do service now or after a year. The treatment for Papa's arm did not help, but they thought he could continue to work. No one went to the train station yesterday. [No closing to this letter.]

From Nicolai
Evacuation Station
Medical Train No. 10/160
Brest-Litovsk, June 3, 1915

With deep sadness I must announce the death of my beloved brother Hermann. He died June 1, 1915, at 12:00 a.m. after a brave struggle with a bad disease. It is particularly sad because he died far away from our dear mother and his other brothers. Hermann will be buried June 3, 1915, at 10:00 a.m. at the Brothers' Cemetery [Mass Grave].[45]

Nikolai Abramovich Rempel

From Nicolai: An account of brother Hermann's death and funeral
Evacuation Station
Medical Train No. 10/160
Brest-Litovsk, June 4, 1915

My dearest Tinchen!

As you have already seen from the post card I sent you on the second of June, our dear Hermann is no longer with us. Who would have believed one month ago that he would be removed so quickly from all the troubles and toils of this world? This letter is really supposed to be an account of Hermann's last days, his death and funeral. However, I don't know if I am in a state of mind capable of doing this very well because it is so hard for me to put coherent thoughts to paper. Right now my mind is rioting with all kinds of thoughts, but you, my dear Tina, understand me,

---

[45] Hermann was interred, not in a mass grave, but in a private plot in a large cemetery in Brest-Lietovsk.

feel with me, will not misinterpret any discrepancies that are woven into this account. It seems to me I have already written about Hermann's illness, but just in case I haven't told you the whole story, I'll start from the beginning.

While I was home on furlough at Easter, Hermann lay somewhat ill with a fever here in the train. However, he was back at work when I returned to the train, although he looked quite sallow. My advice to him that he take better care of himself didn't help much. He simply responded: "But you can see that this work is expected of me? I have to deal with it as best I can." Our Chief Administrator, as you know from my earlier letters, was quite difficult and he made sure that our train was always on the move, never waiting in line with the other trains. The work had to be done and the pace from Easter on continued without a break, often day and night, no rest. All of the medics, not only Hermann, looked terribly stressed and exhausted, but our Chief was always cutting into the line of other trains when he could to pick up wounded soldiers.

When we had finished loading in Bonboringa (Bobruisk?) on the 14th, we left for Fanell. Arriving there, we had a huge workload. Bread, meat and other things had to be loaded into the carriages by us medical workers, all overtired but the work had to be done. Hermann had to see to it that all of the linens were moved from the warehouse into the carriages, doing most of it himself, dragging some fifteen heavy bales into the train on his own. He threw the last bales into the train when it was already in motion. Bathed in perspiration, he stopped into our carriage for a moment before returning to the storage carriage to sort all the clothing and bedding. Although all of us worked as hard as possible, we were screamed at, "Why aren't you working; you, all of you, deserve to be whipped into hell." This was all too much for him, so when we came back to Brest from Fanell, my dear brother was already very ill.

At first he didn't want the doctor to know that he was so ill, but finally at my urging he consented to have me inform the doctor of his condition. When the doctor came, he glanced at Hermann and said, "Well, you do have a fever. I'll give you some pills and you will soon be better." I feared the worst for him, however, and kept my eyes on his every movement and breath because I saw how very ill he was. On May 20th I asked him if he would like to go to the hospital because I thought the situation demanded it. He agreed because he thought it would be quieter there and the air cleaner. The doctor agreed to admit him to hospital immediately. That same day when we took him to the hospital, we were told he merely had influenza, so he was taken to the influenza ward. The next day, I visited him for about half an hour before I had to go back to my train, which was leaving Brest shortly. I didn't realize then that this would be the last time I would speak with him. We returned to Brest about five days later, where the very bad news was awaiting me that I was not allowed into the room to visit with him.

When I last visited Hermann, he was in Intensive Care, and I was not allowed to talk to him. Among other things I was handed a note that he had written in his last hour of consciousness that reads as follows: "My dear mother, sister, siblings and all those who will be coming home eventually. I have been in hospital four days now and already I know what lies ahead of me. In a few days I shall be dead. You know, dear Mother, that I have a childlike faith in Christ." On the 29th and the

31st, I saw him again and he seemed to have improved a little. But on June 1st I was told he could not live much longer. I had this terrible feeling, but believed, however, that God would not take Hermann from us. But God had different intentions for him. He wanted to make an end to his suffering and to take him into the heavenly kingdom. On June 2nd I went once more to see how his condition was. How terrible every step to the hospital was; no one understands, even my good comrades, who usually share all suffering with me. But this time I walked to hear the heartrending words that, "Your brother wished us all of us a long life (to live many years) and then died." And so it was God's will to take him to Himself, and God has never made a mistake.

Now I had to find out quickly when and where Hermann was to be buried. It was my wish to lay him to rest at least with some semblance to the manner that we are used to. So I requested permission to buy a coffin and that he be buried in a separate grave, not a common one. The first request they granted readily, but it appeared that the second would not be granted. But after much negotiating back and forth, and pleading, the second request was also granted. However, when I returned to the hospital a little later, I was told that the body could not be placed in a coffin, but my colleague, Kornelius Fast, had already purchased one. Now I had to plead again. In the end I was granted permission to place him in a coffin, but only after our doctor interceded.

By 12:00 noon on June 3rd, the burial was to be completed. So we had to work from early morning to complete everything. Fast and Dyck went into town to see if the coffin was ready and to see if the pastor whom we had telegraphed had arrived. In the meantime, I went to the hospital in order to see if everything was ready there. Soon the coffin arrived and we (i.e., not we, but the rather the medics from the hospital. We were not permitted to touch him) dressed Hermann in the clothes that he usually wore here, however, very clean: a blue satin shirt, black trousers and boots. He looked just the way he did when he was working with us on the train.

Because the cemetery was quite far away, it was almost impossible to carry the coffin, although all medics offered to do that. And so the coffin was placed in a Polish carriage lined with white sheets and procession began to move slowly to the cemetery. We had not proceeded very far when we were joined by our nurses, the doctor and wife of a colonel (the overseer of the local fortress) who followed us in an automobile. They carried wreathes they themselves had woven, in addition to a metal wreath, with the inscription:

"Eternal Memory to Hermann Rempel, Died on June 2, 1914"

When we arrived at the cemetery, the coffin was lifted from the carriage because the cemetery is large, and carried by medics to the grave. Here we stood around the coffin in silence. Then it was lowered into the grave. Soon the muffled sound of earth fell down into the grave to cover the coffin forever. When the grave was covered, a wooden cross was erected, with the inscription:

"From Doctors and Nurses to Dear Hermann Rempel, June 2, 1915, Age 35"

The metal wreath was placed on the cross and the burial mound was decorated with wreaths and flowers.

Because the pastor did not come, there were no words spoken, each prayed quietly to himself. And so we returned home to our train and in the evening Dyck read a few passages from the Bible. We sang a few songs, bowed our heads once more in collective silent prayer. Therewith our funeral was ended, but the pain not for a long time. I am absolutely convinced that our dear brother Hermann is now much better off than we are, but how very painful the separation. Who knows who will be next? Please, my dear Tinchen, write to me often to carry me through this difficult time.

Your grieving Nicolai

P.S. I do not have time to proofread this letter, so please excuse my mistakes.

Notice to family of his death June 1, 1915

Nicolai and his brother Hermann served on the same train until his death. Hermann was principal and teacher in the Schönfeld Zentralschule before the war. He left in 1911 to pursue further studies in St. Petersburg.

From Tina

Schoenfeld, June 8, 1915

Dear, dear Nikolai,

Yesterday we received the sad news that Hermann is really dead. We had all been playing ball happily before our wagon returned from the station bringing Papa back from Kharkov and bringing your card announcing Hermann's death. All playing stopped immediately. Everyone was stunned. Your sister Tina who just happens to be here in Schoenfeld was inconsolable; she could hardly contain herself. She also had heard talk that Hermann had died, but she didn't believe it—none of us believed it. But because he was so sick [with typhus] she had feared she would hear the news of his death, but because she had heard nothing further, she had breathed a sigh of relief, thinking that things were better with him. We were notified by phone right away.

Yesterday and today many people who knew your family in Mariental stopped by, including Uncle Matthies with Louise and Agatha, Tante Braeul.[46] Mama [Nicolai's mother in Mariental] will get the message tomorrow morning. I'm going to Mariental with Tina tonight and will take it to her. The Matthieses are also going back today and Sara [Nicolai's niece] is going along as well. There will be much grief and activity in that home immediately! Please address your letters to Mariental, even though they will probably be delayed for a month. Write us in detail about Hermann's death and what else that dreadful disease is doing.

Are you still quite well? Mama had Ediger submit an application, requesting the release of one of your [seven] brothers from the service, but whether that will happen is hard to know. How happy I would be if you were freed! Then we would stay with Mama because her provider [Hermann] is no longer with us. In a small way we could be a substitute for Hermann, don't you agree? It almost seems as though your siblings are destined not to die at home. Anna died in the Terek— now Hermann in Brest-Litovsk, and who knows who else will stay in Brest [the front at that time]. If only this horrible war would finally come to an end. It is so very sad when one cannot die at home among family members. Well, it is God's will and we must not complain about it.

During the past week, 600 letters were found at the station buried under debris and manure. All of the stamps had been torn off and the letters had not been stamped. And we wonder why the letters we write don't reach their destination! All of us are well and we hope you are, too. Now I must eat supper, give the children their bath, then pack up and get ready to leave. Again many greetings and kisses from your ever-loving Tina.

From Nicolai
Evacuation Station
Medical Train No. 10/160
Brest-Litovsk, June 11, 1915

My dear Tinchen!

Yesterday evening I received your long letter from June 5th and I thank you. It is really remarkable that the people there already knew about Hermann's death on the 5th. They must have anticipated something like this because no news could get there so quickly. We first knew about it on the 2nd after faspa, and I sent you the

---

[46] *Tante* and *Onkel* used like 'aunt' and 'uncle' in English: —*Tante Tina* or *Onkel Johannes*. But they could be used loosely as Mrs., Mr.. We children called our neighbors *Onkel Unruh* and *Tante Unruh*. The *Ohm* in Plattdeutsch means Old Man but in an affection sense.

news that same night, but you could not have received the letter before the 6th of June. Well, despite sorrow and sadness, people imagine many things. Also, that I am no longer in the Bandaging Ward is a figment of someone's imagination, and I will probably be working there for some time yet as it is probably the most sanitary work in the military medical trains. None of the medics are in hospital any longer, and are back on duty more or less healthy in this train. All experience a certain measure of exhaustion, but we take comfort in the thought that we will regain our health when we are with you again as we all hope to come home to our loved ones again.

But God may have a different plan for us. In a brief time, if God wills it, things can change very suddenly, as we have witnessed just a short time ago. We saw that just in the last days. Hermann was sick only a few days, from May 17th to June 1st. Whatever God does that is done well. His way is always right! Let's never forget this, my dear Tina, and should we never see each other again here on earth, we do have the assurance that we will see each other with our Heavenly Father again. This is my only comfort even now that Hermann has passed away from us.

How is your health? Has your mouth healed or is it worse? Definitely get some dentures immediately. Not for the sake of looks but for your health, because your stomach isn't in the best of conditions. So do get some dentures right away. If you need money, write to me and I'll find a way. If you go to Mariental, we may have to write in Russian as the postmaster in Gnadenfeld is a bit ornery. You won't find any [of our] wagons there because they have been sold. I thought the droshky was long ago at Eusch, but probably Ohm Matthies will not have received my letter. And also about the harvester (binder), it seems that Ohm Matthies has received nothing. Tell Papa that he should not chide Matthies for not having given machinery to Osolien, as I told him he should not give any of my things to anyone without my permission. After all, he was looking out for me. Probably Matthies has been there already and has settled everything with Papa.

I received the package with the butter and coffee and it was all wonderful. It could have stayed at the post office another week and still would have been quite all right. Here nothing has been said of the medics becoming sick from the things that were sent from home. It is plain to everyone that there are other causes for the illnesses here. It's surprising to me that such nonsense was blathered about there. Thank you very much for the last parcel—it was delicious.

Concerning the motorbike, tell Gerhard that if he pays me 100 rubles cash, but no less, he can have it any time. I paid 150 rubles for it then and it is in better condition now. I asked questions in quite a few letters that you have not answered yet. Please read them over again and then perhaps you will give me the answer. Here things are going along as usual. Lately there has been less work for the medics because we have had respite for several days after each trip, and this is good for everyone after such long intense work.

Please greet parents and siblings and I send loving greetings to you and the children.

Your Nicolai

From Tina
Mariental, June 12, 1915

My dear Nicolai,

It's Sunday again today and I'm glad it's over. I was in church in the morning for Communion. After that I had a good nap and then went to Mrs. Loepp's birthday celebration. There were a lot of women at the party but only three old men. And the day after tomorrow there will be a wedding, but it doesn't seem like it at all since the Matthies didn't need anyone to help them. The bridal couple didn't visit us and we don't know if we'll go to the wedding. The Matthies are very peculiar people. Maybe the bride will come to see us tonight; then our going to the wedding will be another matter.

You probably received the things (letters and money) from Voth. Will I be so fortunate in that you will use your money for a trip home or not? From your last letter my hope was lifted again that you would be coming home. I would be most happy if you came. We are doing a lot of sewing. I am sewing shirts for your brother Heinrich while Tina[47] is sewing for others. She actually wanted to go to Alexandertal to do some sewing but mother won't let her go. Tina would so much like to go. Who knows what mother would do if Tina should leave home for good. Then she would have to let go of her.

The hay was mowed for seven rubles. You write about going to Wiebe. All the children are healthy and I will wait until you come home, then things will go better. Hilda is coughing; she's had this problem since she was little, but sometimes it's worse. Well, one problem with our children is that they always want to gad about. It's impossible for them to stay at home. They feel too lonely. I have punished them for it but it hasn't helped at all. I am being calling for supper —must go quickly.

Well, now I have finished supper. Selma is very cranky. She is standing beside me and bawling. There is a wedding in Gnadenfeld on the 16th. Susa, the daughter of the school's headmaster, will likely be there. If possible, mother and I will go, too.

Have you received any news about where Gerhard has been sent? I still don't know where he is. Things will not go well with that boy. I believe it was very difficult for Papa. He [Gerhard] cheated him again. He took some large pieces of cloth behind Papa's back, sold them and kept the money. When Gerhard left the last time, he hid a large bolt of cloth in the wagon, but then forgot to take it out. When I used the wagon later to go to the station, I discovered this big package worth at least 100 rubles. He and I often quarreled about episodes like that. It would be so sad if he were to perish in a strange place. Let's not forget to pray for him, but we too are in need of prayer because we are still not fully committed ourselves.

I was going to write a letter to the folks at home (Schoenfeld) but I will wait. Perhaps someone from the Jakob Matthies family will come to the wedding and then I will send a letter with them. I will write them to let me know if they are very busy, and if they are, I will come right away to help. I am really quite contented and

---

[47] Tina is Nicolai's youngest sister, a seamstress, who later worked in the first orphanage in the Mennonite settlements, in Grossweide. The orphanage was established by Abram and Justina Harder. Tina Rempel married Johannes Harder, son Abram and Justina Harder. See T.D. Regehr, *A Generation of Vigilance: The Lives and Work of Johannes and Tina Harder* (Winnipeg: Canadian Mennonite University Press, 2009).

happy here, arranging things so that when you come home we can take it easy. Stop over in Schoenfeld when you come; your suit and shoes are there. All of us are very well and I wish you the same with all my heart. The children eat a lot of mulberries; however, there won't be any cherries this year but plenty of apples. Tina planted a lot of cabbage seeds and if all the plants mature, there will be plenty of those.

This afternoon the bride herself walked down the street, asking some girls to help her, but she sauntered right past our place without stopping, even though Tina was practically sitting in the street. It was quite dark when Susa came by, wondering if we would help with the decorating [probably for the bridal shower], but she left without even waiting for an answer. Tina is so annoyed that she can hardly control herself. She doesn't want to go to the shower and so none of us will go; nor will any of us go to the wedding either. Tina says the bride is using us as a stopgap. She remarked to Susa, "Who knows if Tina [the bride] would appreciate my showing up." Susa told her she should just go, nobody would say anything to her.

Enough for this time. More after the wedding. Many greetings and kisses from your loving Tina and children.

From Nicolai
Evacuation Station
Medical Train No. 10/160
Brest-Litovsk, June 16, 1915

My darling Katja,

I just came back from Gomel here to Brest-Lietovsk. I want to quickly write this letter and tell you about our recent work. As I told you in my last letter, we are not as busy as before. Now we are taking wounded men from Brest to Minsk or Gomel. Our train is not at the front anymore but at the rear. Being at the rear is much different from being at the front. Now we even have time to rest sometimes. It is so good. There are moments when we can even be cheerful.

Only one sad thing—Hermann is not with us anymore. I am almost well again and so are my friends, the other medical workers, except for Ivan Thiessen who is in the hospital. The rest of us are working—everything is OK, but I cannot adjust to the fact that I'll never see my dear brother again, talk to him or receive his advice, but mainly I don't know how I will come back home without him. We went to war together, together we worked in the same Red Cross Military Hospital Train, and now I will come home without him! My soul is suffering greatly.

But we are not the only ones crying about a brother lost to this war; millions are crying about the brother, the husband, the father and the son they have lost. We are all of us sinners and it seems to me that God is punishing us for our sins. It is time to wake up and confess our sins honestly. Pray, my dear Katja, for me, and teach our children to pray for peace, too. I sent a letter to you and to mother in which I describe Hermann's funeral. Did you receive that letter? Let me know, please.

How are things going in Marietal? Everything the same? Did you receive the grant that all soldiers' wives are entitled to? How are our dear children? Are they in school already? Write me about everything no matter how trivial you think it may be. Tell everyone who remembers me to write to me because I am very lonely after the death of my brother, Hermann. I have very fine friends here on the train, but I feel very lonely after Hermann's death.

Just now we received a telegram telling us to go to Holm to pick up some wounded soldiers. We will take them to Gomel. Yesterday I wrote that Ivan Thiessen is in hospital, but today, June 17, we sent a few more friends to the hospital, all with severe dysentery.

Did you hear anything about the special grant my mother should receive, a government grant when a soldier dies? Has she heard anything yet? I'm waiting impatiently for your letters and thank you for them. I hug you and kiss you and our dear children, too.

Your Nicolai

From Nicolai
Evacuation Station
Medical Train No. 10/160
Moscow, June 21, 1915

My much beloved Tinchen and children!

It seems that Driediger will be going home, so I will try to send a letter with him. I sent one only yesterday, but it is very doubtful that you are receiving my letters. We receive letters so seldom that we seem to be quite isolated from all of you. I received the last one from you twenty-one days after you had written it. The others haven't heard from their families for a long time either. I have written to you many times but received no answers. What would it be like if we could talk with each other face to face? But there seems to be no possibility of that now. Many people believe that once the State Duma is in session, there will be more discussion of peace. However, there we are deceiving ourselves. No one in that body [Duma] really thinks of peace, and the war will drag on for a long time yet. So we will just have to be content with written correspondence, if that will do and look to a long adieu. However, we have no idea what our heavenly Father has in mind. He may have quite different plans, and so, my dearest Tina, let us ask God to bring an end to this horror and mold us into true Christians.

Since this letter will not pass through many hands but will be given to Driediger, I want to address a matter that concerns only the two of us. In one of the letters you wrote that you see a very dark future, that you are fearful of the future. I didn't know how you meant that, whether it is the future of which young women are often fearful or do you mean that hard times are coming for all mankind. Have you experienced any physical changes since I was home or is everything quite in order? Are your periods regular? Please write me everything.

I had written up to here and along comes the mailman with two letters from you. How full of joy I am, you can't possibly imagine. I also received the notice that a parcel is on its way for me. My heartfelt thanks. If you were here, I would hug you and kiss you. Now I have ample of everything. I probably won't receive your parcel for several days because we are about to leave for Brest and on from there. Where, we do not know.

Today I met Aron again, who told me that Lenchen [his wife] went to Marietal. Have you met her? What is everybody in Mariental doing? Will there be a lot of fruit this year? Concerning the money you mentioned, I really don't know what to say. The money for the undercarriage should go to Julius; he probably needs it. What you don't need of the balance should go into a savings account, that is, fifty rubles. But in any case, have dentures made for yourself, then if at all possible, have yourself and the girls photographed and send me the photos. Otherwise I will forget what you look like. As for the rest of the money that is to come in, some should go to Sawatzky and 100 rubles to Schmidt with interest. I believe that is all the money that will come in. Have you received any money from the Crown?

Peter Neufeld is sitting here with me wondering how it is possible that his letters don't arrive at their destination. Recently he has written very often. I know that for certain. Peter is quite well but he needs about two weeks of rest and a healthy diet to help him with his stomach that continues to be upset. Otherwise he is quite healthy. Well, nothing is coming of Driediger's trip home, so I'll send this letter by post.

In the meanwhile, I send you most heartfelt greetings and I am always your Nicolai, who thinks of you from early to late.

From Tina
Mariental, June 22, 1915

Dear Nicolai,

I haven't had any news from you for a long time. Your last letter was dated June 4th. What's been happening anyway? Are you sick or do you simply not have time to write? When I was in Schoenfeld and didn't hear from you, I could always get some news about you from others [on furlough.] I'm staying here in Mariental until July 6th and if you haven't arrived here by then, I'm going back to Schoenfeld, if I'm alive and well. Yesterday a memorial service was held for Hermann in the church here. After the service, we invited the neighbors and Mr. Harder, the teacher,[48] to the house for a bite to eat.

It rained yesterday and also today, so I really don't feel like doing any work. However, I just finished doing the buttonholes for six pairs of trousers. I want to gather up the clothes tonight because tomorrow is laundry day—nice job to look forward to, eh? Well, this too shall pass.

Johannes was here from Berdiansk for one day. He brought the news that you will be released on account of your lungs. He said that Papa had been in Berdiansk and told them that you had written a letter to Schoenfeld with the news that you will be released from service. How delighted I am, hoping that it will really happen. Then I will nurse you back to health and together we will follow the straight and narrow path. Mrs. Harder remarked yesterday what a great privilege it was that she

---

[48] Hermann and Harder were teaching colleagues and, I assume, Harder also served as pastor in the church in Mariental.

didn't have to give up her husband to the service. She said, "How sad if after fourteen years of being together I would have to be alone." Well, she is lucky and I'm happy for her with all my heart. If only all women could avoid this separation from their husbands! Who knows how many more husbands will have to go to war?

I stopped writing here yesterday. Since I've finished with the laundry for today, I'll add a few lines. Looking at the picture of how things are here, it is plain to see that the "boss" [Nicolai?] is missing. Often people come for spare parts. I sold parts for twelve rubles today. Several people came for seed grain but there is none left; nor is there any promise for a good harvest because the grain has been flattened by a rainstorm and so will be difficult to harvest. We are waiting for you to come home to help. I tell them not to count too much on your help because you will not be able to work right away. You have to take a good rest first. But everyone is full of hope that you are coming. Will we be disappointed? Today I delivered the spare parts for the harvester that Hildebrand bought. I have kept an account of all the transactions. I have cleaned all your soiled clothes from last summer. Nothing new is happening here. If I have any questions about any item, I ask Jakob Likov. He has been a great help to me. He bought the brown box-wagon for seventy rubles. Ohm Matthies, who sold it to him, didn't know that these wagons are quite expensive now.[49] When I arrived, he had already sold it. Of the machinery left, there are two grain-cleaning mills and five grinding mills. Otherwise everything has been sold except a lot of old stuff. You might not be interested in this information, but I'm writing about it anyway.

I'll stop now because there is not much content to this letter. I'm so disappointed every morning that there is no news from you.

Greetings and kisses from your Tina. I feel we'll be talking face to face soon.

From Tina
Mariental, June 28, 1915

My dear Nikolai,

I want to write to you but don't know where to send the letter. Lenchen came here last night and told me that Brest-Litovsk is no longer your right address, so I will change it again. Since I left Schoenfeld, I have received three letters from you: June 4, 11 and 16. None of them were opened, so we can write our letters in German.[50] You tell me I haven't answered all your questions; I certainly believe I have, but maybe some letters were lost.

I expected you home here on Thursday, but nothing came of that hope and I was most disappointed. I have to learn to accept disappointments, and I'm trying but will have to work at it harder. I was so sure that your next letter would bring the good news that you are free from further service—but again nothing. So I reminded myself of the proverb, "Hoping and waiting makes fools of many people."

---

[49] Many draft horses, wagons and teamsters had been inducted to transport food and war materials from the end of the railway line into the battlefield. It was part of the supply line. It seems that Nicolai and Tina owned or rented a parcel of land in Mariental. How they took care of their property in Mariental is unclear as Tina was in Schoenfeld most of the time.

[50] For restrictions on the use of German language see: Toews, *Czars, Soviets & Mennonites*, p. 74.

Mika said that is not found in the Bible. An adage says, "Hope will not disappoint!" That is very true. Well, I do hope you will be released from the service soon. I am praying continually. It is said that God hears children's prayers, so surely He will hear prayers of our children, too. The other day while we sat at the table, Hilda said she had prayed to God to send Papa home soon. And what to do with the many questions children have. I am reading a wonderful book by Esther Rind. If only I could be like Esther's cousin, Agnes—a fine God-fearing woman.

I wrote this far until the children interrupted me. Lenchen is here now with her two children [Ernst and Frieda], and on the 5th of July, Greta will be coming with her three [Waldemar, Erna, Gertrude], and then there are our three [Alice, Hilda, Selma], so our house will be full. However, when Greta comes I will go to Schoenfeld for a few days.

I received the 100 rubles for the harvester and paid our debt at the Abraham's store, eighty rubles, and I still have the rest of the money. I sold spare parts for twenty rubles and then there is the money for the box-wagon, about seventy rubles that Jake Likov still owes us, but I can get it whenever I want it. And I have a check in the amount of 300 rubles from Sudermann and Jakob Thiessen, the payment for the harvester to be delivered September 1. Hopefully you will be home by then? We brought the hay in yesterday and the manure will be dry soon so that it can be spread. Tomorrow we are going to Karl Schmidt's to pick cherries.

My mouth is all healed now. Until recently bits of root kept coming out, but now everything is fine. I can't have my dentures fit for three months, but half of that time has nearly passed. You don't have to send me any money. Of the twenty-five rubles you sent me, I've used only nine rubles for the tooth extraction. As for the Crown Grant for soldiers' wives, I won't be getting any of that. Until now all the women here have received it, but the government allotment for soldiers' wives has been cut and I won't get anything at all. Lenchen still received thirteen rubles in Halbstadt the day before the program was canceled. I have written you four letters from Mariental, and told you about everything, but perhaps you didn't get them. I believe we are getting all our letters unopened.

It's getting quite dark; I will light the lamp so that I can finish this letter. The children were playing happily outside until now but it's time to put them to bed. I am anxiously anticipating a letter from you tomorrow. If you only knew how I long for your letters! You probably feel the same way. Mother did receive the letter you mentioned. Things are going well here in Mariental. The children felt quite at home right away. The first families [refugees] haven't moved in yet, because they had to hand in their passports to the mayor. We haven't heard anything about Mama's application to have Heinrich and you released from the service. If only it would be granted!

Many greetings and kisses from your ever-loving Tina.

P.S. Thiessen wants to bring the money one of these days—about 400 rubles. Please let me know as soon as possible what I should do with it. Write even if to Schoenfeld.

From Nicolai's mother
Mariental, July 1, 1915

Dear Nicolai,

    I really doubt that you will receive this letter because your dear Tina says she has already written you five letters and you haven't answered any of them. I want to dare once more to write in German, but if you don't answer this either, I guess I'll stop writing because it's useless. Please write to me telling whether Hermann got the letters that I sent to Brest-Litovsk, and if he mentioned that letter to you and also the one I sent to Kirov. You and Hermann told us at that time to write either to Brest-Litovsk or to Kirov because you would be going through both places and so would possibly receive one of the letters there. Did you get the Kirov letter? I had written about many things and asked your thoughts about them. In the letter to you, I had just alluded to some things I also wrote in Hermann's letter because I thought you each would receive your letter. But because you haven't mentioned anything about what I had written, I conclude you didn't get the letters.

    Oh, Nikolai it is so very difficult for you—first Hermann's illness and now his death. I feel more sorry for you than for our dear, dear Hermann. He has overcome everything. It is well with him forever, and we should not weep any more. But still, I cry all the time. When I think that you have to return home without Hermann, I want to scream loudly. "Oh, don't leave Hermann there alone—so alone." But his soul is with the Lord, saved for eternity. How often I wish that I too could finally find that rest with the Lord and sing praises to the glory of God.[51] I don't think I could endure all this sorrow if our Father in heaven didn't send so many dear people who are comforting us. By this, we see how the people loved our dear Hermann. People everywhere are showing their deep compassion and sorrow for us. Last Sunday, preacher Harder officiated at the funeral in the church. He, too, showed his compassion and deep sympathy.

    Later in the afternoon we had a little gathering in our home to celebrate Hermann's life. We invited the neighbors and young people, adolescents and the older teens. Teacher Harder presented a short tribute there, too. His Scripture text at the memorial in the church was, "Blessed are the dead who die in the Lord. They will rest from their labors and their deeds shall follow them." Then he reminisced about Hermann's life as a teacher and how much the people had loved him and that he [Harder], too, had loved him very much. Harder's sermon was truthful, without exaggeration. He spoke about Hermann just as he would have liked it to be. He was a good example for us in his selflessness and love, even though he too was a sinner like all humans are. He fought the good fight against the world, sin and Satan. His struggle is over and he will now receive the crown of life. May the Lord help us all to have victory over evil and help us to endure because he who endures to the end shall be saved. When will the time come for this war will end?

    We have heard nothing about our application, much less about the result or your release. Johannes was home and told us that Peters' son-in-law talked confidently about your imminent release because you are unable to do any work

---

[51] She died in 1931 in the USSR. At that time she was still living in the Rempel home in Mariental (see photo in Epilogue), although it had been confiscated by the government and housed other families.

and that you will soon be home—perhaps only for six months but most likely for good. You will be discharged even without applying for it. That's what you supposedly told Peters yourself. Now we are waiting for you daily. But be sure you have the proper release papers or you might experience what happened to Hermann Klassen. He had to go back and still isn't home.

Things are going quite well with us. Your dear wife and children are here, and Sunday Lenchen is coming with her two children. We are also expecting Greta with her children. Then we are missing only Susa with her Hans, and Sarah with her four children, and then we're all together. And you could come to us, too. When the war is over, we will discuss everything. But, of course, Hermann is missing! Dear Nikolai, please write to Heinrich often. He is so alone out there. You still have your dear wife who writes to you. Heartfelt greetings from your loving mother, Sara Rempel.[52]

From Tina
Mariental, July 1, 1915

My dearest Kolya [Nicky],

If you want to hear anything from me, I need to write in Russian, which I can do but poorly. Even though this will not be a long letter, you will know something about us. I am planning to go to Schoenfeld on the 6th or 7th, and you can write there again. We are still alive and healthy, so you don't need to be worried. I got money and paid our debt to Abram. In a few days, Thiessen from Sparrau wants to bring the money he owes. What should I do with it? We already brought in the hay, the bricks are almost dry, and we cleaned up the attic. All of us miss you so much and our children always ask why their papa is not coming home. Your medical commando is living now in Krasnopol?

I know that you will be making fun of my letter in Russian, but from Schoenfeld I will be writing in German. If I have to write in Russian, I will not send many letters. I didn't get any further government support because financial support for soldiers' wives has been stopped. Mama got your letter in which you wrote of Hermann's illness, death and funeral. We also had a small memorial service here. The service was in church after which we invited neighbors in for coffee. Someone told us that you were ill and you had written to Krasnopol that you were going to return home for six months, so we are anxiously waiting for you.

It is very hot and even though we had a heavy rain the yard is quite dry. Two days ago I canned thirty jars of berries. Aaron's wife is here now with her two children, and on July 5th Greta will come with her three, so then Mother will have some distraction from grieving so much at the death of Hermann. It is very noisy here now.

Love and kisses and always thinking of you, Katya

---

[52] As mentioned, Hermann had never married and had been the main financial support of his mother, although she also had income from her farm. He had been a teacher and the principal in the Gnadenfeld high school. He was a devout Christian who was greatly admired by the family, especially by Nicolai whose religious convictions were strongly influenced by this brother.

P.S. Elena and children also send their affection. Yesterday I got your letter from June 21st.

From Nicolai
Evacuation Station
Medical Train No. 10/160
Minsk, July 7, 1915

My dearest Tinchen!

It seems that Jacob Ivanovich is leaving for home tomorrow, so I will use the opportunity to send you a little note. I don't know if you are already back in Schoenfeld, but if you have been faithful to your intentions, you, my dear ones, will probably have arrived in Schoenfeld on the 9th of month. The last letter I received from you was written on the 8th of June, just before you were leaving for Mariental. You can well imagine how pleased I would be to be able to read a letter from you. I know that you would have written several letters to me from Mariental if you had been well. However, they did not reach their destination.

I wrote a number of letters in Russian and requested that you begin to write letters in Russian also. A letter from you on my birthday would have been most welcome. Well, perhaps G. Fast will bring me a letter from Brest. The reason for his going there was to get the mail. All of our correspondence is actually sent from Brest here to Minsk.

Please be so kind and send all your letters to the following address: City of Minsk, Evacuation Station of Medical Train No. 10/160, N. A. Rempel

We have the prospect of staying here in Minsk for ten days because the whole train is to be thoroughly refurbished. But there is much work even now in the hospital trains because one train after another passes through here with wounded soldiers. It is absolutely horrible, the mass of humanity being slaughtered, men who just a short while ago were living peacefully and quietly with their families, earning their bread honestly, but now perish miserably far away from wife and child, parents and siblings. How often we ask ourselves: when will this catastrophe end? When will we be able to live in quiet and peace again, even as God has ordained it?

I didn't complete my letter yesterday, so I will continue today on my birthday [July 8]. Fast came back here from Brest, but still no letter for me. All others appear to have received letters, but none for me. Am beginning to read the letters other wives have written because there are no letters from my wife anymore. Just read Hermann Enns's letter that his Anna had written to him. Well, instead of reading letters or resting, we'll become an exhibit, marching and dancing the polka twice daily. How different this day is from the one six years ago, our wedding day. Where has that beautiful time gone?

When we come to Moscow next time, I will probably leave train No. 160 to rest for a while and then take up work on train No. 153. The chief officer (Sobko) on that train was the assistant chief on my first train. As I wrote you then, he is a very good man. When I last met him here in Minsk, he said to me, "I would like very much to transfer you to my train, but how can we do that?" I told him that they wanted me to stay in Moscow because I was not very well and then it might be possible. That sounded like a good idea to him, and God willing, it will probably happen. K. Fast will likely be in that train already. Apparently nothing will come of Dyck's furlough, so I will send this letter by mail and then, of course, it will be uncertain whether you receive it. I have been waiting until the date, the eleventh, for Dyck's furlough but will simply have to toss it into the mailbox.

(Written after July 11)

Because our kitchen is also being renovated and we receive only forty kopeks per day for food, in order to make ends meet we are doing our own cooking on a small *primus* [Kerosene camp stove]. For lunch today we had real Mennonite cuisine: gooseberry moos with ham [*Krestbeermoss mett Schinkefleisch*]. The ham you sent had been untouched until now, so it came in quite handy and it was very tasty. For tomorrow we plan to make apple fritters ["*runde Küake mett Kjoasche*] and cherry pastries. I am, so to speak, playing the master cook. Today my suffering brothers suggested I be awarded a citation for the excellent gooseberry soup. Well, these are insignificant matters and if only other things would run smoothly, we would be quite content with this cuisine. If only the interior of our carriages could have the same luster as the exterior with its new paint and varnish, the mood would also shift from what it now is.

How I desperately long finally to be home with my wife, children, parents and siblings. I am so terribly tired of this soldier's life, I can't even describe it. I just want to get home, to be a free human being, where I can speak openly with anyone without feeling the constant threat of "constraint of the whip" over my head. Now we just look around wildly like a tiger trying to satisfy his trainer, always having to look right and proper, eyes front, always having to march to the drummer, etc., etc. Such a life is not for a human being. Humankind is supposed to be free, to look into another's eyes with a clear conscience, to trust in each other, to love each other. We know the fruit of love from Corinthians 13.

But I'll stop now with the request that you write soon because today, the 11th of July, it is one month since I last heard from you. Rumor has it that the Rempels [Not Nicolai's relatives] want to visit [their son] Peter again. I would advise against it because people cannot go to Brest any longer without special permission because of the danger. Further more, Peter is on the train and in good health.

With warmest greetings and kisses,
Your Nicolai

From Tina
Mariental, July 7, 1915

My dear Nicolai,

We are in the midst of doing a big laundry, but I want to write a few lines to you. My hands are shaky so my writing is poor. We have been washing, getting straw from Mr. Matthies and piling it into stacks outside. Your sister, Tina, and I are building the stacks so who knows how this will work out. We have already brought home six loads. We place our [hand drawn] wagons next to each other and if

Matthieses have time, they load them, otherwise we have to do it. Of course, that gives old man Matthies something to laugh about, and I don't go there to be laughed at. I'd rather stay here to help with the unloading and stacking.

I had a very restless night because of my painful arm and Hilda with an earache, and I had no ointment for her ear. When she cried I told her that crying wouldn't help, so she asked me at least to wash her ear out with water. It helped for a few minutes and then she started to cry again. Then I put peppermint drops in her ear and she soon fell asleep and is still sleeping.

The girls are healthy except for a troublesome cough. As for me, well when you come home, we'll go to Berdiansk to Dr. Dueck to see what says. It is nothing special but I don't know how to explain it. When you come we'll discuss everything thoroughly. Otherwise things are going quite well with the children and me. You will have to excuse me if my page is not filled. I try to write a letter each time the mail is sent out. I forwarded the letters from Mama and Tina to you. Did you receive them? Tomorrow is your birthday and our wedding day. It's amazing when you think back how quickly time has gone by. Now I am counting the days until August when you'll be home. The children always ask, "When will Papa come home?" Hilda never forgets to pray for you. Sometimes she prays, "Let Papa come home the day after tomorrow." Please forgive me for the hurried scribbling.

My most heartfelt greetings and kisses, from your loving Tina and children

From Tina
Schoenfeld, July 12, 1915

Dear, dear Nikolai

I am back in Schoenfeld again. The trip with the children went quite well. Greta is in Mariental now and yesterday Truda went to see her Schroeder [husband] in Ekaterinoslav. If she likes it there, she'll stay several months. How I would love to come to see you for a while, too. I am so tired of living by myself and I know you feel that way, too, my darling.

We have a guest here at present—an army medical orderly—a Mr. Friesen. He is on leave for two months—works on the same train with Heinrich and some others from Schoenfeld. He says things are going very well and they don't have much work. He can earn quite a bit of money while he's here. He went to see a Russian in Kopani to have his motor checked. When I was still in Mariental, the Schulzes were having some problems with one of their motors, too.[53] They had to go to Berdiansk to have it repaired.

I must ask you right now what to do with the money that is coming in. Papa says we should put it into the bank until you come home. Please let me know right away. Papa says he doesn't care what you do with it, but he just wants to give us advice so that there will be some money when you come home. When I go to Mariental, where some money should be coming in now, if you approve, Papa and I would deposit it, too.

---

[53] Bernard Peters, Tina's father, had a business that included a dry goods store and farm machinery sales, included stationary engines and binders—hence, the spare parts.

What kind of payments are you still obligated to make at the Mayors? I don't know anything about that, so write me about it so that I will be informed or we may be giving out money and don't even know what it's for. I thought you had settled all of these matters at Easter. I asked Matthies about it, and he said everything was as before except for the harvester that had been sold and he had crossed it off the list. I took in some money for the box wagon and for some spare parts. I have it here—130 rubles. Some people wanted to borrow it, but Papa suggested that I should hold onto it until you write. If you want to deposit it, he will bring it to you [when he visits Nicolai]. If only you were here, everything could be regulated and organized.

Hilda and Selma are sleeping. They didn't want to nap after lunch, but they faded soon and went to sleep after Faspa. If Selma keeps on growing as she is, she will catch up with Hilda soon. She is growing unbelievably fast and is quite chubby, too—all of them are—Selma, Hilda and Alice. It is like what Aron wrote to his Emi —they're roly-polies. Our girls will mature very quickly and they already want to be "big" girls. Last week there was a very bad storm in a village near here. Ten telephone poles toppled and were broken, probably struck by lightening. All the wires were a twisted mess. Today it is overcast and it's raining with thunder and lightening.

When I had my teeth extracted, I weighed 3N 18 but now a month later I weigh 3N 25. Gained weight. Even though it is wartime, I have a pretty good comfortable life. Before, Truda always weighed more than I, but now I'm catching up, except that her cheeks are very hollow. Her little Schroeder [Margaret] is chubby.

The two letters I wrote in Mariental, I addressed one to Brest and one to Moscow, and now that I'm here they are showing me a different address—Minsk. Well, I believe you have received my letters because I always write promptly. Very soon I'll send you a parcel with cookies. I had thought I would send coffee and butter also, but I heard from Tante Sana that the women take turns sending coffee and butter and now it is their turn. Is that right? Please let me know so that you don't lose out. Write me if you are short of anything and I will send it right away.

Willie [in Forestry Service] came very close to being sent away to serve as forest watchman. They were looking for the smallest and the weakest in the Sagradovka Forestry Camp and Willie belonged to that group. He was afraid of that position, so he went to the head forester and begged that he be allowed to stay where he was. He was told to wait for an answer until the next day. The next day, twelve men were sent away, but Willie didn't have to go. He is now the cook, but the cook has to help with the threshing, also. They don't feed the men as well as they used to when you were in the forestry camp. They get white bread only twice a week, so we women send them cookies and something to spread on their bread.

It doesn't look good with Grandpa, in fact, it is very sad. He is lying in bed swearing and scolding. He is out of his mind, so to speak. I don't know what will happen. I hope there will be a change because it is dreadful to listen to him. That's why I seldom go to see him, because the little children should not hear that language. Old people like that can't seem to die, but young ones must die. Like Etus' sons, the oldest one already died in the war and the younger one is now home for six months. All the shooting and the noise of the cannons affected his head.[54] He is supposed to go back after six months whether he is well or not. When will this terrible war end?

Write and tell me where Peter Rempel is now. They say that he is in Brest and that he can't go back into your train; the administrator won't allow it. Mrs. Rempel is very concerned about him. If she had someone to take her, she would have come to visit you by now. We are sending for Papa tonight and this letter will go along.

There was a prayer meeting in the church last week. It seems that the time has not yet come that peace will be declared. We must experience more testing and afflictions before God will answer our prayers. Let's not neglect to pray, my dear. Let's believe that the war will end soon and we will be together again.

Many greetings and kisses from your ever-loving Tina whose thoughts are always with you.

P.S. Grandma [Toews] was here for your birthday.

From Nicolai
Evacuation Station
Medical Train No. 10/160
Minsk, July 15, 1915

My loving, faithful Tinchen!

Finally, finally I have received a letter from you from June 22. I heard nothing from you for more than a month. You can't imagine how I felt. The last letter from you was dated June 8th. Is it really true that you didn't write to me from the 8th to the 22nd of July? That is 14 days. I didn't want to believe it but if it's really true, then I don't Know what to think.

You write that you can stay in Mariental only till July 6th. You seem to be on the run. I sent a letter there already and one also to Schoenfeld after July 10th so that you stay informed. This present letter I will send to Schoenfeld. As to my being discharged from service, well there is no chance of that. I don't remember whether I wrote home already that there is no prospect for being released; possibly I did write. Several doctors told me that because of my medical condition, my weak lungs, I should be released from the service, but then I never really considered that a possibility and so decided not to write about it, because being released would be most difficult. So we might as well get rid of the notion of seeing each other before the war ends. Our doctor said I should be released from work for at least one month so that I could go south to a resort for recovery, but that request was denied. So I will serve, and serve faithfully, to the end of the war. And you, my dear Tienchen, will have to abide the time patiently there until I come, and that will not be until springtime. So we have a long time in front of us before we see each other again. Should it be God's will to bring us together sooner, well, then we would be much more grateful than we are now, because we have enjoyed much more of his grace until now than we deserved.

---

[54] Possibly shellshock or Post Traumatic Stress Disorder—was most severe in the Western Front where battlefronts moved very little. Meyer, *A World Undone*, p. 392.

In the over all scheme of things I am must say that things are not so bad. It's when I get no news from my wife and children, parents and siblings that I'm about driven wild. You can't really appreciate how that feels. No one from Schoenfeld writes. Is anyone still alive there or do they simply not want to write to me? Even if everyone is very busy there, surely you all have more time to write than I have, except at this time when we are refurbishing the train. You must know that when work starts again after this break, there will be no let up day and night, weekdays and Sundays. No time for rest, and we have to steal time to write.

You write that that you delivered the spare parts for the harvesters and that Hildebrandt took them. I don't know anything about what is going on there. I don't know how it is going with our business in Mariental. You write little, give me very little information, and somehow you have the idea that I am not interested in what's going on. I simply don't understand that! How many times have I told you that even the most minute things that are happening there are of great interest to me. I'm interested in everything, even the smallest bit of information. Please don't forget that. Why don't you write me a letter every day until you have described everything? Tell me about yourself, our children, the parents and the siblings. Are you well? What did you do in Mariental while you were there? What were Mama, Tina and children doing? And what are you all doing in Schoenfeld—parents, siblings, grandparents, uncles and aunts? How is the business doing? Is Gerhard stuck [in the military]? What are the neighbors doing? Also those in Mariental. And what about our livestock, etc.? There is so very much to write about. Remember, I am interested in everything.

Lenchen wrote Aron that you are very skinny. What's going on? When I was home the last time you seemed to be in good shape. Did you get some dentures? Do that by all means. Did your financial support from the Crown come through yet? You do have money, right? The spare parts, the box wagon, the binder were all sold on credit? Did you get my letter in Schoenfeld in which I told about Hermann's last days and his funeral? I sent a copy to Mariental. Did they receive it? Please send me the address of brother Hans, and then I ask you and all the others once more to write me everything that's happening there.

Now I will write a little bit about my life here, although one can't write much from here. I have to be careful not to write too much. [End of letter missing]

From Nicolai
Evacuation Station
Medical Train No. 10/160
Minsk, July 18, 1915

Dear Tinchen and children,

It sounds as though we will be leaving Minsk tomorrow. Then the work begins and it will be difficult to write letters, so I'll do it now while I have time. All of the administrators except the doctor are on board. The train looks very grand now with the new paint. However, I wonder if things will run any better. I doubt it, unless our Zemstvo Commander is not coming along. Where we go from here, none of us knows yet and nothing special has happened while we have been here. At present things are quite frantic in the carriage First Class. Our Zemstvo Commander is having a fit, calling the medics one after another to appear before him and then he cusses them to his heart's content. Of course, he has to make up what he feels was neglected while he was away from the train for a week. It is said that he was given "power of attorney" to give each of the medical staff a good thrashing. Well, that could prove to be a pleasant diversion for us—to get a thorough thrashing now and then.

Today he was actually ready to hand me over to the police. It so happened that few days ago I was sent to purchase some ethyl alcohol for the train, but because no one would give me any, I returned and gave the money and the prescription back to the man in charge, the commander's assistant. Today I was asked again to get some ethyl alcohol and, of course, I had to have the prescription from the doctor. The commander said to me, "But you already have it." I told him that I had returned the prescription and the money to his assistant. So I went to fetch him and then he said, "I have the money but Rempel has the prescription."

"No," I said, "I returned it all to your assistant." And because I stood my ground firmly, they started a search, a long search, but nothing was found. Then he came to me and said, "If you can't produce the prescription, I'll have to hand you over to the police so the situation can be explored." I assured him again, while we two were alone, that I knew with certainty that I returned everything but couldn't provide evidence. Finally he was convinced that I was telling the truth, so he went to his assistant and demanded the prescription from him who had it after all. Later he was very friendly to me again.

Recently, Fast and Dyck and I exchanged thoughts about God's wonderful ways. It is remarkable how we, in spite of all the goodness he has shown us, still remain defiant, disobedient and often despair so easily. If He were not a God of love and if He weren't a God of inconceivable patience with us, we would have been exterminated long ago, like the citizens of Sodom and Gomorrah or the people at the time of Noah. Teach our children the true blessings of God's love. What are the little imps doing? Are they all healthy? Have they forgotten me completely or do they sometimes speak about their Papa? How I long to see you all again, to put my arms around you and kiss you. May the time be near that this can happen.

I did not complete this letter yesterday. I just came from the infirmary (Bandaging room) where I worked all day. You probably didn't work today because it is Sunday. How nice it is when one can work six days and rest on the seventh day. We haven't been able to do that for almost a year. I am closing now and in my spirit I am hugging and kissing you.

Your Nicolai

From Tina
Schoenfeld, July 20, 1915

My dear Nicolai,

I finally received your dear letter yesterday for which I am very happy. Your last letter was dated June 21st. It is strange that you are not receiving my letters. I wrote seven letters from Mariental and addressed six of them to Brest-Litovsk and one to Moscow and you didn't get any of them. It seems that someone is interested in our letters. I even wrote one in Russian as you asked me to do that, but you didn't receive that one either. I think you will probably get them from here. I arrived back here on the 7th of July.

It is exactly five years ago that you and I came to Schoenfeld [from Mariental?]. You were on the way to the Forestry Camp. We had come from Herbert's funeral. Those were good times, right? You will remember that very well. I realize now that we traveled too little during the six years we were married. When I think back, we were together only two years, and the rest of the time we have been separated. Let's hope that we will be lucky enough to be able to spend more time together in the future. Oh, sometimes I feel I must run to you, only to you, hold you in my arms and never, never let you go. I really have to try hard to control my feelings and not to lose courage. Sometimes I feel I will not be able to endure it any longer without you. But I want to be strong even though it is very hard for me. I lack nothing, have a comfortable life, but I'd rather work hard with you at my side than to be so lonely.

Recently we have buried three people here. Yesterday we buried G. Schroeder's 20-year-old son from Kawalicha, who died of emphysema, and today Liestje [Lisa] Dueck's 3-month-old daughter will be buried, and on Wednesday is the funeral of Mrs. Warkentin who lived across the street from pastor Driediger. If this continues, three dead in one week, our population will soon be decimated. May we all be ready when death knocks at our door.

If you will be allowed to go to Moscow for a rest, maybe you can home for fourteen days at that time like Kornelius Fast did. I would be beside myself with joy to see you again and I'm very curious to see you. I imagine you are very thin. If you can't come, I'd certainly come to you if I had someone to accompany me. It's better if you come because then you can see your children, parents and siblings. Let's ask the Lord to grant your complete release.

The weather is cold, just right for catching colds. In fact Selma and Hilda have colds. They cough a lot and run high temperatures at night. Hopefully they will feel better soon. I am well and hope you are, too. Congratulations on your birthday—the second one now [since induction]. May God bless you richly and bring you home soon. I'm so sorry that you didn't get the seven letters I wrote. I had written a lot about our business affairs and I'm hoping you will still get them. Please write me if you haven't received any of those letters. If not, I'll have to repeat everything from the beginning. On the 17th I sent a package of cookies to Minsk but I forgot to write you about them, so I don't know if you will get it, although I did write the number of your train (Evacuation Station) so you really should get it. I'll have to be more careful in future. Tell me if you still have coffee and if I should send butter or honey. Perhaps the post office will send packages with food. Do you need money?

I would love to take a few trips with you once you are in your new train and have your good Zemstvo Administrator. I think I told you that your brother Johannes is home for six months and Hans Friesen for two months. He is working as an engineer and making good money. He is not the "fat Friesen" he used to be. He has lost weight. I want to finish this letter so that it can be sent today. I'm embarrassed that you don't get my letters. It may appear that I don't write any letters. Willie is still in the forestry camp and Gerhard's induction has been postponed for a year. He is lucky and Papa really needs him here. Otovis [employee in the store] has been gone for a long time. Some Jews come to our store frequently. They want to buy a lot of our stock. Last week Papa sold 500 rubles worth of goods to Jews, but now Papa wants to sell it in big lots, not little by little.

Should I send you some fresh plums? They will be ripe soon. It's quite stormy outside and the winter apples are falling. It's a waste but what can I do about it? We will have a lot of watermelons ripening in the fields this year.

Who of the people that started with you in your train are left? Now that Hermann is gone, you can't seem to stay together any more but most of them seem to be leaving. It seems that he was able to keep you all together. If your situation on the train is that bad, I hope do you can be transferred to a better one.

When I was still in Mariental, we packed a parcel for Heinrich. Alice came along and wanted to know whom the parcel was for? When Tina told her, she said, "This is for Uncle Heinrich, and that is for Uncle Heinrich. What about Papa, there is nothing for him? You don't think about Papa at all." What a child to have such thoughts! Alice is very precocious. If I don't answer right away when she calls me, she is quick to say, "You heard me." She is such a chatterbox! And mischievous! She always mixes coffee, oatmeal and rice together when she is in the store. She is a good-for-nothing! Hilda is my little doll, always beside me. Now she is sitting here looking at a picture book. They are much better behaved now because Grandpapa steps in quite often. They were pretty unruly the four weeks in Mariental, but here they are much better.

Tell me what to do with the money that I take in. Should I deposit it in the savings bank? I think so or we won't have any money when you come home. I'm going to Mariental again on the first of September and will collect some money there or should I just leave it there? Papa thinks I should deposit it. Please write and tell me what your wishes are.

Many greetings and kisses from your ever-loving Tina and children. I hope you will be home soon to rest.

From Tina
Schoenfeld, July 23, 1915

My dear Nicolai,

I received your much appreciated letter the day before yesterday, but it is really odd that you didn't get the letters in which I told you from beginning to end in great detail what I was doing in Mariental. But I will write it again—I don't mind at all. I returned here [Schoenfeld] with Ohm Matthies, his daughter Liese, Mrs. Brauel, Agatha and Tina who visited here for three days. The trip to Mariental with the children went well because they slept most of the way. Johannes' wife Sara came along too, so mother's house was full of grandchildren. She had been looking forward to this for a long time. Your sister Tina and I did some sewing—Tina for herself and Mama, and I sewed a black blouse for myself and panties for the children. In between we weeded the garden.

Now to our accounts. Ohm Matthies sold the harrow for 170 rubles. Mama spent that money as well as the money for our cow. You probably hadn't paid her for the cow; I really don't know. Hildebrandt from Hierschau sent the last of the harvesters here. You had written there were five, but there are only three left now that Osolin bought one and Matthies had sold one to Suderman, leaving three. The drivers with transports came on Sunday after *faspa* to get a couple of the harvesters. I asked Jacob Baerg, Heinrich Hildebrand and Ohm Matthies to help load them, which they gladly did. It was dark by the time they were finished so that we had a late supper. After a few days Suderman came to get a harvester. He paid down 100 rubles and gave us a post-dated check for 300 rubles that we can cash September 1. I have the money here and also the check which Papa should look after. We didn't know what to do with it here.

I paid our debt to Abrahms with the money Barg paid us for the wagon, so now we owe Abrahms nothing. I also sold spare parts for twenty-five rubles and now have 125 rubles in my possession and am waiting for you to tell me what to do with it. I already wrote you that Papa thinks we should deposit all money we receive in the bank just in case we suddenly have to leave here. I will soon receive a government voucher as the mayor has notified me that it is available now.

We hired Penner to bring in the hay, at least two hayracks full. We paid six rubles to have the manure spread on the field, so we finally got our field fertilized. Mother has three cows. Although I was there four weeks, I didn't get a chance to see our heifer.[55] We had no horse to take us there. Our calf is quite frisky, and there are some chicks, too, but not much fruit this year. I washed all your greasy clothes and polished both pairs of shoes. Everything is ready for your arrival. We are waiting for you with great anticipation but are so often disappointed. It must have been a misunderstanding that you would be released for six months. That is what Dueck wrote to Manja. Isn't it wonderful that Johannes has been released for six months?

But back to writing about what happened in Mariental. We sold the wagon for cash and the binder with a 100 rubles down payment and a 300 rubles post-dated check due in September. I also sold spare parts for cash. I didn't sell any implements—there are five in the shed as well as the old threshing machine, the boiler, the grinding mill, five grinding lathes, a motor and a motorcycle. I believe Mr. Duerksen from Steinbach wants to buy the latter.

Johannes wanted Mr. Matthies to give him the money for the wagon, but I told him the money belongs to you, Nicolai. Penner gave me a ride to Gnadenfeld to Karl Schmidt's to pick cherries for the winter. I was thinking of canning cherries for the winter, but as I have so little hope of you coming home, I will not go ahead with that. It is too bad that you haven't received my letters. I will repeat what I remember but have already forgotten some of what I wrote about. Ohm Matthies comes over almost every day to romp with our children, which he just loves, no matter how cheeky our children are. Lenchen [Aron's wife] was there too for fourteen days with her two [Ernst & Friedel] while I was there. He [Ernst][56] is

---

[55] Apparently Nicolai and Tina's plot of land that they planned to farm after the war was some distance from the village.

[56] Ernst's father was Nicolai's brother, Aron, who moved to Omsk, Siberia, where he taught after the war. He later disappeared during the Stalin purges. See Epilogue.

such a comical fellow and Friedel [Ernst's sister] is such a gentle songbird. Greta and her three children as well as Anna came to see me before I left. With twelve grandchildren the house was full. It was very lively and very obvious that the fathers were missing. The next day Anna and I and the children left for home [to Schoenfeld]. We took the hackney back to Schoenfeld. The trip home was very good and there was plenty of room to lie down.

All of us are well here. I gained eight pounds during the four weeks in Marienthal. I always seem to gain weight there— life is just too comfortable. When I left a number of farmers were already threshing. Abram will help Ohm Matthies and Gerhard will help the Loepps with the threshing. Both are reluctant to go there because they feel that those people are too strict with them. But Mama says that is good because they [these two grandsons, Abram and Gerhard] don't want to obey her, and when Tina [their aunt] admonishes them, they talk back to her. Mama had to spank Sara one day because she was so stubborn. Then Sara said she would not stay there any longer but rather go to Samara. All in all Mama is having a difficult time with all four of them [The Neufeld grandchildren].[57] They don't want to do any work and they won't obey Mama. We really do miss your presence here very much. Mother mentioned to me that she just doesn't want the boys to live at home during the winter.

I think I wrote about everything that happened here in Schoenfeld. Peter Enns lost their big shed in a fire. Their son Peter suffered severe burns and is in critical condition. This is how it happened: Peter Enns was not at home, so his son Peter Jr. and the hired man tried to empty some fuel into a container that was positioned close to a motor. They were working by lamplight but not careful enough. When the barrel was almost empty, Peter told his helper to wait with pouring for a minute or two while he wanted to move the lamp to the other side, but he didn't wait and because he couldn't see what he was doing, some gasoline splashed on to the motor. It exploded immediately and the gasoline container burst into flame. The hired man ran out, but Peter, who was going to extinguish the lamp first, could hardly find the door because of the fire and thick smoke. When Peter finally emerged from the burning building, he had suffered burns on his hands, face, ears, head and back. The poor boy was in such a state of shock that he didn't seem to feel the pain right away. Everything happened so quickly that the people in the building weren't even aware of what was happening. At first they hardly saw the charred figure of the boy standing there and only the raging fire behind him. Because of the large amount of gasoline, the building burnt down. A strong wind was blowing the burning embers all the way to the village schoolhouse. Grandmother's house was in danger of catching fire too, so she moved a lot of things out of the house into the yard.

The poor boy is supposed to lie in bed for three months. Who knows if he will survive. He can hardly speak. Parts of his body are still badly swollen and he doesn't open his eyes at all, but the doctor assures them that his eyes will be fine. This all happened through carelessness. It's too bad that this young boy was the victim. The

---

[57] Nicolai's oldest sister, Anna, died in the Terek region near Persia [Iran], leaving the four young children with their widowed father, Abram Neufeld. Soon after he remarried, he, too, died and four children came to live with their maternal grandmother Rempel in Marienthal.

hired man suffered a few burns on his hands and face but nothing serious because he ran out of the building right away while Peter was groping around to find the door.

The sale of our binder twine is now past since most of the threshing has been done. We are not very busy in the store either; at least we don't get much business from the Mennonites, but the Jews are steady customers. They bought all the crockery, footwear, hangings, screws, bolts and wire. Tomorrow they are coming to do their own packing. We women have been busy for three days sorting and counting. It was a lot of work. In the place where we had the footwear, we are now displaying the porcelain dishes. We have sold a lot of dry goods also, like drapery. Papa said that if a customer or customers want to buy the dry goods en masse, he is willing to sell everything. He said that if he has to leave, then at least we'd have the money. There's talk about having to leave but who knows what will happen? And what would happen to me then? Then I'll come to stay with you. Well, let's pray that God will protect us from any of that. We are beginning to sew warm undergarments to prepare for winter. Grandpa's Toews health is deteriorating quickly. The aunts, Tante Sana and Tante Tina, are still living with them in their old place. The neighbors are threshing on Franz Rempel's land, where he[58] is staying right through threshing time.

Until now no one here [Schoenfeld] knew that Ohm Matthies had been courting Mama [Nicolai's mother] but Mariechen Dueck brought the news from Halbstadt and now many people know about it. People asked me if I had known about it and I told them I had but I haven't told anyone about it. I will stop writing—more another time. Please write if you have any special needs. Did you receive the cookies?

Many greetings, hugs and kisses. Special greetings to all of your comrades in the train. From your ever-loving Tina and little children who think about you all the time

From Tina
Schoenfeld, July 27, 1915

My dear Nicolai,

As it's quiet here right now, I must take the opportunity to chat with you. How nice it would be if you were sitting beside me or I on your lap and we could talk intimately! Perhaps soon, very soon! How I long for that, my dearest! I received your letter yesterday from July 18th. Don't you get my letters; you have mentioned only one letter? I write to you often, this is the third letter this week, so it's too bad you're not getting them.

I went to Sara's birthday today. There I met many people we know: Warkentins, Duecks, Miraus, Riesens, our Greta with her three children, and me with our three girls. It was lively party! One could hardly understand a word of what was being said; so right after coffee, I left with our three and went to Grandmother's. Uncle

---

[58] Franz Rempel was apparently separated from his wife. Such marriage problems created a big stir in the Mennonite communities.

Peter was there and he romped around with the girls. We just came back from there and the youngsters got on the scale and weighed themselves. I weigh 3N 25 gr., Alice 1N 10 gr., Hilda 1N and Selma 35 gr. She [Selma] is so plump. When I ask her where Papa is, she answers, "far, far away." Our oldest two often ask, sometimes tearfully, "When will papa come home?" In one month, it will be a whole year that you are serving and are away from us, and who knows if we will lose another year. On Friday, July 31st we are supposed to go to the Volost [regional government headquarters] to pick up our Crown grants: about 100 rubles plus a few. I want to deposit it in the savings bank so that we have money when we need it.

I will stop writing now and go for supper. Later I want to go to Aron Rempel's birthday celebration. This is where I stopped writing yesterday. Then I went to Grandmother's to ask Tante Tina to come along to the Rempels', but the Wienses were there and persuaded me to stay at Grandmother's, which I did.

I did laundry all day today and now it's time for evening leisure. While I was doing the laundry, Selma sat in the tub of water next me and playing away; she just loved that. The children run about the garden regularly now, playing and eating plums. They are not very ripe yet but it doesn't matter to them. They have good tummies.

I heard today that Dueck [Manja's husband. She was like a member of the Peters family] is expected to come home soon. Manja came back from the Colony [Molochna] today, telling us that her husband had sent word that she should come home. I won't believe it until I see him. Well, I wish her all the best and rejoice with her. But then having to leave again, well that's so difficult. I wish you could come home.

I must tell you something else. It seems that your mother[59] wants to get married again, but she would like to have the approval of all of you. She hasn't said a word to me about it, only to Greta and Lenchen. I don't know why she hasn't mentioned it to me. I guess she doesn't trust me, thinking that I might gossip about it. I don't know how she can think that because I don't talk about things I am not supposed to tell. Well, I won't hold it against her.

Our weather is not very good for threshing; it's raining a lot. How are things going with you? I don't think you will have fully recuperated yet and probably won't as long as you are there. I would nurse you back to health, my dear, if you were home for a longer time, I often imagine the day when you arrive home and we all rush out to meet you? When I put the children to bed at night and it's not quite dark yet, Hilda sits on the windowsill and asks many questions. Right now she is sitting here waiting for me to talk to her. Alice is more of a scatterbrain; she listens with half an ear. Right now she is still outside running around with the other children.

Well, I hope I have answered all of your questions. Goodnight and again, warmest heartfelt greetings and a kiss from your ever-loving Tina.

---

[59] A neighbor, Ohm Matthies, mentioned in Tina's letters, had courted her, a widow since 1907. Matthies was supposedly a rather coarse fellow who did not measure up to the expectations of some members of the Rempel family, especially the youngest daughter, Tina, although Nicolai's mother, it seems, was quite fond of Ohm Matthies.

From Nicolai
Evacuation Station
Medical Train No. 10/160
Moscow, July 29, 1915

Dear Tinchen and my beloved children!

Now I feel invigorated again because I lately received several letters from you in which I see that all is well with you. My longing for you is becoming increasingly intense but we are quite powerless over our situation, and so I have put my trust into the hands of God.

Just now our train is leaving Moscow and is on its way to Brest. Our last trip was difficult. We had wounded soldiers in our train for six days. We needed almost a whole day to load them, so you can imagine how we fared. Six of them died on the way, more than died at home, as you related in your letter. Among the six was a man named Koop who was my neighbor here in this train. Koop had a stomach ailment and the doctor told him to be very careful and not work too hard and to eat only light meals. And how our Zemstvo Administrator heeds doctors' recommendations you already know from my letters, and so, of course, Koop had to work practically to the end. When Enns made a special plea to the chief to let Koop take time to rest, his response was, "Koop just doesn't like the hospital carriage he has been assigned to so that is why he is sick." But Enns sent Koop to his quarters for a rest anyway and appointed someone else work in his place.

When I got up in the morning, I looked at Koop and asked him: "My goodness! What is going on with you?" He could hardly speak and said that he felt terribly sick. I asked him what he wanted for breakfast. He said that if it were possible, he would like an egg and some milk. I went to the cook and passed onto him the request, and then I had to return to my work. Of course, I first asked the doctor to examine Koop once more because he looked very ill. Our doctors were in no way remiss in their help and did what they could, but their efforts were in vain. About at midnight Koop breathed his last. Even before he died, he was transferred to a special carriage because they suspected cholera. When we arrived in Minsk, the carriage with the body was uncoupled, and so we don't even know how he was interred. Most sad is that we don't know whether he had forgiveness of sin. May God be merciful and grant him forgiveness and peace.

Tinchen, we don't know if we will see each other again, so we must take care of the most important thing first—to demonstrate our love for God by the way we live. When I think that I could die here in this train, that doesn't really matter because then I will be with Jesus. Only you and our little children bind me to this world, and I would love to serve you, to share joys and sorrows, to have you for sometime to come. To live together with you as a family is a mere foretaste of heaven. Married life after all was something that God already established in the paradise.

I wanted to stay in Moscow and the chief promised me that I could stay, but he now has reneged, telling me I had to take one more trip to train a replacement and then I could stay in Moscow, where I will get a thorough medical checkup. Actually

I feel quite well, but it would be better if I got a thorough examination by a specialist in pulmonology to check my lungs. Please send thirty rubles to me in Moscow. Thank you very much for the cookies; they are very tasty, outstanding.

Most heartfelt greetings from your Nicolai. Stay well and God be with you!

From Tina
Schoenfeld, August 4, 1915

Dear Nicolai,

I received your letter you wrote on the 29th. I am very happy for every one of your letters and am so glad that you are getting my letters now, so you know how things are here. Papa has finally decided to write you a letter, too, as he promised. In your last letter you wrote that you are going to Moscow for a rest. I'm glad that the administrator was so gracious to approve it, but he may still regret his promise and change his mind.

Nothing has changed with me, which makes me happy.[60] When I think that I may have to flee with the children someday, it will be so much easier for me, right? May the God protect us from that! If only we could be together again and stay together. When I lie down at night, I often think that we must be great sinners or God wouldn't allow all this misery and grief. How often the children ask me, "Why isn't Papa coming home?" Today Hilda asked me that again and I always have to give her the same answer. Nothing changes. When you get to Moscow, maybe you will get permission to come to see us for a while or be released altogether. Let's pray for that.

Must tell you what I am doing. I sleep in the back room with my three girls. I sleep on an iron bedstead, Alice on the sofa, Hilda in the little bed and Selma in the cradle. I chose that back room because it is quiet and the children can sleep longer. At the moment Susa [Tina's sister] and I are sitting in my room writing. I began writing this letter right after *faspa*; then Grandma Toews came and interrupted my writing and now I need the lamp. We're always glad when Grandma comes because it happens so seldom. Today while we were having coffee, two medical workers came driving down the street, and immediately everyone was outside to see if they would stop by the schoolyard [It was next door] so we could talk to them, but unfortunately they walked right by. They were Dueck and the Matthies from Schoenbrun. I was reminded of our teacher, Dueck, right away.

Tomorrow morning I'll send thirty rubles to Moscow for you, but I don't know if the address is correct. I've have had no opportunity to have the photographs taken yet, so you'll have to wait. We already received the money from the Crown—103 rubles—so we'll have forty rubles left after we pay Papa. We have been mending and patching old clothes. I mended twenty-one pairs of socks already for you, and now I will patch your clothes and then sew some white shirts for you. With all those clothes waiting for you, you should already be here to use them. Well, let's hope.

The farmers are looking to a good grain harvest. I was going to send you some plums, but they are not accepting any parcels right now. I enjoyed two weeks with

---
[60] She may have thought she was pregnant.

Lenchen. We are celebrating three birthdays this week—Warkentin, Mariechen Dueck and Selma. That child will be two years old and by the time you come home, she will be a big girl.

Greetings and kisses from your loving Tina

From Nicolai
Evacuation Station
Medical Train No. 10/160
Vyazma, August 7, 1915

My dearest Tinchen!

It is almost impossible to write; first, because of the merciless babbling that is going on and it is so disruptive that I can hardly hear myself think, and secondly, because writing in a moving train is a challenge. However, I will make an attempt anyway in order to please you a little. Unfortunately, I have so little opportunity to give loved ones any joy.

Just imagine, my dearest Tinchen, I was but a hairbreadth away from coming home yesterday when we came to Moscow. I had requested to stay in Moscow, but the chief wouldn't let me stay, as he had promised. He said, "Rempel just wants to transfer over into train No. 3." But in order to win me over, thinking he was doing me a favor, he offered to have a doctor write me a fourteen-day sick leave and have a doctor at home examine me, and when the furlough was up, I was to return to this train. I naturally agreed to this plan because I was so eager to go home. But knowing the chief, I really didn't put much weight on his promise from the outset and am satisfied to be together with my comrades again now on the way to Minsk and not, as I was promised, on the way home. Oh well, if it is God's will, I will be coming home soon. Perhaps He will hear the prayers of our little ones who, as you write, pray every day that God will bring their Papa home soon.

So far none of the ten Mennonite medics on this train have received any [extended] release time. We would be sorry if our little community here were to break up. We'll be able to wait it out now. I was told confidentially by a nurse that the chief is now probably on his last trip with us; then he is out of here. It appears that his superior won't put up with him any longer. As I said, it's still a big secret in which I really don't put much faith because it seems quite unbelievable that we would finally be rid of that old guy. However, he has been somewhat calmer in the last week, must have come to realize that everyone does not love him. The food is also better in the last week than it's been in a long time. We can always taste it in the thin soup when he tightens his wallet, pinching from the medics' allowance. We do have a new chef and that makes a difference because she sympathizes with the plight of the medics. One has to eat otherwise we just won't make it. Today the Old Man [chief] left for a few days, perhaps for a visit home. For us it's always a holiday when he is gone.

Just arrived at Yartsevo and will, as it sounds, be here for a few days because there is a huge traffic jam of trains ahead of us in Smolensk and Minsk. There are terribly many refugees at every railway station.[61] You feel so sorry for these poor people. Recently a refugee with a little child in his arms came to one of our doctors and begged for some medicine for the child. Among other things, he told us that his wife had fled [the war zone?] with the child while he had been working on the railway. There he received a telegram that he was supposed to come to such and such a place. When he arrived, he was told that his wife had perished when she fell under the train and the child had lost its toes in the terrible accident. His wife was quickly buried and he had to take the child and leave immediately. These poor people have to suffer terribly, terribly much misery, indescribable misery. Let's thank God that you live peacefully where you are and pray that He may let you to stay there in peace in the future.

Recently we have seen many women among the soldiers, dressed, of course, in uniforms like the other soldiers [but not recognized as women].[62] On our last two trips carrying wounded from the front, we had such wounded young women in our train. The other wounded soldiers, however, did not know that there were women among them.

Greetings to you with heartfelt love and kisses, your loving Nicolai

From Tina
Schoenfeld, August 14, 1915

Dear Nicolai,

For a while I heard from you often, but now I've heard nothing for fourteen days. Someone told me that you didn't get permission to stay to Moscow for a rest. Your administrator wouldn't allow it. I sent the money you requested to Moscow, but who knows if you will receive it now? This morning the Schroeders came here. Truda is staying here but he will have to report back to work after five days. He has an easy position—doesn't have to exert himself at all. I did some of my cleaning today because Friday is a Russian holiday. Only Reinhold and Franz Willms are left in the store now. Fritz is gone; he will be inducted soon. I'm waiting desperately for your homecoming. If they will give you a vacation, they might as well discharge you. I long so much to talk things over with you, my dearest!

All the others are sitting in the office, but I prefer to write you, to visit a little with you. The children just got home after they accompanied the seamstress back to her place. She has shortened my fur coat and added a fur collar using the remnant. It wasn't useful to me anyway. Now the coat looks better. I was going to get some material for a dress, but I guess I can get along without it. But I'll need to buy some flannel to sew warm underwear for the children, and I bought another pair of shoes for each of them because shoes are becoming increasingly expensive. Hilda is sitting

---

[61] By now the Russians had been forced back by a German and Austrian offensive that had captured large areas of Galicia (Stone, Chapter 8) and creating hundreds of thousands of refugees who flooded eastwards, see Peter Gatrell, *A Whole Empire Walking: Refugees in Russia during World War I*, (Bloomington: Indiana University Press, 1999), p. 21; some were evacuated to provinces in which Mennonites lived and their presence is reported in later letters by Tina (Urry).

[62] On women in Russian army units see Laurie S. Stoff, *They Fought for the Motherland: Russia's Women Soldiers in World War I and the Revolution* (Lawrence: Kansas University Press, 2006). (Urry)

beside me, scribbling on a piece of paper. She always finds me. Many people here have finished their threshing, and we have finished digging up our potatoes; however, we don't have as many as last year. Father sold all of the cast iron implements to some Jews and also a number of parts for the cheaper implements.

I'm still addressing my letters to Minsk. I hope that's still right. All of us are healthy, and I hope that you are too. What is the situation with the medical workers who were sick? And what about you? Since I haven't heard from you for such a long time, are you ill? You really spoiled me for a while when I received a letter every time the mail came in. Now I've heard nothing for fourteen days. I'm still hoping that you will come home, perhaps indefinitely. I have so much to tell you. They are now conscripting mere youths—18- and 19-year-olds! How terrible! May the Lord hear our petitions and help us to get through this. We are sinful people and do not deserve any better. It could, however, be much more difficult for us. Until now we have really little to complain about.

I must close for this time with the hope that you will come home soon. If your administrator had any compassion for you, surely he would give you leave to come home. Many greetings and kisses from your ever-loving Tina and children.

From Nicolai
Evacuation Station
Medical Train No. 10/160
Moscow, August 15, 1915

My most treasured Tinchen!

We are leaving shortly from Moscow to Minsk, but we can't go much further than that. From Minsk they want to send us farther up the line this time, but where we naturally don't know. As far as I'm concerned, we wouldn't have to go any farther because it is easier to pick up wounded soldiers from the hospital than from the field. I probably wrote my last letter from Yartsevo. You will be unhappy with me because I write so seldom, but I write whenever I have time. I received two of your letters in Minsk and also Papa's. Thank you, thank you many times for them. You are really very wonderful, my heartthrob, to write so promptly. But when will the time finally come that we can talk things over face to face. Would that God grant us peace for which everyone is longing so much. Then this letter writing between us will cease, as it will for millions of others, and instead of this costly letter writing, everything will be discussed by word of mouth. But the time hasn't come, but we have to wait patiently for God's good time to say, "Peace on Earth and to all men good will!" When He brings that about, then all people will helplessly have to drop their weapons and obey.

At the moment Dietrich Cornies is sitting beside me here in the train. He was at home and he tells me that things at home are taking their usual course. In your last letter, you write that Ohm Knals [Note letter of July 29, Ohm Knals Matthies] is courting our mother and that mother would like to marry him. It seems to me that you are hurt that Mama hasn't told you anything about it. There is, of course, no question that Mama trusts you as much as her other daughters-in-law. You know very well that you are Mama's favorite. Let me explain to you how this came about. Already last winter Matthies tried very seriously to convince her to marry him, but mother rejected him. In May, he again courted her urgently, but she told him that she would first have to think about it very seriously, and secondly, she wanted to ask her children for advice. Now mother has received answers from all her sons, and she told Greta and Lena only after you left. They were in Mariental longer than you. They apparently have nothing against the marriage, but should we [her sons] definitely oppose it, then the matter was closed. That is why I have not written you about it until now. You, my dearest treasure, don't be angry with me or with Mama.

Today I received the thirty rubles that you sent me. Thanks much. It seems that you should address my letters to Moscow soon because there is so much work in Minsk.[63] And nothing seems to have come of my staying in Moscow, because the old man refuses to assign me there. However, I have resigned myself to God's will.

How does it look with Gerhard's service? Has it been postponed for a year or merely from one lottery to the next? Will stop for now since I think I can still make the mail train and I send you and the children the warmest greetings and kisses. Your Nicolai

From Nicolai [He had been home on furlough]
Fastov, September 4, 1915

To: Katharina Borisovna Rempel Village: Krasnopol
From: Station, Ekaterinoslav

Dear Katja,

I was luckier this time than last time. I arrived in Kiev at 1:00 p.m. and immediately found my train. After one and a half hours, we arrived at Kamenetz-Podolski and Vinnitza. I came to the station in good time. There were wall-to-wall people there—like fish in a bowl. Yesterday I spent the whole day walking the streets of Ekaterinoslav from 10:00 a.m. to 6:00 p.m. Now we are on the way to Vinnitsa and I hope to see brother Julius there. Please greet my relatives and neighbors.

Remember me. Kissing you, your Nikolai

From Tina
Schoenfeld, September 25, 1915

My dear, dear Nicolai,

I think tomorrow it's already eight or nine years since you came to us here.[64] So much has happened since the first time you came to visit us. I was a young girl and you a young boy, and we've had so many experiences in those intervening years. Last year you asked me if I still loved you as much as when I was a bride. Well, I find it hard to express how very much I love you. At times I have such a strong yearning

---

[63] Moscow at that time was the Zemstvo major center for mail distribution to medics.

[64] Nicolai came to the Peters in Schoenfeld in 1907 after having completed *Oberrealschule*—high school—in Gnadenfeld. He worked in sales and accounting for Bernard Peters, his future father-in-law. Possibly their first meeting was when Nicolai came to interview for a job.

for you that I don't know what to do. That's how it is when one is married. We belong together and yet so often, so often, we have had to part. When will this misery end? I could adjust to anything if only you were finally home with your family again.

I thought I would hear something about you from Hermann Enns. He's been home on furlough since the 23rd and has passed by our place twice but he didn't stop in. I'm sure that if it were you, you would have stopped in to see his family. I'm very curious to hear what he has to report. Sometime during his month's furlough, he will surely come by to see me. I've already heard from Gerhard that the doctors and the nurses are off the train. Gerhard came back from Ekaterinoslav and told me that Schroeder had just received a postcard from you, so I hope that tomorrow brings me one also.

Things are going well here, although it could always be better. We are well and I wish you the same. I still haven't received the photographs. If we hadn't paid for them up front, we'd probably have had them by now. I'll ask Gerhard to write a letter in my name about the delay so that then we may finally get them.

So your big boss on the train is still holding out; hard to get rid of someone like him, I guess. Mrs. Rempel [distant relative] commented to me that she is praying for her husband's discharge from the medical service on the train. Well, it may still happen. If we people show greater faith in God, the war would finally end, but people are so complacent. I'm glad for Mrs. Enns that Hermann is home. I would be enormously delighted if you were finally home with us and we could build our family. We have really not been together very much during the six years of our marriage, and so we don't know how good it would be. In my imagination, I see us sitting here, just the two of us, without any disturbances, the children sleeping. How wonderful it would be! Actually the children are sleeping, but I'm sitting here alone without you, can't chat with anyone. I don't like it! Well, let's not lose courage, but hold our heads high because we have a great God who has our best in mind.

Yesterday I had visitors. Peter Loewen from Fuerstenau stopped by and a Mr. Osolin came to settle his account. Well, our busiest time is over, and we will take a break from mowing. But enough for today. Many kisses and greetings from your ever-loving Tina and children. Hilda always asks if you are coming home soon.

From Nicolai
Evacuation Station
Medical Train No. 10/160
Yzdruckovo, October 1, 1915

My most beloved wife!

At the present time I'm sitting in my railway carriage quite alone. Gerhard Fast went to buy milk for supper. We have to sustain ourselves pretty much now that the Old Man has once again sliced away a big share of the already small sustenance we have been getting until now. For instance, we get only 20 u. [Russian word] instead 28 or 30 u. of meat for forty men, we now get only 20 u., and sugar instead 5 u. per month, we now get 2 u., and tea a mere 1/8 u. And the same is true for everything. There are actually times when one forgets that one is a Mennonite. When I think about the many times the Old Man has taken advantage of us, an overwhelming desire for revenge just rises up in me. Wouldn't it be better that one person were to sacrifice himself than that all should die because of one ruffian? If I didn't have a wife and children, a change would have taken place here already. Sometimes a battle rages within me. May God give me the strength to subdue the desire for revenge and do what He teaches us.

I really have begun to notice how numbed I have become to the voice of God; how powerless my prayers are. In fact, my dearest Tina, I am much, much farther from God than I used to be. Unless you pray for me that God will give me faith and strength, I don't know how I will persevere. Pray for me during these hours of testing that I don't give up. I don't know why, but I have no desire to read God's word, and when I force myself to read it, I find none of the joy and comfort I once did. And in my prayers speaking to God, I don't have the same trust and joy that I used to have. Everything seems cold and numb in and around me, cold and hard as stone. When, but when, will this ever change? We have been torn from each other without mercy or love. Who has given some humans the right to destroy the joy and happiness of others? One person, who is mortal and must die like all others, has the power to tears to shreds the happiness of millions of people. I sit here as in a prison cell quite, quite alone, far from wife and children, far from parents and siblings. How, I ask myself, are things going with you; why can't we live together in peace and joy?

Our train has been standing here on a spur for the fifth day already, forest on one side, and on the other side the rails that carry one train after another roaring past, carrying thousands of 18- and 19-year-old boys like cattle to the slaughter. They [these young men] are moving toward almost certain death. And for whom and to what purpose? For Christians, who Sunday after Sunday preach God's word? God must be repulsed by us hypocrites! We who call ourselves by His name, yet all the while the blood of those murdered flows in streams. These are the humans whom God created his own image? How we have defiled the image of God! These thoughts keep racing wildly through my head so that I can hardly write.

If only you were here, you would be a great comfort to me in such troubled hours. How I miss you and my dear children! What a comfort it would be if I could discuss all of this with you. Your words of comfort were always like a salve on a wound. No one comforts and hugs us, my dear. Instead of being caressed, we are being cursed.

Just now we are told our train is about to leave; that, at least, will be a change. Will close now and get some lunch. A thousand hugs and kisses from your Nicolai.

From Tina
Schoenfeld, October 2, 1915

My dearest Nicolai,

I received your postcard yesterday. I am very sorry that you are disappointed in me, thinking that I don't write to you. This is my fifth letter. I can't understand what is happening to them. I'm sure I have the right address, and I'm so very sorry that you are not getting any of these letters. When I wrote the fourth letter, I thought surely this one would please you. So far I have received two cards and one letter from you, and that quite satisfies me because you probably don't have much time to write.

I am very well and nothing has changed here; all is normal. The children are quite well and ask about you often. We had a visitor today. Lorenz was here. That poor fellow has gone through so much. He had to flee [deserted] or he wouldn't have come here. Greta says she won't tell Julius about it because he would despair in his loneliness [in an isolated forestry station]. Just after Truda left for Rosenthal today, we heard that nine houses had burned down to the ground in that village. All men except for one had gone to Lukashevo with their horses and wagons [to report for possible induction] and so they were not there to help. A woman had been heating her oven with straw and had gone out to feed the animals when the house caught fire. In addition it was quite stormy and windy.

For a number of days it was muddy here, but now it is dry again, and we've had some frost the last few nights. On Tuesday we are butchering pigs, and why aren't you here to help us? Yes, who would have thought that you wouldn't be home for this event? I sold my winter jacket for eight rubles and I'm glad to be rid of that old rag. I can do without it because I have the fur coat. Herman Enns had to sort the mail today because Ohm Dyck is very sick with dysentery. A child of one of the refugees here died. It doesn't go well with those poor people.[65] Some of our people think anything is good enough for these refugees. And they make fun of them because of their different customs, like some Polish refugees who apparently sip their coffee with spoons. But why should that diminish them? We don't know yet if the Schoenfelder will have to give up their high school [living quarters] for the refugees.

Haven't you received any letters from me since you left? That is very strange. I still haven't received the photographs, nor has Gerhard written to the photographer to remind him. We are not very busy in the store. The dentist is boarding with us now and I'm going to let him check my teeth again. If he agrees, I'm going to get him to extract two of Alice's teeth. The office is full of people right now listening

Sketch by Doris Rempel

---

[65] Refugees were coming to the villages from the war zone.

to Lorenz. He has gained quite a bit of weight; he says he has been so hungry at times that his tongue hung out of his mouth. Hermann Enns doesn't have to return to your train, but you seem to have no luck to get off that train.

Write me long letters, even if seldom. But I know how busy you are. We'll just be content with things the way they are. So many people have to suffer a lot more than we. Well, I know you are doing your best, just let us not forget the most important thing—to pray. You for me and I for you. How I long to be with you forever! Greetings again from your ever-loving Tina and children who always remember you.

From Nicolai
Moscow, October 10, 1915

My dear Tinchen and children!

We are still stationed here in Moscow. Who knows when we will be sent to Kiev because further than Kiev we probably won't go for a while anyway. Our train has been side-railed on a spur for much needed repairs for some time. Soon we are going to Ekaterinoslav with wounded soldiers, and then it would seem as though it would be but a small matter of moving a little farther, at least to Gaichur.

This trip home did cost quite a lot, but when I think that I was able to see my dear, dear Tinchen and my dear children, kiss them and enjoy a happy time with them, then no amount of money was too much. We had a wonderful time, don't you agree, dearest? Oh, may we soon see the end of this horrible war and be united with our loved ones! Every day one witnesses such sad scenes of the Ratnicky being sent away to the front. If you stand back and look at this scene, then all kinds of thought go through your mind. Why all of these tears, all of this misery and sadness, families being torn apart. Couldn't we human beings live in love toward each other, accept each other, instead of slaughtering each other in the most ghastly ways, as it's being done now? Evil tongues instigate all of this misery gradually.

We Germans are also in a situation where we can easily be embittered against our fellow man because all kinds of lies are being spread about us. You know me well and are quite aware that I get far to upset about our being so maligned, that our work is not being acknowledged, that we are not seen as faithful citizens. I know for certain that no one can be more for the welfare of the Russian Empire than I and all the Mennonites I know. And yet one is often regarded with suspicion about which one is then quite indignant. Jesus says, "Why wouldn't you much rather suffer wrong than do wrong?" Yes, why are we unwilling to suffer; we have received so much good. Is it because we have not become quiet before the Lord? We are still weak in our faith and still don't quite belong to those who love their Lord so much that all things serve for the best. We must reach the point where we thank our Lord for everything. He may send us whatever He wills, whether good or evil. But God has never wanted our injury, quite the opposite, and thus it will ever be. And for that we must always be thankful. That's not easy for either of us, but especially for me.

Well, what are you all doing? Has everything happened at the Schroeders already? [birth] How long was Schroeder home? Are you always helping Truda or who is serving her? Please greet Trudy heartily from me. Next to us is the train in which Aron is serving. Many trains are being repaired right now, that's why we are standing here so long.

What do you think about coming to Ekaterinoslav if we should come there with wounded soldiers? Should I send you a telegram in case that happens? Since we seldom come to Brest, maybe you should try once more to send a card or a letter to Kiev. For the time being, Brest remains our main post office. You will sense in my letter that I find little joy in writing.

From your loving Nicolai

From Nicolai
St. Petersburg, October 14, 1915

My dearly beloved Tinchen and children,

We have again come to Petersburg where we were more than year ago. Our joy to come to Moscow to get your letters, or better said, to get letters from our families, has almost been transformed to sorrow. Actually we don't know yet what will happen to our letters. We have been assigned to the Veliki Luki district and the distance from there to Moscow or to Petersburg is about the same. So it is possible that we will come to Moscow some time. So please, as soon as you get this letter, send one to the following address: Veliki Luki, Evacuation Station, Medical Train No.10/160 c. N.R.

We will probably leave tomorrow for our assigned destination. Last time we took on wounded from Pigoraleue and from there it was a mere seven werst to the actual battlefield. If the wind came from that direction, we could hear the gunshots, smell the powder. Had the Prussians known that a train was standing at the station that close, they might have shot at us. But we stole in by night and were gone again in the morning so no one noticed that a train was standing there.

The trip was a difficult one because we had just taken on the most recently trained medical staff. The bandaging did not proceed as smoothly as it had before because these new nurses and the new doctor were still somewhat awkward. I have become accustomed to the nurses, but I am somewhat out of harmony with the doctor. He is too haughty and overbearing. It seems to me that he won't last long here because the Old Man does not care for him much either. Now the Old Man has transferred Gerhard Fast from the officer's carriage to a different one and has been replaced him with a Russian, so that I am cut off completely from the other Mennonites. How long I will be quartered in this train is hard to know. He may even throw me out today. The main reason I am having constant conflict with the Old Man is alcohol. This time I was able to get some drink fairly easily, so that he now has a bucket full to guzzle and five buckets to use as fuel. Now I am at peace about that and am quite content.

We now have to prepare many things for the trip. Yesterday I was quite ill. I had a tooth pulled and it was so impacted that I thought the dentist would not be able to extract it, in spite of having an injection. After it was all over I had such dreadful pain that I didn't know what to do. Now it is better except one side is very swollen. Here in Petersburg we're having winter. It has been snowing all day and it's getting quite cool. When I look out onto the blanket of snow that covers everything, I am overcome by terrible homesickness. You feel Christmas coming on and yet no prospect of coming home. May God grant that our service will at least be finished by the following Christmas.

How are things going at home? What are the dear children doing? What about you, my dearest, are you still upbeat and are you managing everything? If Enns has not left yet, then please send my shoes along and a few bars of soap. If only I could pick them myself, how I would hug you to my heart and kiss you, my precious ones. My loneliness is so great for you that I can't put it into words. Please greet the parents, the siblings and also the grandparents, Uncle Peter and the aunts.

Your Nicolai, who loves you dearly

From Tina
Schoenfeld, October 14, 1915

Dear Nicolai,

Today I am on so-called guard duty again. Schroeder is leaving by 2:00 a.m. and I have promised to wake him. I will use this time to chat with you. Fortunately we have a cook again so that I don't have to be in the kitchen all the time. However, we seem to have visitors continually. Schroeder is leaving today and the day after tomorrow David and Mika Adrian are coming to visit. On Friday they leave and want Mika to go with them. I don't want to quarrel with her, but if I had my way, Mika [Tina's sister] wouldn't go along. We have six children here and they have only one. Somebody has to help to look after this little brood. I'll just do what I can and the rest has to take care of itself. I will not overexert myself, but do only as much as I want to do. I wouldn't mind at all if you'd come and take me away from here but that can't happen so I'll adjust and stop complaining about it.

I'm gaining weight again, am 3 u 28 pt., and that without shoes. I had Mr. Isaak to repair a pair of my shoes—new soles and heels—three rubles and fifty kopeks. It's expensive but the shoes are like new. I bought a new pair for Alice but they are too small, so I will try to sell them. I can't tell you everything that's going on, the girls are healthy. Selma is like a log; I can hardly lift her up. Today when Alice, Hilda and I stand back to back there is no difference. Here in the colonies, many little children are dying of scarlet fever or measles, but ours, thank God, are still very healthy. We can't thank God enough that He has given us such healthy children. One can sleep well after committing everything to Him. Then there is nothing to fear. The children are sleeping peacefully without care or worry. Now the sandman is coming after me, too, but I have to stay awake since I promised to wake Schroeder up. If I don't wake him, I could be in trouble. Have you received any letters from Willie or don't you write to him anymore? Did you get the two letters that I wrote in pencil, also the addresses? Probably not since you don't mention them at all.

So I wrote on Wednesday and on Friday and also one on Monday. I have been waiting for an answer. I thought I would get one from you today, but have waited in vain. In your last letter you were most discouraged and seemed to be very angry. I keep thinking about that. May God protect you from hurting anyone. That would have been terrible. Well, my dear, I know you wouldn't do that. It is cold in my room now because the fire has gone out. I don't know how we are going survive this winter. We still don't have any coal. At night we heat with a bit of manure, which gives very little heat. There is no change with Grandpa.

Enough for this time, more next time. Many greetings and kisses from your loving Tina and children.

From Nicolai
Evacuation Station
Medical Train No. 10/160
Moscow, October 30, 1915

My most beloved Tinchen!

Today I received three letters from you, from the 14th, the 16th, and one from the 26th that you wrote from Mariental. I thank you from the bottom of my heart. And the photographs I have also finally received. I don't like the way they turned out and will write the photographer my opinion of them. So you were in Mariental? How are things going there? And what's with the teacher? I would like to drop in there again to see what's happening, how things are looking. Well, perhaps the good Lord will bring this to pass. When it seems quite impossible that our wishes will be fulfilled, it often happens that just then He acts on them. From our perspective there can be no peace for at least a year, but you and I also know quite well that anything is possible with God. It is wonderful how He provides for us with everything. He looks after us even as he looks after the birds in the heavens. We have not worked for ourselves for over a year now (at least not I) and yet we have suffered no want but actually lived in plenty.

I wrote up to here while still in Moscow and then I had to stop to go to work because we were leaving. It is almost unforgivable that other matters are more important than my wife and children, but as you know, my dearest Tinchen, that is not my fault; you are the dearest and most important person in my life. We have been waiting here already for the second day, two werst west of Kreuzburg. I have finally accumulated so much free time that I can now answer your letters. Today is November 5th, Hermann's birthday. Who would have thought that within one year he would be gone! Who knows who will be the next one to go? Well, as God wills it! We could easily pass away just like our dear brother Hermann.

I am sitting all alone in my carriage while outside the wind is blowing, but in here it's quite warm and I feel very comfortable. I have the photograph of you and our dear children in front of me and look at it for some time after every line I have written. When will I actually be as close to you as I am now to this photograph? I always feel that I will be home for Christmas, that is, on furlough only, but I am probably simply deceiving myself.

Gerhard Fast and N. Driediger will probably go home on furlough because both have been released from service on this train, so only five of us Mennonites are left on this train. Dyck and I are probably most firmly planted here and I think we'll be rooted here to the end. I won't even initiate steps to get a release. The hypersensitivity I used to feel when the Old Man would cuss me out I have also overcome, but I have to guard myself from laughing in his face when he scolds me. A good Mennist[66] would probably say: "He is such an uncouth swine!" [*Daut es oba ehn aufjebriechtet Schwien.*] However, we now always get along with each other because I repair all kinds of equipment for him, but especially because I know how to keep the six alcohol lamps in our train burning. He trusts me and I'm careful not to misuse his trust. It is unfortunate that the Old Man doesn't want to go to Moscow. When we take on wounded here, we will take them to Petersburg.

It is rather uncomfortable with our correspondence. Did you write to Velikie Luki? When we were in Moscow, I met Hermann Enns. Well, he told me a lot about the Schoenfelder. The others also received their parcels from home. It is good that you want to send something especially to me. Well, you know that Enns brought about eight pud along with him here. Fast and Enns will take care of everything for me there in Moscow if you want to send me something. We share some of the food that's sent to us from home, but sending things by mail is first of all too expensive for me, and secondly, too inconvenient. Friesen, Neufeld and Klassen are about 1,200 feet away from our carriage. Just between the two of us, not all of us are equally gluttonous here.[67] Let them eat now and I will eat when you send me something. So far I'm doing well with my brown bread. I don't like eating dry brown bread for breakfast but it will do.

If it is at all possible to send brother Heinrich something, I would be very grateful. Maybe you could buy some sausage, butter and cookies, but pay for everything in cash, understand? And send it to Heinrich. At home there are only the wives[68] who send food, so it won't be easy to do. What you send him should not appear to be something gifted. Perhaps you could bake the cookies yourself, but, of course, buy the rest, but do this only if it won't be too much work for you. Can you imagine, that rascal sent me 50 rubles because he thought I needed money and was in real need. Well, I'm enormously pleased by this act of my dear brother, even though I didn't really need it and gave it to brother Aron. How and where to send it? Ask Mrs. Cornies, she has most of her sons on train No. 221 where Heinrich is serving.

You seem to be a little upset that the Schroeders took Micka [Tina's youngest sister] along to Ekaterinoslav to babysit. Well, it's a bit ticklish but let it go. These people are obviously still quite young, always living beyond their means, but their time will come too. They won't always be walking on silk carpets even though they are schoolmasters. [Schroeder was a teacher before induction.] I don't think you will have enough in "your bread basket" at one-and-a-half rubles per week. That is too little for doing so much work, but you can do whatever you please. I prefer that

---

[66] Mennist—Mennonite

[67] Apparently some are a bit reluctant to share the food sent from home.

[68] Heinrich isn't married and it appears that wives of medics frown on sending parcels to the unmarried servicemen through their collective efforts. So Tina is cautioned to send Heinrich a parcel of food outside of the collective efforts.

you should leave things as they are. I think it might be possible that you too could live in Mariental. I'm sure there would be enough room for you there. However, now that it is almost impossible, you want to go there, whereas a year ago when a room was waiting for you, you didn't want to live there. Well, be patient, my dearest one.[69]

Many greetings and kisses from your dearest one, Nicolai, who loves you very much.

From Tina
Schoenfeld, November 1, 1915

Dear, dear Nikolai,

At last I can chat with you a little. It's Sunday and because we take turns, it's my time to stay with the children. I have a maid but as far as looking after children, she is useless. Have just had coffee and the children are presently quiet enough that I can continue writing. Papa went to Kharkov this morning and is coming back Wednesday. During the time you were here, I have been to Mariental twice.

I wrote up to here when the children came and surrounded me and I started making mistakes, but now my little tormentors have left me again. Tomorrow I will send the baggage for you to Kornelius Fast's address in Moscow, and I'll send this letter with the list of contents of the baggage with Mirau, who will bring it to Fast because he is going directly to Moscow. Have they already received their parcels that Hermann Enns took along?

I thought Nikolai Driediger would come to the funeral and then I would take the opportunity to send you something, but the poor man wasn't able to come. I am sure he took that very hard, right? Greta and I were not invited to Cornies and I was a little sorry about that. However, we were actually very busy because we were going to butcher six pigs the next day. So in all we have butchered eight pigs this year. Our house was in turmoil all day long. I could hardly stand it, especially for the sake of our children. Last night Greta and I went to Miraus and we were home by 10:30 already, but still Mama scolded us thoroughly, but fortunately I don't let that bother me so much any more. Papa left to go to the station at 8:00 and I'm quite sure Mama shifted the hands on the clock because when we came home, the clock stood at 11:00 already while in the *Koschke* it showed only 10:30. I have noticed that every time we go away mother is unhappy, although we seldom go away.

I had written up to here and then I went to Riesens for a while to say goodbye because Heinrich must leave now too. All the young folks were there, as well as our auntie, Miss Harder, the elderly Riesens, and I. We sat in one room while the young people in the other room got pretty wild, playing *Schluesselbund*[70] and what not. I don't understand how people still find pleasure in playing those games.

---

[69] The Peters' home was essentially a compound where their unmarried children lived as well as their married daughters with their children, the daughters' husband being away in the service (See Introduction).

[70] *Schlüsselbund* was a game popular among Mennonite youth that includes some flirtation. Something like musical chairs

Soon it will be Christmas again and you will not be home. Who would have thought when the war began that it would last so long? According to some people, the war will continue for a long time. We humans are simply too wicked; we don't want to improve and follow our Lord, who wants our very best. When I pray with our children at night, Hilda never forgets to pray for you and that you will come home soon. Julius, who has been away fourteen months, wrote to Greta he would love to see her and the children, but it is not possible under the circumstances otherwise she would certainly go to visit him. She wants to write to Tina asking her if she would go with her since she doesn't want to go alone.[71] If I were in her place, I would go alone and simply let Julius know when she would arrive.

[Page missing]

From Nicolai
Evacuation Station
Medical Train No. 10/160
Siedlce November 9, 1915

My dearest Tinchen and children!

Yesterday I received your dear letter of the first of October for which I thank you most heartily. The letter was addressed to Moscow, and because our doctor had stayed in Moscow when we left, he brought our mail along when he caught up with us. Was inordinately happy for your letter. I am so sorry, my dear Tienchen, that things don't always work out as you would like, but unfortunately I can do nothing from here to change your situation, much as I would like to. Can merely urge you to practice patience, patience and humility. I am sorry, too, that you cannot be in Mariental, but that's what you wanted (to live in Schoenfeld) at one time and now the situation cannot be changed. If things aren't going well with us, we need to look at the thousands and millions for whom life is much, much, worse than ours.

Sometimes life seems so pointless in doing this work here far, far away from wife and children and especially doing the kind of work that has no benefit at all, work that if fact should not even [have to] be done. The whole world would be happy if this work [as medic] did not exist.[72] It seems that God has struck humankind with blindness, that we don't see the great absurdity of war. Oh, might this cursed murdering soon come to an end. However, we can do no more about this situation (war) than we can about our own immediate situation. So the only reasonable thing to do is to leave it all in God's hands. With His help we can overcome everything that seems so difficult to us. If we lose our courage and begin to despair, every little problem begins to seems insurmountable. To God, the fainthearted are an abhorrence. Of course, difficult, perilous times can strike at any moment, and we may not be able to see our way through, but what seems insurmountable to us, God can see us through. Later we are ashamed that we had

---

[71] Traveling alone with three children is difficult enough, but especially when unescorted by a man or an older woman.

[72] Nicolai is addressing the futility of war. Because war is futile, he regards his work as a medic an adjunct to futility although a necessary labor.

so little faith. Now and then I feel quite uncomfortable here, as you can see from my letter. My patience suddenly runs out, but later when I take a sober look, the matter seems not to have been so serious after all. You may well remember the time when you shed many tears and I almost perished with rage (actually I didn't show it much). It was because of a minor incident. You were tired, I believe, of living together with relatives, the source of the problem.

We certainly have to expect occasions, if it is God's will that we will live together, when we'll have complaints and disagreements, but won't we try to work these issues through without major disruptions, without blaming each other? Shouldn't we be able to do that then when we're living together. It will be demanding, yes, much more demanding than our situation is now. No matter where or with whom we live, if we don't humble ourselves and love each other, it will not go well with us. Eventually everything has an end and so will this war end. How near it is, we do not know, but we do know this, that God watches over us and when the time comes, He will bring us together. Yes, my dear Tina, let's make sure that unity and love always stays with us.

We are still here in Sielan and have no prospect of leaving soon because there are no wounded here. You have prepared a container of all kinds of goodies for me and I thank you heartily, but I have one request. Do not wait to send it with Fast and Driediger. That wait might be too long and I may have lost my appetite or be famished by then. Furthermore, butter may be very expensive so perhaps you shouldn't send me any unless it's possible to send some Mariental butter, that would be a different matter.[73] The Old Man has left on furlough for ten to fourteen days; we feel very good about that and can breathe freely once more. It is too bad that we are scheduled to go to Petersburg and not to Moscow. [Letters await them in Moscow.]

What are our three ne'er-do-wells doing? Probably much work for their mother, right, my poor dear? Well, even if they make unpleasant moments for you at times, you know they do it out of sheer love. How dearly I would love to see you all again! What isn't can be!

Many greetings and kisses from your ever-loving Nicolai.

From Tina
Schoenfeld, November 10, 1915

My dear Nikolai,

Since I have finished my work, I want to chat with you a little. It always takes such a long time for you to receive my letters and to answer them. Right now Friesen is home for ten days. Gerhard Fast is home also being rather silly, gallivanting around in the Colony with his old lady. But you are probably interested in what I am doing. I sorted the clean laundry and put it into the cupboard, something I like doing, and am in my comfortable room again, my bedroom, relaxing.

The son of teacher Bergen from Komarovka, a medical worker, came home for a three-month furlough, had been home only fourteen days and then died suddenly.

---
[73] His mother in Mariental has a supply of butter from her cows.

This month those two old fogies, Johann Warkentin and David Martens, have to leave for the service. Mrs. Warkentin said if her husband had to go, we Schoenfelder will have seen the last of them, and that's it. But she wants go with him. On Sunday I visited Mrs. Hermann Enns and had a good chat with her. Nikolai Driediger stopped by there for a short while. He told me quite a few things about you. He said that if I would bring some things over, he would gladly take something to Moscow for you. Today Mrs. Rempel asked me if I had any news from you. Well, I satisfied her by telling her that we received two postcards from you and that I was satisfied with postcards as long as I knew you were alive and well. Naturally I am happier for a letter, and I believe I will get one from you tomorrow. Mrs. Enns is happy that her husband now has a permanent job here, but who knows how long this joy will last.

When Papa was in Ekaterinoslav, he received a telegram that all those [Mennonites] who work in government offices up to 30 years of age will now be inducted to work in field hospitals, and people not fit for that work will now be placed in the government offices. This may affect Schroeder as well and, in fact, would actually do him some good because he would then really come feel the affects of whole war.[74] I have written this letter so poorly because Gerhard [her brother] is making such a *Katzenjammer*[75] in the dining room on his violin that I would like to flee. Otherwise all of us are well although typhoid and scarlet fever have occurred among the children in our neighborhood. But our children are healthy. They run around outside, then come in crying, warm themselves, and go out again. The streets are neither muddy nor dry, but it is cold. Is there any prospect of your coming home on furlough? How I do wish you could come home for Christmas! Maybe Heinrich can come too, as mother said.

Selma is lying in bed asking for roast duck. She is always hungry and such a precocious child. When I pray with her at bedtime she always says, "Pray for Papa, Papa come home." Sunday night I took out the Bible Story picture book and explained it to them. I told them the story of the birth of Jesus and those little tykes were most attentive. Many warm greetings and kisses from your Tina and children who wish you the best of health.

From Nicolai
Evacuation Station
Medical Train No. 10/160
Siedlce, November 13, 1915

Dear Tina and children!

That our train is still standing in Siedlce may cause you to wonder when you read the first words on this page. There are until now no wounded here, thank God, and probably not in the other places either, whereas things at first were so terribly

---

[74] Schroeder, Tina's brother-in-law, had been posted in a government office in Ekaterinoslav and was later transferred to Odessa, thus avoiding what Tina considered real non-resistant service. There was at times a bit of friction between Gerhard Schroeder and Nicolai.

[75] Katzenjammer: literally means the "wailing of a cat" or caterwaul. A loud disagreeable noise combined with confusion.

frantic. The train on which Aron is serving arrived here this morning. He said there were in Duenaburg no wounded either, so after their train had been standing there for six days, they were sent here. Being stationed here would not be so bad if my longing for letters were not so powerful, and in addition, the pangs of hunger for those things you are going to send me are growing. I hope those things will be waiting for me in Moscow and also that there will, for a change, be a letter from you.

Did you not receive the letter in which I ask you to send my mail to Veliki Luki? The others have already received some letters at Veliki Luki, but I have nothing. Please send all letters to: *Veliki Luki, Train Station of medical Train No. 10/160 of the All-Nobility Organization. N. A. Rempel.*

It appears that the letters from you can't be sent without stamps anymore. Many have already received notice to make payments to retrieve their letters. However, the cost of stamps should not frighten you out of writing to me; I'm sure we can pay for them.

It seems to me that you are much too busy, have to work much too hard, and I just don't like that at all. Of course, I have nothing against your helping out some. I assume it hasn't come to the point where you are the cook and the serving maid also, serving everyone, has it? You have quite enough work with the children. I clearly remember when I was home that you had no time during the week to sit and chat with me, so how are things going when I am not there? Perhaps you think that I don't know when you work so hard. Naturally I can't see how you torture and martyr yourself now, eating your bread by the sweat of your brow. It appears that you stumble around tired and emaciated and that you can scarcely carry yourself about from exhaustion. Once more, keep in mind that when my service is finished, I want to come home to a healthy, robust wife. Refrain from insanely hard work so that you don't make the time of my service here more difficult. If you can't do anything but work hard at Schoenfeld, go to Mariental. There you can do as you please. There you are lady of your estate.

What about Gerhard? Is he completely free for service or has his induction merely been postponed? You write me nothing about it. What about J. Warkentin, has he been conscripted or isn't the count up to that group yet? Has Papa bought a lot of Christmas goodies: cookies, nuts and so on? I would love to step into the store for a few moments and taste all those sweets, but much, much, more I would like to lock you and the dear children in my arms to hug and kiss you with all my heart. It seems like a dream that there was a time when I sat and chatted with you, while the children were playing happily near us or lying with their little heads on our shoulders, listening to our conversation. Again and again I say to myself: yes, there was such a time; yes, there really was such a blessed hour in the quiet family circle. But now! Now I am sitting all by myself and writing. Here I am, close to Riga, and you are there, far, far in the South. What a great chasm lies between us and yet how close we are to each other. But how horrible the roar of cannons here! With each burst of the thunder from that cannon, one imagines that a number of human beings have fallen again, men who probably have wife and children in some far-away home. May God grant us peace soon. There would be no greater Christmas gift for us all than peace. What is impossible with humans is possible with God. Let us pray for peace!

Enough for today with greetings and kisses, your Nicolai

From Tina
Schoenfeld, November 15, 1915

My dear, dear Nikolai,

Today it's already four years since Hilda saw the light of this world. So much has happened during that time. It's very good that we don't know what will happen in the future. When one sees how much a child develops in four years, how wonderful that really is. It is beyond comprehension. We can't thank God enough that the children are so healthy. And I am happy that there will be peace again soon. What joy there will be in the whole world when fathers come home to their wives and children. However, there will be many tears, too, because of the many who will not come home.

It's not very warm in our room because we are trying to conserve heat because we don't have any coal yet, but we are heating with oil and manure [bricks]. I have received your dear letter and quite agree to send something to Heinrich. Peter Papke has come home unexpectedly, but he has to return by the first of December. If I see Papke, I will send the parcel for Heinrich with him, but if not, I'll send it from here. Tina Zehrt agreed to go with me to the Papkes' today but she hasn't come yet, probably thinks it's too cold. As for driving, well, our horses are worn out. I suppose you aren't certain whether you will be coming home for Christmas, so I do want to send you a Christmas parcel. Well, I won't be sending raisin bread because we have neither raisins nor currants. You don't like them anyway.

I sent you several letters in which I told you about Mariental. The new teacher was rather uppity when she first came there and wanted to assert herself with the farmers, but they put her in her place rather quickly. They were not as stupid as she thought. At first things didn't go smoothly, but now she has calmed down. They call the Russian woman teachers *Boltuschka* [a chatter-boxes] and say that they are just "Russe *majals*."[76]

Papa was in Ekaterinoslav. Who knows if we will get sweets this year? He had been promised some, but who knows. Today H. Wiens is going to the station and I'll send my letter along with him. Schroeder has been lucky again. He will stay in Ekaterinoslav and has been assigned a position as bookkeeper. They are not coming home for Christmas. Well, so much the better, then we have less work. You are asking about baking bread. I don't have much to do with that—merely seeing that it's done. The Russian girl has to do the kneading, so it's easier for me. We always take turns with making meals. Today my week begins. Last week I sewed a lot for

---

[76] This teacher is obviously Russian and that may not sit well with the Mennonites because they have had their own teachers from the time they had emigrated from Prussia until 1876 when some privileges were rescinded. They then had to teach Russian in their schools. That had been done by Mennonite teachers until the shortage because many had been inducted. Russians had to fill the vacancy. "Russe majals" is Plautdietsch for "Russian gals", rather derogatory term, but it reflects the attitude many Mennonites held toward their Russians neighbors.

the children—four pairs of underwear, two aprons and a dress for Alice. Gerhard is in the office right now very annoyed about something. Well, you know how he always behaves. Since he's been in Ekaterinoslav for a few days, it's too quiet for him around here. I often have it out with him. [Page missing]

From Nicolai
Evacuation Station
Medical Train No. 10/160
St. Petersburg, November 19, 1915

My dearest, beloved treasure!

    I have time right now to answer your dear letters that I received yesterday. You will probably wonder how it is that the letters don't come to Moscow, but to Petersburg, 600 werst further. Well, yes, my dear Tinchen, what is sent from one person to another whom one loves above all else in the world, which is not too hard to achieve. One spares no effort or cost to sustain a relationship even if it is confined to letters. If I were there, I would take you and lock you in my arms with unspeakable love and tenderness, my dear wife, and thank you for your letters and for the parcels that are waiting for me in Moscow. But how sad that you do not receive all the letters I write and I don't receive all of yours either. Strange that you seem to get only those letters that I write while I'm in a state of depression. It would be better if those went lost.

    But I know, my dearest Tinischka, that you are so good, so loving and kindhearted, that you bear me no grudges when I sadden you. Believe me, dear Tinischka, every time for as long as I have known you and have caused you grief and hurt your feelings, I, too, experience deep pain and conscience pangs afterward for what I have said or done. Seldom have I let you know how sorry I was, you whom I love more than anything in the world. You were so good, so concerned about me, and in spite of that I could be at times as hardhearted as a stone. However, I am not that hard, only my stubbornness and self-love stanched my true feelings. In reality, my heart was nearly breaking with love and compassion for you.

    We must become much more open with each other, hiding nothing from each other. I know you tried very hard to be open with me, to hide nothing from me. I, however, felt that you were never quite free and open, and so I, quite wrongly, became less open with you. Now I realize how foolish that was and from now on I shall strive to look at everything more soberly and to discuss everything with you. This pride and self-love must go. We must discuss everything in humility with each other, and then there can be no differences between us. I was happy to read in your letters that you had been able to capture the children's interest in stories, interest in our Lord, etc.

    That I will be home for Christmas is doubtful. There's nothing new here otherwise. The Old Man, quite unchanged, is apparently happy to be back with us. We will probably stay in Petersburg for three days and then possibly move to Duriensk. We would all love to go from there to Moscow to help G. Fast and N. Driediger with the things they have brought for us from home, at least tell us much news about Schoenfeld. I would be much happier if I could hear the news directly from the Schoenfelder in that village. What a joy it would be if I were home by then! I wish you gentle slumber and God's care and send you thousand kisses and greetings. Your loving Nicolai.

From Tina
Schoenfeld, November 20, 1915

My dear Nikolai,

I'm sitting again to chat with you. We are enjoying good health, except Hilda has sore eyes and Selma has a sore bum. She burnt herself sitting on the little stool and then was hurt more while sitting on the potty. She likes it warmed up, but I didn't realize it was too hot when I sat her on it. She was up in a flash screaming like children always have to do no matter what happens. We've had some frost lately, but now it's muddy again so that means a lot of work when the children run through all the rooms. Luckily the children don't run out in the mud much, then I'd have even more work. But we have a very strict cook who won't tolerate that. Well, generally speaking, things are going very well.

We did our last butchering for this year at the Miraus. It went quite well. But Franz Wiens and that old dodderer, Eitzen, were full of fun. They clowned around like young boys most of the time. Last week I wrote you that Warkentin's furlough was over and was supposed to leave, but the day before he was to go, he got a message that he could stay home a little longer. Right now a number of medics are home on leave and I hope you will be home soon, too, but maybe I'll be disappointed again, which I will simply have to accept. I'm resigned to whatever happens. Thank you very much for your last letter. I would like to be like you—content, no matter what happens. I hope to do that, with God's help.

It is strange that children should be so concerned about death. Recently Hilda was not feeling well and asked me if she would die. I answered, "If God does not will it, you will not die." She said, "But I don't want to die." When Selma wants to punish someone, she always says, "Going to hell." One day I said to her, "Do you want to go to hell, too?" Then she began to cry and said, "Selma not burn, no Mama." She uses the word Mama in every sentence. She is so precocious as though she understands everything. She follows me around wherever I go or sits close beside me. The children are asking how many nights they will have to sleep before you come home. It is quite obvious that they miss you very much. Next week Friesen is coming again. He inquired by letter if we needed a worker and Gerhard told him that he should come. But how long will it be until he's called back and we lose him again? He doesn't want to be a volunteer anymore.

People say I am gaining weight. This year of the war is good for me in that respect only. But don't get any ideas, my dear Old Man. Everything is in order as it should be. I wouldn't be upset if by the time you come home I weigh 4 N. I don't have many grams to go—maybe 11. Well enough about such things—more next time. Greetings and kisses from your loving Tina and children. Your last letter was written on the 9th of November.

From Nicolai
Evacuation Station
Medical Train No. 10/160
Strugi-Belaia, November 25, 1915

To: Katharina Broisovna Rempel –
Gaichur Station, Ekaterinoslav Railway[77]

Dear Katja,

We are on our way to Sielan after a six-day stopover in St. Petersburg. I was sick during those days, but don't worry because I feel better now. It was very cold there, snowing hard, and I think I had a touch of the flu. I have a request for you. As we are no longer with Veliki Luki, please send my letters to Moscow again. I don't know where we will be with all our wounded soldiers or where we will work. Everything is going the same— nothing new. All our hopes for a change for a better future have disappeared forever. What we have now will be in the future, too.

I will write you a letter tomorrow. Please don't worry about me. I'm fine.

Your Nicolai

From Nicolai
Evacuation Station
Medical Train No. 10/160
Kreuzburg, November 27, 1915

My dear wife and children,

I have this great longing to chat with you while we are sitting here once again at Kreuzburg, and it appears that we will be here very long. We would much prefer to be waiting in Moscow than on these wild steppes where only soldiers, war machinery, steeds[78] [horses], and aeroplanes can be seen. I am no great friend of Moscow, but I do love letters you send to my address there—in fact, everything that comes from you. Sent you a postcard yesterday in which I wrote that I was a bit ill, actually hovering between being a little ill and just not being really well. I have decided to take sick leave when I don't really feel well. Others don't care about me when I'm sick, so why shouldn't I look after my health? I regard it my sacred duty to take care of myself. Am writing you about my illness, not because it's worth writing about but because you once told me that I keep such matters secret from you. So just remain calm and be assured that I will keep you informed of every episode.

I'm jealous of you because you have so many things to write about from there— about our dear children, etc., etc. What is our dear little Selma doing? Does she still ask you to bring her a roast duck when she is already in bed? What about Alice, how does she occupy herself? Is she still a little whiney at times? And Hilda, I always imagine her as an unruly ruffian who scraps with other children from early

---
[77] Gaichur was a station on the Ekaterinoslav Railway Line, hence Ek RWY.
[78] Nicolai uses the archaic German word "Rosse." Its equivalent would be steed or charger in English.

'til late and then looks around with her friendly smile. I find myself in a situation that almost drives me crazy because I can do nothing for my wife and children. Especially in these formative years when children need proper care and activities, I can offer them nothing—no parental guidance or proper teaching. One simply has to sit by quite helplessly. There is no prospect for peace, everything going the same old way.

But I'd better hurry because this letter is supposed to be mailed today. Who knows how our plans for me to spend Christmas at home will turn out? God grant that we see each other soon again! I just want to tell you once more that I love you, although you know that! I am surrounded in this room by medical officers who are practicing their writing. So you can imagine what it's like when wandering eyes keep glancing at what I'm writing. Just one more day and Fast and Driediger have to leave their families for Moscow. How quickly the month of furlough has passed for them, and how bad these poor fellows will feel tomorrow night? To say *Auf Wiedersehen*[79] is easier than saying good-bye. But do console Mrs. Fast. You, too, have had to take leave of your husband three times in this war.

Where have the two old fellows, Warkentin and Matthies, from Schoenfeld landed? Or has nothing been heard of them yet? It will probably happen to Rempel [a neighbor], teacher Toews,[80] and Ohm Enns that they will have to leave their homes, too. A Polish man is sitting beside me dictating to me what I should write to someone, but unfortunately he can't communicate in Russian very well. He simply wants some help in expressing his love for someone, but nothing came of it. If things are better tomorrow, I'll try writing again, but for tonight I'll stop because there's nothing more I can write.

I send my warmest greetings and kisses to you and the children, your Nicolai. Greetings for the parents and siblings.

From Tina

Schoenfeld, November 27, 1915

My dear Nicolai,

I sent a letter by mail on the 25th to Weliki Luki and when the mail arrived today, I received a letter and a card from you. I thank you heartily for the letter. You wrote that I receive only those letters that you have written while in an unhappy mood. Well, I believe I have sometimes earned your reprimand in a somewhat sharp tone. I don't fault you for it and I want to change for the better.

Well, your Old Man (boss) is back on your train again, and it is not as people rumored here that he was gone forever. Gerhard Rempel even told me that Peter might be coming on furlough soon because the Old Man had left the train. You ask which singers come to choir practice: Miss Riesen from the Wiens family; Jacob, Mariechen and Kleine [little] Friesen from the Kornelius Enns family; Miss Janzen and Enns from Peter Enns family; Anna Peters, Anna Rempel, Lena and Gerhard from our family; from Peter Heidebrecht family: Abram and Susana, Kornelius

---

[79] The German *Auf Wiedersehen* is equivalent of "I'll see you again."

[80] In Germany, even today, teachers are addressed by title—*Lehrer* or *Herr Lehrer;* hence *Lehrer Toews*, or in English that would be Teacher Toews, like Professor Toews.

Neufeld's son, Maria Mirau and Justina Rempel; from Frank Wiens family: Greta, Liese and Nicolai. Franz Rempel is the choir director.

Today Gerhard Fast came into the store, and I want to send at least one letter for you with him. I can't send other things because he has a full load so I will let that rest. Besides you haven't received what I sent last time. I will ask Fast to forward the letter to where you are stationed most of the time. Well, let's hope that you can be stationed in Moscow or come home for good. I am curious what Heinrich will say about the parcel I sent him. I urged him to try to be home, too, when you come home. Wouldn't that be so great? And what is that old guy, Jacob Ivanovich, doing? Has his hair become even whiter than it was? Why doesn't that fellow come home? We received a letter from Lorenz recently. He is in Red Cross train No. 175. He writes that they were on a trip to Gomel and that they had been on the move for nineteen days but still had seventy werst to go and would probably arrive by Christmas.

This week I have made duvets for Hilda, Selma, Hans and Wolya. Selma is very proud of hers. Everyone has to look at it. Greta [Julius' wife] and Tina [his sister] want to go to visit Julius after Christmas, but he told them to wait because all of the villages are over-crowded with soldiers so there would have no place for them [Refers to quartering soldiers in private homes].

I write so often that I really have nothing to write to you. I just read your letter again. If only I could write letters like yours, my dearest, my one-and-only. I read your letters again and again.

Grandfather (Toews) is getting noticeably weaker. He may not live till spring. But enough for this time. Many greeting and kisses, your Tina who loves you.

From Nicolai's Brother Heinrich
Tiflis, November 30, 1915

Dear Sister-in-law Tina!

Yesterday I received the letter and the parcel from you through Papke.[81] A thousand thanks for them! You don't know how happy I was to receive them. First of all, that you haven't forgotten me, and secondly, it came just at the right time, especially the butter, because it is quite impossible to get butter in all of Tiflis. None has been available in some time. Also for the sausage and cookies, I already had some today, and they are most delicious. My comrades who are with me here think I have the most wonderful sister-in-law. Now, as far as I'm concerned, we could go back to Begle-Almet again where we always have to fast a little because there's little of anything available there. Our train was there all of last week while we were loading wounded. Things are not good there because winter has set in fully, much snow and up to twenty-two degrees of frost. By contrast it is very nice here, don't even have to heat our stoves. Yesterday we played ball in the meadow. I won't be home for Christmas. They have promised us furloughs for January, but then I will have to wait my turn and so I won't be coming home right away. I would gladly breathe some air different from this Caucasus air. It seems that we have been banished to this place—the Caucasus.

---
[81] Note Tina's letter of November 15.

You ask me in your letter how it is with my sweetheart? Well, I hardly know what to say or do. I would be interested in Anna, but I don't like her family, so I haven't made up my mind one way or another. I would like ask you for some advice because it's always easier to judge a case when one is not directly involved. However, there's still time for the whole matter. Your old man is really fortunate with his furlough, but it must be very hard for him on that train; at least I wouldn't want to be in his place with that crazy boss.

How is it with your three girls, already quite grown up? Are the boyfriends coming around yet? How happy I would be to see you all again and chat and tell *Reuberpistolen*.[82] I would have much to write about, but one can't write so much during this time; however, we'll have so much more to talk about later when I'm home, if we're still alive. How is Greta with her little ones? [a son and two daughters] She has had to endure a lot during this war.[83]

Greetings and kisses from your grateful brother-in-law, Heinrich. Please greet your parents and the other siblings from me. My address is: Tiflis

From Tina
Schoenfeld, December 3, 1915

My dear Nikolai,

Was hoping for a letter from you yesterday but none came. You probably got the letter I sent with Gerhard Fast. What about the parcel, did you finally get it or are you still hungry? If you could come home, I would fatten you up so well! Every day I think about you, even after I have gone to bed, hoping that you would have the good fortune of coming home.

Must tell you what we are doing. The laundry has been done and I'm very glad we did it before Christmas. Now I am busy sewing undergarments for Alice and Hilda so they won't freeze when we travel in the cold of winter. I have been sewing all week from early until late. I planned to do all the sewing for my children myself but will have to get one dress for each girl made by someone else. I don't like to do that, but what can I do? You will probably say, "Earning nothing and paying out money for sewing?" However, I have already earned the money for their dresses. I wanted to save a total 200 rubles by the time you come home, but I now had to use some of it. I bought shoes for Alice, new soles for my shoes and other most necessary things. I know you won't blame me for those expenditures.

Friesen showed up here again and has been helping in the store. We are keeping the place warmer now because we had heavy frost. Sometimes Hilda asks, "When will it be Christmas?" Then Alice answers, "Christmas will be here when Papa and Tante Susa come home." Our dining room is quite empty of furniture now, so the children can romp around as much as they please. You have to have strong nerves

---
[82] *Reuberpistolen* is literally robber pistols. They are cock-and-bull stories. Something like a pulp western, the good guys usually winning.

[83] Greta's husband, Julius, was away from his wife and children much of their marriage. He died in 1919 while on his way to Mariental. The Rempel family was notified by telegram. Nicolai and a helper brought the body home where he prepared the body for interment.

to put up with all that wild play. We haven't received our Christmas stock for the store yet. Gerhard is supposed to go to Ekaterinoslav on Saturday to see if anything is coming. People are constantly asking for things we don't have in stock and business is doing quite well even if we don't have any new items yet; the old ones are sell well, too. Papa had bought 159 rubles worth of confections, which seemed like a lot, but he has tripled his profit on them. One package used to cost merely five cents but now costs twelve cents. It is awful how expensive everything is becoming.

Come home and get your Christmas gift! You don't have to spend any money on a present for me. I'll be perfectly satisfied if only you can come home. If not, we must be contented with that, too. Once again, greetings and kisses from, Your Tina

From Nicolai
Evacuation Station
Medical Train No. 10/160
December 4, 1915
The trip from Veliki Luki to Sielan

My deeply loved Tinchen!

I wrote a card the second of the month to inform you that we would be going to Moscow. This is what they told us and I believed it, and we were looking forward to that trip but things took quite a different turn again. When we arrived at Veliki Luki, we were told, "This is as far as you can go!" All of our requests were summarily turned down. So we had to unload and return to Sielan. How long we will be sitting here no one knows. We do know that three medical trains are ahead of us, so ours is the fourth in line. It could take one month before we can take on a load of wounded, so we can expect to get to Moscow after the holidays. By the way, we don't know anything and can't say anything. Should those in top positions suddenly be seized by the inclination to start warring again, well then anything can happen and everything will be changed in a few days and then all the trains could be filled with wounded soldiers very quickly.[84]

When and how we will receive our parcels is not at all clear to us. Fortunately Jake Ewert received a parcel at Veliki Luki with butter, sausage and coffee, so we are well provided for. I arranged with Enns and Fast while I was in Moscow to have them open a parcel of food if it arrived so that it doesn't spoil. I am quite sure that everything will be taken care of in Moscow. I am much more concerned that you are not receiving all of my letters and you might believe that I am merely too lazy to write. Well, I certainly can't complain about not having time to write.

As I didn't finish my letter yesterday, I will try again now. It is approximately 295 werst from Veliki Luki to Sielan, where, we are told among other things, we have just arrived. To cover that distance should take only ten hours, but it took us thirty-two hours. It is a very poor stretch of railway and many accidents happen on it. We got a taste of that on this tour, but luckily no one was hurt. Once some

---

[84] Apparently the fighting had come to a standstill or a temporary truce. The Russians had been suffering severe losses, being driven back by the Germans.

carriages became uncoupled from the rest of the train so that we had to sit there for quite a while, and the locomotive broke down a second time. Fortunately we rested unharmed in our rail carriages. Until now, thank God, we have been protected from all misfortunes, except that my plan to come home for Christmas was derailed. It is difficult to accept not to be able to do what one has planned. I can't do anything about it and I have committed everything to God and you probably feel as I do.

Again I postponed another day sending this letter off. Yesterday we had several officers in our compartment and some even stayed for the night. They asked me for ink and a pen to write letters and today they went directly into battlefield where writing would be more difficult than here, and so I postponed sending this letter until today. It is Sunday and in addition it is a major national holiday, Coronation Day—December the 6th, and it is a wonderful day for me because I received three of your beautiful letters today. You can't imagine how thankful I am to you. How I wish I could whisper into your ear what a great joy you have given me. I wish I could come to you and kiss you heartily, my darling. But these are idle wishes that cannot be realized, and we must move on without them. It will really be unspeakable joy when I am reunited with my wife and children to live and work in peace, in love and patience, and to make life easy and delightful. What can be more beautiful in this world? No burdens, no problems then can weigh us down. We can go through everything as lightly as a deer. Dear God, may that time be much closer than we believe it to be and may we never relax our prayers for peace on earth and peace in our hearts. I think that all the preaching about peace will not vanquish war, quarreling and strife. Who knows where we will celebrate Christmas? Just now I was told that they want to send us from here to Durensk, and then we will probably have to stay there over Christmas.

Now to answer your questions—I want to express my concern about Hilda's eye problem. You wrote me once that Hilda had a severe fall, now is that true? So then it is possible that she has strained her neck ligaments. I suggest you take her to the doctor or to Wiebe in Lichtfelde. It would be too dreadful if she suffered an eye defect. Please, my dearest, do take this problem with her eye seriously. I am not really troubled about Selma's backside. Next time she will probably take care to sit down on something cool. And I am very happy and pleased that you are keeping well. Soon you may be like N. Thiessen, but I really would not want such a fat wife, yet if you put on a few pounds that wouldn't hurt. Then you wouldn't look so fragile.

Thank you so much for sending brother Heinrich a package. He will of course have been enormously happy for everything that you sent him including your letter. Write me if you paid for everything you sent to him. What do you think, my dear, about buying cloth for a suit for me, that is, of course, if Papa sells it for that price that I always pay. If you think this is a good idea, why don't you get some for yourself also, if you need it. Better to do it now than later, because the price for those goods will not decrease.

What is Papa occupied with? He probably finds things difficult. He doesn't answer my letters any more. As a matter of fact, no one from home writes me. Actually I owe Gerhard an answer to his letter and I will do it soon, but Susana and Mika never write. Nor does Willy. I received a letter from sister Tina today. They seem to expect us for Christmas, but they will probably be sorely disappointed.

I will close for now. Please greet everyone, the parents, siblings, grandparents, Ohm Peter, Tante Sanchen and all the neighbors, especially Jakob Franzovich. Jakob Ivanovich sends special greetings. That poor fellow has a tough life. He has to be in his office from early morning till late at night, even if there is no work. I feel sorry for him. His old boss has no sense.

Many kisses and heartfelt greetings from your loving Nicolai

From Tina
Schoenfeld, December 9, 1915
My dear Nikolai,

I want to chat with you a little, but of course, it would be much better face-to-face. You will have heard by now that Grandpa [Peter Toews] is dead. Our Grandpa died very peacefully. He lay quietly one day and two nights and then fell asleep. It is so quiet at Grandma's now that he is gone. Aunt Tina is taking it the hardest.[85] I wonder who will come for the funeral. Truda, Mika and Gerhard are coming Friday and staying for the night and leaving on Saturday. We also sent a telegram to Julius and Willie. Julius certainly won't come, and I don't think Willie will come either. And, of course, you won't come.

Have you been to Moscow and did you get your things? It would be too bad if everything was spoiled. We are very busy sewing. I have already finished five little dresses. Until now I sat in the living room where Greta, Tina Z. and Anna are sewing, but they are chattering so much that I can't get on with my writing so now I'm in my bedroom. All the children are sleeping. Last week Selma stuffed two beans into one nostril. We tried a long time to remove them but just couldn't get them out. Suddenly they came out by themselves. Alice has been very sick for two days. Her tonsils are quite swollen. Mrs. Dueck thinks it is not serious but her throat is very sore. I thought it might be diphtheria but she says that the discharge would be gray then. I am using iodine ointment on her, which is supposed to help. Our weather was very foggy until now, just right for catching colds, but now we have some frost again.

I have everything ready for Christmas. I ironed the bedclothes as well as I could although they don't look as good as store-bought linen. So what are you up to? Anything new? I'm glad that you wrote me about everything including that you were sick. You want to know what Alice is doing? She sits and sews together little pieces of cloth or she looks at picture books. I often tell them stories that they really love. Selma and Hilda are good little girls; you know, the old sort. If only everybody would come home soon, the joy would be overwhelming.

What would you say if I were to get a passport? Papa thinks it would be good because who knows when we might have to flee? Well, enough for today, more and better next time. Many greetings and kisses from your Tina. Greta and Tina Z. send greetings.

---

[85] The Peter Toews, Tina's grandparents, had three daughters and one son. The eldest daughter, Margarita, married Bernhard Peters. Margareta and Bernhard were Tina's parents. A brief account of the escape of the other two sisters, Susana and Tina, from the Soviet Union in 1944 is in the Epilogue.

From Tina
Schoenfeld, December 15, 1915

My dear Nikolai,

We just had a very busy time. Our Grandfather was buried two days ago. Grandma found it difficult to say good-bye to him even though she had had a very difficult time with him the last while. Everyone felt sad. When we go to Grandma's now it is quiet and seems so strange. Only Susa, Mika, Greta and Truda came for the funeral.

I just heard Papa scolding Gerhard because he had hidden [stolen] some things again.[86] Papa just can't tolerate that. Schroeders are leaving on Friday. They will not stay for Christmas. Mika and Susa will stay here a while and go home after Christmas. Alice has been very sick for a whole week. Yesterday it didn't look good at all. There is something wrong with her throat. When I made a compress for her, she felt much better immediately. She has difficulty talking. I also gave her some herbal tea that helped a lot. I was beginning to think that you might not see her alive again. God heard my prayers. Hilda's eyes are much improved. It was just a common ailment. Selma's legs and backside are better, too, but she is very careful now not to sit on a hot seat again.

You asked me what I sent to Heinrich. I told you about it already, but you may not have received that letter. I sent him raisins, cookies, butter, four rings of sausages (three long ones) and some *Pfeffernuesse*. I paid Papa for everything—about five rubles, and I gave Papke two kopeks for delivering it to Heinrich. On Saturday the 12th, I received your letter and postcard, also a letter from Heinrich. He thanks me heartily for the parcel. It came just at the right time. I don't know where to send your Christmas parcel? I guess to Moscow to Hermann Enns. I'm still hoping that you will come home for the holidays. Kornelius Fast has come home for one month and ten days.

Had you heard the news about Grandfather's death? We wrote to Hermann Enns and he was supposed to send you a telegram. Greta has had no letter from Julius for a whole month and she is very concerned. All of us are well except Alice, but I believe she is improving. This year we will celebrate Christmas Eve in the high school again. We are pretty well ready for Christmas and you are included, too.

Just now the telephone is ringing and then I always think it might be news that you are coming home. Greetings and kisses from your ever-loving Tina. [Nicolai did come home for Christmas, albeit for only a few days.]

---

[86] Gerhard Peters, brother of Tina, was considered a rather amusing, colorful ne'er-do-well by the family, the black sheep. He came to Canada with his parents et al. in 1924, and allegedly never did a good day's work in his life. He was master at conning relatives and others out of five or ten bucks with the convincing assurance that the loan was as secure as gold in the bank and would be returned promptly. Of course, he never repaid. His hale-fellow-well-met spirit probably saved his life and that of his parents when some brigands who occupied the village of Schoenfeld 1919 entered the Peters store to make off with whatever they wanted. He happened to have had a friendly relation with one of those brigands, whom he met with a warm greeting that was returned by the brigand (See Epilogue).

Julius and Anna Lange—
Nicolai's paternal grandparents

Abram & Sarah (nee Lange) Rempel—
Nicolai's Parents

Nicolai at 18

Tina at 18

Peter & Justina Toews—Tina's grandparents

Margareta & Bernard Peters—Tina's Parents

Tina's Family—Peters Family 1906: Standing left—Gerhard, Gertrude (Truda), Margareta, (Greta), Katharina (Tina), & Willie. Seated left—Susanna, (Susa), Bernhard, Mika, Margareta holding Hans, Anna. All except Hans immigrated to Canada in 1924. Hans died at 14.

Katharina with Alice 1911

Nicolai in his quarters

Nicolai center seated and colleagues in Forestry

Nicolai (long coat) with Forestry Colleagues and a curious onlooker

Red Cross Hospital Evacuation Train No. 10/160; Nicolai circled on right. His brother Hermann on left. Initially the Red Cross Hospital trains consisted mainly of boxcars fitted with beds, and etc. By 1915 boxcars had been replaced.

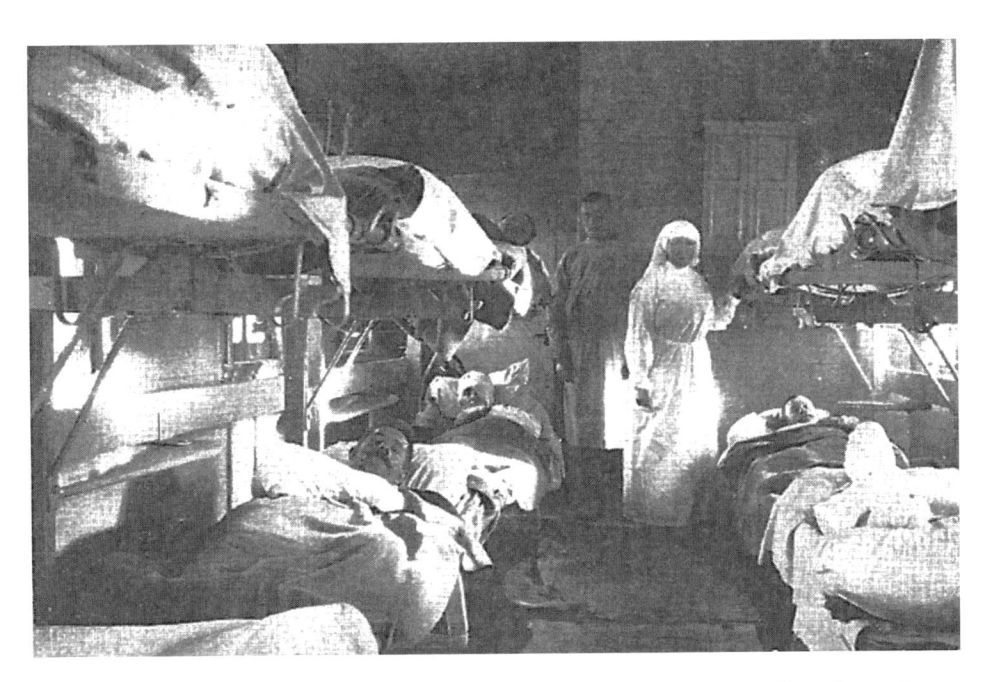

Wounded soldiers in Red Cross Hospital Evacuation Train: Quiring & Bartel, *Als Ihre Zeit zu Ende War* (Saskatoon ,SK Modern Press, 1964), p.181

THE LETTERS

PART THREE

Letters of Nicolai and Katharina Rempel 1916

Because of the intensity of their work, the burnout rate among medics taking care of injured and wounded while they were being evacuated from the battlefield to hospitals was initially quite high, but over time they were granted more R & R. Nicolai's requests for transfer out of his work as a medic on the Red Cross Hospital Evacuation train was finally realized in 1916. Initially he was assigned to work in a hospital in Moscow, but was soon transferred to Zemstvo Command Headquarters in that city where he performed secretarial tasks among other responsibilities for the remainder of his service. Even though his work load is much lighter, he complains to Tina about his frustrations, trying to meet the demands of the fumbling Russian bureaucracy. His initiation to the complexity of this big city opened his eyes to a world from which life in the small village had sheltered him. This year may have served as an apprenticeship for the dramatic changes that took place in 1917.

From Tina

Ekaterinoslav,[87] January 2, 1916

My dear Nicolai,

You will see from the address that I am at Truda's. The decision to come here to Ekaterinoslav went very quickly. Truda wanted to stay in Schoenfeld longer, but Schroeder sent a message asking her to come home right away, so we left New Year's Eve. Again we had to wait five hours at the Gaichur station. The train was to leave at 3:00 p.m., but left at eight o'clock, and so we arrived 2 a.m., so Truda and I spent New Year's on the train. Schroeder will know by the 4th of January when he'll be transferred to Odessa. She and I might return to Schoenfeld rather than going to Odessa because Schroeder's transfer may even be postponed, but you could send a letter here. Truda will be coming with all her belongings to Schoenfeld, but reluctantly. She plans to pack a trunk today already.

It seems strange to sit around without any work. I am just not used to it. All but Truda and I have gone to the government office. You will be unhappy that this is only my first letter—time has slipped by so quickly, but I will try to be more punctual. When I left home, Alice and Hilda did not want me to go, but Selma stomped her foot and said, "You should go." How was your trip back; not the best I suppose? The hamper you sent back is still here, but I don't know who the sugar and the other things are for. Please write me again to whom these things belong.

---

[87] Tina is visiting her sister Truda whose husband, Gerhard, was stationed in Ekaterinoslav but was waiting for a transfer to Odessa. It appears that he held office appointments throughout the war.

The men in the military here in Ekaterinoslav look very depressed. They are being sent by boat on their assignments and that is apparently quite dangerous at this time.

The page is full and Truda can't find any more paper. She sends greetings. Many greetings and kisses, your Tina.

P.S. January 5th. We are going to go to Odessa instead of returning home to Schoenfeld. Katya and Peter will go to Krasnoyarsk [Siberia]. My address is: Odessa Main Post Office, Kr. Uns. Dern. T. P. Ung.

From Tina [while visiting her sister Truda]
Ekaterinoslav, Jan. 6, 1916

My dear Nicolai,

We are still here. Although every day it is rumored that we will be leaving, so far nothing has happened. Maybe they'll keep us here for another week, but that can change suddenly.[88] My things are already packed for the return home. I am bored, having no work. Schroeder noted that we may be ordered to stay here, and what happens then if our baggage has been shipped? It seems an eternity that you and I have been separated. I so would love to be with you, I can hardly stand it, especially knowing that you are really not far away. How I long for March when we plan to meet here in Ekaterinoslav.

I don't care for city life at all. All you can do here is stare at your four walls. If you were here, we would rummage through the town. Today there will be a big ball in Schoenfeld at David Dueck's. You have a holiday where you are, too, I think. Who knows what our girls are doing? When I return home from here and Heinrich has already gone home to Mariental, I'll go there.[89]

This is how far I wrote last night. Schroeder is taking a nap for a few hours, Frieda is reading stories, and Gretel went to visit the Martens. I'm not used to it being so quiet as at home there is always so much noise. I am lonely. If I had the courage I would run away. If I were sure that it would be another week before we can leave, I would go with Susa and Anna Willms on the vehicle they want to take. I don't know what else to write; one experiences so little. By the time I arrive home we will have a new apprentice and I'll will be my task to train him, if that's possible, not like that Hans Wilms. What has Hermann Enns heard about his wife or has he gone home? Fast is returning to Moscow today or tomorrow. If I were there I would send you a message or a parcel. Please forgive me, my dearest, but there's nothing that can be done about it this time.

How quickly the time passed when we were together, those three days went so fast it seems as though you weren't here at all. I should have taken Selma with me, but thinking I would be away only for a few days I didn't, but unfortunately things

---

[88] Tina is waiting to return home, but cannot return for some reason. It may be that the infrastructure (railway system) is beginning to collapse.

[89] Again it becomes evident how difficult life has become for these servicemen's wives who have no place of their own. Tina and several of her sisters, whose husbands are in the service, shunt back and forth between in-laws, Tina between Schoenfeld and Mariental.

have changed. Please send your letter to this address. If I'm gone they will forward it. I feel miserable without a letter from you.

I stopped writing here. Today is Saturday, there is nothing to do; it's cold and I haven't really spent much time outdoors during these six days. I'm pampering myself too much.

Many greetings and kisses from your ever-loving Tina.

From Nicolai
Evacuation Station
Medical Train No. 10/160
Moscow, January 13, 1916

My dearest Katja,

Forgive me for not answering your dear letter sooner, but because of circumstances beyond my control, I find myself in the situation where I could not respond sooner. Do not pay attention to rumors you may hear about me from other people. I will tell you everything myself.

The other day I went to the sauna with a few friends. The water was cold so I turned on some hot water and I slipped and fell onto something sharp and injured my forehead and nose. My friends got some first-aid supplies and I dressed my injury with bandages and whatever. Then I went to the doctor who stitched the wound on my head and wrapped it in bandages. I tried to get some rest, but the pain in my head would not stop. So some people here urged me to go to the hospital, where I have been since yesterday. Even though I feel fine now, I will have to stay here in hospital for six or seven days before I'll return to work. I'm sorry about my bad handwriting. My left eye is completely swollen shut and I can barely see out of my right eye. The room I am in is very small. Four of us share it. The nurse is an old friend of mine whom I know from the old hospital where I worked at one time.[90] But I am doing quite well now. I hope you get this letter in Mariental. I got your sixth letter on the 11th. Please don't worry about me. I have told you everything that has happened, and as I promised haven't kept any secrets from you.

Give everyone my love. Greetings from Nicolai

From Tina
Schoenfeld, January 19, 1916

My dear Nicolai,

We have just returned from an awful trip. The three girls and I left from here (Schoenfeld) January 18th in the evening to the Gaichur station and waited several hours for the train that naturally arrived late. From there we went as far as Nelgovka, where I had planned to get a driver to take us to Mariental. However, because of a severe blizzard I found no one, and it was below zero and the waiting room was not

---

[90] Possibly in the hospital in Ekaterinoslav where he had taken basic medical training and where most Mennonite medics were briefed before leaving for their assignments.

heated. Otherwise I would have waited there until the blizzard let up and I could get someone to take us to Mariental. I offered ten rubles to a Russian man, but neither he nor anyone else accepted the offer. However, that was probably good since I could have been stuck in the drifting snow with the children. So the only thing left for me to do was to return to Gaichur. The train was to arrive in at 6:00 P.M. but we didn't arrived until 10 p.m. The telephone station was closed, but they opened it for me. I called home and told them where I was. They were all asleep already, so I told them we would lie down in a second-class compartment in the parked carriage. At six o'clock someone came to fetch us. Now we have just had breakfast and are happy the ordeal is over.

The children were so chilled, they said they did not want to travel in winter again, only in summer. I have a cold and a headache. It was unfortunate that it happened this way, but what could I do? I was hoping to meet your brother Heinrich [in Mariental]. I wanted him to help pack the spare parts for the motors that were there and bring them back here, but that didn't happen, in spite of my good intentions. I thought I had organized my trip quite well. In Mariental they don't know about all of this. I should have written them long ago to send a wagon to pick us up, but the letter would take a month to arrive there and the trip was a quick decision. The cold weather is letting up some.

You probably sent me a letter to Mariental. Because of my traveling back and forth [from Mariental to Schoenfeld], I often receive your letters late. What is the condition with the wound on your head? Has it healed? Are you coming home on furlough soon? Perhaps you could still meet Heinrich. I believe his furlough ends February the 13th.

Now I will lie down and sleep till evening, I hope, because I have not slept well for two nights. Yesterday while I was gone, Hermann Enns sent money to have us pack his overcoat with things to be sent to you. For how much can you sell the butter I send you? People don't want to sell their butter under two rubles. I asked Mrs. Wiens if she had any butter to sell, I would give her whatever the price was. She said she had some and I asked if she could spare some, but she has not sent any yet.

Selma has been sleeping for a while. I will wait for you before I travel again. A good opportunity will come along I hope. Enough for today. I received a letter a few days ago from your mother. Your sister Tina is in Einlage again. Many greetings and kisses from your Tina.

From Tina
Schoenfeld, January 22, 1916

My dear, dear Nicolai,

Thank you so much for your very dear letter that got here yesterday. I sent you one the day before yesterday, the 5th as you were home on furlough. Traveling back and forth between Schoenfeld and Mariental, I was unable to write so often. My headaches have stopped, but I still have a runny nose and a blotchy face. I am so thankful that you did not injure yourself more severely when you fell. Recovery will take time. Will I find a scar when you come home? It doesn't really matter to me since I would love you just any way you are.

Sometimes have the feeling that I am not worthy in God's eyes. Then nothing seems to matter. I feel as though I really don't know how to train our children. When I am annoyed or upset, I am sometimes quite severe with them. Afterwards I always feel very sorry that they had to suffer because of me. I don't want to do that anymore. Also, when I am not busy, have little to do, I find little joy and tend to mope. So I have to work hard—better than merely sitting around. Papa is supposed to teach me better calculating skills so I can help him more with the accounts. I think I can do it.

You asked in your last letter how we have arranged our living quarters. Well, it's like this. Mika sleeps in the parlor; Susanna Reimer, Anna, Truda and little Margaret sleep in the guest apartment; Gerhard, Hans W., and a new student occupy the office; and I with my three girls and Greta with her two girls [Erna and Kurt] are in the children's rooms. Papa and Mama and Wolja [Waldemar] sleep in the back bedroom. The German girl with her child sleeps in the room next to the kitchen. We have no other servants at present.

Last week we celebrated Greta's birthday. On the 28th is Papa's birthday, and I suppose that will bring in many guests again, so we have a lot of preparation ahead of us. Even the war does not stop us from celebrating birthdays. You were home at one of these celebrations, but will probably not be here for these. It would be best if you were to come for Easter and we certainly want to go to Mariental then, too. We'll have more time this furlough, so what would you like to do? Whatever suits you the best we'll do. It is only two more months until then. I am so elated already about being with you. In March, everything will be stirring and in bloom. Truda doesn't want you to come then, because she won't be here and she would like to see you. Well, we will do what is best for you and me. Before I left for Ekaterinoslav, I sold a pair of trousers that I sewed and the sugar that you sent. The money will almost pay for your trip home.

I can hear the children playing in the living room while I am sitting here in my room writing. I just took a break from my writing to check on them and I really bruised my finger. It is blue and quite painful. Today after *faspa* [afternoon coffee break] I want to take this letter to Hermann Enns, but am not sending you anything else. Peter Neufeld is going to Moscow the 29th and I will send a package for you then. He mentioned it to me already.

For Papa's birthday, we want to slaughter the sheep, and I will make meatballs with gravy to send you so that you can share in the celebration. At Easter or whenever you come, inform Sinelnikov by telegraph, and I will come to the station with the children to get you. They want to do that so badly and you must allow them to do it, even if we have to wait from noon until evening. That long wait won't be bad for them at all since they know that you are coming. The children and I are well and I wish you the same. Selma has just found me and won't give me any rest. She insists on sitting on my lap and is making a mess on my letter. The weather is just right for sledding.

Has Heinrich written you that he might be getting a furlough at month's end? I am really sorry that I didn't see him when he was home last time. Maybe the war will end soon and then, if we are alive and well, we will all see each other again. Enough for this time. All the children have already come inside, so it is time to stop.

Many greetings and kisses from your loving Tina and children.

P.S. We are all looking forward with joy to see you soon.

[Nicolai must have been home on an extended furlough, perhaps recuperating from that head injury or the letters between January 22 and April 2 may have been lost.]

From Tina
Schoenfeld, April 6, 1916

My dear Nicolai,

I just finished wrapping the parcel I want to send you. Unfortunately the raisin cookies flattened out too much and are like little pancakes. As for butter I wanted to send you, well, there isn't any available. It's been a busy day, what with laundry, the twelve pans of cookies for the Easter holidays, and your parcel. Heinrich Loewen will probably be home for Easter. I expected a letter from you today, but unfortunately none arrived. I'm sure you are very busy and tired.

I have to tell you about my misfortune and also fortune at the same time. You left some money for me and I hid it—you know where. Gerhard came and asked me for a loan. I gave him as much as he requested and then wrapped the remaining 25 rubles in a piece of paper and hid them in Papa's desk, intending to put the money away in our secret place later. Well, as misfortune would have it, Papa decided to organize his desk that day and tossed out papers that included the money I'd put there. Well, the papers landed under his desk. Later when I went to get the money, it was gone and I just couldn't find it. All day long I felt so terrible and disappointed about the loss of the money. I even cried about it, not that I'm so greedy, but because I had lost something for which you had worked so hard. The day after Papa had organized his desk, our maid cleaned the room and tossed all the rubbish out of the window, not realizing what was among that stuff she had thrown out. When she washed the windows, the papers she had thrown out got a bit wet. Later that evening Reinhold walked by that part of the house and happened to see the papers lying under the window. The twenty-five rubles had fallen out of the wrapping and were now plainly visible, none the worse except for being a little wet. I'm glad that God hears prayer.

Last year you came home for Good Friday. That won't happen this year, but let's hope that you will soon be home for good. Have a blessed Easter, even without me. Just be as happy as you can be. If you have any needs, please let me know. I have no way of knowing unless you tell me. Let's not forget the most important thing—prayer, you for us over here and we for you over there. And pray that I will have strength and wisdom to train our children.

We are all well and we wish you the same with all our heart. Are you feeling better now? For now *Auf Wiedersehen* very, very soon! P.S. I'm sending you two little parcels of goodies.[91]

---

[91] Nicolai was no longer on the Red Cross Hospital Evacuation train, but had been assigned to a hospital in Moscow. In this letter of May 9, he informed Tina of his transfer from the hospital to Zemstvo Command Headquarters where he performed various secretarial tasks for the remainder of his service. He was also during much of this time taking accounting courses, hoping to develop advanced skills that he could later

From Nicolai

[Addressed from—Moscow, Hospital of High Society, Povar St. 13, Nikolai Abramovich Rempel]

Moscow, May 9, 1916

My dearest wife and children,

From the last lines of my last letter, you see that I am no longer working in the hospital, but am again at work in the headquarters. Wrote that letter before noon but had neither reviewed it nor prepared an envelope. I went to take a nap, not anticipating any changes. When I had slept about an hour, one of the medics woke me up, urging me to come to the telephone. The chief had been asked to come to the phone, but he was not there, so I was to respond. When I introduced myself, someone from the local office, where the medics are quartered, instructed me to pack my bag and go to Command Headquarters, the general had transferred me out of the hospital. Of course, it did not take me very long to leave the hospital and appear at the office where I had been requested. Here I was told that I would be working in Command Headquarters with Hermann Enns and Driediger. Well, you can imagine how happy I was about that and how my heart rejoiced. Felt as though I had been sprung from prison. Naturally the way you are treated here is quite different from the work atmosphere in the hospital, and this work, of course, is much easier.

Let me describe our daily schedule. In the morning we get up between seven and eight, drink our coffee; then we write letters and read something until nine-thirty. Between nine-thirty and nine-forty, we go off to work so that we're there ten o'clock. Then I answer the letters and the telegrams that arrived in the evening, at night and in the morning. And that takes care of the important work. Naturally one is able to find something to do in the remaining time. At eleven o'clock we are served tea and half a pastry per person. At one or one-thirty we're served lunch. The cuisine leaves something to be desired but is much better than in the hospital. At three o'clock we are again served tea. We work until six but are often excused at four-thirty or five. So you see, my dearest Tinchen, there is a huge difference between the hospital and the office work here at headquarters, and because of this improved atmosphere, one is in a better mood, and so I believe my health will improve quickly. I already feel significantly better after working here only three days. The day of course has not ended yet, so when we arrived at our quarters after work, we prepare coffee and a few eggs for supper and are satisfied and happy with that. The remainder of the evening is spent in various activities.

The ways of God are remarkable. It is unfathomable how he governs. It was incomprehensible why I was transferred and now everything is clear. I will stop for

---

apply in business. He stayed in Moscow until the collapse in October 1917. The approximately 7,000 Mennonite servicemen were performing some kind of alternate service not under the army's jurisdiction, but under some other governmental or private agencies. The main agencies were the All-Russian Zemstvo Union, the Red Cross, and the United Council of the Nobility. The costs of maintaining the Mennonite servicemen were to be borne by their home communities. The money for their support was funneled through the agencies under which they served. In addition, families of the servicemen sent foodstuffs as often as they could: to wit, Tina's parcels.

now because I want to go to my old work place to see if any letters have arrived for me. The men from Schoenfeld send their warmest greetings. These good fellows have done their utmost to get me to my new posting.

Kisses and greetings to you and the children. Your Nicolai

From Nicolai
Moscow, May 28, 1916

My dearest Tina and Children,

I thank you for your dear letter of the 22nd. If nothing has interrupted your plans, you should just be arriving in Mariental now and so I will send this letter there. Why don't you arrange our room in the comfortable way it was when we were living there? In case I get a furlough, we can settle right into it again. Actually, I don't expect to be furloughed 'til October, but one never knows. What Franz Wiens has been saying about me [Rumor about Nicolai's being ill] you should take with a grain of salt because my health has improved since he saw me. Working here in the chancery [headquarters] seems to agree with me. I have a healthy appetite and am in good spirits. However, I am terribly homesick for all of you. How I would love to see you, hug you all and kiss you. Often when I sit here, I imagine you, my dearest Tinchen, putting your soft arms around my neck and caressing me all the while and kissing me passionately on my lips. I have wrapped my arms around your waist, and without any shame I would look into your faithful eyes that in their purity are focused only on me. Eternal faithfulness and love can be seen clearly in your beautiful eyes. Happily and without worries, the little girls are playing near us as though they already understand the joy of their parents and are busily trying to make our joy even greater. In purist innocence, they often ask questions that we answer with great joy. What a great fantasy, but if only it were real! How wonderful it was when I was with you but now we are separated, that happiness destroyed for some time.

Didn't finish this letter yesterday and will try to finish it this first day of Pentecost. Had intended to finish this in the morning because I was alone here in charge of headquarters. I thought I would sit back and write in peace and comfort, that is, while the others are enjoying a holiday. However, I had just begun writing when I was disrupted because the members of the High Commission decided suddenly to hold a meeting here. One of the Commissioners, a nobleman, [a Prince], who arrived early and found the place empty, it being a holiday, stated emphatically "In wartime there are no holidays! Today we are working!" And he then asked me to tell the cook and the handyman that everything was to be run as usual. Tea was to be served, as well as lunch, so I went down immediately to see if anyone was there to prepare and serve the food, but I could find no one, yet by two o'clock everything was to be ready. Well, good advice is expensive. I then informed him by telephone what the situation was; however, the "gentlemen" [die *Herren*, i.e., members of the Commission] arrived in spite of it all and proceeded to conduct their meeting.

I am now sitting here up in the second story writing while down below the Commission is holding its meeting. Now and then they call on the telephone, requesting certain papers or files, and then I have to scurry about to locate them and carry the requested files down to them. However, at least for the moment the storm has subsided, but for how long this calm will last, I don't know. I would be very happy if things were to run quietly like now until eleven at night.

Hadn't quite finished the sentence above when I was called by the chairman of the Commission to bring a letter written by some doctor down to them. Well, with sweat pouring down my forehead, I scrambled about until I found the letter. Just imagine trying to find something in this office complex that who knows when it was written or where it was filed. After all, I've not been here very long and am only vaguely familiar with this whole setup, especially with the cubicles where the others work. Well, it worked out O.K., thank God, and if He does not withhold His help, things will also go well in the future.

For a while it seemed as if I'd be going without eating today, but they took pity on me, so at two o'clock I went to get some food; however, it simply was no match for the food we are accustomed to on holidays. It is now five o'clock and I have to sit here for another six hours. I imagine things are happier there on this holiday. You will not be sitting locked down as I am. But in spirit I am there visiting with you, doing some lawn bowling, walking with you over to the cemetery, then over to Isaacs' fish pond, and I hear your voice and the voices of the children.

But my reveries have been interrupted for two hours. But, thank God, everyone has flown the coop and I am here alone and an uncanny silence has enshrouded this place. However, suddenly everything springs to life again, although not in this building. Bells are ringing nearby, a group of children have gathered and are playing happily and yelling in the yard below. Even the crows have congregated here. Until now never noticed that this type of bird exists in this area.

If you write to Mama [Nicolai's mother], ask her if it would be possible for her to sell our furniture, unless, of course, you're planning to spend some time there in Mariental, then selling it would be foolish. In the meantime, our release from service has been postponed to the fall of 1917, so we should be coming home then. Meanwhile there will be things enough for you to do in Mariental. No scarcity of that. Who is taking care of the lambs in Schoenfeld or did you sell them? I actually bought them for the children as pets, but they probably didn't get to play with them much. It would not hurt, if the opportunity arises, to take Hilda to Dr. Wiebe. I regret that I did not take her to him when I was home in the winter. It wouldn't hurt to have him examine Alice, also. Selma looks as though she has no bodily flaws, but there may be some caprice behind that facade that will clear up when she comes to the age of reason. How wonderful to be with all of you again, but I hope that there will be no more misunderstandings between us.

With the most intimate greetings, Your Nicolai

P.S. Regards to Mother, Tina, Mika, Gerhardt, Sarah and also Old Man Matthies

From Tina

Mariental, May 30, 1916

My dear Nicolai,

I've been here in Mariental for three days, but you will probably know that already. As there's a moment of quiet, I must write you. Things are going quite well now. A number of people have showed up here in the last few days, some even without leave-of-absence. The trip here was not very good, however; we had to stand all the way to the first station [Probably from Gaichur to Pologi, about sixty to seventy miles]. The passengers who were sleeping paid no attention to us, no matter how much complaining I did. Our children were sleepy and begged to sit down somewhere, but that simply didn't happen. We finally arrived here after we paid someone four rubles to drive us here from the station. Abram [a nephew] and Tina Zehrt were also with me, so that, at least, was a help and I wasn't alone. We are all fine now, but how are you? Feeling better or still the same?

I was quite surprised to hear about a wedding here, something I would never have guessed. Tina Matthies is getting married to a Mr. Penner from Siberia—a widower with three children, the youngest is 2 years old. What a responsibility she is taking on! Penner been here only one week and the wedding will take place in fourteen days. Some people predict a double wedding, but we'll see what happens. We probably won't get to invite the couple to our place, but we'll see.

As Heinrich Vogt is going to Moscow this week, I'll send this letter with him to be sure that you'll get it. I will also send you some baking, if he agrees, to take it. If you get a furlough while I'm here, can you stop in at Schoenfeld on your way and bring your clothes along. My baggage was over-filled, so I could't take them. I hope that's all right with you.

Yesterday was a holy day, so we went to church in the morning. Agatha Matthies was baptized in our church today. We wanted to go for a walk in the forest after faspa but a heavy rain stopped those plans. In preparation for the wedding, the Matthieses have scrubbed their house and storehouse and decorated them beautifully. Old Ohm Matthies still says he doesn't want to put on a wedding. Well, I think it will be good for Tina to get married. Maybe it will bring a change in her. Ohm Matthies told Mama that his daughters had said to him, "Just like mother, she [Tina] will deceive him [Penner], too. They still can't forget that. Well, what else can I tell you about Marienthal?

I guess you know that Reinhold is coming back to us [in Schoenfeld] after Pentecost. He has leave until October. That's very good because Papa is having a hard time, especially delivering spare parts. The evening I left, your brother Johannes came home for one month. He was lucky again. Well, I do not begrudge him that. The time will come, too, when you will be home with your loved ones, who miss you very much. The children often ask about you. There are rumors that the forestry workers will be released to go home, but I won't believe it until it actually happens. It would be great if Julius [in the Forestry service] could come home. Well enough for this time. Many greetings and kisses from your ever-loving Tina and children. My ink is running out—will buy more when I get to Gnadenfeld. Do you have to pay extra postage for my letters? I don't for yours.

From Tina
Marienthal, June 5, 1916

My dear Nicolai,

I just prepared a basket of cookies for you that I'll take to Vogt since he is leaving for Moscow tomorrow. He will gladly take the things for you and deliver them personally. I am also sending two washcloths, a towel and the Bible. Send the basket back if there's an opportunity or bring it yourself when you come to Schoenfeld. As for buying the overcoat, I have second thoughts and I will wait until fall when they may be cheaper. I am now wearing Greta's fall jacket and will manage with it as I won't be going to Moscow to visit you. You ask about money. I will send fifty rubles for you with Vogt. When I left Schoenfeld, I gave Greta twenty-five rubles. She wanted to buy cloth for a suit for Julius that he requested it. So don't buy any cloth for her; she can get it cheaper here.

We didn't go to church today and have just finished lunch—*Schnetje* [pastry] and milk. The children are playing outside on the swing that Abram built for them before he left. He had to walk the eight verst because no ride was available,. He asked Johann Neufeld to take him, but he had no time. Thursday a Russian man was struck by lightning in Elizabethal, killed instantly, and two farmhouses burned to the ground. How terrible to be killed by lightening. Our final hour can come without warning, so we should always be ready.

It would be wonderful to chat with you in person. Whenever I hear a wagon arriving, I wonder if it could be you. Only disappointments so far, but one day my imagination will prove real. The children never forget to pray that you will come home soon. All three of them are healthy, as am I, but I may be pregnant, although I can't feel any movement. I menstruated last on March 13th, but after that, nothing. I have not felt any changes yet, and am not any bigger. I am convinced that nothing has happened but I may be wrong. The main thing is that I am healthy.

Mother worked in the garden yesterday so she couldn't sleep because her feet were very sore. She wanted to go to bed very early, but then Ohm Matthies comes and he always stays long. I was already sleeping when he finally left. It seems to me that the two of them like each other very much. But don't mention in your letter what I have written about staying up late. This week we got a letter that was included in yours and I don't know what it means, so I am sending it back to you. People don't need spare parts right now, and it would be good if I could sell what we have. The money I am sending to you could be used for your trip in case you come home. The garden is beautiful, the roses are blooming, the vegetables and everything look magnificent! But all things do perish and we with them, longing for relief.

Many greetings and kisses from your Tina and children.

You ask about shoes. Alice needs 23 cm., which is the measurement from the toe to the heel on the outside. Hilda's measurement is 21 cm.

From Tina

Mariental, June 16, 1916

My dear Nicolai,

Fortunately the wedding is over. It was nothing special. At first we had decided that no one would go to the wedding, but then we had second thoughts. Tina and I had attended the *Pultaowent* [a gift-giving party the night before the wedding], but that was nothing special either. We never did see Ohm Matthies or the Esaus there, but, of course, we all went home early. We had expected mother to attend the wedding the next day but she refused to go. Furthermore, the visitors had to fend for themselves pretty much. Only Ohm Matthies paid any attention to us at the wedding, but Esau had that sour puss face. The wedding lasted until dusk.

Today we really wanted to go to Gnadenfeld where there was another wedding, but we could not get a carriage, although we tried at six places. Perhaps it was for the best because the weather is unpleasant, and it has just started to rain heavily. I wanted to have a nap with the children, too, but the chickens in the barn [it adjoins the residence] are so noisy that I couldn't sleep and am sitting here writing instead. The mail hasn't come yet. I will send this letter with Ohm Matthies since he is taking his newly married couple to the station. They are leaving for Siberia.

Concerning the money, I have already sent it. I had taken eighty rubles along from Schoenfeld and that was good because Mama (Nicolai's Mother) hadn't yet received any money from Mantler. It was rumored that he may no longer be in Nelgovka. He has been dismissed from the flourmill, and now Siemens and some Jew have taken over. Ohm Matthies is going there today so I asked him to see if Mantler is still there and ask him for the money and to bring it back with him. If I had been able to get a ride, I would have gone myself.

Yesterday the men from Mariental were requested to bring their horses and wagons to Chernigovka[92] but only one team was taken for service. At Steinbach[93] and Kleefeld some horses and wagons were destroyed by fire. Some Austrians had carried straw on wagons to the field and thrown it on some embers, and immediately everything burst into flames. They jumped from the wagon, but the poor horses died in the flames, neighing terribly. Next week farmers want to begin harvesting, although there is much blight in the grain. The people are concerned about the high cost of labor and the poor quality of grain. Many have hired Austrians [prisoners?] at twelve rubles per month, but then they also had to clothe them. The Russian full-time workers charge 200 to 300 rubles per year. Ohm Heide did not buy the threshing machine. He found a different one.

The mail has just arrived but I received no letter. I did got one on Monday, the 13th. Thanks. Concerning the shoes, I will wait until fall to buy them. The girls can manage till then. You ask me in your last letter how I occupy my time. Well, none of us are overworked. Yesterday Mika, Gerhard, Sara and I brought in four loads of hay from the pasture and another two from the back field. In between I was sewing shirts for Heinrich and when I have finished those, I want to sew some for you, too. From lunch to *faspa* everyone takes a nap. We are all very lazy. I believe Mama received a letter from you Monday.

It is enough for now. Many greetings and kisses from your loving wife. I dearly love you though you may be in doubt of that.

---

[92] As already mentioned, sometimes farm draft horses and even the farmers themselves were conscripted to serve as transport at the front. This deprived the farmers of service animals they needed for farming and by 1916 was creating shortages as things were siphoned off to the war effort.

[93] Steinbach was a large Mennonite estate that still exists but is now a home for seriously handicapped adults. Selma recalls that they would go there on church picnics several times a year.

From Nicolai
Moscow, June 18, 1916

My most intimately loved Tinchen!

Just arrived back here at my quarters and found your dear letter of the 12th of the month. Thank you so much for it. I had to wait far too long to get this letter. Just imagine not receiving a message from you for ten days. Now isn't that too long? The one you sent with Vogt took only two days, but this one wandered about for seven days. That makes the difference even though they were written only six days apart. You, my poor dear Tinchen, still hope that I will soon be home. I am really sorry but that won't happen. I do not know where in my last letter you got the idea that I might be coming home soon. Perhaps you drew that conclusion from my suggestion that you tidy our room and arrange it in such a manner that we could be quite comfortable in it for the time when I really do come home. No one would be as happy as me if I were released from service, but as I wrote you in my second-to-the-last letter, there is no prospect of my coming home before October. Good or bad, we'll have to come to terms with whatever happens.

If my health continues to improve, I will soon be fully restored soon. Well, it is better, I believe, to regain my health completely and even I have to forgo coming home for a while. It will soon be two years that we have been living apart.[94] That will eventually change, but until then we have to be patient! "God neither sleeps nor slumbers." He knows what we need.

Well, the whole gang has returned here and my writing will have to stop. There is so much nonsensical chatter that you cannot really collect your thoughts. I got a letter recently from Papa that he wrote from Ekaterinoslav on his trip from Kharkov. He did not seem to be very pleased and made several accusations, among them that I, after ending my forestry service, had not stayed in Schoenfeld. I answered the letter immediately and reminded him that I had not moved to Mariental [To help his mother and to set up his and Tina's farm] without his consent and urged him not to become discouraged as he still had some young energetic children who know quite well that it is their sacred duty to honor their parents.

It seems to me that you have the yen again to go back to Schoenfeld. My feeling is that you should stay in Mariental. As there was not much work for you in Schoenfeld, the family will be able to get along without you. Just stay in Mariental a while longer even though the children prefer to wander about and don't always stay around the house. Those little urchins should be free to move about, and you shouldn't be so strict and confine them so much. If nothing can be done to keep them at home, just let them run off steam. No spankings, even if Mother thinks it should be done. Punishment upon punishment is useless and the children are merely embittered by that. I feel so sorry for the poor little things that I'm almost reduced to tears. In your last letter you say nothing about your health. How is your health, same as before? Is everything OK? And how did the wedding turn out? Did you attend? When the bride went to other homes to invite them and did not stop by your place, you did the right thing not to go. I feel sorry for old Ohm Matthies, because he will feel miserable that you were not invited. It is his daughter's doing.

---

[94] He is referring to the time of his induction in September 1914.

About the 300 rubles, you write that they're not in yet, but say nothing whether Ohm Knals is dependent on Mantler or if Mantler is still in Nelgovka or where he is, you say nothing. I wrote Mantler that he should send the money to Mother right away, but have no answer yet. When you return to Schoenfeld, please take my old shoes along and give them to Kornelius Fast so he can bring them to me and I'll have our cobbler repair them. Well, nothing is going to come of my writing. These people are sitting so close to me that it is quite impossible to write.

I send you many heartfelt greetings and kisses. Your Nicolai

From Nicolai's Nephew Abram
Zalinovnoe, June 22, 1916

Dear Uncle,

I received your most welcome letter. Please excuse me for waiting so long to answer.

You want to know what my daily expenses are:

First of all a note book - 15 kopeks; a knife – 55k.; a brush - 15 k.; envelopes – 33 k.; writing paper - 24 k.; a comb - 35 k.; shoe polish - 24 k.; body lotion - 45 k.

For Sunday, candy - 30 k.; 2 bottles of perfume - 35 k.; pen (pencil) - 20 k.; an eraser - 35 k.; a mirror - 30 k.; a pair of shoelaces for my shoes - 20 k.; buttons - 20 k.

The ten rubles you gave me paid for all of the above. Another time, I'll write you what I buy from my own salary. I'm so glad that I took all of those clothes from home otherwise I would not have had enough to get by. I have to get new soles for my old shoes; that costs five rubles each time. Nobody would do it for less. A new pair would cost at least twenty-five rubles. Boots cost only fifteen to eighteen rubles, but for now I will make do with my old shoes. Now I know what it means to be a shop boy (Ladenbursche) I must close. Your loving nephew, Abram Neufeld

P.S. I was home for Easter and Pentecost. It gets more difficult for me to say goodbye each time. Wishing you the best of health!

From Tina
Mariental, June 22, 1916

My dear Nicolai,

This is my fifth letter here from Mariental. Strange that you didn't get the first one. I wrote on the first day of Pentecost and sent it along with Loepp on the second day. I got your letter on the 20th, thank you so very much. My sister Susie also sent me a postcard, asking me to bring a certain book for her when I return. Please let me know by July 1 whether you are coming or not. If possible I want to be in Schoenfeld for your birthday. That's three weeks away. You thought it would be six months before you got a furlough and four months are past already.

We are looking after Toews' garden—drying apples and also canning some, so if you are not going to be here in winter, I can send you some produce, although as preserves. On the 24th there is a funeral for the Marten's 6-year-old boy who died of tetanus. He died after a two-day illness. I'm sure the whole village will go to the

Sketch by Doris Rempel

funeral. I'm surprised and pleased how Sara [Nicolai's niece] has changed. She never complains as she used to and nothing is too much for her. She is far ahead of Mika [her sister] in that respect. Because it's very hot today, it will be a good beginning for the farmers to harvest their barley. Before we know it, summer will be gone. Fortunately, I always keep busy. I sewed seven shirts for Alizchen[95] and seven for Heinrich, and now I am sewing four white shirts for you. I hope you will like them. I am trying the best I can, but my sewing machine sometimes doesn't sew smoothly. Tina [Nicolai's sister][96] and I are sewing four shirts and two pairs of trousers for Abram, too. When I go home Tina will probably come along to do more sewing and help to clean up everything. The streets are very dusty and we need rain badly.

Yes, we went to the wedding but no one noticed us. The Esaus didn't even shake hands with us, as though we were invisible. Well, we also pretended that we didn't see them. We went along to the singing[97] after the wedding and Liese was there, too, but she also treated us like strangers. Tina always says, "Well, they don't have a brain so what can you expect?" She was quite upset the other day and said, "The boys have caused this trouble with their love affairs, and now I have to bear the consequences."[98] Well, that's how it is, but we aren't really angry with them. You say that I will think you are asking for too many things, but that is not the case; I don't mind at all, as long as I have something to send to you.

But enough for this time. Many greetings and kisses from you ever-loving Tina and children.

P.S. Aron wrote that you are not feeling very well [Aron was also serving as a medic but in a different train].

I had already sealed this letter when I received your letter via the Mayor's office. I have just written to tell you that I am going back to Schoenfeld at the beginning of July. I was disappointed when I read your letter. If you don't want me to go, I'll have to stay here. However, there is enough work for me at Schoenfeld if I want to work. You tell me that I should let the children go wandering about the neighborhood but mother tells me that I shouldn't let them go gallivanting around;

---

[95] Alizchen: little Alice. In German the suffix—*chen* at the end of a noun signals a diminutive, as does—*lein*, as in *Männlein*, little man, the diminutive for Mann.

[96] Tina, Nicolai's wife, and his sister Tina were both trained seamstresses. Nicolai's wife, in addition to many other tasks, sewed much of the clothing for her family, and to earn a little extra, she sewed for others as well.

[97] Note custom of singing on all occasions. It was customary for the youth in villages to meet in the evenings at the end of the village boulevard to sing and flirt, but under constraints of Mennonite customs.

[98] It may have been that the Rempel brothers in their youth had treated the Matthies' daughters with less than respect.

yet somehow they seem always to get away and go anyway, and then I have to spank them. I don't know why, but at Schoenfeld they stay at home, but here they always want to go visiting. I guess they are lonely here at grandmother's.

Again, I'm sorry that you don't want me to go to Schoenfeld, but if that's how you feel, I guess I'll have to stay here. When I left Schoenfeld, Papa asked how long I would stay away. Papa wrote you that he is very busy, and he really is. It is too bad that I was so set on doing all that sewing here before Pentecost. I should rather have helped him with delivering the spare parts for the machinery; now he is left to do it all alone.

I had better stop writing as I am just not in the mood. That's what happens when something upsets our plans. We still don't have the money from Matthies, that is, the 300 rubles, so I'll wait 'til you to come home in October to settle it.

From Tina
Schoenfeld, July 18, 1916

My dear Nicolai,

Tomorrow it will be one week since I returned, and it is the third time that they have gone to Kharkov. Twice Gerhard went to get some parts, and now Papa and Gerhard are going there to see Weinberg, who insists they be there tomorrow. I am really curious how the matter will all turn out. Weinberg told Papa to change the payment or he would go to prison. I would feel very sorry if Papa would go to prison. If only this situation could be resolved.

The Schroeders will stay here 'til the first of August. Mama was very ill but has improved and I am not well either. Miss Harder was here to examine me and gave me some medicine. I must have overdone it while stacking straw; I don't know what else it could be. I am trying to look after myself but I've some lost weight. Miss Harder said I should stop some of my activities. I cut Selma's hair yesterday and now she looks like a boy. Well, you always wanted one. I have a room in the new addition. It is much more comfortable and no longer a thoroughfare. When you come, it will be more suitable. Willy wrote us that he was engaged on July 19th and asked us to inform the preacher. He is set in his wedding plans, insisting they get married soon and have a small wedding. Our parents are not in favor of all he is planning at this time [He is a medic also].

Instead of sleeping, Selma is tumbling around in her bed. She is trying on the wooden shoes Frieda brought her. Do you know that my brother Gerhard has been freed from induction for a whole year? He seemed to have changed, not getting as angry as he used to. Sister Mika just passed by to the veranda where she can read undisturbed. Susa is very busy taking instruction from Schroeder in three subjects. She will be going to Ekaterinoslav soon for ten days and then has to be in Berdiansk by August 16th when school begins.[99] She has had no summer vacation. She is always studying. Anna Willms, the teacher, is back. She gets thirty-five rubles a month; that's quite reasonable. Selma has finally fallen asleep and the other two are

---

[99] Susan Peters, Tina's sister, began to teach in 1920 after completing teachers' training in Berdiansk. Several of Susan's nieces were her pupils. She continued her teaching career in Canada.

playing outside in the sunshine. They can tolerate a lot of heat. I wonder what you are doing at this moment, also napping or don't you get an afternoon break in the office? Are you getting any salary? When you come home, you can tell me about Sinelnikovo. I will come to the station with the children to get you, that is if you come during the day. I can hardly wait, I am so happy. Bring back the basket I sent you with the baking. Do you ever meet Toews or Dueck? Do you still have coffee or do you buy it ready ground? That may be cheaper. You must not be getting all of my letters since you often do not answer my questions.

Many greetings and kisses, thinking about you and loving you forever, your Tina and children.

From Nicolai
Moscow, July 21, 1916

My dearest Tina,

Received your letter of the 15th. Thanks much. It is, however, something like a letter from Job. First of all, you write that mother is very ill and that you're not quite well either. I wrote you day before yesterday that you should go to the doctor and I still hold that opinion if you're not feeling well.

I was interrupted at this point yesterday. It is now six o'clock and the others have gone home, so I am here alone in the office, thinking of you. Driediger just stopped by, in spite of the rain, and brought me your dear letter of the 18th and a couple of boiled eggs so that I might not starve, yet I have no desire to eat eggs or to eat at all for that matter.

Your letter that fills me with the greatest joy but at the same time seems to be quite sad. I can't get rid of the idea that you are ill and that this is an illness that women can't usually get rid of easily, or even at all. That's how I understand it from your letter. I would blame you bitterly if you had not taken care of yourself, but I can do nothing about that now. I warned you and pled with you to take care of yourself. It is possible that you will carry the mistake for a lifetime. Now please get a carriage to take you to the doctor in Gulyai Pole and don't wait until I come home. *Fräulein* Harder has not studied medicine yet, and so she isn't be competent to prescribe medication nor to make a diagnosis. But do what she has suggested, but be most careful. Avoid lifting the children into bed, they can do their own lifting. Then write me in detail the symptoms of your illness: how you feel, where the pain is, etc., etc. Does *Fräulein* Harder think you are pregnant? Tell me exactly what she said. If it is not possible to get good medical care there, I will bring you to Moscow; perhaps they may be able to do something here. You will surely be able to be away from the children for a month. I regret that I still don't know when I'll be coming home—beginning or end of August. Will do my best to be there by the 10th. When something like this happens, I sometimes feel quite out of sorts. Then I curse everything that has separated the two of us. Yet these are God's ways and His ways are not our ways. Who knows, this may all accrue to our welfare.

Now to your questions—Because some of your questions go unanswered, you believe I haven't received some of your letters. Well, you know it's possible that some letters are lost, both from me and from you, but that should not keep us from writing. Will make a greater effort to write more often and you do it also if your illness won't hinder you. But my dearest, be careful, I beg you. I am quite well again, except for occasional headaches.

Driediger and I drink a bottle of milk each day. It costs seventeen kopeks and so far I can manage with my board money and even save some. My salary is still seventy-five rubles per month. The Prince asked our general to increase our allotment to six puds per month and the general concurred; however, he wrote back to the Prince that the Commission must first approve it. So now the Prince is waiting for the general to come here to discuss it with him before presenting the matter to the Commission. So the thing is still far afield. It is fortunate that we are fed the noon meal here at headquarters, and so we get by; otherwise we wouldn't manage. Now we drink coffee with cream and eat fresh white bread. We have to go and buy the cream and the bread every day, but since that job is alternated, it falls on each of us only every eighth day. As for the coffee, well we also have to purchase it; freshly roasted and ground is 1.60 rubles, and for three pounds of coffee, add one pound of chicory, making it even more tasty and cheaper. The white bread costs twelve kopeks per pound and we use about half per man per day.

I never meet the two teachers, Dyck and Toews, presumably because they never come to Moscow. And here in Moscow it is not very pleasant because of the rain and the cool weather, so our summer uniforms are almost too light. You ask if we take afternoon naps. Well, we haven't given any thought to that because we begin work when you are about to start your noon meal, but, as I wrote you, we are free around four o'clock. However, it does happen that we are not released until seven o'clock.

If I do come home, I will telephone from Sinelnikovo for a carriage; that is, if one is still available there. I would be overjoyed if you and the children would come along to the station to fetch me when I arrive. If I miss the Rostov train in Sinelnikovo, I will go to Ekaterinoslav to the Schroeders, who in the meantime must be home again.

Will stop for now and talk with Papa a bit, i.e., by letter. Yes, who told you that I had written a very nice letter home? I wrote them just what my heart dictated.

Please accept heartfelt greetings and kisses, Your Nicolai

From Kornelius
Moscow, August 16, 1916

Dear friend, Nicolai Abramovich!

Many thanks for your letter of August 12 that I received the day before yesterday and also the one from August 8. Many thanks, too, for the grapes that I also received yesterday; they are delicious. I ate some of them and will share the rest with others as you suggested. I brought a basket to the chief this morning. He was all smiles and called out to me even before I saw him, "It is Rempel, right!" I had actually prepared him for this gift the day before. Yes, those grapes are very tasty, and if you bring some more, no doubt you would get rid of them all. Unfortunately we had no keys for the hampers and so had to break them open. I gave the chief thirty-five pounds, and tomorrow I will give Orlov his part, but probably not half of them as you suggested, because Shimonovski asked for some too, and it would not be good to leave him out, especially since our chief is going on holidays to the Caucasus the first of September, and it is rumored that he won't be back. That's why I will give Shimonovski about fifteen pounds and divide the rest among the office clerks and us medics. Time will tell if you will agree with this division, but I think you have no other choice. By the time you return, it will be too late.

Nothing has changed here. We go to work every day and you will not have forgotten how things run there. Our bosses usually play cards until the wee morning hours and then they wake up sleepy and irritable. In our detachment, everything is going as usual if one doesn't count the episode with Toews for whom Dr. Pozdnyakov signed a three-week release because of his "illness." Generally speaking, it is boring here; the evenings are getting longer and there is nothing to do, so one is in danger of going berserk.

We ordered English correspondence lessons again, so at least we'll have something to do. I am looking for something else to do in the winter, but so far I haven't come up with anything. I have learned about some courses in law and have already sent for the program. If it appeals to me, I'll probably try legal studies. Of course it would be wiser to try something that would bring in some money instead of always spending money. But I'm not smart enough for that. Our daily wage has been raised to one ruble, so now our monthly earning is thirty rubles. Of course we gobble that up. Well, I must stop writing. I hope you have received the telegram informing you that your furlough time has been increased by one week. If you haven't heard, I am notifying you herewith. Heartfelt loving greetings from afar, dear friend, to your dear wife, parents and siblings, also.

Your Kornelius

P.S. I am enclosing a note from Mr. Orlov with an urgent request. My colleagues—Fast, Penner and Driediger—send greetings and please give my greetings to all from Schoenfeld [in Moscow], especially David Petrovich.

[Nicolai was on furlough for a month.]

From Tina

Schoenfeld, August 26, 1916

My dear, dear Nicolai,

Well, I must start writing again, but I would much rather have you here so that I could hug and kiss you. How quickly that month of your furlough passed! Two and a half days have passed since you left, and so it's a little closer to your next furlough. I will count the days again. Reality hasn't quite hit me yet. When I go into the empty bedroom, I nearly fall apart because you are not here. I've shed many tears. Why does God allow a couple to be separated like this? May we soon have peace for which everyone is yearning. Yesterday I put away your clothes, shoes and your coat, but I haven't found your galoshes, yet.

Now you will be in your living quarters again with your fellow sufferers. You will do better than I tonight because you have many friends there, a diversion makes the time pass quickly. The children are in their beds chatting away, but I can't sleep. Mika often comes to spend the night here. How do you like the photos? I like the ones with only the top half best, but the others will do. You are really so handsome. I just can't see enough of your photo.

What about the grapes, were they still good or were they beginning to rot? I repaired a winter jacket for father today, and next week I want to do some other mending. Don't worry about me. I take good care of myself and the others help me. After you left, my period also disappeared. Very strange—it lasted the seven days that you were here and then it stopped. I sent Enns's trunk along to Wiesenfeld yesterday. I'm jealous that Mrs. Fast was able to travel with you. It would have been such fun to travel with you. I heard from Mary Dueck that Lenchen is coming to Mariental for the winter with her children, and Mrs. Willms is going to live with Nickels in Tokmak, and Tante Minna is coming to Duecks with all her belongings. Sara [Johannes's wife] will really be moping again in her loneliness as a grass widow. I must go and see her. Gerhard is coming back from Berdiansk tomorrow.

Hilda is praying that you should come home soon. A thousand greetings and kisses from your loving Tina and children who love you dearly and will never forget you. How great our joy would be if we could be together at Christmas. Good night!

From Nicolai
Moscow September 14, 1916

My dearest Tina,

I just answered your letter of the eighth of this month, but my letter was written so badly that I tore it to shreds. You know that my letters are usually not written very carefully, but now and then I do manage to scrawl really badly. I could, of course, write slowly and beautifully, yet if you sit and wait for dismissal from duty, as I am doing at the moment, one can't truly write in peace; first one doesn't know how the authorities will regard writing letters instead of working, even though there is no work at the moment, and the others are merely fooling around. And secondly, writing becomes quite difficult when so much idle twaddle is filling the air. You are familiar with the atmosphere that exists here; it's more like a saloon than a chancery. In recent days, I have not at all been well disposed to writing letters; I really don't know what that's about.

My accounting course will probably have to share some of the blame. I notice that I am sometimes just as edgy as I was at home when I was trying to keep the books [in his father-in-law's business], trying to do it right. Now, however, accounting is giving me some measure of joy because I'm competent at it or perhaps it's merely my curiosity that is the appeal. There is, of course, so much to learn here in the Chancery that I can hardly keep up with it, especially because there's so much written work. I've become quite discouraged at times with the pile of work lying on my desk. However, if I don't get it all done, my head won't go to the chopping block.

I wrote this far in the chancery, but we were suddenly dismissed at four o'clock quite unexpectedly. Most of the fellows went to watch the airplanes flying about the sky, but I stayed on to finish my writing, and it seems as though I've done nothing but write all day. Now it is ten o'clock and all of the men have gone to bed, but I want to chat with you for a few minutes more. Quite a few of the men of our commando have their wives with them here today. I should think that they will be having a much better time than you and I are now. They sit together, talk to each other, love each other or more accurately said, love each other up. We do, of course, love each other even though we are not together, but we can't caress today and probably not for a long time. When do we have Easter? Is it very late this year? If it is late, I'll come home when I've finished my course work and won't wait until Easter. I will probably finish by the end of February or beginning of March. You can expect me at the end of March 1917, if we are alive and well.

Enough of this nonsense, let's talk about something more sensible. I am now, however, poorly attuned to writing a sensible letter, although I would love to write a letter that will make you ecstatic, comfort you, encourage you to stay strong in everything until I come home. I am incredibly happy that I am being carried on prayerful hands, even by my children. Let's remain true disciples of Jesus—a light for Him. So many wicked things are going on here, and one can easily become inured to them. For example, those conversations that would formerly have offended me I can now listen to quite coolly and even laugh at them. We have reason to be on guard. In closing I who am thinking of you constantly, say goodnight and kiss you warmly,

Your Nicolai

From Tina
Schoenfeld, September 15, 1916

My dear, dear Nicolai,

I received your dear letter yesterday. Heartfelt thanks to you. I am inordinately happy when a letter arrives from you. I won't criticize you for the infrequent writing because I know how busy you are with your office assignments and your studies. Studying accounting diligently will help you and benefit us in the future. I am happy that you can learn something while you're in the service. God will see you through.

We have just eaten lunch and I took Selma here to our sleeping quarters. I'll use the time she's asleep to write. The sun is shining quietly through the window and you can't hear a sound from the sofa where she is sleeping. Mika and I always go here right after supper because it is quieter than in the rest of the house. We have made these quarters more comfortable since you were here and I wonder why I hadn't made these arrangements sooner? Probably because I was not feeling well then. The laundry is done but we still want to iron it today. I did not help with the laundry this time because I was in the store all the time and there were enough hands in the laundry anyway.

Gerhard and Hans have been going back and forth to the station for two days transporting salt. A wagonload has been distributed and five hundred puds were sold to customers who took it directly from the station. The rest we brought here with our horses. We have just four blocks left and want to keep two of them. I wanted to go to Hermann Enns's place, but his whole family was together, so I postponed it until this Sunday. Yesterday I drove to Abram Driediger with Alice about her sore leg. When I heard that Mr. Friesen was there, I went to see him right away to have him examine her. He said it was a type of herpes. I have to apply an ointment twice a day and give her some medicine four times a day. The area had become quite large and swollen in five days. If I apply the ointment and give her the medication regularly, it should soon heal. She has little pain. The Abram Driedigers had a little girl on Tuesday. He came from the station at night and a few hours later he was holding his little girl in his arms. He sends warm greetings. He did not know that you were working together with Enns.

It is getting late and the letter should go to the station today. As Papa is going to Apostolovo about the purchase of brown sugar, he can drop it off. But first I want to ask if you will possibly be going to the wedding [in Mariental]? If you don't go, I plan to stay here and Greta will go. She should go since she always has to sit here at home. Instead I would like to go to Truda's for one week, perhaps later in October. Well, it will sort itself out who will go. Why doesn't that boy, Willie, write exactly when they are planning the wedding? I'll write him today as the others refuse to do it. I owe him an answer to his letter anyway. You ask if I want to come to Moscow. Yes, of course I would like to come very much. But I want to come only if you think I should and when it suits you. I will probably wait until May.

Warkentin has paid me ten rubles for the cloth I gave him. He has always said to Papa that Julius still owes him ten rubles from the time when Julius was conscripted. I gave Greta the money and she paid him. Now he won't continue to press for it. Some of the foreign laborers are still here and will probably stay for the winter. One of them was at Driediger's but only stayed one week, then returned home.

Don't worry, I am taking care of myself, have no pain, sleep well at night and have no disturbing dreams. I know what a good husband I have and that he is untouched by the evil in the world. I have never had any fear that you would fall into temptation. I ask God constantly that He protect you and me from such a sin.

This is enough for now. I will write more another time. Many greetings and a thousand kisses from your ever-loving Tina.

From his nephew Abram Neufeld
Brasilovski, September 19, 1916

Dear Uncle Nicolai,

So much time has passed since you left us. I have been lazy for such a long time, but now I will try to keep my promise and finish a letter to you. I remember very well what you said to me at the doorstep of your house in Krasnopol. Do you think you might come home for Christmas? We hope you are in good health. The government has started to collect all the cattle from the farmers. They will be slaughtered and the meat will be sent to the front. During this night all the cattle are in our yard.

The passport was already sent to me. Gerhard Duerksen and I are sitting here and writing letters. We are living together in one house because Duerksen was sent to Krasnopol. We will live here till winter. The trousers that you gave me look good on me. The jacket is not so good because the sleeves are too long, but the seamstress promised to fix it up. I haven't taken the suit yet. I wear the shoes that you gave me as casual wear, i.e., every day, but I wear the boots only for celebrations. They are my favorite present from you. I calculated how much all that cost; it's a very good present. The shoemaker put spurs on my boots, which cost eight rubles. I hope I can wear them for another year. I don't know what else to tell you.

Your nephew, Abram Abramovich Neufeld.

From Tina
Schoenfeld, September 20, 1916

My dear Nicolai,

Today I finally had the good fortunate to meet Enns. The first Sunday he was home, his whole family was together. The following Sunday I went to the Ennses with Greta, Sara and Tina Zehrt, but we did not find him home. So we wanted to return home right away but the Duecks, the old couple, would not allow it, insisting we stay on, and so it went. But today Enns helped slaughter pigs at Wienses and afterwards he dropped by our store for a while. He believes he will be notified that his furlough will be extended longer. He was at Wiesenfeld when he was notified that he could stay home until the 5th of October. I trust the time will come soon when you and I can live together again as it should be. Evenings I sit and dream of having a place of our own, sitting comfortably after a day's work by the warm hearth with our children and chatting , resting comfortably together. I miss the time so much when you were sitting here talking about your experiences.

What about your health, quite good? The children are healthy and me, too. They just love to snuggle in the niche by the oven where it is warm and comfortable.[100] I have not menstruated since the morning of September 18th and then I started again but not as heavy as last time when you were home. If it should last as long again as last time, I will probably go to Dr. Dueck. We have not been very busy but after *Pokrov* [Day of Intercession] that will change. We have seamstresses sitting here sewing wedding dresses. Willie still has not sent us any further news about the wedding. I would go but Papa says he can't rely on Gerhardt, so I will have to stay home, and in that case, you should not go either. But do as you please; I allow you to do whatever you want. I would rather save the money and go to visit you in Moscow. I imagine Mrs. Fast is allowing herself a good time, right? I feel jealous of the women who can go to be with their husbands. I often help in the store, but they really need someone to do the custodial work. We got a letter from Truda. She says they have taken in four boarders. They have one cow, four piglets and fifteen ducks, so soon they will have an regular farm. She wants us to come for a visit, but I don't have the time. We will be getting a maid right after *Pokrov*, then, of course, we won't have the honor of doing everything ourselves.

The children are sleeping already and I will follow their example soon. Papa and Mama went to Wienses for spareribs. Maybe we will slaughter a pig before

---

[100] Russian oven—a unique heating system usually in a central location of the house. It had benches on its sides, favorite warm places in winter where the children (and adults) loved to sit or lie down to rest. Straw or even cow patties could by used as fuel in the Russian ovens.

Enns leaves and then I'll send you some spareribs. I believe you'd love them. I'll go to Enns's on Sunday again. Maybe I can find them at home this time.

This is enough for this time. Greetings and a thousand kisses, from your Tina and children who love you.

From Tina
Schoenfeld September 23, 1916

My dear Nicolai!

Since there is no one in the store right now, I must take this opportunity to chat a little with you—something I really love to do. I just finished dusting the tables. I sent Hans to the barn to do the chores on time. If Papa didn't check the barn, I think the horses would be dead by now, and that's just how it is in the store, too. Gerhard shows little interest in anything other than dressing up and stepping out with girls. Yesterday and today he took the four o'clock train to Ekaterinoslav where he will have his fling again!

The two aunties, Tante Susanna and Tante Tina,[101] are supposed to be transferred to Gar Constantin [the telephone central], but they are thinking of declining because it is too far away from grandmother. Tante Tina got a telephone telling her to come to Alexandrovsk, but she doesn't know why. Perhaps they want her to work there. It would be unfortunate if she lost her place here. Maybe Papa will be going to Alexandrovsk with her tomorrow. Well, we have to accept things as they are.

Now I'm being interrupted because a number of customers are coming. If a Russian comes, we usually know what he wants—tobacco that's sure. They come for tobacco from far and wide. We now sell the regular tobacco, two packs and two packs of paper for fifteen kopeks. We have been selling petroleum oil[102] at five kopeks per pound. Some places are already charging twenty to thirty kopeks. We ordered some from Ostrovka, but the container came back empty. They had a lot but wouldn't sell us any.

Well, I have locked up the store and eaten supper. Selma is asleep but Hilda is still with me. The girls always want to go visiting. They will turn out to be real gallivanters. Franz Wiens came home today. He has completed his service and is totally free. Who will be happier than Mrs. Wiens! Well, I wish her much happiness from the bottom of my heart. When your service is over, I will be beside myself.

I know you are very busy with your studies and I thank you so much for your letter that I got the day before yesterday. I'm always grateful even when your handwriting isn't so good. I'm sorry that I seem to have written one letter so poorly that you couldn't read it and tore it up right away. Thank you very much for the brush and the detergent that Kornelius Fast's brother-in-law brought. It's too bad that we have four horses in the barn and can't even drive over to the Fasts. I would

---
[101] These aunts, Tante Susanna Toews and Tante Tina (nee Toews) Dyck, were telephone operators even later in the USSR. Their great nephew, Herman, with the Canadian military, located them in a refugee camp in northern Germany in 1945. Their escape from the USSR in 1944 as refugees was written by Susanna. (Note Epilogue).

[102] It was probably kerosene.

so much like to hear all about you, and Papa would like to know if you have done something about the laundry detergent because people ask for it every day.

I wish you the best success in your studies. I'm not at all surprised that you have difficulty studying when there's so much noise in your living quarters—almost impossible to concentrate. All of us are well? My period lasted only three days this time and I'm glad I didn't have to see the doctor.

Many greetings and kisses from your ever-loving Tina and children.

From Nicolai
Moscow, October 1, 1916

My Dearest Tina,

I just sat down, my little treasure, to chat a little with you as all is quiet around me and I can write undisturbed. First, I have to clarify the misunderstanding that seems to have slipped into my last letter. You say you're sorry that your last letter was supposedly written so badly that I had torn it to shreds. Actually the situation was quite the reverse. Either you misread or I miswrote. I intended to say that my letter had been written so poorly that I tore it up.

Your letter of September 23 arrived on the 29th (five days) and my heartfelt thanks that you wrote the last two letters so soon and did not wait until you got a response from me. Now that I'm writing fewer letters, I am receiving fewer as well. Of course, I receive the most from you and those from Mariental but none at all from the others. Sister Tina is quite despondent, mother is ill, people gossip all kinds of things; they probably receive few letters, so she is quite depressed. So I am not at all surprised that they at times become frantic. Please take a bit of time and give them a report of what you are doing. They would be overjoyed.

You will probably be having some difficult times now because you've lost some help and the weather won't be very pleasant either, especially for the children, who do not like staying indoors. Here the rain doesn't let up either, but in spite of the nasty weather it is not too much for the people to stay on the street throughout the night, many bringing chairs and staying all night so that they can get a few pounds of meat the next day. And the same thing is beginning to be true for bread also.[103] The city administration has announced that within two or three weeks white flour will become available again, but in the meanwhile the citizens will have to be satisfied with the coarse rye bread [Schwarzbrot]. But in your area the good cuisine will just now be starting with harvest. If it is possible, could you buy a few pounds of sausage and send it to me through the mail? Sausages don't spoil so easily and here the cost is unbelievable, and even then the quality is very poor.

---

[103] This is an important comment on the impact the War is having on food supplies in terms of production, distribution and prices, especially as winter approaches. The winter of 1916 was severe and these shortages, especially supplies to key urban areas now containing enlarged factories producing war supplies, was a major cause of discontent that would fuel the revolution of February/March 1917. This was especially true of the factories around Petrograd where the revolution was to begin. In the rural Mennonite settlements food was more abundant, although the need for sugar and sweets for Christmas (p. 154) is amusing: The Mennonite sweet tooth. But with their highly mechanized agriculture, Mennonites were facing difficulties. Spare parts for machinery, including binding twine, were in short supply while many horses and wagons had gone to military service. There are hints of this in the letters elsewhere as well. (Urry)

Driediger and I rarely eat an evening meal. We drink coffee at six but we're always hungry before retiring. In order to save a bit of the money that we get for board, we don't eat. I am fine as long as I concentrate on my studies and don't think of the fact that I am a soldier. I have put a table in the guestroom so I can sit here quite undisturbed and quite content, even when I am thinking of you because I know that I am doing something my family. In the beginning I tried to study at command headquarters, but that was useless because of the noise, so I asked our chief if I could use the guestroom, to which he consented without hesitation.

Am very much looking forward to your visit in May, yet I hope to come home before that. In closing I send my most intimate greeting and kisses,

Your Nicolai

From Tina
Schoenfeld, October 7, 1916

My dear Nicolai,

I received a letter from you today—many thanks. Although my hands are still hurting a little, I'll answer your letter so it can be mailed in the morning. Anna and I have our busy week almost behind us. In two days Greta and Mika will take over responsibility for the kitchen. There is much so much work without a servant that I have not helped in the store at all this week. So Greta had to fill in and so then they don't always have to ask me where things are. Anna and I feel more tired in the morning than when go to bed. In one week our girl returns and then I'll get a real rest. To do that, I will go to Truda's. Of course, I'd much prefer to come to you to rest, but I will postpone that until it is more suitable and we can discuss things face-to-face, right? With good fortune you may come home for Christmas?

I received a letter from Willie who says that if he marries before Christmas, they will come here for Christmas. He hopes you will all be home then. That would be such a happy occasion. Papa arrived this morning from the Schroeders. I went to Thiessens to see about buying some dried fruit, but of course I did not get any because they were all in mourning. Greta Thiessen's fiancé died in Bandoraia a few days after an appendectomy. That is so sad, but it is even sadder when a wife loses her husband and children lose their father.

Tonight I visited Hans [Nicolai's brother] and Sara. That fellow is home again for thirteen days. It seems to be the right timing as Sara is so lonely without the girls. I received a visit from the neighbor next door, the dentist who is boarding here again. The man thinks he's freezing to death in his room, but it is really a quite warm room. Twice I heated the place with straw. You've been heating already since the end of summer, right? If you men don't have your wives with you, you freeze, right? If I can buy some sausage I'll send you a pud right away. How do my cookies taste? They were nothing special, but the next time I will send you some nice zwieback.

Papa is thinking of going to see you, so I must send something with him. The children are still playing outside during the day, but when we have to keep them inside there's much more work. Did Herman Enns arrive back safely? Were the ribs and the liver sausage still good or did you have to throw them out? It is quite late but my neighbor is still sitting by the stove. He will catch up on his sleep in the morning. I have to get up early with the children to feed them so I can have two breakfasts.

On Sunday I'll write to Mariental or they will lose hope. If it didn't cost so much, I'd hire someone to drive me there to see them.

Many greetings and a thousand kisses, your Tina and children, who love you.

From Nicolai
Moscow, October 23, 1916

My most dearly beloved Tina and children,

I would love to hear even a small whisper from you, a sign that you are alive and well. The time from one letter to the next is unbearably long, even though it's merely a few days or at most a week between them. I have unfortunately little to report from here, but I do all the more long to hear from you. Because writing materials are becoming scarce here, I am tempted to keep a journal and then send you a copy of it. Then at least you will know how I feel, what I'm doing and so forth. But doing that is merely the imagined stage, far from becoming a reality.

According to what we read in today's paper, a number of the soldiers [*Ratnieky*] of a certain age will be mobilized as of the 25th of October, among them also Frank Rempel, Henry Wiens, Peter Driediger and others and the heartbreak will be great [These are older men in Schoenfeld]. I've heard that Wiens bought a mill and will likely remain free from service until after Christmas. Well, he's had a lot of good luck. Ohm Peter (Driediger) will probably also be passed over because of his poor eyesight. Greet these gentlemen heartily from me and tell them not to lose courage. If we are alive and well, we'll all be home in three years [Tongue in cheek?]. Actually, I secretly believe we could be home for New Year's 1918, but that's also debatable. However, we want to thank God that we can perform our [non-combatant medics] duty quietly without having to experience the fate that most soldiers have to face. That this privilege will continue for us is merely a matter of time. That there are many different points of view concerning this issue is clear, differences also held among the top brass [*höheren Kreisen*]. According to our rights, this privilege cannot be taken from us because it has been promised us with the strongest of assurance (*alles hoehst verspochen ist*).

I'd begun to write this letter in headquarters, but stopped when we were dismissed from work. I've already told you that when we have early dismissal, we don't hesitate one moment. Recently there was an interesting event with train No. 10, again because of a medic. As I told you, the Old Man had been restrained [by his superiors] from always putting medics on report (*runterschreibt*) for any minor infraction. But now he had begun again to really go after the ones he didn't like, and so one of the medics (whom he had been harassing) complained to the general about the Old Man's harassments. However, the general had forgotten about the matter, and that's where it remained until one day when the chairman of the High Commission visited the train. It so happened that this medic was under room arrest (*Stubenarrest*) just when the chairman made the rounds to inspect the train (naturally, in the company of the Old Man.) When he came to the medic's room, he, the medic, complained about the arrest to the chairman in his presence of the Old Man. Well, of course, the Old Man could do nothing at that moment. When, however, the chairman was gone, he gave the medic such a terrible dressing down, yelling at him, "I'm going to hand you over to the military court to have you court martialed." (*Kriegegericht übergeben*). Since the poor medic was now even in deeper waters, the general was reminded by someone that a medic from train No. 10 had registered a complaint with him, where upon the general sent a written order to the Old Man that he was, without a moment's delay, to release Karpov, the medic, from house arrest and transfer him to another train.

The Old Man, as obdurate as always, remained true to that disposition this time, too. He did not transfer him to another train, but took him along on a tour his train that same day. Now the commission notified him in writing that he was supposed to release that medic from his train forthwith. But instead the Old Man wrote that it was quite impossible to release him. Now the commission has written him again, ordering him to send the medic to Moscow immediately. I'm curious whether he will do it, and I'll let you know how it turns out. But enough of this for now.

When we came back to our quarters today, we prepared some very tasty fried chicken, the one you had sent with Papa. We had eaten one half with him when he was here and the rest we saved for today. It tasted wonderful. We have also finished off all the sausages and ham that you sent, so now we have to fend for ourselves and find food. It may be quite a while before Driediger comes back here, so you will have ample time to prepare the things we requested. Today I received a letter from Heinrich in which he informed me that he was feeling somewhat better—was, however, still quite weak. I feel terribly sorry for that young man, but one can do nothing about it except pray, which we have done and God has answered our prayer. Ask others to prayer for him, too.

I feel very well, but I am terribly homesick. If at all possible, I want to come home for Christmas, but there is no prospect for that yet. It is likely that Hermann Enns will go home for Christmas because something else is going on there [wife pregnant].

I send you a thousand kisses, Nicolai.

From Tina

Mariental, October 26, 1916

My Dear Nicolai,

I want to leave from here, so I have to write to you right away. Everything is much the same here except someone has knocked down the fence. It is hard to find out who did it, but if you had been home I believe you would have found the culprit. Mama wants to know if she should report it or if we should let it go. Well, I suggest you write her and advise her. Jacob Bartsch was here and he wondered if it wouldn't be better to have our horses put down [shot]. The stud is completely worn out and you'd get only ten rubles for the pair. It is probably better to retire them. I am going to the station today with Bartsch as he offered me a ride.

I was also in Gnadenfeld for a day with Susa, who had been home for two days. This time we went to Gnadenfeld via the Waldheim station even though the ticket was slightly more expensive—two rubles and ten kopeks. I came back from Gnadenfeld on the Schmidt's carriage. The two boys are still as they always were. Sara [Johannes's wife] is also here—wants to stay until April.

When I return to Schoenfeld, I want to prepare another parcel for you and send it to Wiebe in Moscow. Then you will probably get it. I wanted to send it with Enns, but when I was at Enns's last, he worried how he would load all of the baggage. I think you can lift more than he can. I should really send it with Enns. The others will receive theirs parcels from home, but there will be nothing for you. They do not accept any mail in Gaichur for delivery anymore, so I will send a one-pud package by freight.

I wanted to write with ink, but it was left in Baden, so I am using the teacher's ink to write the address. There is really not much to write about as Mama and Tina will have described everything to you. I don't know what happened in Schoenfeld while I was gone the four days, but I will write as soon as I arrive there. The children will be very homesick for me, especially Selma. Alice asked me to bring her some halva, but here at Abram's store there is nothing. It is nice and sunny outside. Abram and the two girls [his sisters, Sara and Anna] have to rake the leaves together. Well, everything is the same here—it is so boring. If only I could travel with you. Hilda keeps asking,[104] "When will the war stop and when will Papa come home? When he comes, we will go back to Mariental." Have you received the pictures I sent? How do you like them?

Enough said for this time. I must write you that Tina, Sara and I stopped in at Matthies. When we came in, Tina Matthies was there in the house, but she stayed only a few minutes and then went out and did not come in again. Just as ridiculous as always.

Many greetings and kisses from your Tina.

From Tina
Schoenfeld, October 30, 1916

My dear Nicolai,

Uncle Peter [Toews] is going to take this letter along. He did not get the exemption he had hoped for. If he should get an assignment where you are, perhaps you can use your influence to make sure he gets an easier position, but it's not likely that you'll have a chance do that. His work order states that he is to perform lighter duties. I surely hope he gets a good position. Two other people from here have also been drafted—Abram Janzen from Hirkoj, and Gerhard Wiens, who lived at the Franz Wienses. They together with Enns and Rempel will be leaving too after the New Year. Then all that's left are the old men. I just heard that Gerhard Fast is home. I don't suppose he brought a letter for me. I will telephone and find out. He arrived yesterday. In the evening three ladies went to the station with their hired man. While he was helping to take the girls' baggage into the train, someone stole

---

[104] It appears that Nicolai was home on furlough for a few days.

the horse and wagon and they haven't caught the thief yet. There is a lot of this kind of thing going on here. Last week they stole six horses from the Janzen farm at Hirkoj. Janzen is very sick. While butchering a pig last week, a sharp bone splinter cut his hand and now it is badly swollen. He is not supposed to use his hand at all and it doesn't look good.

This week I gave the living room a thorough cleaning, installed the storm windows and caulked all the cracks. I spent two days getting ready for hog butchering. On Friday we butchered the four that we had bought from Aron Rempel: two for us and two for Schroeder. Schroeder helped us a lot. He left today and Gerhard went with him for two days. I have to do a big laundry tomorrow. I wouldn't mind at all if I could rather go visiting than doing the laundry. Brother Willi will probably get married on November 13. Papa, Mama, Greta and Anna are going to the wedding. Maybe in November it will be my turn to go somewhere. If all goes well, Hertha and Frieda, Willi and Greta will come home for Christmas. I'm glad they are coming, but my greatest joy would be if you were coming home, my darling. We will probably hire a maid for one month during Christmas, but until then we will have to do without. We do have Susanna Reimer working for us and so things go quite well without a hired girl;[105] then mother doesn't scold so much. Well, we don't pay much attention to her scolding any more.

Father bought two hams and seventy pounds of sausage. If there is something else we should buy for you, please let me know right away. I just inquired at the Fast's if he had a letter for me, but had forgotten that he came from Tiflis and not from Moscow, so he won't have a letter for me. Thank you very much for the letter you sent a few days ago. Today it's dull, quite foggy and even muddy. Everyone was at Grandma's until now, but I hear the children coming in with much joyous cacophony. All of us are well, even my sciatica has disappeared. If at all possible, do come home for Christmas so we can all be together again.

Many greetings and kisses from your loving Tina and children. Grandma sends greetings to everyone.

From Nicolai
Moscow,
October 31, 1916

My dearly beloved Tinchen,

In this terrible hour I reach for the quill to make one more attempt to win my wife back to myself. Have not quite lost the hope that there are still persons somewhere out there who still love me, although according to all indications such hope is quite futile. Have made every effort to contact you, but all these attempts by letter and also by telegraph have been disregarded. All of this has brought me into a terrible rage and then again down to the deepest sorrow. How terrible it is to be forgotten by people, to be homeless and to have no one to whom you can pour

---

[105] It seems that Tina makes a distinction here between Mennonite help [Susanna Reimer] and a Russian domestic servant. Furthermore, Tina's mother probably doesn't want to create a scene in front of the Mennonite woman.

out your heart. And as more is heaped onto this sorrow, I am beginning to feel like Job. But how can I compare myself to Job of whom God himself said that his equal none could be found in all of Israel.

On the 3rd, I received a letter from sister Tina who said that mother lay ill in bed and since then I have heard nothing; don't know if she is alive or not. Today I received a letter from Heinrich's friend, Peter Matthies, saying that Heinrich is very ill and there was little hope that he will survive. Yesterday I received a telegram that the train on which brother Aron was serving had been derailed, that is, it collided with another train and the carriage that served as office had rolled over, injuring the medic in it. I am assuming that that medic was Aron. On top of these distressing messages—the deathly silence from you—and all of this is just too much for me! I am convinced that you have written, and if you haven't, it must be because of illness. But if you haven't been ill and yet have not written in fourteen days, well, then we might as well stop corresponding all together. Then I will know once and for all not to expect a letter and will accept that calmly.

But please do understand me—you, the very life spring of my heart—and if you have without reason remained silent so long, well then! Please write more often because you don't know how difficult it is to be without message or letter from you. And help me and the other siblings to pray that God will make Heinrich well and create for us all a joyful reunion soon. Until then accept the most heartfelt greetings from your Nicolai.

From Nicolai
Moscow, November 3, 1916

My Dearest Tina,

It was only yesterday when I wrote you, but as N. Driediger is going home today, please be so kind as to send with him the things you bought for me. And please tell Papa that a gauge box was still available. But I have not been able to buy the faucet yet because there were none in the store and the factory lies so far out of the city that I haven't been able to go there yet, although I've made an effort to go.

Otherwise everything is as always. I've heard nothing about Heinrich; have no idea how things are with him. I have to stop now to attend a hearing. Most heartfelt greetings, Your Nicolai

From Tina
Schoenfeld, November 15, 1916

My dear Nicolai,

I thought I would have some peace and quiet for a change, but that won't happen. It's Hilda's birthday today and she demonstrated how naughty she can be. All three are in bed now but not asleep, just chattering nonstop. If I would walk out of the bedroom, they would create a big scene. Warkentins brought your coat today. I had to cancel a visit to the Cornies because their children have diphtheria. Driediger told me that he is waiting for a telegram approving an extension of his furlough. His brother, Abram, is home too, and Jakob Dyck is coming home tonight because of his sick children. Your brother Johannes came home today for a seven-day leave. He wants to butcher his pigs. He's lucky again.

The folks went to a wedding but aren't back yet—must be having a good time. Well, I wish Papa were home now to discipline the children a little. They simply won't listen to Gerhard. I worked in the basement until noon today, culling out rotten apples to make sure we will have some good ones for Christmas and also for you. I do so hope you will be home for Christmas. If I weren't so sure that you were coming, I would go along with Driediger to visit you. What you would say if I suddenly surprised you with a visit? I received your postcard yesterday and will mail the money tomorrow. I would have sent it with Driediger, but he is not leaving yet.

What news do you have about your brother Heinrich? Is he better or worse? I will ask Jakob Driediger if he has any information about him and I've written to Mariental twice already, hoping to hear from them but our postal service is so very slow. Maybe you would be so kind as to write to Mr. Matthies and ask him to send the sleigh. I should ask him myself but I think it's better if you do it, right? I'm writing to you twice a week now hoping that you'll get one of the letters. I even enclosed stamps last time. You don't seem to be getting any of my letters no matter how often I write. The children are well and so am I except for the continued trouble with my face from getting so stiff and chapped. I can't seem to get the face cream that usually prevents this condition. Neither wind nor weather seem to affect my hands, only my face is so sensitive. Maybe you can find some ointment over there.

Selma is standing beside me watching me write. If I could just get away for a few minutes, I could finish this letter. She just told me that when she finishes sleeping, her Papa will be home. She often asks for you. None of the children are sleeping yet. Selma is warming her pillow by the stove because she likes to be cozy. That precocious little thing is something else! Now at last she is lying down and sucking her thumb. Well, I hope you don't mind me telling you all these things. If I want to send you the two hams plus one-and-a-half puds of sausage, I will have to pack them and send from the station or maybe you'll get this letter and can tell me what to do. If I had sugar, I'd bake a batch of cookies for you, but I'll bake some zwieback and send them to you instead. A thousand greetings and kisses from your ever-loving Tina and children.

From Nicolai
Moscow, November, 19, 1916

My dearest Tina and children,

The clock is at 11:30. Yours there will be 1:30 already. Just got back from my class and want to answer your letter of the 15th that I received today of our headquarters. Am grateful that you are writing twice a week, although I am still not getting them all. Of the last six that you wrote, I have received only two. So do not be surprised that I may seem to be a bit nervous. Believe me, my dearest Tina, I really struggle with anxiety and at such times I am not the master of myself. Every time I get a letter from you I am happy and cheerful and stirred to great energy.

In the office recently we are almost worked into the ground in an attempt to make up in a few days what has been neglected in the last two and a half years, and this has to do mostly with my work here. Yesterday the executive secretary came into the chancery to check how the place was being run and so the prince got a good dressing down. This was brought on mainly because a number of papers had disappeared that I have given the prince but that had not been returned to me. Of course in such cases my journal cannot determine exactly where these can be found. Well, I suppose this storm will pass and then there will be another crisis. Last night Enns, Koop and I had to work till 10:30 or eleven o'clock with the Prince. Fortunately he doesn't like to work in the evenings either.

So today I was not prepared for my evening class and so will have to do double the work for next time. And that's the way things are going here. Life is quite monotonous. Today together with your letter I received one from Mother. Among other things she writes that Loewen, the painter, died quite suddenly. His son had also been inducted so now Mrs. Loewen and Nehta [her daughter] are alone.

You keep writing that I am coming home for Christmas so that I almost believe it myself. Just get rid of the notion. I am not coming home for Christmas and you're not coming here until I write you. You would not like it here now because I don't even have one hour of free time. So we'll postpone our getting together until Easter, my dearest Tina? Do as you see fit with the hams and sausage. My advice will arrive too late anyway. I have heard nothing from Heinrich since the 5th.

In closing, I greet you and kiss you most affectionately. Your Nicolai

From Tina
Schoenfeld, November 25, 1916

My dear Nicolai,

In one month from today it will be Christmas, and how wonderful it would be if you were home then. But unfortunately, it won't happen, as you wrote in your last letter. But we don't know; suddenly events can turn favorable. Driediger is arriving in Moscow tonight, but he has no letter from me, and that just makes me want to cry.

We have already put the sweets out in the store. But candy is so expensive this year; the cheapest is one ruble eighty kopeks and the most expensive, three rubles twenty-five kopeks. We have only white and brown cookies and they cost close to one ruble. But people buy them regardless of the price. And butter is one ruble and eighty kopeks. We've had frost and snow already so the children are happy to stay inside. I went to visit Sara for a while before dark today. She is sewing slippers for people. Papa has ordered slippers for each of us so we won't make so much noise when we walk across the floor. When I came back from Sara, the folks had already eaten supper, so with the help of our maid, I quickly mixed some dough for bread. She also heated water so that father could soak his feet because he has a cough. After that I made myself comfortable with a cup of coffee and ate my supper in peace and quiet. All the children are sleeping now. When their Grandfather is here, they are more obedient, and yet do quite enjoy themselves, too.

It is so much more convenient now that we have a maid again. When I have to go away, I know things will get done. I have just finished unpacking some candies and cookies and as everything is quiet and peaceful now, I can write again. We have pretty much finished our Christmas sewing. Yesterday the maid, Mika, and I cleaned the floor in the store. It looks so much better now, but the boys will soon mess it up again with their dirty boots.

Let me know right away if I should buy sausage and ham at the current price. How did you like the last sausage I sent? When I bought them from Matthies, I didn't weigh them again, and now while packing them I noticed it was short some nine cp., and the ham, too, had a quarter missing. Father says it is his fault, as he shouldn't have taken Matthies's word for it but weighed it again himself. So we will add the missing amount from our own stock. Heinrich Wiens is busy grinding whole wheat flour. Today he went to the station to pick up his own scale. Mrs. Cornies was in our store today, bought nothing; she thought everything was too expensive.

Fortunately, my wardrobe was not ready or I may have surprised you with a visit at this time, but from your letter I see that you are very busy anyway. You must be totally exhausted scarcely being able to cope. We still don't have Uncle Peter's address, but as soon as I get it I'll send it. Well, I really have nothing else to write about, but I don't want to send you a blank page. Our envelopes are so poor that one can see through them and maybe that's why our letters go missing. What other reasons could there be? Choir practice will begin again on Sunday. The Rempel girls aren't going, so our dear Gerhard doesn't want to go either. Their parents [separated] have made peace again, but I heard that the preachers want to expel the girls from church. Well, I'm not going to worry about that; furthermore, it's none of my business. They have not harmed me.

Enough for this time. Many greetings and kisses from your loving wife Tina and children. You are always in our thoughts.

From Nicolai
Moscow, November 27, 1916

My Dear Tina,

Unfortunately you will get this letter one day too late because what Driediger told me you had said came as quite a surprise, namely, that you were quite unhappy with me that I haven't written more often. In recent times I have written weekly. If you don't receive the letters, I can't do anything about that. My accounting studies do not keep me from writing, as you seem to suggest. Of course, when I write you a letter, I have to rob the night of a bit of its time, but even then I get plenty of rest. I assure you that I am well and will not over exert myself. But I am sorry, my dearest, that not all of my letters reach you, and that those that do reach their goal don't seem to delight you very much. Will make a special effort not to be so nervous when I write letters.

In part it may be that I too am becoming more hard-hearted. We are now fortunately rid of the chief of staff, the old prince, from our headquarters, but the one who has replaced him is even more heartless, so to avoid being driven into some useless corner I, too, must become more hard-hearted. There is a huge pile of work here in this office. Don't know if I can keep up with it. Otherwise things are going pretty well again. And we have enough to eat again so that we are really lacking nothing. My deepest gratitude for all that you have sent me. The cases arrived here in good condition. Whether I will ask to send more, I don't know yet, but will give it some thought.

What do you think, Tina, should I send something for the children for Christmas? If you were living alone, I would certainly send some gifts; now, however, it doesn't seem quite right that our children should receive gifts but Greta's children wouldn't get any. The others have all purchased something for their children, but I haven't, although I love my children quite as much as they do. Please write me what I should do. If I could afford it, I would send gifts for Greta's children as well as ours, but now I don't know.

Most affectionate greetings and kisses to you and the children, your Nicolai

From his niece Mika Neufeld
Mariental, November 28, 1916

Dear Uncle Nicolai,

We received your dear letter in which you scolded us for not writing to you sometime. I know it was not good of me not to write. It is so quiet and lonely here, but Aunt Tina is coming soon and then things will be more lively. She is lots of fun. Brother Gerhard comes home often, but he is not coming before Christmas. Even if he wants to come, it's impossible because it is terribly cold here now. He always has to walk. Abram wrote lately too that he is often lonely and can't wait for Christmas when he'll come home. Well, it will soon be here and I hope things will liven up a lot then. We are waiting for Uncle Heinrich every day because his friend Reghier wrote that he is coming home. It would be so nice if he were here for Christmas. He would love that.

It's easier to do chores when it's not so cold. But Grandma says we should always be happy when we are doing our work. It must be extremely cold in Moscow, right? There is a lot of talk about peace here but that's all wishful thinking. You probably know that Mr. Loewen died. He didn't feel very well, was undressing to go to bed, fell down and died right there. Such a sudden death scares me very much. Otherwise nothing new is happening here. We have no teacher here now. The last one left a long time ago. She had room and board at Huebert's. We probably won't get another teacher.

I must stop writing. It is late and we have to feed our livestock. Have a very good night! If I stay up 'til twelve o'clock I will be very sleepy.

Hearty greetings from your niece, Mika [Neufeld]

From Nicolai
Moscow, December 4, 1916

My most dearly loved wife and children,

How quickly time passes. In only three weeks Christmas celebration is on us again. It is the third Christmas we are celebrating during this wartime. But the question is where and how are we going to celebrate it? I asked my superior today for a furlough for several days. He seemed to agree that there would be a prospect for this, so perhaps I'll come home for two to three days to be with you this Christmas. What a great joy that would be!

Please don't speak to anybody about this, but buy a few good hams right away, approximately one pud of sausage, also ten bottles of wine (port). I will take those things back with me when I come, and should I not come, well, one way or another we'll get these things transported here, and I can get rid of them very easily. But again, keep all of this under wraps so that we won't be laughed at if nothing comes of this. But let me know immediately if you can get the things I am requesting.

As for the accounting course, it will take a rest for fourteen days during the Christmas holidays, so that won't keep me from coming home. The course seems to be getting more demanding every day, so I will really have to buckle down to get it all done. The suggestion you sent with N. Brugyles that I abandon this whole accounting project, I can unfortunately not do at this time. I will in spite of its demands always answer your letters. Once I have all of this behind me, you will love me all the more once again—even though you might be somewhat unhappy now. Once I am with you, we won't even recall what is happening now but will be most happy that we will be with each other once more. I always have that feeling that we will be home permanently before Whitsun. Until recently I had a different view, but now I believe we will soon have peace.

I will be finished with my accounting business in March, giving me some time to scout around for a position. Of course, to be discharged and then to go home permanently would be most important. What great jubilation and joy that will be when we will be free like human beings to be home with wife and children. If I do come home for Christmas, what should I bring for the children? Or have you already ordered everything from Santa Claus? Recently I sent you Heinrich's letters. Did you receive them? It's been rather cold here the last few days, so we don't spend unnecessary time outside. But for you and the children a white Christmas will make it merrier.

A thousand kisses, your Nicolai

From Tina
Schoenfeld, December 4, 1916

My dear Nicolai,

I received Heinrich's letters that you sent a few days ago. Thank you so much. How sad if neither of you can come home for Christmas. If you come, we should go to Mariental because we hear nothing from them. Your Mother may still be ill, but Mika and Sara could surely be writing you. I'm sending my third letter to them but am still waiting for a response for the others. But maybe they haven't received any of my letters.

Jakob Enns, home for two months from Tiflis, was here yesterday and brought greetings from Heinrich, who is still in very poor health. We have had no news from Uncle Peter and Grandmother is greatly troubled about that. Lorenz sent us a letter with some photographs. He is working in the food department where he has to buy hams, butter and eggs. He is quite happy in his job. Our weather is gloomy, the sky is overcast, and the roads are icy so that one has to be careful when walking. Because the roads are so bad, we won't be going to Willie's wedding.

We are so busy in the store that there is hardly time to eat. The ration cards for sugar create a lot of extra work. It's rationed, as you know, so sometimes ten people are waiting in line to be served. Our Christmas wares are pretty well sold out, but in a few days, more will arrive from Kharkov and many people are waiting for those arrivals. My first task each morning is to clean up the store and prepare for customers.

Today is Sunday. We have just finished our *faspa* coffee, the children are romping in their room boisterously, and I am now hiding in the parlor so that I can write in peace and quiet, but it won't last long. After I cleaned up everything last night, I sat down to do a bit of reading, but they didn't give me five minutes peace, constantly milling around me wanting this and that. At times I think I'll lose my mind, but then things calm down again. Father has the flu and I feel it in my limbs, too, but we really have nothing to complain about when I think of your brother Heinrich who was so sick, all by himself without mother or brother near him. What we suffer is nothing compared to what others are going through. This is the sixth year that I am waiting for you to come home for good to be with your family.[106] Greta received a letter from Julius in which he writes that a mad dog bit him. The head forester[107] told him it was absolutely necessary that he go to Kharkov or Kiev to tend to this matter because it could have serious consequences.

It is getting dark and in one hour we have to go to choir practice. Our young people don't like to have choir practice on Sunday, but we need to practice for the Christmas Eve service. There are so many people in the choir that it seems there won't be room for them all in the school on Christmas Eve, besides all of the parents and our children. Who will decorate our Christmas tree this year? You won't be here, but maybe Willie can do it if he comes a few days before Christmas. Of course, I'd much rather have you do it, so please write us if you are coming or not. If not, I want to send you a Christmas parcel. How did you like the zwieback I sent? People often asked if my Old Man is coming home. When I tell them you aren't coming, they say, "Oh, sure he will come, just wait and see." But now I'm off to choir practice and will finish my letter later.

Well, I'm back. All of the young people came here to our house after practice and played quiet music and a game called "telephone" in the parlor. We had a good time. All refugees are to assemble in the municipal [*volost*] hall tomorrow—all males from 16 to 60 will be ordered to dig trenches.

Tomorrow I'll soak the clothes and do the laundry the following day. I dread it and would be happy to do something else. What else can I tell you? The children are asleep except for Hilda, who is talking to herself in bed. If you get a letter from Mariental, write me what they are doing there. I'm curious to know how things are in general, if the Matthies are still there, and if our cow calved yet.

---

[106] Nicolai did his alternate serve in forestry late 1910 through 1912. He was again called to serve at the onset of WWI (See Introduction).

[107] Johannes, Nicolai's oldest brother, was doing his service in forestry at this time.

Well enough for this time. Most affectionate greetings and kisses from your loving Tina and children who think of you always.

From Tina
Schoenfeld, December 8, 1916

My dear Nicolai,

Only Mika and I are at home and right now I'm alone in the store. All the others went to Aunt Tina's birthday party. The quiet is a treat. Gerhard is off to Kharkov again to see about more Christmas wares. Today the maid washed the floor in the store and I put a large sign in the window reminding people to take off their galoshes when they come in, but they pay little attention to it.

I received your dear letter today, requesting the wine, the ham and the sausage. Papa had already ordered a ham and sausage, but it was meant for Schroeder; however, because you wrote requesting some, he'll put it aside for you. If Gerhard or Mama goes to Berdiansk they will bring the wine. And about gifts for the children, I don't know what to say. It would be very nice if they received presents, but maybe it is just as well to wait with buying gifts for them. I haven't bought anything, but I did sew some pretty dolls for them and fixed up the little doll beds with pillows and blankets. They'll get some other little gifts and then they will be satisfied. We already bought a Christmas tree, so it's beginning to look quite festive. Hans Willms and Wolja just came from the station. Hans has to go there often so at least that's something he's good for. Greta received a card from Julius today. He is now in hospital in Kiev. He has to have twenty injections because of the bite by a rabid dog. He is not allowed to drink any coffee or liquor for a whole year or he could become rabid. It's terrible to think that something like that can happen so quickly.

We were terribly busy in the store today—we got some more cookies and all kinds of other goodies. We took in 300 rubles within three hours. They brought us one pud of sausage and it's quite good. We are not selling many dry goods now, however. I got several letters from you this week —thank you so very much. I also got the one from Heinrich you sent. I had sent him a letter a few days ago addressed to Tiflis. About Uncle Peter, he was sent to the Persian border, a very dangerous place. He is taking some provisions to the front on a two-wheeled wagon and picking up wounded soldiers. I wonder if he's going to make it. We don't have his address yet.

I'm really looking forward to your coming home. It would help to know for sure, even if only for three days, so that you won't be without a Christmas parcel. I can't describe how much I long to see you. We will bake enough cookies and zwieback so you'll have some to take back. Doing it now I'll have more free time while you are here. And if you should come home, please bring some dark envelopes; these white ones are useless.

Suddenly we have heavy frost again so we feel comfortable wearing our warm shoes in the store. When I look back, I see how quickly a year goes by. I am getting older and, soon I'll be 27, an old woman by the time you come home. Well, it doesn't really matter, as long as we love each other—nothing else matters. Bring warm underwear and a warm shirt as all your warm clothes are in Moscow. The children are well but they always want to be in the store and that is not suitable at all. So Mika has to play with them.

Many greetings and kisses from your ever-loving Tina and children.

From Nicolai
Moscow, December 13, 1916

My dearest Tina and children,

Before we were dismissed from headquarters today, I received your dear letter of the 8th of the month. My most grateful thanks for it and that you have purchased for me the hams and sausage. Today I received a positive response to the application that I had submitted requesting a furlough at Christmas, so if nothing intervenes and God's wills it, I will arrive at the Gaichur Station at twelve noon on the 24th. I would be very grateful if someone would fetch me from the station. Could you please arrange a room for us so that we can live those three days together in comfort and privacy? Even though it is only for three days, I am simply overjoyed that I will finally see you again, fold you in my arms, caress you and kiss you.

So that the time with you will not be too busy, could you perhaps package the things beforehand that I will be taking with me? Two puds of sausage if they're available, six hams or at least four, and one pud of butter. I suppose butter will cost two rubles at home by now, and I'll let you know if the butter is to be salted or not.

I hardly know what to write for the great joy in anticipation of spending the holidays with you. It is hardly worth writing very much because we will have peace soon, but I am coming home before that and we can discuss everything in greater detail. Here things are about the same in headquarters and in our living quarters. My hands are quite full with things to do, but everything is going well, i.e., at work. I am so terribly tired of this military service that if I didn't have this outside activity, I would go mad.

My dearest Tina, please forgive that the page is not full, I really can't write anymore. Furthermore, it is almost 1:00 a.m. Good night my darlings, may God protect you until we see each other again. I kiss you all, Nicolai.

From Tina
Schoenfeld, December 18, 1916

My dear, dear Nicolai,

Soon, soon the Christmas festivities will start and you are not home yet, but there is still a whole week until Christmas, and many things can change, right? I would regret it very much if you could not come. But when I think about the many who will never be with their families, we can be very thankful that we had the privilege of having been together. Alice has recovered from her illness but is very thin. It is quite difficult when your child is sick and your husband is far away. How nice it is when you sit at table with us and we can talk as a family. But when you are home, so often others have your attention. I have decided that we will enjoy the evening hours in our room when the children are asleep. Lord willing, it will happen.

In the months after you first left for the service, I wasn't anxious. But now I'm filled with anxiety, when we will ever see each other again or if at all. If I work hard I don't worry so much. Whatever happens, I want to accept. Tonight Truda and Greta are leaving after having been home for a week. We received a letter yesterday from Willie telling us that he is coming home for twelve days. Anna Willms is also coming here for the holidays. We have a busy week ahead of us. Greta received a letter from Julius on November 2nd. That fellow is having a hard time. He has no money. He has already spent the money he got for his heavy winter overcoat, and he has used up his complete board allotment for all of next year. He can't even write any more letters because he has no money and everything is very expensive. I sent him 30 rubles yesterday, but if everything is so expensive, it won't go far. I will send you your Christmas package December 20th, postponing it until then with the hope that you will still write that you are coming, so do forgive me if it arrives late.

Here everything is the same. We have good weather and the people are traveling by sleigh. We received a letter from Otto yesterday. He is asking Papa for a letter of recommendation on his performance in Papa's business. He probably wants to start to work in a store somewhere. I wish him success.

Many greetings and kisses from Tina and children who love you.

From Brother Heinrich
Tiflis, December 20, 1916

Dear brother Nicolai!

Thank you for your letter of the 9th of December. I'll send a short reply because I don't have much to write about. Yesterday I went to see the train on which I had served when it arrived at the station. I got quite excited when I saw all my comrades. They were all very tired. The commissioners are coming tomorrow, so if I'm lucky, I'll be home the day after tomorrow in time for Christmas.

It is Friday, December 23rd, and the commissioners have not arrived, which means that I'll have to spend Christmas here, which will be very difficult for me. Our weather is dull and rainy. Winter has not arrived yet. Some flowers are still blooming. Hearty greetings from your brother Heinrich.

[Nicolai came home briefly for Christmas.]

THE LETTERS

PART FOUR

Letters of Nicolai and Katharina Rempel 1917

Sketch by Doris Rempel

For the mystery of the human existence lies not in just staying alive, but to find something to live for. Above all, love little children for they are sinless, little angels, and they are there to arouse our tenderness, to purify our hearts, and to, in a sense, guide us.[108]

Nicolai was home for Christmas for a few brief days, and on returning to Moscow, he found himself deeply unhappy because of the increasing disconnect from his family. Like many soldiers away from their families during war, Nicolai had formed a close relationship with his comrades under the stress of war, and he seemed not to be able to fit into the home situation. It is well known that soldiers in war usually bond strongly with their comrades, yet long to be with their families, but once at home, they seem to feel out of place. Nicolai complains about the lack of intimacy with Tina, asking Tina to tell him her deepest feeling, something she appears to have difficulty doing. Because there are no letters from the end of January to the beginning of March, one can assume that Nicolai was home during that time. Whatever the case may be, his first letter after he returned to Moscow, reported the dramatic changes were taking place there.

The war had seen an immense expansion of Russian industry that put severe strains on Russia's backward economy. The large-scale recruitment of soldiers reduced agricultural production while other peasants moved to urban area and into the factories. Decline in food production, compounded by transport chaos, meant the cities and their populations were no longer properly supplied, as the correspondence between Nicolai and Tina reveal.

These economic problems were tied to the worsening military and political situation. The Russian offensive of June 1916, lead by General Brusilov, while at first successful, was not sustained. The winter of 1916 was severe and by early 1917 the situation had become critical. The Tsar, who had moved to command headquarters, was increasingly unpopular and was blamed for Russia's military failures. His wife was even more unpopular. Her constant interference in

---
[108] Fyodor Dostoevsky, *The Brothers Karamazov*, Pever and Volkhonsky, Translators (New York: Farrar, Straus, Giroux , Paperback Edition 2002). p. 214

government affairs, guided by the dark monk, Rasputin, saw ministers dismissed and replaced by her favorites. Late in 1916, members of the nobility assassinated Rasputin.

The Russian people were now fed up with war and longed for peace. Matters came to a head in early 1917 when in Petrograd strikes broke out among factory workers over food and demonstrations calling for change took place. The soldiers in the city refused to intervene and eventually mutinied. In February the Tsar was forced to abdicate and the Duma (parliamentary assembly) formed a provisional government. This was the Revolution that promised land reforms and equality for all. The promised reforms were met with widespread enthusiasm by most Mennonite servicemen.

Nicolai, too, was drawn into this cause of the Social Democrats. On May Day he had joined thousands marching down Tverskaya Street to Strastnaya Square [now Pushkin Square] to celebrate the revolution with its promise of the new freedom and equality for all.

A few days later, on May 6th, he joined some 700 Mennonite medics in Moscow who drafted a proclamation that was sent to all Mennonite settlements. The statement warned of big changes coming and urged the home front to adopt a more just attitude toward attitude and treatment of their servants, especially Russian servants and their peasant neighbors. This proclamation sent by Nicolai to the elders in Schoenfeld was summarily rejected and ridiculed. When Tina related to him the response of the community elders, Nicolai was so incensed that he wrote a scathing letter rebuking the rich elders back in the colonies, accusing them of treating their horses better than their servants, of failing to keep the promise they had made to the servicemen that they would support them and their families, a promise unkept. The elders had encouraged the young men to enlist as medics at the beginning of the war. The reaction to the rebellion of the medics, stirred their elders at home to send a delegation to Moscow to calm their rebellious sons. Nicolai records that meeting.

These letters of 1917 are the observations of Nicolai, a common soldier, as he saw the city slide into civil chaos, the overthrow of the Provisional Government by the Mensheviks who were then deposed in the November by the Bolshevik coup. Nicolai was in Moscow till the onset of October Bolshevik coup. What happened to Nicolai and Tina until their immigration to Canada and their years in that country is sketched briefly in the Epilogue.

From Nicolai

Moscow, January 1, 1917
[Nicolai had been home briefly on furlough for Christmas]

My dearest wife and children,

Greetings to you with God's richest blessings for the New Year in all that you do. Thank God we have survived another rather difficult year to see this New Year. I am unaware of what had happened during the few hours I spent at home with you. Even now I can't remember if we had any meaningful conversation. I have a very guilty conscience that I was with my family, for whom I live and who are my everything in the world, but didn't have a meaningful exchange with you while I was there. Indeed, we did talk to each other, but about what and how much? We talked about others and that is all. Did we sit with our children even one hour and speak in confidence with each in joyful chat? Did you and I talk intimately with each other, as married couples should? Did we read the Christmas story together and speak about the reason for Christ's birth? No! To all of these questions that our innermost being asks at the end of the old year and the beginning of the New Year, we have to answer, "No!" And where will this "no" ultimately lead us?

If we place our hand on our hearts and are honest, we have to admit that a small rift lies between us. Neither of us can explain it. We seem to believe that the best relationship exists between us, and yet the atmosphere between us seems to be somewhat foggy, though this rift is rarely noticeable even to us. But a furlough like this last one can lead to a deeper rift. I am quite unhappy about it, as though there is no one on this earth who understands me. How difficult when there is no one to whom you can open your heart, one who truly understands you. To you I can confide everything, yet you don't seem to confide in me. So I remain alone, shut off from you. I let things gnaw at me that would under normal circumstances be removed from the full heart. This is not a reproach of you in any way; you do your best to make everything as agreeable as possible. But I am probably an odd person whom no one on this earth understands. But please don't worry, my dear, we'll work it out. Let's determine to redeem our time more profitably if there is another furlough.

Enough of this for today. I have been here working for two days but am only now writing to you. I may have wronged you because I did not write to you immediately, but I could not force myself to write. Please excuse my shortcomings. The trip back was very good, that is, I had a seat. It was quite crowded up to Sinelnikovo,[109] but from there I got a seat assignment and was quite comfortable all the way to Moscow. The other coaches were indescribably full. Felt sorry for the passengers who did not have assigned seats. I easily got rid of the produce I brought with me. Too bad I hadn't brought ten puds of butter—could have realized a nice profit. Perhaps you could send me a few more puds. One can always earn extra money that way.

Most heartfelt greetings to you and the children, Your Nicolai Please greet all the others heartily, too.

From Nicolai
Moscow, January 5, 1917

Dearest Tinchen,

You probably weren't pleased much with my first letter in the New Year. I am truly sorry, my dear, that I often cause you such grief, but I had such a heavy heart that I could not help writing what I wrote. And certainly at times you will sympathize with me and notice that in many cases we do not really understand each other as well as we used to. As you will have seen in my letter, I have difficulty dealing with it.

---

[109] Sinelnikovo—station near Alexandrovsk on the rail line to Moscow via Kharkov.

Now I am happier because I had a chat with Hermann Enns who said he experiences similar struggles, but he does not dwell on them but simply takes these things as they come. If you wives were honest, you would have to admit that we men are quite insufferable in many situations. While here in the service we become rather one-sided so that it must be difficult for you to contend with us. I have sometime caught these quirks in myself, but in most cases a person is blind to his own failings. And so my treasured, my dearest truly beloved wife, forgive me when I create problems for you. I do not mean to be hurtful, but rather quite the opposite. I do from the depths of my heart want to make you and the children happy, but have become so inept through this life in the military, but after this time of testing, I believe, God will make us very happy again.

My plans, which often seem so silly to you, will come true, and I want with all my heart to make you and our dear children happy. In a way the joy begins with our children, that is, they have brought us joy since they were small. Now a different joy begins. It was the first time that I noticed how our children had learned to voice their wishes, and that gave me unspeakable joy. Just imagine how our joy will increase as the children will learn to express themselves more clearly. If at all possible I will provide for you all comfortable living quarters, a place you can arrange into a comfortable home. You long for your own hearth. I regret that I have not paid enough attention to your wishes, have not been able to fulfill them.

For some remarkable reason, we will have another free day tomorrow. The chancery offices[110] will be closed and I will probably go to church again. I find great joy in attending church services here. They lift my spirits right away. Have you heard anything from brother Julius? He doesn't write and I feel worried about him. Nothing has changed here. The talk about peace has subdued. It is seldom mentioned.

Heartfelt greetings and kisses to you, my Tinchen. Your Nicolai

From Nicolai
Moscow, January 7, 1917

My dear Tinchen,

Only today I received your letter of January the 2nd [It was enclosed in a letter from Tina's mother]. Heartfelt thanks. However, the letter is actually very short. I almost came to the conclusion that you and Schroeder had colluded to write me very brief notes. At least yours filled half a page. But Schroeder, he sent me a mere scrap of paper! If I had been you, I certainly would not have enclosed his in the letter to me. Then at least then I would have saved myself this indignation. I don't know if Schroeder is crazy or if he thinks I'm demented. I will give him a piece of my mind regarding his letter even if it will cause our friendship to be severed forever. I would not write to anyone on such a small, lousy scrap of paper, not even to the persons of lowest caliber. He has a nerve to send me such a letter! I am so full of rage that I simply can't write any more about anything. I need to take time to cool off.

---

[110] Headquarters in Moscow of the All-Russian Union of Zemstvos, functioning with the Red Cross under government supervision.

I put this letter aside for two days. Now that I have cooled off, I find it easier to write. I thought I would have received another letter from you by now. I was wrong and I hope I can endure the waiting period until I get one. How have you arranged your living quarters at home or is Truda not in Schoenfeld yet? Are you women occupying the children's room, or how have you arranged your living quarters? Please tell me exactly how you have arranged everything.

It is very difficult to write because a number of men are sitting on this bed, playing cards and prattling so that I can hardly concentrate on what I am doing. Sorry I am not happy about writing. When the opportunity is there to send a letter with someone, I should be able to pour my heart in it. You can see by my scribble that I don't really feel like writing. You say among other things that you have nothing to write about to pass on to me because you are in Ekaterinoslav. You went there because you had not been there for a long time. You must surely have seen things that were new to you and yet you have so few words to write. Then put yourself into my position—day in, day out I do the same thing, walk the same path. What then should I be writing? You have many things to relate to me from home. I hope you see what I am trying to tell you.

Hermann Enns is probably going home tomorrow, so that is why I am writing this letter. My best wishes to the people there. So as not to forget, let me tell you right away to whom the things in the wicker trunk belong. One of the round boxes is mine, plus the enamel container with the sugar in it. The sugar in the other two round boxes is Driediger's, as well as the sugar enclosed in a pillowcase.

I hope the writing is not too harsh. I am sending a few sweets along with Enns that was a treat our commander "prepared" for us. You can take some for yourself and the children. As far as I am concerned, you can sell the rest. I paid two rubles for them, and I am sending them to you to try them out. I am including a letter for Schroeder. Look it over and then send it to him.

Heartfelt greetings and kisses, Your Nicolai

From Tina

Schoenfeld, January 11, 1917

My dear Nicolai,

We arrived safely in Schoenfeld today. The children really missed their Mama. I was in Ekaterinoslav for ten days and enjoyed it somewhat. Truda came back with me, bag and baggage. Now it's lively in our house again. If nothing changes I want to go to Mariental at the end of January and stay until March when you come home. I received two letters from you during the time I was away, thank you so much. I appreciate what you wrote in your first letter, making me feel renewed in the spirit again. I agree we must be closer to each other, must learn to understand each other better so we can enjoy a happy married life. Sometimes I feel so bad when you're away that I could just scream, but then when you are at home, I don't have the courage to talk things over with you. God give me the courage to tell you what's on my heart when you're home. You can't imagine how happy I will be to see you!

I wrote you only two letters from Ekaterinoslav. Please forgive me, it just so happened. Well, what does Hermann Enns say to his little, new daughter? Please congratulate him for me if he hasn't left yet. Maybe he is on his way home already. Truda found it pretty hard to leave her husband in Ekaterinoslav now that she is so close to having another baby. She has been worrying about it a lot, but I try to comfort her that giving birth [her second] will be easier this time. We could perhaps take her to Berdiansk to Dr. Dueck, but she would rather stay here. I came home at the right time from Ekaterinoslav; the laundry was done, clothes were already hanging on the line. I got away scot-free this time. I was secretly hoping for that.

I stopped writing here yesterday because I went to the Enns's for a birthday celebration. Naturally, almost all of Schoenfeld was there. Of course, Enns's little boy Jascha was there, too. He had been staying with the Wieneses while his mother was having the baby. I asked him how he liked his new little sister. He didn't seem to be very thrilled about her. "They can throw her away," he said. Well, he will get used to her. Someone asked Jascha if he would like to sell the baby? He answered, "No, Mama has enough money in her chest of drawers; she doesn't need any more." Mrs. Enns thinks her husband may come home today. I want to go to see her again if possible tomorrow. Our little girls are awake, up and about bringing life in this place again. Eight little children and my brother Hans is the ninth.[111] You can imagine what it's like here now.

I just heard that Hermann Enns arrived home tonight. I'm so happy for his wife. I do hope he brought a letter for me; I can hardly wait. There's not much going on in our store these days —selling mostly spare parts for the equipment. This year I want to learn how to assemble some of the machines so that there is something else for me to do. If only the war would end soon so that we could have our own household! But I'm afraid it will not happen very soon. Our girls will be grown up soon. Now all they talk about is going to their grandmother's in Mariental. That's very important to them.

Many affectionate greetings and kisses from your Tina who can think only one thing— which you will soon be home for good.

P.S. We'll send you two puds of butter as soon as possible.

From Nicolai
Moscow, January 16, 1917

My most beloved Tinchen and children,

I have not received an answer to the letters I wrote you this year, but I long to chat with you. The last letter from you was of the 6th of this month. If you are in Ekaterinoslav still, you will not have received mine, and, of course, will not have answered it. You postponed your visit to Ekaterinoslav so long that you certainly will have no joy of it now. I feel sorry for you that you have been sitting there all the while bored and have used up your Christmas gift [money sent her] for what, nothing? And I regret that you will not get the needed rest you had hoped for on

---

[111] Tina's three: Alice, Hilda, Selma; Greta's three: Waldemar, Erna, Gertrude; Truda's daughter, Margaret, and one other child? Hans was killed a few years later when roughhousing with other boys he was struck on the head with a brick.

this visit in Ekaterinoslav. Well, we'll have to postpone all of our wishes till after the war as nothing can materialize at this time.

I have not given up hope for your visit here in May, and many things will have to happen before I'd give up that hope. I long terribly for all of you—Several times I could just have cried because I longed so much for you, and yet, yet—we are becoming more and more estranged from each other. Some people seem not to weather these trials and ruin their lives and the lives of their loved ones forever. Recently, I heard that the wife of Johannes Enns in Memrik had a child by another man. Whether this is true I don't know, so please don't say a word about it to anyone. When you hear something like that, however, you imagine that life is simply over for those who suffer that way. God grant that it is merely a rumor. But such things happen when we are far from our God and love for each other vanishes, and for some people life somehow ends.

Where do you and I stand in our relation with God, my dear, and with our children? Dear Tinchen, our responsibility to them is not small. At present, it is you who must show the children the way to the truth. Woe to the mothers who neglect to do this! When I think of our dear little girls, my heart aches. These poor, innocent children who might lose their way because of our neglect. That would be terrible!

I ended this letter here yesterday but did not send it to you because I definitely expected a letter from you; today Kornelius Fast brought me your letter of the 11th of this month. This is the first letter from you in the New Year written from Schoenfeld, and I thank you much for it. This letter seems evident to me again that you have this great longing to open your heart to me, but you do not do it. I have often pled like a child that you not hold your deepest feelings from me—tell me all that is burdening you. I feel it again now, my dearest, and your silence is causing a riff between us. If there is something on your heart that is troubling you, I can sense it so clearly you wouldn't believe it. If I were to ask you, "What is troubling you?" and you answered, "Oh, it's nothing," let me tell you, a slap in my face wouldn't hurt as much. You know that I truly love you, that I am yours without reservation, so don't close yourself off to me, please. You should hide nothing from me and we will become more united and happy once more. It will then be easier to fulfill our duties.

Now to your other question. When I will come home, I have no idea, so I can't answer that. Currently I am still in hospital; however, I want to get away from here tomorrow or the next day. The wound has healed nicely and my nose is not swollen, and even the swelling around the eyes has subsided. I received a letter from home in Mariental. They write, among other things, that the cow had a bull calf on the 6th. The cow gives a fair amount of milk and remains calm during the milking. Sister Tina has gone to Einlage again. My second page is full and I have to close.

I send heartfelt greetings and kisses to you and the children. Your Nicolai with painful longing for you.

From Tina
Schoenfeld, January 17, 1917

My dear Nicolai,

Our house is full of visitors. It is Greta's birthday. Although the visitors are still all here, I would rather chat with you than sit out there with them. I received your letter that also included your response to Schroeder's note. I have not sent it to him. Unfortunately, Truda read it. This is how it happened. A group of us was sitting at the table—Truda, Greta, Anna and I. When the mail came, I found your note to Schroeder enclosed in mine. Assuming it belonged to Truda, I gave it to her and then read my letter and immediately realized my unfortunate stupid mistake. Of course I shouldn't have given her the letter, but how could I know its content? I asked Truda not to write Schroeder anything about it in order to avoid any further conflict. I don't know if she will send it to him or not.

But going back to what happened. Mama had written you a letter and I enclosed one from me in it. I asked Schroeder to mail it but had not glued the envelope shut properly, so it was partly open. So Schroeder wrote that little note to you and slipped it into the envelope and then mailed it. And that's how you got the brief letters from the two of us.

Yesterday I got the letter where you describe your accident. You are accident-prone like your middle daughter. She's just like her father. She also often hurts herself. Thank you very much for writing me the truth about your health. Isbrandt Riesen is leaving tonight for Tiflis, so I want to send this letter with him. If we're alive and well, we will leave for Mariental tomorrow evening. I'm not sure how long we'll be away. At present our roads are quite icy so I have to go now before the thaw when the roads turn to mud again. Your brother Heinrich stopped by here on his way home to Mariental In a recent letter, your mother writes that Tina has gone to Einlage again. She plans to stay one month, but I think she will come back sooner because brother Heinrich is home for only one month and that month will pass very quickly.

How is it with your furlough? Are you coming home in March? I haven't been to see Enns yet, and you know the situation with our horses, and no one else is driving out there [neighboring village] to see him. He was at the County Office today as well as at the Wiens's but didn't stop by to see me. I think it's rather strange that he doesn't care enough to stop by. I'm sure if it had been you in his place, you would have stopped in, right? But I can't demand it of him.

Papa will send you some butter soon although the price has risen to eighty kopeks. How about your head injury? Will it be healed soon? That must have been a very bad accident. We were thinking that if you could home on furlough now [because of the injury], we would be overjoyed. The children are giving me no rest; they want to go to Mariental right now. The trip won't be very comfortable, but then it's not really very far [about sixty miles]. Address your letters to Mariental so that I will have one soon.

Enough for now. All the visitors have left and so that noisy storm has died down. We have many birthday celebrations here. Greetings and kisses from your loving Tina and children.

P.S. Must tell you that I sold the trousers for seven rubles. Should I sell the white horse, too? I will ask thirty rubles for it. A Russian fellow was almost ready to buy it. Let me know.

From his Sister Tina
Kichkas, January 18, 1917

Dear brother Nicolai!

Yesterday I received your dear letter of January 13. Thank you so much for writing right away, so now at least I know how things are going with my brothers. I am here all alone today; the others went to the funeral of our neighbor, Mrs. Petker. There is another funeral tomorrow for a Mr. Dick. Both died suddenly. Mrs. Petker went to bed, fell asleep and didn't wake up again. She died after three days without having spoken another word. Mr. Dick died of a heart attack. How quickly our life can end; we see that every day! And few people think about eternity. I'm surprised that people are so blind. They rush about here and there but peace and happiness eludes them. One does not see so much of that in our quiet Mariental. I'm getting to like it here more and more. Everyone here knows about the devil's amusement [cards], even little children know about it. Graying men and even young women play cards. Of course, I find that very strange.

I understand from your letter that you are hoping to come in February. By that time Heinrich will be home, too. I hope the maids will be gone by then. At first I thought I would hire a few more girls, but Mother says it is much too hard for her to be alone with the girls, so I'll be glad when this month is over. I'm really looking forward to your visit in February. Of course, you will bring your family, too. There are a lot of things to discuss that we can't do by letter.

We must finally make a decision regarding mother's situation [A neighbor has proposed marriage to their mother, widowed some 10 years]. We will have to become resigned to the fact that there is no other way. We could have solved the matter at Christmas if it had not been opposed so strongly. I don't want to be alone when this matter is discussed. When you are here, you advise and support me, and I am much stronger then. Sometimes I think I must get used to the idea, but my whole inner being rebels against it [the marriage]. In my opinion, this decision can't be postponed any longer. I can only imagine what the result may be.

My answer always seems to result in [family] warfare! Strife! Payday is coming for you one day and then you will remember how you have harassed me. We will talk about the rest when we see each other. Please write and tell me about the condition of your injury, whether it is any worse and if you are suffering with wound-fever. You must have had a lot of pain.

Heartfelt greetings from your sister, Tina

[Since there is no correspondence from late January to March 17, one can assume that he had been home on furlough for two months, possibly recuperating from an injury, but he is now back at Zemstvo headquarters in Moscow. The letters below show Nicolai's enthusiastic awakening, as it were, to the changes that are taking place.

From Nicolai
Moscow, March 17, 1917

To all my dear ones in Schoenfeld,

Yesterday morning I arrived here in Moscow. The trip was difficult but very interesting. I will describe to you briefly the trip Gaichur to Moscow. I just barely had enough time to get my baggage on board; it weighed 16 pud [nygr]. The conductor and his helper said I could take only 10 pud on a ticket Class II. But when Lapenko came, he told them that one could send as much baggage as you wanted to Moscow. I rode the slow train to Chaplino, where I had a six-hour layover, and then I missed the connecting train at Sinelnikovo that went to Moscow and so had to wait in Sinelnikovo the whole day. But by no means did the time drag because there was so much to see and to experience. It was all very exciting and went quite well.

At nine that morning, it was announced publically that a [special] train from Kharkov would arrive at noon with a representatives of various trades or professions.[112] Near midday people from surrounding areas began gathering in little clusters, chatting about goings-on in their regions (In their towns and villages). At the designated time, workers from various trades also arrived carrying red flags and banners with inscriptions, so that by noon a huge crowd had assembled. Exactly at twelve the train from Kharkov pulled in. Attached to the front of the locomotive were large red placards with slogans like: "Great is Russia's freedom," "Welcome the Revolution," and so forth. The train, consisting of six or seven railway cars, each elaborately decorated with red flags, was welcomed to great jubilation by the crowd. After this enthusiastic welcome, speeches by the representatives on the train were made. Among them were some excellent speakers. One of the finest speakers was a Jew [Trotsky?] from Sinelnikovo who had been exiled for political reasons.[113] The whole thing lasted until two o'clock, and then, again to great jubilation and thunderous applause, the train moved on.

Toward evening, the train I was to take to Moscow finally arrived here. I had an assigned seat to Kharkov, but could not get one beyond there, and it was pointless to try to get one as each carriage was as crowded as the next one. That is how I arrived here this morning. I had my coffee and went to work. But I did not last all day at my desk and asked my supervisor to give me some time off to recover from the trip and catch upon my sleep. Much has changed since I left here, but I'll write you about that soon.

Your loving Nicolai

---

[112] The word in the original letters is *provisionen* (provisions) but should probably be *professionen* (professions or trades or trade unions).

[113] This sounds as though he may have been Leo Trotsky, but James Urry believes that it could not have been Trotsky. He had returned to Russia from his lengthy stay abroad in February 1917, shortly before the Tsar's abdication, He was well known for giving inciting speeches. Although initially with the Menshevik, he joined the Bolsheviks and was a major figure after the Bolshevik seizure of power in the October coup. He was assassinated in 1940 in Mexico on Stalin's orders.

From Tina
Schoenfeld, March 18, 1917

My dear Nicolai,

Must finally write. I was sick this whole week, always felt like lying down my stomach hurt so much. But that is minor compared to what happened today. Around three o'clock, Truda went into labor and by eleven o'clock little Peter was born. Truda is doing well. Schroeder had come home quite soaked during a heavy rainstorm the night before.

To add to this, we had a lot of visitors because it is Mama's birthday. Mika and me and our three girls have moved into the upper room where I am now sitting and writing. I'll have to stop now because it's six o'clock and time to make supper. We are having meatballs and I wish you could join us. That would make me truly happy.

Last night we had a terrible ordeal with Greta's cow calving. That poor creature was five hours trying to give birth in the field, so finally we called Wiens and Enns to help bring her into the barn. There they worked half an hour longer until she delivered. The hired man had been propping her up until it was no longer possible, and then a problem developed with the afterbirth. That was even worse than the birth. So finally we called Mirau and Peter Neufeld to help slaughter her. At least that way we could still use the meat. We worked till after midnight cutting up the meat, making a short night. Greta sold the calf (it was large) today to Peter Enns for 50 rubles — that is good money. We also sold meat today for 50 rubles, so now Greta has 100 rubles. The hide will bring a good price, too, so Greta will get what belongs to her. Before the birth, the cow had been perfectly healthy. What a night!

Well, supper is behind us now but I didn't eat anything. The smell of the cooking was enough. It's still pretty busy downstairs but I came back up because Selma wanted to sleep. Our accident-prone girl, Hilda, hurt herself once again today. She injured her head quite badly. There are no wagons on the street any more but mostly riders. The road is still in poor repair. I am glad that tomorrow is Sunday. I will sleep in. One gets tired after a busy day. This is how far I wrote yesterday.

(Sunday) I got up at nine o'clock this morning, the others went to church. Mika and I stayed home since we had a lot of work to do. Anna and Gerhard went to bid farewell to the Rempels, Selma is taking her noon nap, Hilda and Alice went to the Wienses, Greta and her children, Waldemar, Erna and Gertrude, went to the Dirksen's— so the majority has gone away. We are having the most beautiful sunshine, but it is windy. If it doesn't rain again, we'll soon have good roads and the children can play outside for which they have been waiting. Tomorrow the mail will likely bring us a dear letter from you. Now you can feel freer to write and won't have to be so careful. [Unclear why]

Well, what did your comrades say when you arrived back in Moscow? Were they happy only because of what you brought them or also that you were back again? And how was your trip? Did you have enough to eat? What was the situation there when you got back? Good or bad? I imagine things were bad for you. You must have been happy to see your brothers again. It was different for me. Always a feeling of emptiness after you leave. I keep looking for you everywhere, but there's no Nicolai. It was a bad feeling. Even Papa felt lonely right away. If only there were peace again, we could live alone. To own your own hearth is worth a pot of gold. Have you heard any news from brother Heinrich? Is he well? If Willie can get ten days furlough, he wants to come home, too. I will send the cloth we bought for your mother to Mariental with Greta.

Your brother Johannes had to walk to the station. As you know, it almost impossible to find carriages to take you any where since so few horses are left. He took only the things he needed most. He hopes to come home again at Easter time. I will send this letter with Peter Neufeld because he's returning tomorrow to Moscow. He is finding it hard to leave.

Enough for this time. Many, many hugs and kisses from your loving Tina and children.

Selma says you are coming home again tomorrow.

From Nicolai
Moscow, March 20, 1917

To all my loved ones in Schoenfeld,

I have spent four days here in Moscow since my return. A significant change has taken place since I left on furlough [late January]. At home in Schoenfeld people were happy also that we Mennonites now have equal rights with other citizens of Russia who can speak up and are no longer under the thumb of the old Regime. Here in Moscow one sees and feels much more clearly what it means to be a free citizen. A number of changes have already been made in our organization. Much of what is happening we can read in the papers, but not everything by a long way is reported. Let me give you an approximate picture what has changed here and what we are doing.

As soon as I arrived, I was told (and this greatly interested me and will also interest you) that Commander Korsakov of the train on which I formerly served, had been blocked by the medics from entering their train and that was lucky for him because he smelled the rat and took off; otherwise he would have been arrested right there in Petrograd [St. Petersburg]. The commander of the Garrison himself had boarded the train together with the medics to catch that other scoundrel, Rorsakobr, but again fortunately for him, he had already taken off [Both Korsakov and Rorsakobr were very unpopular with the medical staff]. Then the medics together with other staff telegraphed that they intended to topple the Old Man himself [Commander in Chief]. Of course, our High Commissioners, whom I mentioned in an earlier letter, now had to bow and scrape to all demands [of the staff—the common people]. Besides Rorsakobr, the medics and other staff members had toppled another High Commissioner, one Baron Stael von Holstein. This happened the day before yesterday. If it had happened earlier, we know well what the result would have been. But now the old regime is quickly being swept away.

We have now organized a committee of seven persons. The chairman of this committee [Soviet style] is a serviceman, a bureaucrat also from here, a true red, a lawyer; two men, members of the former commission, real blacks [anarchists?]; and two medics with high school and university education, also reds; plus two bureaucrats, both reds. This committee represents, or better said, functions, as mediator between the service personnel and the Executive Committee of the Old Nobility Organization and deals with the organizational matters. For example, if my superior wants to fire me, the whole matter has to go before this committee to see whether valid reasons exist for the dismissal. In fact, if I have any complaint or issue with my superior where I'm working, I can turn to this committee, and they will adjudicate the matter, all the while keeping clearly in mind that I am a citizen of equal standing with my superior. In one word, the judgment is just. Similarly, if I want a furlough, I turn to this committee with the request and not, as formerly, to the prince where my request would lie on his desk for weeks before it was given any attention.

Furthermore, we have elected two of our medics to the Soviet of Soldiers' Deputies. They are Hermann Enns and a certain Achnickov. In the C. P. and C. G., frequent meetings are also held to take up the serious matters whether we want to continue this war, in what manner; how the needs of the workers and soldiers are to be met, etc. Among other things, they have decided to join (*in Verbingung zu setzen*) [114]the Social Democrats of the World. Yesterday we had a meeting of all Mennonites here in Moscow. There we discussed the article in the newspaper, *Pyccr. Cr.* [115]of the 17th of the month and in the newspaper, *Pyccr. Bug* of the 19th that dealt with granting unrestricted civil rights to everyone except those émigrés from Germany and Austria-Hungary. We all protested vehemently this restriction. We are not mere lackeys. We demand all the rights that are granted all of the other Russian citizens. Should these equal rights be denied us, then they should find an open door in a country where we will have equal rights with their citizens.

We chose three delegates who will go to Petrograd as soon as possible to meet with Minister of Justice; Kerensky[116] to find out what is being planned for the citizenship of us Mennonites and to convey to him what I mentioned above. If our delegates find Mennonite delegates from the Halbstadt and Gnadenfeld districts in Petrograd, they should immediately set up contact with them, unless they are the same old cadre who were there formerly kissing the hands of the Ministers and giving them huge bribes and even attempting to contact Rasputin. However, if those same old slackers are there still, who were representing us before, we want to have nothing to do with them. That old, obtuse, humdrum pace set by them has to be swept away out of our *Mennonitentum*. If they [old guard Mennonites] don't want to bow to our demands willingly, we just have to give a signal and those bootleggers (*Schmuggler*) will get their just reward. Furthermore, we decided to make contact

---

[114] This could also mean, "to make contact with".

[115] Pyccr. Cr is possibly *Russkoye Slovo*, a liberal newspaper; Pccr. Bug is undoubtedly the Kadet newspaper *Russkiia Vedomosti*; the Kadets had strong links with the zemstva organizations; both were Moscow newspapers at the time (Urry).

[116] The provisional government was initially composed of the Kadet coalition led by Prince Georgy Lvov, which was replaced by the Socialist coalition led by Alexander Kerensky. He was elected Deputy of the Fourth State Duma from the "Labor Group" (trudoviki) in 1912 and became the faction's leader. By March 1917 he was Minister of Justice in the Provisional Government, initiating such acts as the amnesty of political prisoners and ordered the return of all revolutionaries from exile. He became one of main leaders of the Social-Revolutionary party and was made Military Minister in June in the Provisional government. His effort to reignite to the Russian army's offensive in June failed. After the Bolshevik coup in October, he escaped from Russia (Urry).

with all Mennonites who have been mobilized and also with all of the Mennonite municipalities and districts. If we are united in one alliance, we are much stronger than if we all go the way we have been going till now—each for himself. In order to inform all Mennonites of our decisions and our work here, we plan to publish a report covering all decisions made here and forward that report to all points of the compass where a Mennonite can be found.

At our meeting the discussion then turned to those who live in dire poverty, alone and isolated in forests [doing their service there]. It was reported that seven persons living in such isolation in the forestry service were driven to despair and suicide because of deprivation. If at all possible, we want to help such persons, although currently funds are not available. In fact funds are not even available for our own organization, i.e., to publish and forward the aforementioned "Report" to Mennonite communities. So, immediately donations were requested but not much was collected, only 250 rubles. The suggestion was then made that we turn to our home communities; perhaps there can be found some magnanimous persons who might find some joy in contributing their widows' mite to the worthy cause of bringing all Mennonites (*Mennonitentum*) into closer communion. Inspired by this good prospect, we decided then and there to call this whole matter to life as soon as possible by having each of us appeal to friends and acquaintances to contribute something so that all Mennonites would stand united: "All for one and one for all."

Without a doubt, we mobilized servicemen do **not** have less power than you at home, and we want to apply all of our youthful energy to secure our future existence. Attempts are being made wherever possible to accommodate the demands of our servicemen, i.e., our demands and wishes are given special emphasis. Without a doubt, now is the propitious moment to secure our rights as citizens. In conjunction with this issue, our delegates in Petrograd are supposed to report to the soldiers and the workers there what the intention of the government is for us Mennonites. A genuine Social Democrat can never support an unjust situation [withholding equal rights].

Please tell all of the neighbors what we have determined here. Undoubtedly all of you and the other Schoenfelder will concur with us, even agree to support this project financially, so that that this whole matter can be started (actually it has already been set in motion) and we would accept this with gratitude. I send to all the Schoenfelder warmest greetings, to grandmother, the aunts, Mieraus, Dürksens, Sara, Frau Rempel, Warkentins, Dycks, Wienses, Riesens and especially to Aron Rempel, and also to you my dear parents, siblings, wife and children, I send heartfelt greetings.

Your, Nicolai Rempel

From Tina
Schoenfeld, March 21, 1917

My most-loved Nicolai,

While the others are strolling up and down the street, but I want chat a little with you. After you left on Saturday, I went to my room and had a good cry. The first night without you was very difficult; I thought about you all the time and slept very little. Even now I can hardly sleep. But I will get used to being alone again. I'm very glad when the each day is over. It means one day closer to you. On Sunday I went to say good-bye to brother Johannes. It's not good that Sara is so alone now. I'd gladly help her but it's not possible. I went to see her for a while today and she complained that even the food doesn't taste good when she has to eat alone. I believe her. I'd feel the same way if I were alone.

I have so many people around me and yet sometimes I almost despair. Fortunately I am very busy. Today I sewed undergarments for Alice, Hilda and Selma, and then I went to look for the lambs, thought someone had stolen them, but they were in the meadow behind the church. The ram was there, too. We will have to lock them up so that they can't stray. Selma often asks, "Where is my Papa? Did he go to Mariental?" She, like me, hopes that you will soon be back here with us. Excuse me, but I'm fighting back tears all the time. Enough for this time even if there is still room on this page. I hope I won't have to write many more letters to Moscow. Many greetings and kisses from your Tina who thinks about you all the time. Auf Wiedersehen very, very soon.

From Tina
Schoenfeld, March 24, 1917

My dear Nicolai,

I received a letter yesterday dated March 17 and today I got one from the 20th [The account of events in Moscow]. It is a very important letter. It has been read by many people today, and they are very interested in what it says. I read it as soon as it arrived and then gave it to Papa, who took it to the *volost* administration office across the street right away where the mayor, H. Schroeder, G. Enns and some others were present.

Mr. Rempel [separating from his wife] hasn't been seen today so we haven't given him your greeting. There was a meeting again today at the Rempels, but I don't know what they accomplished. Mrs. Rempel refuses to give him what belongs to him. The Elder from the church was at the Wienses and said that Mrs. Rempel is obligated to give Rempel his half. And now she is afraid. She had had come to Jakob Duecks last night at nine and lamented that her husband wanted to leave for good and she was wondering what she should do. That's the kind of talk this woman spreads around. However, we can't be judgmental. Whatever they are destined for will happen to them.

Everyone here is chipper. Truda is up and walking about already [after birth of Peter] and Schroeder has gone to Rosenthal for two days. Aron's wife, Lenchen, has been here with her children [Ernst and Frieda] for a week already and will stay for quite a while longer. They are living at Sara's who has enough room. Someone went to the station to fetch Susa [Tina's sister]. It's ten o'clock now and she should be here by noon. We paid our maid her final salary today. Another one has offered her services, but we are not quite sure about her.

I cannot write as interestingly as you. I heard today that the Commerce School students from Halbstadt are supposed to have written to Fast, I believe, that it is Trenkenschuh's son-in-law who has deserted. I have forgotten his name. Lenchen remarked today that Heinrich Ediger from Gnadenfeld will likely also take off (disappear) suddenly.[117]

We did a big laundry today. Everything has been mangled, ironed and put away. We have a very good manservant now. Nothing is too much for him, but we are very careful not to overload him or he might leave us also. We'll soon have a dry road again, and the children are eager to be outside, but they are so strange. They always seem to look around for a mud hole to play in. When we were at Mama's birthday, Hilda fell and hurt her head on a stone. It's pretty bad. I have been cleaning it regularly with peroxide and daubing it with iodine several times a day but it doesn't seem to get better. I can't even comb her hair—will have to cut it. I am sitting on the floor writing while the children are sleeping peacefully—everything is quiet. I had really wanted to wait up for Susa but that will take too long, besides tomorrow is Saturday. I'm in good health. What we were expecting hasn't happened so far [pregnancy?], but that's all right.

I'm not sealing this letter just in case we can't send mail tomorrow, then I'll write a few more lines. Many greetings and kisses from you loving Tina and children. I didn't complete this letter yesterday. Dueck is going to the station today so I'll send the letter with him. Nickels and Minna have arrived. More next time. Your ever-loving Tina and girls

From Nicolai

Moscow, March 27, 1917

My dearest Tina and children,

Two weeks have past since I left you and not any news from you. All letters you wrote during this time must have been lost. Am in agony waiting to hear from you. We hear all kinds of reports about the Schoenfelders' responses to the medics' recommendations, reports that are not very pleasant, indeed. We heard that the Schoenfelder make fun of our meetings here, of our organization and that we have sent delegates to Petersburg to gain clarification to questions, especially concerning the Mennonites status as citizens and about the Russian Germans in general. If it is true that the Schoenfelder are of that disposition, then they are indeed quite ignorant of the directions the new politics are taking. They are really quite daft [verrückt]. But I can't believe that those people who have an interest in what is going on in the world would hold the view that has been reported to us here. That there have always been blockheads is of course nothing new, but those guys will fortunately soon have their tails cropped.

My impression concerning what is said about us in Schoenfeld is that they look on us here as though we are little children who still need the guiding hand of the old fogies (old Mennists). That time, thank God, is past. For some three years now,

---

[117] Trenkenschuh is probably the son of the long-time secretary of the Halbstadt volost who was likely not a Mennonite (most likely Catholic) and thereby liable to military service (Urry). On Heinrich Abram Ediger, publisher, editor, banker and buromaster of Berdyansk see Benjamin H. Unruh, "Ediger, Heinrich Abram (1858-1943)," *Global Anabaptist Mennonite Encyclopedia Online. 1956. Web. 8 Mar 2014*. Why he had to disappear is unclear, but he was extremely wealthy and may have been involved in the bribery conspiracy. (Urry)

we medics have looked on in dismay and disgust as we have been betrayed and lied to by the very men whom we looked to as our leaders—those who said to us when we were conscripted, "Brothers go out in joy. We will look after your families. They shall lack nothing." How shamefully they deceived us whenever possible. Not only that, but no one (other than our parents) has even bothered about our families. They have even turned down what the government wanted to give us; furthermore, whenever possible, they placed additional levies on the families of us conscripted men. Where no levies were possible, as in the case of Mrs. Papki, they charged her with the most bitter accusations that she was a spendthrift, had no ambition, and this poor woman was made to feel responsible for letting her innocent children starve. Yet all the while most of these persons (accusers) have done little more until now than to stuff their own insatiable maws.

My hair stands on end just to think about it. When will this egoism finally be put down? The time is now and I have no doubt that it will happen! When you attend one of these meetings of the Social Democrats, you become increasingly convinced that everything will soon be put in order. Saturday while we were attending such a meeting, the *Babushka* of the Russian Revolutionaries, Brezhko-Brezhovskaia, came there and gave a speech that erupted in tremendous applause. Saturday evening we were in the Polytechnic Museum where professor Speransky gave a most interesting lecture about the past Czar, his upbringing and his governance.[118]

Just now someone came and told us the delegates whom we had sent to St. Petersburg to discuss our citizenship claims have returned. They report that they were received politely and were assured by the Justice Minister Kerensky, "There is no question. You are citizens just like all the others. Especially you Mennonites, you have always brought much prosperity to this country, and you now fear that someone will take away this your country from you? No, never will that happen!" Then he sent warm greetings to all Mennonites. And so the situation looks good. If only this war would stop soon then we would be on top of things. Hopefully we will come home for the winter and then the happy life begins.

I will close for today as some are already asleep. Yes, and you can tell those who made sport of us that these "children" have really accomplished something here! Again warmest greetings and kisses from your Nicolai.

From Tina
Schoenfeld, March 29, 1917 (Before Easter)

My dear Nicolai,

You probably received my letter even though the person I'd asked to mail it didn't do it, kept it for two days and then brought it back to me. I heard from Mrs. Fast today that you haven't received the baggage yet. It would be unfortunate if

---

[118] Yekaterina Konstantinovna Breshko-Breshkovskaya (1844-1934) was a woman of noble descent who had spent twenty years in Siberia for revolutionary activity and returned to Moscow on her release in 1917. She was known as the Grandmother of the Russian Revolution, hence Nicolai's use of the word Babushka. Professor Georgy Nestorovich Speransky (1873–1969) was a pediatrician at the University of Moscow. (Urry)

some of the produce would spoil. Getting around is difficult because of the mud from the frequent rains. We have both sunshine and wind today so that the ground dried a little before it rained again. Lenchen [Aron's wife] is waiting for better roads so she can go home to Halbstadt for Easter. I'm looking forward to Easter when we won't be so busy. We cleaned our store today, had hired a maid to do the work. Father has a bad migraine again today.

Yesterday we sent the boys with horses and wagon to get a load of sugar from the station. Our boys had already loaded it when the agent suddenly appeared and told them that without the necessary papers they could not have it. So they unloaded it and took containers of syrup instead, only 160 pounds. Papa said that that Jew had really cheated us again. The syrup is bitter, only good for cookies. We will try again tomorrow. I thought you would come home for Easter, but you must be very busy since you have a new administration. You will probably have more work now that there is a new government.[119] Oh, that the new government would soon announce PEACE. How everyone would celebrate! Hilda is in bed but can't sleep. She has all kinds of requests for you to bring when you come home.

Must tell you about the Aron Rempel [distant relative]. He left for Gnadenfeld on Saturday after complaining to people about his situation and went about crying like a little child. He had told his wife that whatever you did is fine with him. He looked so miserable, as though he might even be losing his mind because of their separation. They have divided their property between them: 14,000 rubles, two horses, four cows, five pigs and then his furniture. Mrs. Rempel had already moved his furniture into his room. After the division, Rempel had asked his wife, "If I should come back to you, Mother, would you take me back?" (*Mutta, wann ekj too die trigj komme wud, wuds du mie trigj name?*) She had answered him in a very condescending way, "Well, you can come if you want to" (In Plattdeutsch "*Na, kaust komme wann du welst*"). The mayor and the secretary were present at the division of property. They said the Rempel girls had been romping about, laughing and carrying on like idiots, as though such behavior was expected of them. I just can't understand that woman. It is sad. Well, she might come to her senses someday but that may be too late. I don't like to gossip about people, but you did want to hear about the Rempels, don't you?

We are well and wish the same for you. I must tell you that mother is very fond of you. I overheard her say when no one saw me that you worked so very hard during your furlough. Mother always says that Schroeder is very lazy. She hopes he will leave soon.

Many greetings and kisses from your Tina. Happy Easter to you and all your comrades!

From Nicolai
Moscow April 6, 1917

My beloved wife and children,

I have just received your letter of March 29, a heartfelt thank you. You indicated that another one is on the way, one you had sent with someone to the station, but

---

[119] The Provisional Government came into power on March 14, 1917, after the abdication of Tsar Nicolas II.

he had not posted it so you took it back from him. We have not received very many letters from each other in the last while. I sincerely regret that I have not written more often. Your letters come very irregularly too. When we will have more navigable waters, this situation will correct itself.

I am terribly sorry that I hurt you so much with the thoughtless words you had to hear from me just before I left to come back here. However I said right away that you had misunderstood me, yet it seemed to me I couldn't convince you. I want to assure you again when I said that I did not want to come home before the end of the war it was **not** because I did **not** want to be with you, but rather because I don't like to be without some steady work and don't enjoy merely loitering about. In all honesty, my heart is in pain when I see that my dear family doesn't receive from me what I want to give them and rightfully would wish to give them. I understand quite well what you mean when you write that you would like a home for yourself and your loved ones, no matter how small. I have that yearning too, and I have no doubt that both of us will make every effort to reach that goal. It will be a joy to build our own hearth. You will then come to know my more positive sides, not just the constant complainer that I have been and have thus created unhappy hours for you.

I am indescribably sorry that I have saddened you, you whom I honestly love. You have always carried out your obligations to me in an exemplary manner, doing much more than any wife owes her husband. I, on the other hand, always fall short of my responsibility to you and the children. But with God's help this will change, and we will come to know how to express our love for each other in word and in deed. The time will come soon when we will be able to move into our own home, if God wills it and gives us health.

Tell me what do you think about this suggestion. I have decided to stay here till August even if we have peace. I have to stay here to complete what I've taken on, i.e., my accounting studies. But I would like you to come here in May. Who knows if there will be another opportunity to show you and explain everything to you that is happening here in Moscow, so please get yourself ready. Someone told me that technicians could now be released from service quite easily. Help Father to think about this. I believe he could get Willy and Julius released from service. I will write you next time about the things that are happening here.

Greetings and kisses, Your Nicolai

P.S. What are the children doing? Are they always well behaved? How is Hilda? Is the wound on her head healing? Tell Alice I have not found shoes for her yet, but she should be patient that I will find shoes. Does Selma still chatter as much? Oh, how dearly I would love to have you all around me.

From Tina

Schoenfeld, April 8, 1917

My dear Nicolai,

It is Saturday evening, the work is finished and the children are in bed. It feels quite comfortable in here, but it is stormy outside, heavy rain, thunder and lightning. I spoke to Driediger by phone but the connection is poor. To visit the Driedigers is almost impossible. Two days ago we had such a severe storm that our outside privy was knocked over, its windows shattered and the shingles torn off. We thought the tin roof would start to fly off, too. The horses had to do a lot of fieldwork this week so using them to go visiting is out of the question. We have already planted the vegetables and potatoes.

I received your dear letter of the 30th of March this week.[120] You write that you have little information, but I am always satisfied with your letters. Julius came from Mariental for one day; he had been there for three days of a short furlough. He looked quite thin and I packed a large hamper of food for him. When will this traveling back and forth stop and you can stay home for good? In church earlier I wanted to meet Nikolai Dueck about the matter you mention before he returns, but he was outside before I got to the hallway.

Tante Sannah is going to the eye doctor since her vision is poor even in her best eye. Papa is going to Kharkov tomorrow to see if prices of wares are cheaper there. The shoes cost seventeen rubles in Berdiansk and that is more reasonable than the twenty-five rubles in Moscow. Have you bought shoes for Alice, yet? If not, it would be better that I buy them in Berdiansk. Today Susie is leaving for Berdiansk, so I asked her to check the prices of clothing there, to look at the summer jackets and their cost. If they are more reasonable, it is better that I buy a ready-made jacket. I am willing to forgo my trip to Moscow because of the cost; however, if you really want me to come, I will do it willingly. I would love to see you. If I come it will probably be after Pentecost and perhaps by then we will see an end to the war.

In your last letter you wrote that the Schoenfelder are having fun at what you suggested and that father also made fun of it. Wiens said that Papa had written many things, but he denies that he has written anything. People make up these stories, and if you believe everything you hear that would simply be quite stupid. If you turn in an application for my supplement under this new government that would be very helpful. The teachers have all gone to Alexandrovka for a meeting about the situation here [shortage of teachers] and will return home tonight.[121]

We are all healthy. The children have a nice tan and are walking barefooted. Alice and Hilda are visiting at the Wiens's. Selma is romping around with Gretel [Schroeder, Selma's little cousin]. It has cooled off and is raining. Write me if you want me to send you some baking, and I will send it by mail so that you don't have to starve. I will buy some flour. By now you will have received the letter I sent with Schroeder. Had you insured the things that have been lost?

The day after tomorrow we celebrate a birthday—our oldest daughter is turning seven. She is a big girl now and in another seven years she will have completed her education. She asked me to bake cookies for her graduation and wants to invite her

---

[120] Nicolai's letter of March 30 was not included in this collection.

[121] One of the first things the Provisional Government set about doing was release teachers from service. This happened to Nicolai's brother Aron. Three of his brothers were teachers: Herman who died in 1915 (note letter June 4, 1915) had been principal in Schoenfeld Zentralschule. Aron had taught in Gnadenfeld and later in the Omsk area in Siberia where he was later also active in the All-Russian Agriculture Union. Heinrich, mentioned frequently in the letters, began teaching after the war. He disappeared in 1937, a Stalin casualty like his brothers Abram and Aron (Note Epilogue).

friends. [In 1910 when Nicolai entered the compulsory Forestry Service, Alice was not yet born. He has been away from his family most of those seven years—two years in the Forestry Service and three-and-a-half as a medic in military service].

Many greetings with love, Tina and children. I wish you the best of health and may you soon come home for good. I am sending you buns and cookies. Enjoy them.

From Mika, Nicolai's Niece
Mariental, April 9, 1917

Dear Uncle Nikolai!

My conscience bothers me a lot that I haven't written for so long. In your dear letter that we received, you express so much hope for the future. Grandma worries that we might be disappointed. We have hardly seeded anything in our garden except for a few flowers because no one was willing to plough our potato field. But tomorrow morning Tessmans will do it and once the potatoes are in the ground, it won't take long to seed the vegetables. Uncle Julius came home on Easter Monday and Aunt Greta was very happy. Abram and Gerhard [Tina's brothers] were home, too. You can imagine that it wasn't very peaceful around here with those two, plus Wolja and Kornelius Peters from the Old Colony who was at our place during Easter also, especially when they all started horsing around.

Right after Easter Uncle Julius and Abram walked to the station. They had wanted to catch a ride with Braeuls, but there was room for only one person so Uncle Julius walked with Abram as a favor to him. Abram appreciated that very much. They had sent their baggage along with Braeuls. Abram had a difficult time saying good-bye this time. He would have forgotten his leather jacket if Aunt Tina hadn't reminded him. But Uncle Julius was jovial and clowning around.

Last night we went to sing for David Schulz who is suffering with tuberculosis and probably won't make it much longer. We were surprised by a rain shower and came home drenched to the bone. We sang on Easter Sunday, too, and had very good base voices in the choir. They were Heinrich Voth, the teacher's son, Hans, our cousin Gerhard and Abram Braeuls. Gerhard is happily back in Gnadenfeld. School starts tomorrow. Now I must close.

With greetings and kisses, your niece Mika.

From Nicolai's Mother
Mariental, April 10, 1917

Dear Nikolai!

We received your precious letter. Thank you so very much. I'm glad that you are full of good cheer and hope. It's my heart's desire that you will not be disappointed. I guess I'm too old to be easily swayed. If God is in something, it will stand, but if not, it will pass away. So whatever you do, seek God's counsel first. Trust in the Lord and lean not on your own understanding. In all things we must first seek God's blessing. Man proposes but God disposes. Yes, God disposes and may he direct the hearts of the new government to do what is pleasing in his sight. That's my heart's desire and my daily prayer. If the new government will not follow

God's ways, they cannot expect to prosper. God bless you! I'm sure that you will not undertake anything before you seek the will of God.

Nikolai, your letters are so cheerful, but Aron is so careful what he writes. He writes very little and in the Russian language and his letters have always been censored. He says that Lenchen should write in Russian too. Are the old laws still in effect there? Aron just doesn't seem very happy. You write that I should give Lenchen some money. What for? Her mother is paying for her trip and her sister Minna is coming to get her. She will bring the money for the trip. Tina gave Aron ten rubles and I gave him some too. He didn't want to accept it. I think Mrs. Wilmsen [Aron's mother-in-law] can help him because she has only the one Lenchen [daughter] to worry about. Maybe some of our own people have greater needs, but if you insist that I give her some money, I'll do it. I still have 145 rubles in cash that belong to you.

All of our land has been leased. On the one dessiatina behind the Leopp's property [one dessiatina equals approximately 2.7 acres], Kornelius Matthies has seeded grain. He rented it for ten rubles. A Russian farmer planted corn on three dessiatinas, also paying ten rubles rent. Another dessiatina is rented by Matthies for ten rubles, and four dessiatinas behind the Rudnerweide road are rented by another Russian farmer.

I would like to go 50/50 with someone to seed the remainder of our land, but so far there are no takers. All we can plant now are potatoes, pumpkins and grain, but so far we haven't even done that. No one wants to plough the land. I've talked to the Peters, old Loepps, Abrahm Klassens, young Loepps, the Bergs, but no one is interested. Tessman promised to plow half the acreage with the five-gang plow [five shears]. Reimer says he will prepare the acreage for seeding potatoes with the sulky plow [one shear], but I doubt that it will ever happen. I think we will have to resort to the five-gang plow for the potato field, too. We have done no planting in our garden so far. On the 8th to the 9th of April we had a heavy rain. The farmers haven't completed their seeding either. Because of frost damage most of the winter wheat has to be reseeded.

How we long for PEACE! Julius was home for three days at Easter time. After his furlough, he and Abram walked to the station. Braeul would have given them a ride, but there wasn't any room since Brauel had teamed up with Voth and together they had so much baggage, including Julius's things, so there was no room for anyone else. Many people were home for Easter—Abraham Isaak; Abram Loop; Heinz Tessman; Hans Hubert; Hans Hildebrand; W. Nickel; Aron and Abram Braeul; Heinz Martens, the teacher's son; and Jakob Loewen from the Crimea came with Abram on the Thursday before Easter, and Kornelius (Cornish) Peters arrived on Easter Day before noon as did Julius.

Now I want you to tell me a lot, too, especially your thoughts about what we have done with our land. I don't like it at all but there seemed to be no other solution. We don't get any feed for the animals now, and what can you buy with the few rubles? If we had seeded winter wheat, we would have had double expense. I thank God that at least someone is using our land. Maybe next year we will be able to rent out all of it.

Every day I am waiting for PEACE to be declared! Heartfelt greetings and kisses from your Mama (even without Papa)

From Tina
Schoenfeld, April 14, 1917

My dear Nicolai,

A month has vanished since you were home and who knows how many months will pass until you come home for good. You hear much talk that we will soon have peace. You ask about the children. They play so hard all day that they willingly go to bed early. Hilda's head wound is not better. Selma still poses questions that I sometimes don't know how to answer. Alice thinks she is quite grown up now that she is 7 years old. This morning a film of ice covered the chicken trough and the air during the day is very cold. The boys built a fire in the orchard creating smoke to prevent the blossoming trees from freezing.

Today here in Schoenfeld the people voted in a policeman. You probably know him well. He used to be in Gaichur and his name is Nicolai Kirilovich Shamrayev. He is renting four rooms at grandmothers and pays twenty rubles a month. He receives a salary of 1,800 rubles. Next week he is moving here with his family [It is probably the first time the village has had a policeman, and this suggests increased threat and theft].

Don't feel bad that you made me feel sad at one time. I have done the same to you, my dearest. Apparently we are similar. A wife can't do too much for her husband and I feel the same as you about that. You ask whether you should complete your studies. Of course, I am in total agreement that you continue them since that will be helpful in the future. Sometimes I sit and wonder what we will do when peace is finally declared. Peace! Peace?

It is so cool in the room, especially when I sit so still and write. I am very warm when I am in the kitchen that is heated all the time. Alice is lying in bed already and sends greetings. We have almost finished planting the garden. The cost of butter is one ruble and twenty-five kopeks. The Jews are driving the price up. The people are paying them cash and so they don't bring us any butter [barter for goods in the store]. If we would pay them cash and used their way of calculating, they might sell us butter. Have you received the things I sent in your container? What about Driediger, has he received all of his things?

Well, our parents are just coming home from visiting the neighbors. It is time for bed. Mrs. Jacob Enns is lying on her deathbed. She will probably die soon.

Many greetings and kisses from your Tina and children who love you.

From Nicolai
Moscow, April 15, 1917

My treasured Tienchen and children,

So I have spoiled my credit in Schoenfeld, because, as I hear it, the people there are quite indignant about my letter. If I had had an inkling that my letter would be read by those people, I would have written even more indicting charges. But what I had written was to you, telling you what was weighing heavily on my heart, about the most abominable injustice that has been perpetrated even among our Mennonites. But finally the measure of unrighteousness is full and God has given that situation a dramatic reversal. We can now expect big changes, changes that have in part already taken place. It is quite clear to me that this has not registered yet with many of the Schoenfelder. I'm referring here not to the Schoenfelder of our more intimate circle, but rather to the community as a whole, especially the estate owners.

But now begins, as the saying goes, "Give the dogs that lie at your door what they truly deserve and not, as it has been until now, just enough bones to chew on to keep them from starving." How many tears have the poor workers shed and how much sweat has flowed from their brow just to satisfy their masters (*Herren*). And what was this sweat of their brow brought them, only scolding and shame with but a few exceptions. When did these masters speak a kind word to their laborers? When did these workers get a square meal from these "mighty" masters? When was he paid a just wage for his labor? I believe I can rightfully say, NEVER!

Yes, I will admit that now and then an estate owner spoke a friendly word to his worker, but those are rare exceptions. Rarely has a worker been given a decent meal by these rich landlords—as it is proper. In the true sense of the word, most workers have had to eat their meals like dogs. Take for example in summer time. Always there is near the horse stable a large trough where the horses are fed, and it is very good that livestock can feed in the fresh air in the shade of a tree. Not far from this trough there is the summer kitchen, outside of it the servants eat their watery borscht sitting on wooden blocks or shoddy benches. And that is the food with which the landlords attempt to salve their conscience, a conscience that pricks them now and then. You'd often heard these masters say, "We, too, always get our borscht from that kitchen and it's really good, as is the kasha and fruit soup [*Plumemous*]. But when has there been chicken or goose or duck on tables of the workers? When have the workers enjoyed zwieback or cookies or plum *perishki* with their tea? NEVER! These masters always say, "It is too expensive to feed the servants the way we eat. If we did that, we would not make ends meet."

Well, their estates would survive even if the workers were treated like human beings. But then, of course, the master would not realize so many thousands in profit. This egotism of the sovereign masters will now have to give way. They will be forced to reduce the workload of their servants, stop overburdening them and they will have to feed them better. If you stand back in objective judgment and ask isn't the worker a human being just like his master? Why he should exist in subservience all his life and be debased through his labor and reap no benefit? You must conclude that this situation is inexplicable and that the worker would be justified if he were to rise up in indignation and claim his right by brute force [And thus it came to pass].

Does this laborer not have the same human feeling as his employer? Does he not have the same desire to live, as it is proper? Does he not have the same desire to eat decently like his master? Everyone who is fair-minded will have to admit that he is a human being just like his master and has the same needs. Why then should he live so miserably compared to his master whose wealth this laborer creates. Well, it has always been thus until now, but the page has been turned and the bourgeois will learn to see in his worker a respected human being. However, he will be seized by deathly fear when he sees that his bank account can no longer be filled by the brute force was used to fill it formerly. He will clutch his wallet to his heart and scream half in delirium and despair, "Damned be anyone who dares to cut my income and gives it to my workers. Futile are all organizations that seek justice and truth. Just let me continue to live as I have until now. I don't want to know anything else. The afflictions of my neighbor are of no concern to me." These masters dare to mock that which is most noble [the laborer].

Our Mennonite brothers dare to scoff at us, the servicemen, because we have united in an effort to alleviate the suffering of those who are famishing in the forests and also to help our dear wives and children. But that is not our only goal. We want all Mennonites to unite as one to improve our collective situation. Isn't it already a major step forward that our delegates brought the message from the Minister of Justice that we Mennonites are Russian citizens who have equal rights with all others—which our lands will not be taken from us unjustly? But why then are the Schoenfelder scoffing at us? Why are they making light of our efforts? Was I not speaking the truth when I said that those who were laughing at our efforts were daft? I did not write that all Schoenfelder were crazy, and yet they seem to be all stirred up about my letter. Well, if the shoe fits, let him wear it!

As I have heard, the Schoenfelder would for the life of them like to know who carried the report here to Moscow that they are mocking us, apparently to wage revenge on that person. Naturally I would not disclose who this person is, but the Schoenfelder should not forget that not only we Mennonites who are in the Dvorianstvo (All Nobility Organization) receive letters from Schoenfelder, but also those who are in the Zemstvo Union and the City Union with whom we were in contact. I would be very grateful to you, my dear wife, if you were to keep me informed what is happening there. It would be most interesting to know how they are reorganizing their lives to make things more practical for themselves.

Now just one more little matter and then I'll close. Please let me know what Schroeder has been doing and what he has said. Did you talk to him about me? And what does Julius report? How is your health and what about your coming here? If you come here do take Class II and wire me about your scheduled arrival so that I can meet you at the station.

My telegraph address is: Moscow, Spiridonovka, Tovarishchestvo, and Rempel.

My letter address is: Moscow, Spiridonovka, D. 19, O.D.O. N. A. Rempel. You have lately written my address incorrectly. Apartment No. Moscow, Novenski, D. 97, K 32. Please don't mix it up.

Our baggage has finally arrived. Fortunately nothing was spoiled and I realized a good profit, about eighty rubles, almost enough to pay for your trip. In addition I made twelve rubles and fifty kopeks from the cloth brought by Kornelius Fast. If Fast had wanted it for himself, naturally I would not have taken a profit. And the cookies you sent with Driediger I have received. I am very, very thankful for them. Now we are not suffering any shortages. Have enough of everything.

Warmest greetings and kisses from your Nicolai.

From Tina

Schoenfeld, April 18, 1917

My dear Nicolai,

As Wiens's son-in-law, Friesen, is leaving tomorrow for Moscow, I have to take advantage and send the butter with him. He is very willing to take it. The price is sixty kopeks for twenty-one and a half ounces. What I'm sending is all I could get now, but if you need more, let me know.

About the motor, it's still at the station in Gaichur. According to what I heard, he wants to buy it soon but is short on money. Papa says if you had put him in charge, I would have had the money already. But probably you didn't think of letting him handle it. Well, I hope we will get our money.

Yesterday was Sunday and we played ball on the Riesen's yard. Of course, I had my girls with me and they had great fun. They picked grass and played their little games. Your brother Abram was home visiting here yesterday. This is my week to cook. I already have three days behind me. Right now I have a break between lunch and faspa.

We're all of us well. Papa and Mama, Selma, Hilda and Greta are taking naps. Anna, Mika, and Lischen Federau are chatting away in the living room. Gerhard was napping too, but just now he jumped up and chased children out of the house—Wolja, Alice, Erna—because he thinks they're too boisterous. Reinhold is busy working on songs at Aron Rempel's. There will be a horse auction here again on the 22nd and the 23rd. If only you were here now to see the trees in full bloom—what a magnificent sight. If we don't get a late frost, we should have a lot of fruit this year. We have taken over a garden and will get half of the produce. Our lambs are quite fat and frisky.

Right after the commencement in the school, Mrs. Toews is going to the Crimea to her parents. She will sell some things and store her furniture at Hermann Enns's. I'm sorry she is leaving. She is such a good woman, I often visited her and I will really miss her. Selma is up already and looking for me outside. This morning she was in the kitchen, grabbed a piece of meat, then came to me and said, "Mama, Selma not naughty, no?" She is such a little dickens. I had better to go out and get her because I hear her crying, "Where is my mama?" All the children are well and so am I. I'm not sure how things are with me as I have not had my period since then [As he was home? Probably pregnant with Bill, born November 28, 1917]. I don't feel anything so I'll wait a while yet. I suppose everything will fall into place, sooner or later. I will write you when I know. I received the photographs and also your last letter written April 9. Thank you very much. Mail delivery is so irregular now, it seems as though the letters never arrive on time.

Ohm Doft and Mirau are still having their differences. A few men here have been freed from the draft, having drawn the right numbers. Another lottery for the service begins on April 25. Reinhold and Gerhard will have to enter the service in one month. Then father will be left alone with the women to run the business. Well, the two Johannes are still here. When Abram Driediger leaves on the 3rd, I may send something with him but I dislike asking people for favors. I would rather spend sixty-five kopeks and send it by mail. Did you get that last parcel already? How did the cookies taste and the butter? After I have finished this letter I'll go over to the Wienses and take the butter to them. Is there anyone you know in your hospital train?

Yes, I have to mention something about your moustache. Why don't you shave it off before others start pulling at it? I know you wanted to shave it off but I wouldn't let you. Are you gaining or losing weight? Are you still carrying a fever? Every day I think about the time you will be able to stay at home with your loved ones. One just doesn't appreciate the time enough when we are together at home. Thing are going quite well with the children but sometimes I have to do some spanking. Alice is very stubborn so sometimes I just don't know what to do. Lately I had to spank her hard and then she had to sit still in the house until she would ask to go outside again. I went in to see her once but she was still angry and would not ask so she sat there for half a day. When I went in later, she was very friendly and asked about supper so I finally let her go. In that way Hilda is quite different. She is quick to change her attitude and be good again. I hope you are well which is my heart's desire for you. The girls send many greetings and hope that you will come home soon. I'm writing poorly because I can hardly see the lines any more but it's too early to light the lamp. Once more, greetings and kisses from your ever-loving Tina who thinks about you all the time.

From Nicolai
Moscow, April 24, 1917

My dearest wife and children,

Again another Sunday has passed, a day of rest one would think, yet we were quite busy—if I may put it that way—even though we did not go to work in the Government office. We had Mennonite guests from various regions and so a general conference of all of the Mennonites who were here in Moscow took place. Actually the guests had come at the invitation of professor Lindemann to attend a general assembly of all German Russians in Moscow, or more accurately one could say, a convention of representatives of all Mennonites in Russia.

First, I will name who these guests were: from Halbstadt, Benjamin Unruh, I. Willms, Heinrich Braun[122] and a Matties, a bookkeeper of the Orphan Treasury; Elder [Johann] Klassen[123] from Schoenwiese; Epp[124] from Berdiansk; and a few

---

[122] Heinrich J. Braun (1873-1946), Mennonite Brethren leader and head of the influential Raduga publishing House. In 1915 he was threatened with arrest and managed to escape deportation by fleeing to Petrograd where he came under the protection of Assistant Minister of Internal Affairs, Prince Volonskii, where he remained working for the Mennonites on land liquidation issue until the abdication of the Tsar. See David G. Rempel with Cornelia Rempel Carlson, *A Mennonite Family in Tsarist Russia and the Soviet Union, 1789—1923* (Toronto: University of Toronto Press, 2003), p. 166.

[123] Johann P. Klassen (1868-1947), influential Elder from the Frisian Gemeinde, Khortitsa, immigrated to Canada where he founded the Schoenwiese congregation in Winnipeg.

[124] David H. Epp, minister and later elder in Khortitsa, at this time living in Berdiansk. Editor of the pre-War Mennonite newspaper *Botschafter* and author of a number of historical accounts. A member of a powerful and influential family in Khortitsa that had supplied religious and educational leadership, he remained in the Soviet Union and died a natural death before the terror began: James Urry, "David H. Epp: Intellectual, Spiritual, Cultural Leader, 1861-1934," in Harry Loewen, editor, *Shepherds, Servants and Prophets: Leadership among the Russian Mennonites, ca. 1880-1960* (Kitchener, ON: Pandora Press, 2003), pp. 85-102.

others unknown to me. Because Zemstvo Union has a large auditorium for medical officers, we always gather there and it was the same yesterday. In the morning session, J. Klassen and B. Unruh made fine speeches. Then we adjourned for lunch and congregated again at two. Some 700 men had assembled [Men in footnotes- influential leaders].

First Benjamin Unruh[125] spoke about the present situation of the Mennonites and about the situation in general in Russia. He then addressed the matter of the differences in (disposition) attitudes between the mobilized men vis-à-vis the people at home. After Unruh's speech, one of our men spoke. Here then these other speakers followed: Heinrich Braun, teacher Sawatzky,[126] Epp from Berdiansk, and finally Willms and Matties from Halbstadt. Then Heinrich Braun took the podium again to report about his life in St. Petersburg as a member of the Land Liquidation Commission, a very interesting report. And last Jakob Janzen[127] from Orloff, representative of Bransker Commando, also spoke.

There followed a lengthy debate about a general meeting of all Mennonites. This caused feelings to run a bit high. Then Benjamin Unruh spoke up a second time in an attempt to bring us to a consensus. Among other things he said, "It does not surprise me that we hold such different views, and it is, of course, self-evident that those who are not experiencing the whole revolution as you here in Moscow will lag behind. Secondly, we knew each other well three years ago when we still lived together. But now we do not know each other at all any more. You are not by a long way the same as you were three years ago, and we who are at home there in the South are not the same by a long, long way either, so if we are to realize full accord between us, we will first have to live and work together again. But now let us see if we can't come to a general agreement so that we can, as much as possible, organize and stay in constant communication with each other." The meeting went from two o'clock past seven. A few delegates were chosen to attend the next meeting of the mobilized that will take place on May 2nd and 3rd in Halbstadt. [128]

Now to a little business. I sent seventy-five rubles to Susa for shoes and rubber boots for the children, i.e., for Alice and Selma and also for Hermann Enns's son Jasch. Shortly I will send you 300 rubles. Please send me, if it is possible, one pud oatmeal. We are close to starving here. In May we will receive only half a portion

---

[125] Benjamin H. Unruh – teacher at the Halbstadt Commerce School, a leading figure in the community deeply involved in the political events. Following the revolution he stood as a candidate, and may well have been elected to the Constitutional Assembly which the Bolsheviks prevented assembling. He left to negotiate with the Germans in 1918 and never returned to Russia and became a representative of the Russian Mennonites in Germany where he established questionable links with the Nazi regime: Heinrich B. Unruh, *Fügungen und Führungen: Benjamin Heinrich Unruh, 1881-1959*. (Detmold: Verein zur Erforschung und Pflege des Russlanddeutschen Mennonitentums, 2009).

[126] Sawatzky is most likely Gerhard Sawatzky from Khortitsa, he served in the medical services and had strong left-wing views and helped the early Soviet government introduce educational reforms.

[127] Jacob H. Janzen (1878-1950), a minister and later elder from the influential family of Janzens based in Ohrloff/Tiege in Molochna. He later immigrated to Canada where he played an important role in the immigrant community in Ontario. He served as a minister to Forstei units and attended the meetings with Kerensky in Petrograd: See Jacob H. Janzen, *Lifting the Veil: Mennonite Life in Russia before the Revolution*. (Kitchener ON: Pandora Press, 1998), p. 125. The notes about filling in historical details above were provided by Professor James Urry.

[128] Nicolai's three brothers attended that meeting: Julius, Abram, and Aron. See Tina's letter May 7.

of bread per person. Somebody asked me if possible to have some rye flour sent. But it's probably not possible, otherwise I'd like ten to fifteen puds of flour. Didn't you receive my telegram about the butter? I asked Papa to send me three puds of butter, not as baggage but the way one sends butter. Tomorrow I will finally keep my promise to Gerhard concerning his request for the drapery. I am ashamed that I did not do it sooner but I had no time. Now we decided to work only from 10 a.m. to 4 p.m., so that I'll have some time at my disposal.

Tinchen, please write me what is happening. I don't know anything that is happening there, what is going on; no one is writing to me about what people are doing for the revolution. I may also stop writing to you about what's going on here because you don't write me anything which is evidence that you are not really interested. You also don't write me about our children or don't we have children any more? Best greetings, your Nicolai.

From Nicolai
Moscow, April 30, 1917

My dear Tina and children,

Again I have postponed my writing for so long that you have the right to be displeased with me. I should have an excuse for not writing, but I cannot give you any. I felt myself deeply indebted to you when I heard suddenly that a hamper full of bread had arrived for me on the 2nd. In fact that hamper of bread was a gift that gave us great joy. It may seem rather peculiar to you, not to be able to get bread, but this is really the situation here. It has to be kept quiet around here if someone has a small supply or it may be commandeered. So I give you my sincere thanks for the bread and my comrades also thank you heartily for it.

You are afraid that a trip here will not be worth the expenditure. Well, I don't think we will be threatened by starvation just because you come here, you'll see to that at home already. For the life of me I would just once like you to see something other than Schoenfeld. You must be bored stiff with everything there, and I think if you were here, I would be able direct you for once to some other ideas and you would return to the children with renewed courage and devote yourself to them with greater joy. Naturally it will cost money, but if you could bring some butter along, the expenses could be covered with the sale of that. I leave it up to you when you want to come.

Hermann Enns and another fellow from our division are going home for Pentecost so that only Driediger and I will be left here, and we'll have to work very hard to keep up with everything. It might be better if you came with Hermann Enns when he returns here, then you could celebrate Pentecost at home (as probably no one will want to look after the children during Pentecost anyway). Secondly, I would have time to visit with you then. But I do have to set aside the evenings of Tuesday, Thursday and Saturday when I attend class and you will have to be content to stay alone on those evenings. Gerhard Fast tells me that you have no interest in coming here. Is that true? I don't want to pressure you to come, but I do believe you would enjoy it.

Now there is another question and that is your health. You have written me nothing about that. Please write to me if it is the same as a year ago. You wrote me that Alice will start school in a week and I am not quite in the clear about that. Please let me know more details about it, and if a kindergarten is to be organized, see to it that Hilda and Selma can also be taught there. That Aron was transferred to the government office where Schroeder works I have known for some time since the transfer was initiated from here and I had written you about it. What other important things have happened, please inform me about everything?

Heartfelt greetings from your loving Nicolai.

From Nicolai
Moscow, May 1, 1917

Dear Tinchen,

You will be surprised that the date of this letter has jumped forward so far. We are celebrating MAY DAY in Moscow. At this celebration here, most of the banners carry the inscription, MAY FIRST, so I am joining them and instead of writing April 18, I write May 1.[129]

There is a magnificent spirit of celebration here today and I am sorry you can't be with me. I have had a most wonderful day! There is such a celebratory atmosphere so that I feel as joyful and content as one can possibly feel. Everyone at headquarters had been given the day off; no one was working. From nine o'clock in the morning, one long procession filled the street: one group after another, one long stream. But let me describe from the beginning what I heard and what I saw.

As I mentioned to you before, the processions started at 9 a.m. Several of the units passed by this place where we live, so we joined them, marching along toward the center of the city. The order of the festivities was planned ahead of time, numerous service groups marching in units: for example, the factory workers from the various factories, each in their own unit; soldiers from infantry, the artillery, cavalry, Junkers,[130] students and teachers, cooks, cleaning women and street cleaners, etc. Each group had their own standard with various inscriptions. Before we had gone very far, other groups came toward us, these groups that had likely chosen a different route. They carried large white banners with red inscriptions such as, "LONG LIVE PEACE AND PEOPLES FRATERNITY"; another one read "BROTHERS LOVE ONE ANOTHER," etc. Among other things, flyers were handed out; one of these I will send you. When we came to Tverskaia Street, groups from all directions of the wind were coming in to join those already assembled in the square.

I must mention that in these processions, men walked arm in arm, about eight men abreast, and everything was organized in truly dignified manner, so that the really fine order prevailed. You heard none of those harsh commands from the police they usually give. Here you heard only commands such as "Comrade, please do this" or "Please move out of the way," and everyone responded promptly. And so we marched alone Tverskaia to the Strastnaia Ploshchad [now Pushkin Square], and

---

[129] Some changes were made unofficially from the Julian calendar to the Gregorian.
[130] Junkers: James Urry suggests that it may refer to students of any military or Junker school in between 1864 and 1917.

from there to the residence of the former Governor General which is now the Headquarters of the Soviet (Council) of the Worker's and Soldiers' Deputies. There on the balcony stood the Executive Committee of Workers and Soldiers. The balcony was decorated with green boughs. High above on the wall was a white banner with the inscription in red letters, "MAY 1," and at a lower level hung a large banner of red cloth, approximately three yards by ten, with the inscription "WE DEMAND A DECREE FOR AN EIGHT HOUR WORKDAY"— "THE LAND OF FREEDOM LONG LIVE PEACE," etc.

On either side of the balcony were similar cloth banners with various inscriptions on them. In the large square in front of the residence a huge crowd had assembled. However, the street running in front of the residence was kept open; the people standing at curbside formed a cordon so that the procession could move through. The front of the residence was decorated with cedar boughs and red flags. After we had been standing a short while, a large automobile, also adorned with green boughs and red flags, moved in along the street. On this vehicle stood a soldier holding a gun; attached to the bayonet was a banner with the inscription "MAKE WAY FOR WOMEN," and so on. Next to the soldier stood a woman in the traditional Russian dress, holding the other end of the banner that was fastened to the bayonet. Slowly and solemnly the vehicle moved along the street, a mass of people followed in song and jubilation. After them came a military band playing the "Marseilles." They also carried banners with various inscriptions, such as, "SOLDIER CITIZENS"—"LAND OF FREEDOM"—"LONG LIVE PEACE, BROTHERHOOD OF THE PEOPLE" (Peoples Fraternity, etc.). In the procession officers marched arm in arm in brotherly manner with the common soldiers. Then came a group of workers, singing the funeral march for the fallen that had died for freedom. This group was followed by the artillery, its cannons decorated with pine boughs (trees fastened to the cannons) as well as many banners. One of them read, "DOWN WITH HOHENZOLLERN & GERMAN IMPERIALISM." Most of the others carried the banners, "LONG LIVE PEACE AND BROTHERHOOD"—"PEACE WITHOUT LAND SEIZURE (Oppression)," etc.

After this Governor General[131] rode (horseback) with his staff. And so on in this manner, one cadre after another, an endless line, passed down this street without interruption until two o'clock in the afternoon, each carrying many inscribed flags so that there was a stream of red flags as far as one could see. These were truly very impressive flags made of silk, velvet and other materials. The slogans adorning most of these read: "PEACE AND BROTHERHOOD"—"LONG LIVE INTERNATIONALISM"—and "WORKER OF THE WORLD UNITE PEOPLE UNITE." Besides these, there were thousands more. It is quite impossible to describe all that happened today, but to be present at such a celebration is certainly worth it.

Estate owners are probably a thing of the past because all citizens agree that the land must be redistributed. How difficult it will be for those who own so much land!

---

[131] Nikolai Kishkin was Governor General from March to September 1917.

What I have described to you, you probably would also have enjoyed experiencing. However, there is a shadow moving over Moscow and that is the problem of bread; it is becoming scarcer each day. We decided that it would be good to have white bread sent from home, so could you please pack one pud of butter with it and send it as baggage. But tell Ivan not to send it by slow train but rather with the mail train. Or if Gerhard Fast should be home, it would be better to send a container of food with him.

Now to the question that I have not answered so far. I did not buy any shoes for Alice in Moscow nor have I bought boots for Wiens either. They say there are none available. Nor have I, even with the best of intentions, been able to fulfill Papa's request. But enough for today. I write so often and you so seldom. The problem may be a faulty address that I don't receive your letters. May I suggest that you not be so indifferent. The letter from the 3rd that you are supposed to have sent with Schroeder I have not received.

The most intimate greetings send you your Nicolai.

From Nicolai
Moscow, May 6, 1917

Dear Tina,

I am taking time to answer two of your letters. Please forgive me for being so deeply indebted to you. You are so much better than I am because I hear no accusations from you concerning my long silence, whereas I express my disappointment immediately when you don't write often enough. But before I begin answering your questions, I will give you a report of recent events.

I just returned home from a general meeting of our Organization of Servicemen [O.D.O.] [Mennonite Medics?]. You can easily imagine how hard it is for monarchists, like most of our superiors, to get used to the idea of a republic, and it will be clear to you that a Social Democrat or even a Progressivist cannot possibly reach consensus with monarchists. As you know, we had in our Organization of Servicemen [O.D.O.] a committee consisting of five medics plus two members from the Administrative Commission. Four of these men from the O.D.O. (Organization of the Nobility Office?) were absolute gems, and the two from the Administrative Commission were certainly more progressive in their outlook than any of the other members of that Commission—however, they do belong to the Black Hundreds.[132] Our Committee of Servicemen had worked for approximately in the two and a half months, and, one must say, very diligently, in spite of the fact that they had to do constant battle with persons who were terribly hostile toward democracy. Yet in spite of this obstructionism and hostility, our Committee accomplished much, and had, to some extent, influenced the Commission delegates so much that the latter began to look at issues more seriously. But taking note of the drift of things, the other members of the Administrative Commission began

---

[132] The Black Hundreds (Schwarzen Hundert) was the name of an extreme nationalistic, right wing organization in the last decades of the Tsarist Empire. They supported monarchy and autocracy and opposed democracy and any revolutionary movement. Known also for anti-Semitism and instigating pogroms.

pressuring and harrying their delegates on our Committee so much that the latter resigned.

Now other delegates were to replace them, but our committee members, seeing this manipulation, resigned from Committee of the Servicemen, telling themselves that if it was almost impossible to work with the former delegates of that Commission, it would be utterly impossible to work with these new ones. Of course, emotions ran high and everyone was agitated. A few of the servicemen were in favor of setting up a separate committee without Commission representatives, but unfortunately, the majority was opposed to that suggestion because there are still too many bootlickers[133] among the men (admirers?) of the nobility. It is incredible how a meeting like this can make peoples blood boil, especially if they don't get what they were aiming for. However, we are fortunately not done with the elections, and we still have a small chance to carry out our plan, but, I'm afraid, not without much agitation.

There seem to be ongoing elections here in Moscow, and it will probably begin to be the same where you live. One becomes tired, dead tired, of all the meetings and all the speeches. I don't know how the Minister of War, Kerensky, doesn't lose his mind. Recently the Mennonite Committee was also enlarged because the committee members were unable to keep up with all their correspondence that comes in. All Mennonites are joining in to help and all or almost all have contributed financially to the Committee. What the Committee plans to do with this money, I've already written you. Only Schoenfeld has enshrouded itself in silence, and people there, who don't know what to do with their money, have until now not contributed one thin kopek to this noble cause. Isn't it a shame that they can't even agree to support the high school. Of course, that's not surprising since Schoenfeld does nothing charitable except for its church [*Gemeinde*].[134] Well, people here are getting a pretty clear picture of Schoenfeld! The Schoenfelder can't even agree to support a high school, even though there are persons who have resources to quite comfortably support a school by themselves without the help of others, quibble over a few lousy rubles. Isn't that outrageous?

One should not forget what Jesus said, "Make friends with the unrighteous mammon."[135] Well, it may have taken a long time, but socialism will win, and how will the many treasures that these people have laid up help them then? In the days of Noah's, it took 120 years of preaching, but no one listened. And that's the way it is today with the citizens of Schoenfeld.

All right, my dearest Tina, now that I have calmed down a little, I will answer your questions. On the 26th of April, I received the bread you sent and it was baked just right and not squashed at all, as you feared. Of the five loaves of bread, we still have one-and-a-half. Once more, heartfelt thanks. So you'll be coming here with Enns after Pentecost, and that will give us more time to be together and to discuss

---

[133] Nicolai uses the term Speichellecher, literally lickspittles. It means toady or bootlicker. In current German he would probably have used the coarser term, *Arschkriecher,* a brown-noser.

[134] *Gemeinde*: A German word that could mean church fellowship or a civil community; here he is probably referring to the latter.

[135] Luke 16:9 "And I say unto you, *make* to yourselves *friends* of the *mammon* of *unrighteousness*; that, when ye fail, they may receive you into everlasting habitations."

matters. I won't be coming home on furlough until September, so you should come here now if you feel up to it. The rail traffic will be lighter and the living quarters here in Moscow more readily available.

Tomorrow we are expecting delegates from the south who had been sent to Halbstadt to a meeting of all delegates representing all of us servicemen. Am really quite curious what happened there. Need to report that the situation with the soldier ration of the Mennonite soldiers wives (*soldatka*s) looks rather shabby, because we received a message from someone who was sent to Petersburg to investigate the matter at firsthand that the money does not belong to the Mennonites[136] [*dass den Mennoniten das Geld nicht trifft*].

I must crawl into my hole since it is 1:30 a.m. Heartfelt greetings from your loving Nicolai.

From Tina
Schoenfeld, May 7, 1917

My dear Nicolai,

I received your letter that I had been waiting for eagerly, although I was afraid it would tell me not to come there to visit you, something I would very much regret. To go with Fast after Pentecost is really too long to be away from you. I have a great longing to be with you again. Fast suggested that he might not even go by the 14th. Then things will be different, of course.[137] If I go now, I don't have to prepare for Pentecost. I am getting the children ready, that is, their clothes. Of course, the folks here would gladly take care of the children until I return. Even if you don't have much time for me, the time you will have will be so much the better. I will prepare everything for us so that we won't be hungry. I wonder what you will say about clothes I have chosen to wear for my visit. I bought a black coat for the occasion. I am so impatient—it is all taking too long.

Julius is home for a few days. He came from a meeting, May 2nd and 3rd, in Halbstadt. Your brothers Abram and Aron had been at the meeting, also [Note letter of April 24—Perhaps the meeting was to be held in Halbstadt in May. This meeting could have meeting of medics with the elders in Moscow]. They discussed many things about the service. The forestry guards are now receiving thirty rubles monthly. Julius and the other two have their earnings for two months in their pockets. I suppose that will enable him to express his own ideas more "clearly."[138] We also received a letter from Willi yesterday, telling us about their gatherings and that a complete turnabout has occurred. He hopes he can come home for a few months. If possible, he wants to come to Greta's for Pentecost. All that is fine with

---

[136] Soldiers' wives were to receive a pension. Perhaps the fund meant for the pension was used for other purposes.
[137] Wives who visit their husbands prefer to be accompanied by a male on the trip. Explained earlier.
[138] This is perhaps a reference to Julius's frequent financial problems and absence from his family (Greta) even before the war. He was on his way to his family home in Mariental from a business trip when he died of a heart attack on the train in 1919. Mentioned in an earlier letter. His son Waldemar (Wolja) suggested to me once many decades later that his father may "have been given to drink."

me, if only I can come to Moscow I will be overjoyed. But I am always anxious that something will happen to stop me from visiting you. What then?

I wrote you about Alice's enrolling for school [in fall]. The teacher, Dirks, said he wanted to take these children now before school closed into the classroom so that he would come to know them a bit. But because of the heavy rain, nothing came of it, so his plan couldn't be implemented and Alice's "great expectations" were frustrated and she was reduced to tears. However, the weather has turned lovely now and the grass is growing too quickly. I am having difficulty writing, feel a bit addled, because I am so excited—as if you are close to me already, but that is impossible. I would be beside myself if I were suddenly told that you were at the station and I was to get you. When will that happen, my treasure. I wrote you in my last letter what my situation is. You probably have received it already. I want to send this letter right away by train. Aunt Tina is going to a meeting in Alexandrovsk with other telephone operators.

We are all healthy, especially the children who usually eat bread with onions and salt between meals. It is very healthy, but their breath, not very pleasant. Earlier today the three were with Susa, Hans, Abram and me at Grandma's [Toews] for coffee—but not Gerhard, of course. Well, for today this is enough. Many greetings and kisses. What I haven't written you, I will tell you personally when I visit. I kiss you again, your loving Tina.

From Tina
Schoenfeld, May 11, 1917

My dear Nicolai,

I am sending you a letter instead of coming in person. I am very sorry but I can't do anything about coming before Pentecost. Besides, I have such a warped nature that I think I will be a bother to people who would take me along. Then I think of the time you had to be troubled with Fast's wife going with you to visit her husband in Moscow. My parents could suggest something that would change the situation but they won't. Now I will wait until after Pentecost and see if Enns will have the pleasure of my company. I am not a small child so he really won't have to look after me. If I come to visit you after Pentecost, you can possibly accompany me home, and then we'd pack up the children and go to Mariental. Isn't that a good suggestion, my dear? Otherwise there will simply be too many people here in one place. Mother can hire the maid, Maria, who was here last year, to do the work I ordinarily do.

Today mother gave us a good scolding. We stood at the street when Franz Rempel stopped by and told us that workers were going to be in short supply, but then he said to Mother, "But you don't have to worry, you have many 'soldiers' [meaning her daughters] here." Mother responded that as soon as the work begins, they [we, her daughters] want to leave. I said to mother that she was the one who wanted us to leave. "But who says that?" Mother asked sharply. Truda said they [the parents] have more work than she can comfortably cope with. So Rempel wondered where we would go if we left. Well, we can feel it increasingly every day that they don't want us around here. They always complain at the table how much flour is used in one month and how much it all costs. When I hear that I could despair. To hear mother, one would think that we do nothing now, but she doesn't take into consideration that we have been without a maid since *Pokrov* [Day of Intercession] and we have taken up the extra work.

Well, that's the way it is in this world. When you read this, you will think, "Yes, Tina wanted it this way. I have always told her that it would happen sooner or later." Of course, we eat here at their table, but the work we do apparently isn't taken into consideration. Usually Greta and I are the last ones to leave the kitchen, taking care of cleaning up, and I do it willingly, but that counts for nothing. The situation is really becoming deplorable. I just want to get away from the nagging. Sometimes I'm ready to burst, but I have to keep silent. That is why I so much want you to come home and take me with the children to Mariental. I don't like to travel alone with them.

Tomorrow Fast is going to Moscow. I ordered some butter from Aron Rempel that I wanted for baking zwieback for you to send you with Fast, but then your brother Johannes came and took it with him. So I have nothing to bake with and we can't get any butter here today or tomorrow. Truda and I want to go to Miraus for coffee. I have not been anywhere since before Easter. But first I want to see where Selma is and then take a nap.

This is where I ended my writing. But in between, I have been to Miraus, have eaten supper, and put Selma to bed, but the other two are still outside. I have cried a lot this week. First, I did not know how I would arrange my trip to Moscow, and today Mama accused me of writing only complaints to you and said that you have often written to me complaining about her. I told her that you had not written anything complaining about her. I then said that if it were not possible to leave the children here [when she goes to Moscow], I would take them to Mariental. Then she was really upset and said that this suggestion of mine was the result of my stubbornness, but my suggestion to take the children to Mariental was really for her benefit.

I just don't know what to think any more. We really can't stay here, and if I go to Mariental, it seems as if that's not the right place either. I just don't know what to do. I doubt Mother has spoken to Papa about us in this manner or he probably would have reprimanded her. Please don't mention to anyone what I have told you about this situation or it might cause a real scandal. I will put up with it until after Pentecost and then a solution can be found. I don't like to complain, but just have to unburden my heart, especially in this situation where I find myself right now. It is not good to be so depressed, right? I believe you will support me in that. I would rather take the children to Mariental before I come to Moscow, but I don't know what I should do. Please write me what you think is best. I will stop my complaining, but if there is no one to comfort me, I despair. Usually things go well, but lately it has not been very smooth. Until now, the married daughters here were of value in Mother's eyes, but I guess the recent daughter-in-law [Willie's wife] will be favored until Mother finds some fault in her. And who knows how soon that will be.

We are all healthy except that I have pain in my sides especially in my abdomen when I cough. and I had a severe toothache last night, but I am fine today. It is probably all about the difficulties I'm having about visiting you. Encourage Enns to let me go along with him when he returns to Moscow, although he probably won't want that. Right now, rye flour is available, but who will take it to the station be sent to you? Gerhard is seldom at home and Papa is occupied with other things, so nothing gets done and I can't do anything about that. Gerhard is leaving on the 15th [for the service?], and he may not return, so I wonder what Papa will do. Susa now has to help in the store.

Day after tomorrow, Mrs. K. Enns is moving and will do some house cleaning at the Heidebrecht's because they want other people to move into their place. It is difficult for her because she has been living there quite long and now she is moving to her parents' in Blumenfeld. It is a good thing that Enns [her husband] is still at home on furlough. Wiens is home on furlough, too. He was with Uncle Peter near Persia [medical service] but now Uncle Peter is the only Mennonite still there. His letters indicate that he is lonely. We heard he is in Chelfa, waiting for the commissar to release him from the service.

My page is full, so I'll close. Tomorrow I will find more paper and then I will add some things to it to make a long letter so that you have something to read. Good night, sleep well and sweet dreams. I did not seal your letter last night. Everything is calm today. Some calves were taken [stolen?] last night but how they did it I don't know. There are workers here from Siberia and Papa has also hired one. He pays him one ruble and fifteen kopeks per day plus room, and he can sleep eight hours. He is a good servant but needs to learn a lot. I have roasted some zwieback [*Reesche Tweeback*] in the oven that I want to take to Fast's tonight. Mother repented of her sins and is very friendly today. Please don't mention what I have written to you.

Many greetings and kisses from the one who loves you, your Tina and children. Send the basket back home if at all possible.

From Nicolai
Moscow, May 18, 1917

My Dearest wife and children,

I just awoke, am sitting on my cot still not dressed, and want to try to answer your letter that Fast brought me. I said, "try," as I don't know if I can give you an appropriate answer to your question. First, because I have in the last while had so little will in me [so depressed] that I can scarcely drive myself to do anything, and second, because it is not easy to respond to the contents of your last letter. Am certainly not in the position to describe to you how painful it is for me when you have such difficult problems [with her mother] that you mention, and ultimately it wouldn't make matters easier for you if I could do that.

It is especially difficult in such situations when I so much want to be with my wife and children to help them, to comfort them, but all I can do is stand by and look at my own helplessness. You write about moving to Mariental. You know quite well what I think about that. Repeatedly you have made attempts to stay there, and again and again you have said, "I can't stand it there; I am so bored in such a isolated nook." And I understand quite well that it is not easy for you to resettle in Mariental after you have been living in a place [Schoenfeld] for three years where you can't hear your own words because of the noise. I am quite certain that if you were to move to Mariental now it would probably be only a few months before you would be drawn powerfully back to Schoenfeld. Without a doubt, you would experience many difficult times, and you would see that it would be impossible to move back. It seems to me that the timing is not good—as mother has said—now that the work has begun "they are leaving." Unless you are absolutely sure that you will hold out to the very end, that is, until I have completed my service, you should be careful what you do. If you leave now when there is work that you are still able to do in your condition [pregnant with Bill, fourth child] and return in winter when the work is not so demanding, and they then have to wait on you (for a while you will need that help,) that does not seem to be appropriate to me.

I hope to be home by fall, but if I am not home then, you will be dependent on others, i.e., your parents. Well, I believe you will take a careful look at the matter and somehow resolve it. I have always allowed you to have your own free will [not interfered] during the time of war in these matters, and you should continue to choose where you want to live. Be careful what you do; don't let your feelings carry you away without giving the matter serious thought. There are always times when one doesn't know what to do, times when you even feel that life has passed you by, and yet we know there are only *few* times when life is that difficult. When mother doesn't get her way, she wanders about complaining all day, so don't be surprised and don't listen to it. It has become her second nature not to be satisfied with anyone or anything and to find not one good person here on the earth. Well, the time may come when our parents will be living with us, and we will repay them, not for what we don't like about them, but just the opposite.

[End missing]

From Nicolai
Moscow, May 21, 1917

My dear Tienchen and children,

I am sitting in my room alone and my thoughts are far, far away from Moscow. My thoughts are in your midst. How I would love to spend these holidays with you to replenish my soul, taking in all the magnificence around us. How lovely were those walks through the meadows and along the streams that we used to share, those wonderful times. Now I am not interested in the least to walk along the boulevard here, which is also very beautiful. But once you are here, it will be so much better, and the whole city of Moscow will then appear to me much lovelier than I see it now.

I am always afraid that something will happen and you will have to postpone your visit to me. It would be most disappointing to me and no less for you, I would imagine. You will enjoy the time you spend here if the trip is not too arduous for you. However, I feel confident that you'll manage this trip well because you have traveled this way often enough. Besides, you have a good travel companion in Hans Enns. Don't let anything discourage you from traveling here with him, even though the relationship between our parents is not exactly smooth. That is a matter between his in-laws and my in-laws. I am referring to that incident with Hans. In spite of that, the relationship between Hermann and me is the best. Simply decide with Enns when you want to leave to come here, and then come if, as you have written, your health permits it. I am waiting impatiently for you.

If possible, and I believe it will be, I will escort you home. Naturally I will just take you home and come right back. However, I believe Lieschen has a real desire to see Moscow, too. Perhaps it is possible for her or one of the other women to come with you, and in that case you can return home with her. And be sure to travel second class since traveling third class today is quite undesirable for women, and it really is not that much more expensive.

I hardly know what else to write. I feel as though it is unnecessary to write much more because we'll be seeing each other soon and then we'll discuss everything. Have you heard anything there about Heinrich? Will he be coming to Moscow or is he staying in the Caucasus? Driediger's brother wrote that four of our Schoenfelder are traveling from Tiflis to Moscow and will make a fourteen-day stopover at home. But I don't know if Heinrich is among them. He hasn't written in a long time.

Now then, my Tienchen, I am closing and forgive me that my letter has so little content. We will be together soon here in Moscow. Soon I will fold you in my arms and hug and kiss you. Would that it were now.

Loving you, your Nicolai

From Nicolai's brother Julius[139]
May 25, 1917

Dear brother Nicolai!

Excuse me that I waited so long with writing. It is not fair and I will try to do better after this. I received your letter and I also forwarded the one you wrote to Lieschen. She sends warm greetings and promises to write soon. The others, and your dear one, send you greetings. Otherwise nothing has changed here. So far your old lady has remained true to you and misses you very much. My vacation has nearly ended, only nineteen days left before I have to return to duty, but there's nothing I can do about my lot at my work place. Even the Devil would show some compassion, right?

From the last letter that you wrote home, it seems that you don't like it there anymore or that you are very bored with your work. Just hang in there, Nicolai. I have to endure my service for two more years, having already served for eight years, and my job is no better than yours. I'm helping out here in the business, too. Sometimes it's hard to keep going, but you just have to resign yourself to it. When you came back from Ruekenau, we believed you that it was impossible to work there, but now we must blame you. However, I don't believe you would let your present feelings stand in the way of completing your service? So keep your chin up.

With heartfelt greetings from your brother, Julius.

[The letter below suggests that there was no correspondence between Nicolai

---

[139] This letter from Julius may be in the wrong place. I am guessing at its date because year is not given. That he has been serving eight years would suggest that the letter maybe from 1917.

and Tina from May 25 till July 16. Nicolai was possibly on furlough part of the time, and we know that Tina spent some time with him in Moscow, as this first letter below suggests. The duration of his furlough, if he had one, and the length of her visit to Moscow is unclear. His opening sentence below, "For almost two months I was not allowed (I did not have) to write letters, or better said, I did not do it," which does not tell us why he has not written for two months. Whatever the reason, the sentence is ambiguous. The sentence of his letter of July 18, "Now our painful communication begins again," seems to suggest that their communication now will be in writing rather that verbal, a correspondence that is dependent on a mail service that is in chaos

From Tina
Schoenfeld, July 16, 1917

My dear, dear Nicolai,

    I am not sitting as comfortably now as I did last Sunday with you. I can't quite adjust to your absence—I have to be here and you there. On the whole I had a good time, though I frequently had to be alone. If it were at all possible, nothing would hold me here and I would come to you with the three girls. Then things would go better between us and I think you would agree with that.

    But let me describe our trip back from Moscow. When we left, we were twelve persons in our compartment all the way to Kharkov. When we arrived the compartment was empty, but six others soon joined us, making it eight. We drank coffee in Kharkov on the train. In Sinelnikov we had to change trains and from there we went to Chaplino. By the time we got there, we were by ourselves and with plenty of room. When we came to Gaichur, Driediger sent a telegram that you probably received. After a short wait, Kornelsen came to get us with his wagon and took us home where all the children came to greet me. They were shy at first then asked why their Papa had not come along. To comfort them I told them that you would come soon. Now they follow me everywhere. When I asked no one was home. Schroeders and Willi Peters left a few days ago to Rosenthal for a few weeks until the prunes are ripe. The same day I arrived, Anna and Susa D. went to Gregarievka to visit Gerhard Peters for one week and so the village is emptier.

    We have a new student from Zagravodka. Willi's father-in-law, Warkentin, brought him to our place. Today is a meeting concerning the opening of the Secondary School. They will hire Unruh and Schroeder from Pastwa as teachers. They may have notified Froese already that he will not be hired. I came home quite angry and informed Papa about Froese. He said this was really stupid, as we have teachers here but may end the contract with Froese simply because they don't want him anymore. So they want to get Schroeder released from the Army, which seems easy to do as he is a medic. I asked Greta if Schroeder looks very ill. She said he has a very good appetite and shows no sign of illness. He has so much money he doesn't know what to do with it. He bought his daughter a gold watch, Peter a silver watch and Truda a sugar box for approximately 100 rubles.

    This is where I stopped my writing because I had to get milk and eat supper. I've had a cold for two days so I slept poorly and my throat felt raw when I coughed.

It is still lingering. Compared to Moscow this place is very mundane. Last Sunday when you and I were at Friesens, I felt a lot better. Well, the children are calling me; they think I have abandoned them.

Friday night thieves broke a window and entered at Jacob Peter's place and stole a lot of stuff. You probably already heard that the Schoenfeld Municipal office is closing. And that we now belong to Brazol Municipality. The new line of division starts at Fasts and ends at Rozhdestvenka. Farmers are now starting to harvest. Gerhard is home for two months. Your brother Hans is home for one-and-a-half months and will leave August 7th.

Time will drag very slowly when you are not home. If you should find some blue cloth for about four to five rubles for five meters, please buy it if you have the money. The children's shoes now cost about fifty rubles. That is a horrendous increase. However, the children are more interested in the ball I brought them and Selma is playing with it right now. I have a headache and you may not enjoy this letter. I will wash the children's feet and lie down. Tomorrow is blue Monday and may be a better day. But today I have no joy in anything, but I have to find it since the children are quite out of sorts. When you will be home things will look up again.

Many affectionate greetings and kisses from your Tina who is always thinking about you. I really enjoyed being with you in Moscow.

The butter costs two rubles seventy-five, and Schroeder does not want to sell me the ham I asked for to send you. Says he needs it for himself in the winter. There is very little fruit available this year either. We've canned only ten containers of cherries. While I was with you, Anna (Tin's sister) was at the Wiebes. She is having back problems and takes frequent salt-water baths and has to rub down her back with salve often. That's what happens when there is no money to hire a maid.

Greetings from your Tina. The children are all healthy and how are you faring in your cubical?

From Nicolai
Moscow, July 18, 1917

My beloved wife and children,

For almost two months I did not have to write letters, or more accurately said, I did not do it. Now our pitiable [painful] communication begins again. How wonderful it was when we could talk over everything and did not have to depend on a mail service that is now in such a terrible state.

As I see from your telegram, you arrived safely in Gaichur and with little delay. How you fared on the rest of your return trip, I don't know, but it was a big load off of my mind when I saw you lying so comfortably in that second-class compartment waiting for the train to leave. I assume that the trip was tolerable to Sinelnikovo. When I observed those poor people standing outside on the steps of the carriage, your seat seemed quite luxurious.

I was very sorry that I showed myself in front of your coach window. While I stood out there for a while looking in at you, you seemed quite relaxed and happy [Said tongue in cheek?], but when you noticed me watching you, your tried to put on a happy face. Oh well, by now you will have got over it. How I feel in my little cell here, you can't even imagine, nor does it really matter. It is dreadful to feel so alone, so abandoned. If I didn't have so much work with my accounting course, I would have moved into the Command Headquarters [commando], but now it is impossible. You can imagine what kind of mood I am in while I sit here writing at my table. However, the sour countenance I wear most of the time, you probably can't envision. But how else should I react? Now no one greets me warmly [as you did] when I come in from work or from my evening class. Now no one has a tasty meal ready for me when I come home from the office, and no one prepares tea for me the way you always did when I would come home away from the office maelstrom. In one word, I FEEL MISERABLE! You can at least delight in the joy of the children at the return of their mother. How did you deal with the toys you took along for them?

Brother Heinrich is in Moscow again. As it sounds, he will be getting a position here, apparently in the store. Brother Aron has been released from the service and is beside himself with joy. The first thing he'll do is to visit his family in Siberia. [They had moved there during the war.] What do you hear from Julius? What is brother-in-law Schroeder up to? And what about father, what's he doing now? Please write me everything. How are our dear little ones? Let me hear from you.

Heartfelt greetings and kisses from your Nicolai

From Tina
Schoenfeld, July 22, 1917

My dear, dear Nicolai,

Again a monotonous Sunday is almost past and I don't regret it at all. You really don't know what to do. The little girls were running about visiting. They don't mind scampering about in such heat, and it is so dreadfully hot and no rain. You will hardly be able to bear it out there in your quarters. On the way home from being with you it seemed quite cool as if autumn had already set in, but how weather can change.

You are probably not taking an hour of free time for yourself, just sitting there with your books and studying. How I wish you could soon see the end and visit your family. I long for my husband, and the children for their father, as never before. How is it possible that we did not think of your birthday on July 8 (20),[140] or did you remember and did not tell me? I remember talking about it shortly before, but then I simply forgot it. Do you remember that we had cherry pancakes for lunch at that day?

When I came home, I was immediately asked if Friesen had a Russian bride [Mennonites rarely intermarried with the Russians; those who did were held in low esteem]. I asked from whom they had heard that. Well, it had been rumored about. It had actually been Frank Peters who had talked about it here when some of us were at the Friesens. So then I had to tell them what really had happened. We hear very little about what will be happening with the school, but I believe it will open, although there may be no teachers. The Schoenfelder are depending on Schroeder

---
[140] Gregorian calendar: See earlier explanation.

[Tina's brother-in-law] and a certain Unruh to come here to teach, but both are at present employed elsewhere. They think the two will be released from service to come here. I asked Papa why they didn't want Froese. He said the people had heard something about him that did not please them. I should have asked if the people here, the Schoenfelder, had at any time liked *any* teacher who had taught here! Well, it might serve them right if they didn't get a teacher at all because they are so hard to please. I don't like it here at all anymore. These people seem to begrudge others anything good. Now they have Aron Rempel to blabber about.[141]

The motor of Mrs. Rempel's threshing machine broke down after they had threshed for a week. Now they blame old Rempel, saying he bought a poor motor for the threshing machine. If he were here in person now, I believe they would stone him. He was here briefly to get his horses from Fast where they had been boarded, and he wanted to stay, but that simply did not work and he had to leave promptly. Mr. Peters recently got a letter from him saying what he thinks of the Schoenfelder—-pretty sad indictment. You should see how Mrs. Rempel now flourishes, puffy cheeks and a wonderful life with her Abraham, who does everything for her from early morning to late at night.

Gerhard has been away to purchase produce, coffee and tobacco. He did get some, so he says. Coffee now costs up to six rubles here and it will probably be more expensive soon. Papa got nine puds of honey from Tesski, and all except three puds at two rubles per pound has been sold. I bought ten pounds for one ruble and fifty kopeks per pound. Perhaps I should have bought more because there is no more available now. If you stay there for the winter, you'll have something to spread on your bread. If you come home in September, there will be no fruit left in the garden. We women and children have spread the manure on the field. We have brought in many loads of straw with the help of a hired man. So that's what we have been doing. Willie has a month's vacation in September but will come home alone and for only one week. Your brother Aron has now completed his service. I am happy for him. He is probably with his Lenchen [in Siberia] now. When will you come home and say, "I am completely separated from Moscow." I enjoyed myself very much when I was there with you. I would move to Moscow without hesitation right now if you were to take a job there.

And who washed your floors yesterday? Is Thiessen cooking a decent noon meal now and then? How are the bedbugs fairing in your bed? Is Heinrich staying in your quarters now? Greet your landlord and Friesen's old lady. I really enjoyed it at their place. Our girls keep asking me whether we will soon all go to visit Papa in Moscow. They think that I will soon take them to Mariental, but that probably won't happen. You may ask why I am writing in such choppy sentences, but I like to write in short sentences rather than long ones. How are things going there now? Can you notice any big changes? Are the trams still running as before?

It's been so quiet in the house until now and I've been very comfortable by myself, but suddenly the place has burst with noise. I don't want to leave the house in my condition [pregnant]. I always feel the people are staring at me, so I stay home. Until November I will not let myself be seen in public very often.

---

[141] The couple is separated, not acceptable behavior in the Mennonite communities.

I wrote this far yesterday. I got some visitors tonight, Franz Wiens's young people. I regret that I did not know that Peter Peters and Mrs. J. Peters left for Moscow tonight, otherwise I would have sent something along with them, at least a letter. Apparently there is a lot of cloth to be had in Moscow, and if that's true, then Papa also wants to go there [to purchase some for the store]. The children are all lying in their beds humming and yawning. I feel a lot of movement within me especially when I am lying down so that at times I can hardly stand it. I did not sleep well when I was at your place, but in spite of that I would gladly come back to be with you. Everything went so well, even when I had to be alone, but then you'd come home. Who makes tea for you in the evening now or don't you get any?

Tomorrow is laundry. Many greetings and kisses from the one who loves you, who longs for you, as do the children. Your Tina. Greetings to Enns. Enjoy yourselves.

From Nicolai
Moscow, July 25, 1917

My beloved Tinchen,

I received your letter July 16th some time ago. I am sorry that I did not answer it immediately. I intended to answer it on Sunday, but I was invited to visit Kornelius Wiens, so I sacrificed my free time that I designated for you and gave that up to visit some poor fellows in prison.[142] So brother Heinrich, Isaak Friesen and I drove down to visit them on Sunday. Wiens was enormously happy to see us and I no less to see him. Unfortunately, it was raining, so that we had to spend the time indoors. I met quite a few acquaintances there; among them were Doerksen and Liese Dueck's husband. The fellows are generally rather undernourished because the meals in prison are inadequate, but they at least get enough bread to satisfy their hunger and they are happy about that, and are generally satisfied with the food. However, the way they are treated leaves a bit to be desired. The barrack in which these fellows are housed is really not arranged very comfortably. It is quite impossible to feel comfortable on the makeshift beds and straw mattresses without sheets.

Quite a few wives had visited their husbands, and some wives were still there. I really felt sorry for those fellows because they look with envy on us who have as much freedom as we have. Friesen brought a basket of eggs, some meat and bread and a bottle of schnapps so that we had a nice lunch. Wiens is known to enjoy a Morgenstern [schnapps] from time to time and was quite pleased to get one. So this is the short report of our brief visit there at the prison camp.

But now a word about our situation here. Our work is going as usual, but it is now certain that our organization [United Council of the Nobility] will be shutting down here in September. We will then have to find employment elsewhere or others will find places of employment for us.[143] If brother Johannes is still at home [He was stationed in Berdiansk], please ask him if there may perhaps be a place of

---
[142] It is unclear why they are in prison.
[143] Nicolai would like to be transferred to Berdiansk, closer to home, not far from Mariental.

employment for me in Berdiansk. If there were, I would move there. But the request for me to be released from my post here and be transferred there has to be initiated from that end. But his request has to be made before the end of August, and then they would be happy to transfer me I think. I would write Johannes about this if only I knew how long he is going to be home.

Well, I just reread your letter where you clearly state that he has to leave by the seventh of August. How is your health? Have you recovered fully from your visit? If I am lucky and things work out, I will be in Berdiansk soon, but for the time being it is still a big question mark.

Heartfelt greetings from your Nicolai.

From Nicolai
Moscow, August 3, 1917

My deeply loved wife and children,

Again time has elapsed since I received your letter of July 22 and I have not answered. You will be very dissatisfied with me and for a good reason. I beg you to be patient for another month, and then I'll be out of this soup in which I find myself drowning at the moment and will answer your letters more promptly.

At present I am terribly busy. In addition to the work at the chancery, I am studying for the final examinations in accountancy but will be finished on the 20th. I am so sick and tired of this military service and all it entails; if it weren't for you and the children, I would wish to die—that's how tired I am of living under these confining conditions. When will we be able to live a normal life, have a normal family life? When will I be freed to return home? I see no hope for that. I sit here as though in a prison cell. All I do is go to work and when hunger really drives me, I go out and try to buy something to quiet my stomach. For two days I've lived only on coffee and tea again, but in spite of it, feel no hunger. Several times I've cooked borscht and a tasty one at that, but that takes time.

People here fear a very severe winter, look to a bleak future, and feel there will be nothing to eat. And in general you sense a massive despondency descending on the public. Everyone is trying to secure various documents in order not be arrested and imprisoned. Endless numbers of deserters are caught, and the officials sniff into every nook and cranny for persons without documents. Actually, one's life is not at all safe. Just a minor altercation and immediately a large mob gathers, ready to lynch anyone whom they see as a culprit. Yesterday I witnessed a scene I shall never forget—-soldiers trying to rescue a man from a mob who would surely have killed him except for the soldiers. He had already been beaten severely and could see nothing but the face of a mob that was ready to tear him to pieces. Several soldiers tried to persuade the mob not to kill him and rather turn him over to the court, but the rabble screamed, "Kill him! Kill him!" The man I am writing about was the superintendent of the hospital. And his "crime" was that he had placed the bodies of some soldiers, who had died in the hospital, naked into coffins and this was the result. But enough! Enough of this!

You asked whether I remembered my birthday on July 20. Yes, I thought about it and remembered it even while we were eating the cherry pancakes. However, you forgot the occasion? I guess it wasn't that important. I always remember your birthday without anyone reminding me. I didn't think it was suitable to ask you to wish me luck. The floors in my room are no longer being washed, and the bed bugs have more freedom now than when you were here. My landlords are well and send you greetings.

Could you please send me twenty kilograms of butter with Driediger when he returns to duty here? Alice's shoes will be ready soon. I have not looked for the cloth you requested but will do so soon. What does Alice say about entering school soon? Please write me everything that is happening there.

Affectionate greetings and kisses from your Nicolai.

From Tina
Schoenfeld, August 13, 1917

My dear Nicolai,

I am sitting in the veranda where it is quite cool and conducive to writing, with no flies around. Yesterday Selma received her birthday card. She was very happy for it and everyone had to have a look at it. Today there was a horse congress here [Horses and drivers requisition to the war effort]. It was voluntary and so there were so few. As for fruit in our orchard, well, there's actually not much: three trees of late plums and some late pears. That is all. By the time you come home, there will be nothing left. We picked some of the plums while they were still green and canned them. The fruit and vegetables in the gardens are being pilfered. One night even our bucket together with the rope was stolen and several trees were stripped of their fruit. In the evenings now we always take everything valuable from our summer kitchen into the house. The workers are dragging off even the green watermelons from the field, so unfortunately I'll probably not have any left for pickling.

On Sunday we had a visitor after church, Henry Loewen's brother, a widower. He has been working at Jacob Klassen's to help with the threshing. Loewen told us how very poorly the workers there were being fed. He had been there for two months and had not been served butter once. Well, the butter does cost three rubles twenty-five kopeks per pound and that, of course, is much too expensive for a man as rich as Klassen. They have really gone overboard with greed. Driediger is here on furlough until the first of next month. I am pleased for him, but your furlough keeps being postponed, always being pushed back further. Perhaps with luck you can come home for two months, October and November. That would be wonderful!

Nickel is teaching in Mariental. He used to board in Johannes's home but now Epp lives there. Schroeder is off to Rosenthal today to get a cow. When he returns, they will be moving into a residence at the teachers training school here. Our children are very happy about that since they will then have one more place to go visiting. Yesterday Julius drove someone to Kharkov and earned 300 rubles and he also sold some things there. Quite a good income in two weeks. He swapped his two tables for some clothes with Schroeder. If Greta had allowed it, he would have sold many other things, and that would have been quite stupid, but she wouldn't allow it. Suddenly he had enough money to take on his trip. Well, it's really none of my business. I have to keep my concerns to myself.

A little livewire, Selma, is sitting beside me and I can't get rid of her. She is such a chatterbox, so I am continually interrupted to answer her questions. Just now she asked me, "How did you say to Papa that he should buy you a hat? Can you buy me a hat?" She goes on chattering away at my side. We recently received some merchandise for the store, so I bought some cloth at only one ruble fifteen kopeks per meter to sew clothes for the children. But I have to stop writing now to go and milk the cow as there was no one home except Susa, and she always wants to be begged to do it. Mother, Father, Loewen and Mrs. Doerksen are sitting in the front veranda. They are still talking about the teacher situation here that has not been settled. Unruh first sent a telegram and followed that with a letter, saying that the decision to come here would not be made until August 15th, and further decisions concerning the school can't be made till then. But now our wagon just left to take the visitors home. Klassen has no horses to fetch them.

I got to this point when I had stopped my writing because and I had to make supper. Everyone had gone visiting except my girls and I. It's 10:00 and everyone has returned from their visits but the girls are still running about the room. Today at noon I wanted to take a nap but it did not happen. First one person came through the room and then another one and in between Father came through taking the mousetrap outside to fill it with fresh water. By then I was so annoyed that my sleep was gone. When you come home things will improve. Do write me if I should go to Mariental or stay here.

The parents are talking about taking in boarders. Then the house will be quite full. If I knew that I could get a competent midwife in Mariental, would go there, and I would not be so anxious and unsettled. The family will soon decide if we will hire a cook or not. Mika [her youngest sister] has been at the Wiebes and has been complaining of a bad back, so she has to take care of herself. But who will finally do all the work around here? I can't do as much as I want to, nor can Greta. Mother will have to involve herself more in the daily chores. When Greta, Anna and I all leave home, mother will realize what we have been contributing to this household. You may see my list of grievances as a preachment, but I am writing this so that you will understand our situation here.

Alice has little ambition to learn and she does not like to babysit, but in time she will improve. Tomorrow I want to sew her a dress for school, and she is happily looking forward to that. The children are all healthy as am I, but that stitch especially in my right side continues to bother me. I wake up at night from it. Sometimes I shift around for hours until the pain subsides. Mrs. Harder is not here or I would have asked what the problem might be. Business in the store is going as usual. Yesterday Fast bought 200 rubles worth of rather expensive cloth but everything is expensive now.

I left off finishing the letter yesterday because I wanted to add something. So now that I have had breakfast; I'll finish and then I'll go to clean up the kitchen. Anna, Susa and the two girls went to pick cucumbers and that will take them until eleven o'clock, so I am alone. Selma is a real early bird. She is up while the others are still in bed and that works out better since I still have to help her to put on her stockings and shoes. Butter will probably be four rubles per pound, so should I send some with Driediger at this price? The price is going up every day and besides, it is not even available here in Schoenfeld. We got butter from Wiens fourteen days ago, but 2 percent of it was water. We have hold our tongues about that or there will no butter at all. Are you surviving like a hermit in your little prison? For how long is Enns coming home? I wish that you could finish your exams soon and then have a chance to rest a while. Maybe information about the school here will be announced soon [Alice will begin first grade].

Many greetings and kisses from your Tina and children who are desperately waiting for you to come home. Truda sends greetings.

From Nicolai
Moscow, August 15, 1917

My dear Tina,

For some time I have been carrying two of your letters in my pocket that have been unanswered, and I don't feel good about that. I will report to you with what I have been occupied lately, and then you will understand why I have been silent for so long.

Tomorrow I will go to my accounting courses for the last time until I sit for the examinations in December, so that's all behind me. But for tomorrow I have to prepare an inhuman mountain of work. Lately I have had so much to do that my letters to you have become rare. And in addition to all that, I was promoted to supervisor here at the chancery.

As you know, we no longer get our noon meals here at the chancery, and the Commission won't even hear our request to supply our meals. Furthermore, this whole matter of our organization, whether it will continue to exist or not, has always been in question and even to this day it has not been made clear [Contradicts letter of July 25]. To our request that they give us something to eat, not merely the handout of two rubles per day, we got this answer: "We will give you two rubles daily, a stove and fuel, so then cook for yourselves whatever you desire." For better or for worse, we accepted this offer, chose an "economist" to buy the food and to make sure the noon meal is prepared every day. And I have been designated as that person, for the time being at least, and I accepted simply because they asked me to do it. I have been released from the secretarial work, but I now have the "pleasure" of running about from six in the morning to five or six in the evening trying to find food for us.

It is not an easy task to buy the food in such a large city when there is always a shortage. Vegetables are still available, but you can get meat only with a certificate [ration card] from a government agency. It is the same for bread, cereal, barley and so on. You need to get a permit for everything you buy. I have been to the all food committees (agencies) and supply services in order to get the necessary papers to buy the produce we need, but have achieved nothing. Tomorrow I am going to the city council and maybe a decision will be made there. The products that are still available become more expensive and scarce every day.

What will happen in winter, I don't know. It looks very grim to me. If it were possible to have these products sent from an outlying region, then I would requisition them from the South. However, you are taking a chance in doing that because you may find that the requisitioned food is as expensive and as scarce as it is here. But I will stop with this matter now.

It is soon time for my furlough. In September I am at the front of the line. However, I don't know what to do. Should I come home in September or mid-October to stay with you until everything is past? [She is pregnant with Bill.] If I were to come in September and stay with you for one month, I would probably not be allowed to come home until November and only after I received a telegram from you [informing him of the birth] and then at most a stay of only fourteen days. We can assume that the birthing then would take place without me. If I came the middle of October, then naturally you would have me beforehand for fourteen days. And you, I believe, would be quite comfortable, that is, because you would have your husband with you sooner. If we agree to the latter, we will still have a full two months before we will see each other. And I long to see you all so very much, even now. Please let me know what I should do, what would please you the most, my dearest. And I will do that. If you tell me to stay here until October, I'll do that with joy. And the time for me, if I am fulfilling your wish, will seem like a mere blink of the eye. I am prepared to do everything for you. It gives me great joy to please you. Please write me immediately what you want.

Now I'll move on to answer your questions. I see, my dearest Tina, that you don't feel too well at times. Although you never complain, I sense it clearly in your letters. It would please me if you were more specific about how you feel when you write. Wouldn't it be possible for you to spare yourself a little more and stay off of your feet, even though you think you can bear up well? I am sure that everyone at home knows you are not lazy and that you work as much as you possibly can. No one would fault you if you were to give your own welfare a little more attention. If I could comfort you, be with you, and lighten your load, how gladly I would do it. Were I in a right relationship with God, even a letter from me would ease your burden. Yet I don't want to desecrate God's Word because if a person does not stand in a right relationship with God, and yet speaks God's words, he brings more harm than good.

Let's be patient, my dear, the sun will break through for us and the dismal, dark, difficult time will change to a time of happiness and good fortune. When I sit here alone in my quarters, I always recall the lovely time with you here. How much better it will be when we can be together again as free people. I still don't know what the situation is concerning my being transferred to Berdiansk. I have been to see Friesen twice. Brother Heinrich does not live with me. I have not been to the eye specialist yet. If at all possible, send me twenty pounds of butter with Driediger and some zwieback, but not too many. I will use them only with my coffee. Actually we are eating well enough now.

Tell Papa that if he wants to order something, I will gladly try to get it for him since I am running around the city all day anyway. I bought shoes for Alice and will send them soon. Greet the parents and siblings heartily. I send you most heartfelt greetings and kisses. Your Nicolai.

P.S. Our superintendent, Franz Wiebe, is very ill with typhus. I think Berg from Schoenfeld will soon be home.

From Tina
Schoenfeld, August 20, 1917

My dear Nicolai,

It is Sunday again today, but no church because it rained so hard that no one could go. It began raining on Friday and stopped a little while ago; now we have beautiful sunshine. Willie has a month of vacation and was here alone for a few days and left today. The rest of his furlough he will spend over there with his wife. That fellow misses his Greta so much [his wife, nee Margaret Warkentin]. Maybe he will get another month's furlough in October, then they both want to come here. He bought this month of furlough for thirty-three rubles [Bribe?]. If you come at that time, you can meet them again. But his Greta has said she won't let anyone see her [pregnant], and I feel that way, too. In public one always gets teased and that is to be avoided.

Yesterday morning, the teacher from Johannesheimer arrived and Toews' things were to be transported on the same wagon, but they can't go on account of the rain. Toews said one more year in the government office and he would die. Mrs. Toews was moved to tears when she talked about their time here. She had been so happy then. She was anxious to see all the girls. She thinks Selma looks like a boy, but what's wrong with that? We have a German[144] farmhand now who likes Selma very much. He tells her that she is his sister, but she says, "No, I am not your sister," and then goes to him readily. He is a very good farmhand and we have so much work. Most of the straw has been brought in. Two loads of chaff and three loads of straw are stacked in the hayloft. Last year I helped to stack the straw, too, but this year I will leave that to others. If only November were here! [The baby was due then.] Alice is standing beside me and wants me to order a slate and a box of slate pencils. We can't buy any slates here in the store. Maybe you can buy one there and send it with Enns.

How did your bookkeeping courses go? Were you successful and satisfied with the results? Days will probably be easier for you now, and if you could come home permanently that would be the very best. Your brother Johannes is home again for two months. He probably didn't accomplish anything in Berdiansk or he would have told me about it. I hope he will be good enough to bring in the straw at Mariental so that when we go there for the winter, we won't have to freeze with our children. I received a letter from mother recently. Annie Tessman is finally relieved of her long suffering. The poor children so young and already without a mother. L. was here for two days and did he tell stories again!

I stopped writing here to give the children their supper and to put them to bed. Then Anna, Susa and I went to visit Truda briefly while Mika stayed here with the children. Truda was home alone with her two children. They had three big

---

[144] The German farmhand is undoubtedly a prisoner of war as they were used widely in the Mennonite settlements; these were more often Austrian than German, but Mennonite attribution of identities could be hazy (Urry).

watermelons, very good ones, from Rosenthal. Yesterday we harvested three baskets full, little ones, a bit bigger than a fist, just big enough to pickle. But the crop is poor.

I must write you what kind of teachers they have hired. First of all is Schroeder; then a Thiessen, unmarried, and 29 years old; and a Miss Loewen. I don't know where she's from. We are hearing more and more about that teacher Froese. He is supposed to be the biggest skunk [Schweinegal] you can imagine, and it is high time that we got rid of him, but the people here are stupid enough to keep him on. Unruh has declined the position. So that's the story of what's happening here at Schoenfeld. Schroeder bought a buggy and a 15-year-old horse and they also have a cow here.

It is half-past twelve, but I'm not sleepy. Tomorrow there will be in a mad rush again as soon as we get up. Mother is out and about at six o'clock already and I had no nap at noon. I went to bed around twelve last night but couldn't sleep until two. My sides ached so much but I feel fine now. Today we had a heavy thunderstorm and in Liubimovka lightning struck a house and a barn, burning them down to the ground. At one time the thunder was terribly loud. Had news today that teacher Dueck and his wife are waiting to be picked up at the Gaichur station. Our team and wagon came from the station at eleven o'clock before they arrived, so I don't know what they will do. Perhaps Father will send our horses and buggy for them, although the white horse is quite lame. Now they want to make Father overseer of the refugees, as though he hasn't got enough work to do. Even now he can't keep up with everything. It sounds as though the trains are going to stop running entirely here beginning August 22. What is the situation there? Probably not too good either.

It is cold today. Selma is sitting beside me chattering constantly. She asked me if I was going to spank her. It seems as though I can't write letters any more. Perhaps it's because I always feel that you will be home shortly and then we can discuss everything. Miss Harder is not here or I would have her examine me.

Well, many greetings and kisses from your loving Tina and the children as well.

From Nicolai
Moscow, August 27, 1917

My dearly beloved wife and children,

I feel the same as you that it really doesn't pay to write many more letters because I hope to see you all soon. I had actually planned to come home on furlough before the 1st of September. Now, however, it will drag out a bit longer, approximately till the 10th. In fact, I still don't know how you are going to respond to my letter whether you want me to come now or you prefer that I wait until October to come. If you would prefer that I come in October, I'll cancel my September vacation.

Am working to get a hearing with the Commission, but I don't know how it will turn out. Went to see a doctor about my eyes and he merely scolded me for not wearing my glasses. Then I went to see an ear, nose and throat doctor, and he gave me such a litany of things that should be done to me so that I really don't know what to think. First of all he said I had a serious ear infection. He then found that my nose was not as it should be and that I definitely had to have it corrected surgically. He says there is no open passageway between the two nostrils, so the nose bone [septum] needs to have a hole bored through it, so that the ears can heal. Our doctor says that such an operation is very complicated, so that I am rather reluctant. Tomorrow I will go to the best nose doctor (*Nasen Arzt*) here in Moscow and see what he says. Well, let the doctors say what they want, I can always make the decision whether I'll have it. I would like from the depth of heart to be freed from this detestable service and be with all of you.

As for my job here, I am continuing it for the present at least. I buy whatever produce I can find for the kitchen and keep accounts of them. It would be child's play to serve "in this position" if Moscow were not so short of everything for which the stomach craves. Now, however, you have to run around a lot. When I come home, I want to see if I can buy things for our kitchen there, things that may, however, be in short supply there already also.

This is what I had written before lunch and will try to finish it now. Enns has been staying here in my quarters for a while already because the compound where the commando stays is being used for training. I feel better now that I am not sitting alone in my prison. Enns has gone to bed early, and I will take advantage of this time to have a chat with you. Usually we don't get to bed before twelve o'clock. This past week has been very difficult. You may have already heard Phillip Wiebe died on Monday, and we laid him in his grave on Thursday. The interment was postponed that long because we believed some of his relatives would come, but only his good friend came, a Mr. Friesen from Millerovo with whom Wiebe's youngest daughter, a 6-year-old girl, had been staying. Naturally he had brought the little girl along. Wiebe's oldest daughter (17) had sent a letter here in the hope that someone would read it to her father if he was no longer able to read it himself. It was a very sad letter. A number of Wiebe's friends here in Moscow came for the funeral so that about sixty persons followed the coffin. It was about fifteen to sixteen versts from the hospital to the cemetery, a "nice walk" on Moscow's cobble stones. In spite of the weather, the old general and our doctor walked almost the whole distance behind the coffin. Until now, no one has become sick with typhoid, seemingly no one was infected. God protect us all from such a severe disease.

Again my letter was not completed. I will make another attempt today, the 29th, maybe I will get it finished today. Everyone here is very much disturbed by General Kornilovs conduct. [*Verhalten*] The fellow wants to bring the government down but will probably be brought to the gallows himself for his behavior. People are really quite outraged about Kornilov.[145] The soldiers as a whole are generally in support of the government. I have heard nothing further today, but it is still early. Well, you will have also heard all about it and the rest we will discuss when I come home.

Until then, heartfelt greetings from your loving Nicolai.

---

[145] This was an attempted coup d'état by General Lavr Kornilov in August 1917 against Kerensky's Provisional Government; he attempted to send troops to Petrograd but was thwarted by the railroad workers. He was later killed by a shell at the start of the Civil War. See George Katkov, *Russia 1917: The Kornilov Affair. Kerensky and the Break-up of the Russian Army* (London: Longman, 1980).

From Nicolai [Nicolai had been home.]

Moscow, September 26, 1917

My beloved Tienchen and children,

I have been in Moscow again for a few days. I haven't settled in yet, nor have I organized my living quarters. Up to this point, I have been very busy selling the butter and the lard, but now that I have gotten rid of it all, I'll finally let you hear something from me.

As usual, I will describe my trip back here first. In Gaichur it was with some difficulty that I checked in the produce. Then at Sinelnikovo, I gave the porter a healthy tip to load my baggage onto the train I was taking. So I managed to get all of my things safely and quickly to Moscow, even from the station to my living quarters. The train was quite overcrowded, but we were eight in one compartment, and it wouldn't hold more even though people almost broke in the door a few times. And so I arrived here whole and happy.

Am back living in the barracks again, but I find this scene here so disgusting that it's beyond description. My manager asked me why I had returned so soon, and when I told him, he said he would gladly give me permission to leave at the end of October. Putting my request to the Commission is a bit precarious; I don't know what their disposition is at present. Brother Heinrich's request for a month's furlough was granted but not without difficulty. He has also been released from government service. There is no talk of peace here, at least not among the ruling wealthy (Besitzenden-propertied class) who see no prospect for peace. But the poor have a different view. There is great fear that our soldiers will soon return from the West and matters could become as bad as if the enemy were here. On the whole, things are running as usual. The old soldiers who had reached the age of 21 in 1895–96 have been discharged already, and orders have been given to discharge those of 21 years in 1897–98. But how long will it be before the 1909 [Nicolai was born in 1888] will be discharged? Well, eventually our turn will come.

How are things at home? Are you still quite healthy, my dearest? Has Miss Harder arrived in Schoenfeld yet? What about Gerhard, is he home already? Please write me everything. I will write more when I am settled in.

Heartfelt greetings, your Nicolai. Regards to the parents and siblings.

From Tina[146]

Schoenfeld, October 18, 1917

My dearest,

Ah, finally it is Saturday evening and although we have guests, I am in the annex and have settled in here with my children. Recently I received your letter, and the most important thing you wrote is that you will come home at the end of October. I have arranged the front room so that we can be alone at times. The other good

---

[146] This letter of October 18 is possibly last of the correspondence between Tina and Nicolai because this was written shortly before the November takeover by the Bolsheviks (the coup d'état). Some notes among his papers suggest that he came home at the beginning of November.

thing is that I have started to heat the place but not too warm. We want to install the storm windows and that will improve the situation, too. This week I washed the feather bedding and filled the blankets again. Now I want to patch and knit so that the children are well dressed when I will be laid up. If only my delivery were today rather than one month from now when it should all be over—that is, if everything goes well [Bill was born November 21, 1917]. No one will be happier than me or you, of course.

Horses are being stolen almost every night around here now. We have a lot of binder twine in the barn—two wagonloads were brought here. The Halbstadt Committee bought some of the twine today as well as a binder [harvester]. I don't seem to enjoy writing any more. I guess it is because you will be coming home soon. I will be waiting for you on the 23rd. I feel rather uncomfortable sleeping in this house, but when you come, things will change. Friesen is sleeping in the spare room that we have arranged for him.

[End missing.]

— End of Nicolai and Tina's correspondence —

The letter below of November 17, 1917, was the last in the bundle of letters that Nicolai gave me in 1956. He was home in Schoenfeld with his family then. A fragment of a note among his papers and from the few times I recall him relating his last days in Moscow. These suggest that he was in Moscow later than November 7, 1917. The letter below addressed to Herr Steiniger shows Nicolai looking with optimism to the future, hoping to set up a business where he can apply his accounting skills and the business experience he gained in retail and farm machinery sales working in his father-in-law's firm. It seems a bit ironic that Nicolai would appear so optimistic at this time. Wanting to sell meat products to the military? However, he did move rather freely across the emotional landscape during his years in the war. Perhaps someone who has studied the effects of war on soldiers can explain what seems rather paradoxical in the situation. Of course, looking back at that time in history, we see how quickly civil order was mutated into civil war and the misery and suffering that followed.

From Nicolai
Schoenfeld, November 17, 1917

Honored Herr Steiniger:

I have discussed this matter of the slaughterhouse with H. E. Loewen. As I told you some time ago, H. E. Loewen was the foreman in the Schoenfeld slaughterhouse for some time and is willing to help build up a similar slaughter business, that is, to act as foreman until someone can be found to manage the whole business. The company that developed the slaughterhouse in Halbstadt had a contract with the government agency roughly outlined below.

The company financed the entire project, including purchasing the hogs, slaughtering them and then delivering the hams and the bacon to the military. The rest of the hogs they could dispose of as they wanted: the lean meat, feet, head, liver, lungs and so forth. Because the company was able to keep so much of the meat that the government did not want, it made sense for the company to set up its own sausage manufacture. So they produced a variety of sausages that they were able to sell without any problems. Sausages, of course, have the advantage over fresh meat in that they can be more easily preserved.

If we should agree to start a business modeled on the one in Halbstadt, then we would have the following expenditures:

Two large water kettles @ 60 rubles each	120 rbl
One large sausage-kneading trough 40	40 rbl
Three large slaughter tables (7 feet x 3½ feet) @40 rubles ea	120 rbl
Two meat grinders @ 80 rubles each	160 rbl
One sausage machine	120 rbl
One large scale	180 rbl
One small scale	100 rbl
Twenty various knives	200 rbl
One sprayer for salting shanks	150 rbl
Two axes @ 20 rubles each	40 rbl
Three barrels @ 50 rbl each	150 rbl
Eight crates 3 feet deep X 1 1/2 wide for brine @100 each	800 rbl
One grindstone	30 rbl
One steel scraper, rope, hooks, other small items	150 rbl
Other unforeseen expenditures	400 rbl
The sum is	2,600 rbl

This sum is required to set up the facility.

Then we also need a wagon or at least horses. I have a wagon and harnesses.

The horses would cost at least	1,500 rubles
The travel cost to arrange all this is	300 rubles
A small mechanism to make the sausage would cost	500 rubles
The rental, fuel and the salt to begin with	1,000 rubles
To start the whole business, we would require a minimum amount of	10,000 rubles.

We would also require workers, as H. E. Loewen suggested. In addition we would also need:

One eviscerator (would also be the manager) at a monthly salary	400 rubles
Four men to lance, singe and hang the carcass @ 200 rubles per month	800 rubles
Two dissectors @ 250 rubles	500 rubles
Two men to clean casings @ 200 ruble each	400 rubles
Three men for various jobs @ 200 ruble each	600 rubles
One laborer @	150 rubles
Total sum of	3,350 rubles

We would payout in monthly salaries of 3,350 rubles and could slaughter 200 hogs per month with these employees.

In total 2,000 puds @ three rubles per pud works out to 6,000 rubles. This leaves us 2,650 rubles. From this sum we subtract for salt, pepper, etc. at least @ two rubles per hog, an amount of 400 rubles the above cost. Amortization of the inventory is 10 percent, that is, 600 rubles. Feed for the horses and unforeseen expenses are 150 rubles per month.

The sum total is 1,500 rubles and leaving a profit of 1,150 rubles per month.

Now I don't have the faintest idea what the income from the sausage production would be. The other question is whether we could get a commitment to provide 200 hogs per month. In my opinion, we should insist that they provide us at least 200 hogs per month; we could in fact slaughter more. We are then guaranteed that the business could run without a loss. Whether we have to deliver only the bacon and the ribs, as it was done in Halbstadt, or the bacon and the hindquarters is not known.

Concerning the site where to build the slaughterhouse, we would have to discuss this together. Concerning the fuel, the building and the wagon, *Schoenfeld* would be most preferable, without a doubt. It seems to me what is most inconvenient is that the veterinarian is so far away. I would like to make a suggestion. Because I currently have no capital and do not have the possibility of putting any money into the business, I would gladly offer my service. I would commit myself to this endeavor as a responsible person. For this service, I would get a specific salary and a percentage of the net profit. Naturally I would like to be a partner in this endeavor and share in the profits, but that expectation would be wrong and so I am making such a suggestion. Should you agree to take responsibility for the business and agree to my suggestion, then be so kind and inform me as soon as possible.

In expectation of your quick response, I remain your N. Rempel.

A year after the above letter was written, Nicolai and Tina received the letter below from Susa Peters, Tina's sister, who was in Berdiansk preparing for a teaching career. Her letter points to the encroaching civil war, the threat of renewed marauding and pillaging that had been begun churning at the end of 1917, especially in the Mennonite colonies.

From Susa Peters
November 21, 1918

Dear Tina and Nikolai!

I thought I would get a letter from you by now, and you were probably expecting one from me, right? I've been trying to prepare for my classes tomorrow but have given it up. I get terribly sleepy when I try to study at night Actually I will have time to study tomorrow morning because I don't have to go to school [Gymnasium] until after 12:00.

I was at home (Schoenfeld) about two weeks ago and found out that you had just been there shortly before. Mika Wiens came with me, too. As soon as I got back to Berdiansk I was ill (naturally the Spanish flu) and had to stay in my room the whole week. I would have been bored if Mika Wiens hadn't been here. She kept me company all week and didn't go to school either.

Nikolai, I always thought you would come to see me since you were here often last year. What occupies your time now, Tina and Nikolai? You, Tina, are probably knitting, sewing and mending like all mothers do and you Nikolai are reading the newspaper, smoking and grumbling. Am I right? Alice is studying diligently, Hilda and Selma are working hard at making a lot of noise and Willie (born November 1917) must be running about by now.

Nothing is changing here. My petty worries are how to get my shoes to the shoemaker and my jacket to the dressmaker, but my big worry is that the teacher doesn't call on me very often to answer a question. Then, of course, all of us are great fear that the Bolsheviks will dominate again [*die Oberhand geniessen*]. I haven't heard from home for two weeks [since she left], don't even know if they are still alive. They say Makhno is not too far away from here now, and that the German army is leaving, perhaps tomorrow already. Many German soldiers have already left. There won't be any left [German military] in the villages. Berdiansk is again in wartime preparedness: We have curfew from 12:00 midnight to 6:00 a.m.

Our light is so poor that my eyes smart especially when I try to read or write. You probably have no light at all? Please write soon, that would be such a comfort in my loneliness. I am fed up with this place and can hardly wait till Christmas. My address is Berdiansk, Vostochni. PR. No 40, S. Petuos. I'm staying in the same room that I had the first year but I'm eating with a Russian family.

Greetings from Susa.

EPILOGUE

Civil War

These letters cover the three-and-a-half years during WWI while Nicolai was away from his family. They began with Nicolai leaving his family in September 1914, when he entered the service as a medic—a loyal subject of *"the father of this land, Tsar Nicholas II."* Three years later in February 1917, he was no long a monarchist but a social democrat heartened by the forced abdication of the Tsar whom he so revered in 1914. On May Day 1917, he marched to the drumbeat of "La Marseillaise" through the streets of Moscow with thousands of others who called for freedom and equality and for the *workers of the world to unite*. He asked Tina if the citizens of Schoenfeld had joined the Revolution yet, and warned that they had better shape up because great changes were coming where the privileged rich would have to share their wealth with the poor. But as time wore on, the rosy picture began to fade. He reported increasing food shortages, violence, and the breakdown of civil order in the streets of Moscow. By the time he returned home for good in November 1917, those calls for equality and freedom were muffled by Russia's collapse into the chaos of civil war.

These letters are a slide show, glimpses into the lives of this couple separated by war and its impact on them during that interval. Nicolai came home a bruised man, quite different from the man who left in 1914. The hardships Tina had to endure, although not as defined as Nicolai's, were trying, caring for their three daughters and helping in her parents' household where the atmosphere was sometimes thick with stress. Often several of her sisters lived under the same roof with their children while their husbands were also away in the service. In the letters Tina again and again expressed the wish for a place of her own, a wish that was finally fulfilled a decade later, in 1928, in Alberta, Canada, when the family were able to buy a farm and moved into its dilapidated, clapboard house.

Their war correspondence ended in November 1917, with Nicolai standing at the door, being greeted by his family with hugs, kisses and tears of joy. As I said in the introduction, these letters are unique only in that they take us directly into the day-to-day struggles of Nicolai and Tina as they try to hold their marriage together. We come to know this couple quite intimately, perhaps too intimately. When my father gave me those two bundles of letters some six decades ago, he told me to take from them what I thought fit for the family, possibly as a reminder to his grandchildren of their heritage, and then to burn them. By publishing these letters I have exposed my parents to the public, but not without considerable self-questioning, doubt and guilt. The letters do show some of Nicolai and Tina's weaknesses and blemishes: Nicolai's unjust castigations and preachments, Tina's agonizing guilt and feelings of inadequacy. But they also show their finer qualities, their sacrifices, the love they have for each other and their care for others. If that were all these letters show, publishing them would not be justified.

However, they do show more than that. They take us into the very edge of the battlefield to the smell of gunpowder, the roar of the canon and to the shattered bodies of dying soldiers. They reveal the utter stupidity that ignited and fueled the war that consumed millions of lives. They show the daily struggles and sufferings of families who are the innocent victims of this cataclysm. They show refugees fleeing the war zone, begging for crusts of bread and safety. Days after Nicolai returned home, the Bolsheviks overthrew the Provisional Government. The immediate results and long-term effects of that coup d'état we know only too well. If these letters induce us to work as diligently, as tirelessly, against war as war demands of us, then, I believe, Tina and Nicolai would consent to opening these letters for all to read.

We can assume that Nicolai and Tina would allow the camera to be turned to their future. To make that transition we need to look at the last two letters above, written a year apart: Nicolai's November 1917, and Susa's (Tina's sister) November 1918—an interval when grim changes take place in Russia. His letter reflects an optimism that stands in contrast to Susa's bleak view. He had just returned home when he drafted that business proposal to start a slaughterhouse that would produce sausages for the military. We might pause to scratch our heads at this anomaly. He had just witnessed the disintegration of the army, soldiers deserting by the thousands, and Moscow in the grips of civil war. Had he forgotten that only months ago he warned the citizens of Schoenfeld that big changes were coming to the Mennonite colonies, and those warnings probably did not include starting a sausage business. However, that plan was soon abandoned as the chaos and violence moved from large cities into the villages and estates like those of the Schoenfeld colony, Tina's family home. As these growing attacks by the Makhnovtse increased, Nicolai and Tina moved South to the safety of his mother's home in Mariental.

The Maknovtse were a revolutionary anarchist army of brigands named after and led by Nester Makhno. His hometown, Gulai-Polye, lay only twenty-five kilometers from Schoenfeld, and that colony being so close to the Makhnovtse headquarters was among the first to suffer their attacks. Tina's parents, the Peters, fell under increasing threat by these marauders who soon took full control the village of Schoenfeld. By the end of 1917, the civil war with its warring factions and open banditry had spread throughout Ukraine, striking Mennonite communities especially hard.

However, in March 1918, with the Treaty of Brest-Litovsk, Lenin made peace with Germany, giving her Ukraine. And so German troops moved into that region, and the unrest and civil chaos was checked somewhat by the presence of the German military. The Mennonites welcomed the German occupation, feeling sheltered against attacks by the Reds (Bolsheviks) and the growing Makhnovtse brigands. However, only eight months later on November 1918, the Great War ended with Germany's surrender, and her troops were withdrawn from Ukraine. Now the Mennonite colonies and others were exposed again to unrestrained attacks by the Reds and the Makhnovtse.[147] It was this anticipated renewed threat of the

---

[147] The Whites, an army formed loosely of some counter-revolutionaries, former Tsarist officers (Kadets) and some Cossacks groups struck battle with Ukrainian Socialists led by Petliura. "Jumping into the melee shortly thereafter were the Reds (the Bolsheviks) and partisan bandit groups named for the color

Makhnovtse and the Reds that Susa voices in her letter. She is in Berdiansk at that time studying to become a teacher when she writes to Nicolai and Tina, who now live in Mariental:

> *Of course, all of us are in great fear that the Bolsheviks will dominate again. I haven't heard from home for two weeks, don't even know if they [her family] are still alive. They say Makhno is not too far away from here now, and that the German army is leaving, perhaps tomorrow already. There won't be any left [German military] in the villages. Berdiansk is again in wartime preparedness. We have curfew from 12:00 midnight to 6:00 a.m.*

The concern for her family in Schoenfeld was well founded. Just weeks after she expressed that concern, some Makhnovtse bandits commandeered Schoenfeld, and moved into an estate across the street from the Peters' home and business. Within the year, Peters' (Tina's parents) home and business were ransacked by these bandits, and Peters himself barely escaped with his life. He fled South with his family to the village of Lichtefeld, not far from Mariental. But very soon even that region was exposed to warring factions, especially the Reds and the Maknovtse.[148]

But the Mennonites having collaborated with the German military before its withdrawal now came under brutal attacks. These attacks precipitated a dramatic change that severely challenged Mennonite integrity. In early 1919, some Mennonites formed armed militias, called Selbstschutz (self-defense) to protect their families and communities from attacks by the Makhnovtse and Red Army forces. These self-defense units had been encouraged, trained and supplied with arms by the departing Germans. But to take up arms was a violation of one of the foremost principles of the Mennonite faith, the principle of non-resistance.[149] "All those who use the sword will die by the sword." The issue of "taking up the sword" at this moment created great controversy and heated debate in the various Mennonites congregations. However, the Selbstschutz won the debate—the church leaders gave way. The few times my father, Nicolai, spoke of the Selbstschutz skirmishes with the Reds and the Makhnovstse suggested that the Selbstschutz initially held off their enemies. But very soon even they were overrun and then a vengeance was turned loose on the Mennonites in a measure reminiscent of a Greek tragedy.

This situation is perhaps best illustrated when General Dobenko marches into Gnadenfeld (municipal headquarters) with his Red troops and was met by two elders with the plea, "Comrade Dobenko, forgive us!" Dobenko responded, "You damned renegades from the faith of your fathers. For 400 years you could not take

---

symbolizing revolutionary anarchism." Consequently, civil war raged through the region and throughout Russia until 1922 when it became the Union of Soviet Socialist Republics: Rempel, David G. *A Mennonite Family in Tsarist Russia and the Revolution*, p. 208.

[148] Sometime in 1921 Bernard Peters returned to Schoenfeld with his son only to find the village razed to the ground. Nothing was left, not even the foundation of his home. An account of Peters' experiences during this period was written by him in 1929 and published in the "Steinbach Post" in 1937 in series. In this account, Peters identifies persons only by an alphabetical letter, he being 'S'. Why he names no one is unclear.

[149] Matthew 26:52 (Common English Bible) This freedom from bearing arms had been one of the privileges granted the Mennonites under the Great Charter issued by Prince Potemkin in 1774 and was renewed with some restrictions by Tsar Alexander II in 1878.

[up] arms, but now for your damned Kaiser.... I will not kill all, but my soldiers can plunder for three days and where they find Selbschützlers, they may execute them."[150] And his soldiers, joined by the Makhnovstchina, killed and plundered with a vengeance.

When some thugs came into the Rempel home in Mariental, they lined Nicolai, Tina and their children up against the wall, ransacked the house, looking for weapons, and taking whatever they wanted. Had they found weapons, Nicolai and perhaps his family would have been shot. Some time later, Nicolai came within seconds of being executed by a one of these brigands who accused him of having been with the Selbschütz. He forced Nicolai at gunpoint against a tree and was about to shoot him when another brigand intervened, insisting that Nicolai was innocent. But when the executioner persisted, they began to scuffle, giving Nicolai tome to escape. "An angel of God saved me," Nicolai still insisted decades later when he lay dying.[151]

Those experiences and others fortified Nicolai's belief never to take up arms, a belief he held throughout his life and urged on his sons. However, that instruction did not take root. Early in WWII his two oldest sons, Bill and Herman, enlisted in active duty with the Canadian armed forces and served in Europe throughout most of that war. But ironically the disappointment and worry that Nicolai and Tina endured turned to joy when they heard in 1945 that their son Herman had located through the Red Cross some relatives among the hundreds of Mennonite refugees in northern Germany who had fled from the USSR in front of the retreating German army. These relatives were two great aunts, Tante Susanna (Toews) and Tante Tina (Dyck), and an aunt, Tante Agatha. The latter came with four children teenage children. Herman had last seen these great aunts in 1925 as a six-year old when his family immigrated to Canada. The aunt with the four children, Tante Agatha, was the wife of Heinrich, Nicolai's youngest brother, frequently mentioned in the letters. Heinrich and two brothers, Abram and Aron, were disappeared in the 1930's during the Stalin purges.[152]

The reunion with these relatives in 1947 when they arrived at the Rempel home in British Columbia was highly emotional with tears of joy and sadness. The joy of course is easily understood, but the reunion rekindled in Tina and Nicolai memories of those dark days of revolution, civil war, banditry and the great famine of 1921 to 1923 that claimed two of their children. Nicolai summarizes what they had experienced during those darkest years in the piece below that appeared in a book by D. M. Hofer.[153]

---

[150] Toews, *Czars & Soviets & Mennonites*, p 90

[151] It was a relative who himself had participated in the Selbstschutz and when confronted by the Reds, he said it was not he, but Nicolai who had participated in the Selbschutz. When my father told me this, he excused that relative by saying that under such conditions it is hard to say what he himself might have done.

[152] Both, Great Aunt Susanna and Aunt Agatha, wrote autobiographical accounts of their experiences in the USSR and their flight that brought them to Canada in 1947.

[153] Nicolai Rempel, "Sleepless Nights" printed in D. M. Hofer, *Die Hungersnot in Russland: und, Unsere Reide Um die Welt* (Chicago: K.M.B. Publishing House, Illinois, 1924), p. 329

Gnadenfeld, June 1923

Sleepless Nights (Schlaflose Nächte)

The loud sobbing of our little daughter sent our hearts pounding again. There was no sleep for my wife and me because we lay in fear of the Maknovtsi brigands to come cursing and beating against the door or window, demanding that we unlock the door and let them in. Why but why did these brutes insist on coming at night as well as by day to do their plundering and butchering with nothing to stop them?

In spite of our every effort to protect our innocent children from this terrible fear, they too often lay wide awake in their beds anxiously listening for the thumping boots coming to the door, boot steps that made our blood curdle. Even the slightest footsteps brought sobs and cries of, "Papa, they're coming again. I'm so afraid."

⚜ ⚜ ⚜

Slowly these times subsided to a quieter life. Life became safer but a different enemy, a cry prompted not by the footfall of brigands but by a silent intruder, hunger, now raised our child's cry. The little voice now was raised not in fear but in pain. "Papa, the Americans will soon bring us some bread, won't they?"

"Yes, my dear child, but you must sleep now."

"But Papa, then we'll get some soup in the kitchen, won't we? Will the beggars eat there, too?"

"Perhaps, but now close your eyes, sweetheart, and go to sleep. We'll see what happens tomorrow."

Hours seemed to pass in this nightly chatter between my little 2 1/2-year-old daughter, Irma, and me. Our kitchen cupboards had long been bare. The only thing people could talk about, all conversation, was focused on food—how and when we would get some food. Even the smallest children had been promised that food parcels would arrive from American Mennonite Relief, and so we tried to comfort our children with this assurance that food would arrive—soon.

Yet as day followed day, anxious night followed anxious night, and still no relief came from starvation, and as thousands around us starved, my hope for the promised food began to fade. But my little chatterbox, Irma, repeatedly turned my despair to hope, kept the embers of faith alive, gave me strength.

But God had given us this little comforter, this 2 1/2-year-old chatterer, for but a brief time. Shortly after the food packages sent by the AMR[ii] had arrived and she had enjoyed a taste of them, it was too late for her! God took her back to Himself.

Except for the song of the nightingale that breaks the quiet of the spring nights, everything seemed to slumber in sweet peace. However, veiled behind this tranquility, lay sleepless parents, mothers and fathers, in their beds who could find no rest because of the anguish for their children. In these our most trying hours, we found comfort in the words of our Lord and Master. Our children too listened eagerly to the accounts of how a higher Being rules everything.

Yet today our children are told (in the presence of parents and teachers), "There is no God, there is no higher Being and if anyone tries to convince you, don't believe them. Don't listen to your parents and teachers if they try to convince you of a life hereafter." We have accepted all of the suffering and deprivation of these terrible times [the war, the revolution, the starvation] with the help of our trust in God ~ but to take away from us now our faith too would mean the destruction of our children. So we are driven to looking for a place where we can live out our faith in freedom and peace.

Nicolai Rempel

Sketch by Doris Rempel

PREPARING TO EMIGRATE

The last photo of Grandmother Rempel with some of her grandchildren, 1924. Standing: left Selma, cousin Abram Neufeld, Hilda and Alice right. Second row: cousin Mika Neufeld, Bill second from right next to Sarah Neufeld. Herman standing left of grandmother.

Nicolai and Tina at the time of emigration from the USSR 1915

Selma, Alice, Hilda and Eduard. Eduard died a few months before the family immigrated to Canada

Rempel Home in Mariental, Russia

Peters Home, Store & Machinery Sales in Schoenfeld, Russia

THEIR FIRST HOME IN CANADA

The farm Rempels purchased in Swalwell, Alberta, Canada 1928. Tina's parents lived in the cottage (front left) until 1931 when grandmother Peters died. The house set back was the first Rempel home. It was a 322-care farm, bought under heavy mortgage that was finally paid off when they sold the farm in 1944 and moved to British Columbia.

Off to church in their first means of transportation in Canada.

Family summer 1932: Back row—Nicolai, Bill, Alice, Tina, Selma, and Hilda. From left—Nicky, John, Irma, Herman: Teo, Looking away. Bernard is present but not yet visible. 1932

Home in East Chilliwack, B.C. 1945

The Family in 1949: Front row left: Hilda, Tina (Mother), Nicolai (Father), Selma; Second row: Irma, John, Teo (editor), Herman, Bill, Alice; Standing: Nicky, Bernie.

Nicolai and Tina 1953

Tina died in November 1955. Nicolai Died May 1956

IMMIGRATION TO CANADA

It was two years before the hopes and wishes expressed in the last line of Nicolai's letter (June 23) were realized. In September 1925, having been granted exit visas, they were able to leave the Soviet Union for Canada. Tina's parents and all of her siblings had immigrated to Canada in 1924, as had Nicolai's brother Johannes and his sister Tina (Harder) with their families. They had sent back favorable reports of their new life in this Promised Land. However, it was not easy for Tina and Nicolai with their five children to say farewell to their homeland, Russia. Their leave-taking was fraught with the pain of tearing up their roots, leaving most of Nicolai's family behind, including the graves of their two little children, Irma and Eduard. But this new land, Canada, offered the hope for a soil that would restore those broken roots and let their family, their faith and their Mennonite identity flourish in peace.

So on a morning in late September 1925, they found themselves at the same railway station near Gnadenfeld from which Nicolai had departed for the war eleven years before. This time again hundreds had gathered at the station, some leaving, others to bid them farewell. About a thousand émigrés boarded the train made up of a series of boxcars outfitted with bunk beds, some crude cooking facilities and primitive toilets. But the preceding decade had prepared them for these minimal survivor facilities on their six-day trip to the gate of departure from Soviet Union into Latvia. The trip to their final destination in Canada took one month. From Riga, Latvia, they went by boat to South Hampton, England, where they were given physical examinations, and then on by train to Liverpool where they boarded the ship Mountcairn for the ten-day sail across the Atlantic to Quebec. From there an immigrant train carried them across Canada, dropping off individuals and families along the way, most of whom would move in with relatives or be hired as domestics.

And so it was that Tina and Nicolai with their children, Alice, Hilda, Selma, Bill and Herman, arrived in Acme, Alberta, on October 25, 1925, the farthest point west that that train would take immigrants. They arrived essentially penniless, with a debt to the Canadian Pacific Railway for steerage, with their few belongings, and even fewer words of English, some treasures in photographs, and the letters enclosed between the covers of this book. They with other immigrant families were warmly received by local Mennonite farm families and were fed in the Mennonite (Holdemann) church. By the end of the meal the farmers and others had looked these new people over and selected those whom they would take home to serve as farmhands and domestic help. The Rempels with their five children and Tina heavy with another child, were not exactly what the farmers were looking for, so they were the last to be selected. One Wilhelm Redekopp, a Mennonite bachelor who had not known the bathtub in some weeks, took the Rempel family into his home, a clapboard house on his farm four miles from the nearest village, Sunnyslope, where he gave them free reign, so to speak. But they soon learned that Redekopp lacked in cleanliness was inversely proportional to his generosity and big heart. And so Tina and her daughters took the free reign in hand, cleaning and scrubbing until the place was livable and insisted that Ohm Wehlem (as he became affectionately known to our family) to take a bath. It was Ohm Welhem's goodwill, good humor and generosity that reignited the family's courage and helped to set them on the path to a better life.

It was also through Ohm Wehlem that Nicolai came to his new vocation, a Knoake Dockta (bonesetter), as he came to be called in the community, a vocation he would pursue the rest of his life. It happened that in the dead of winter Ohm Wehlem fell on the ice and fractured his leg. Because there was no doctor within miles and the snow lay deep, Nicolai's experience as a medic came to the rescue. During his service as a medic, he had assisted doctors with literally hundreds of similar and much more severe injuries. So he set the fracture, placed the leg in a cast, and the family took care of Ohm until he was able to walk again. Soon Nicolai was mending fractures, dislocated joints and other injuries of persons within the larger community. All the while, like most immigrants, the Rempel family took whatever jobs they could. By the spring of 1928 they had saved enough to buy, under heavy mortgage, a somewhat neglected farm from Mrs. Mildred Browning, who had been unable to maintain the place after the death of her husband.

So the family moved onto the farm with its clapboard house, dilapidated outbuildings and poor farm machinery, some draft horses and a few cattle. It was an answer to the great yearning so often expressed in Tina and Nicolai's letters. It was a place of their own. Because the farm came with grain already sprouting, they were able to harvest enough wheat to meet their first mortgage payment that fall. The insurance company that managed the mortgage for the widow Browning also managed to splice into the contract fire insurance on the house, on the rickety barn and even on a henhouse. In 1935 when hail struck destroying the wheat crop records show Manufacturers Insurance Company squeezing Nicolai to make payments on the arrears in principal, interest and insurance. Had it not been for Mrs. Browning's kindness to renegotiate a more lenient contract, the Rempel family would have found themselves homeless once again.

In spite of these and other difficulties, their years in that community served them well. Nicolai's popularity as Knoake Dockta had grown as had the size of the family. They had added five Canadians by 1932: Irma, John, Teodor, Nicholas and Bernard, bringing the count to ten. Tina's parents, Bernard and Margareta Peters, had also joined them on the farm in 1928, moving into a small cabin, not quite meeting the standards of the residence they had enjoyed in Schoenfeld. Tina's youngest sister, Mika, with husband David Klassen, had moved into a farm house nearby where they too grew their family, eventually to eleven children. So it was that the Klassen and Rempel cousins grew up together and became life-long friends. Susa Peters, Tina's sister, who wrote the last letter in the series, was the dynamo that pushed the Klassen and Rempel children to higher education.[154] Tina's brother, Willie, and his family lived within driving range, as did Nicolai's brother Johannes. And so with a few other relatives who would come to visit now and then, the

---

[154] Aunt Susie (Peters) had begun her teaching career in Ukraine and took up teaching again in Canada. She encouraged and funded the education of many nieces and nephews. Her teaching career ranged from Ukraine to isolated village schools in Alberta, to a Hutterite colony, and to Inuit People at Reindeer Station in the North West Territories, even accompanying them on a whale hunt to the Beaufort Sea one summer. In 1945 she worked with the Mennonite Central Committee caring for war orphans in London, then in Holland and Germany to help locate Mennonites refugees who had fled from the Soviet in 1944.

Rempel-Peters extended family was re-established. Missing were Nicolai's other siblings and his mother.

The Mennonite Brethren in that community had begun a church fellowship; initially meeting in homes but soon had their own little church. Nicolai served as minister and Uncle David Klassen the choir director. The most cherished memories of my childhood church experience was the singing of old hymns in four-part harmony, rarely heard in congregational singing today. Sunday afternoon visits with relatives or friends were never without a religious devotion that included the singing of a hymn or two, usually a cappella.

And so the years rolled by in Alberta through good crops and bad, drought and hail, terrible snowstorms and beautiful summer days. In five of the last eight years that they farmed, hail damaged the crops. One year, just weeks before harvest, hail drove every wheat stalk into the black earth. After the storm subsided, Nicolai walked out onto the blackened field, stood there silently for many minutes, talking to his God (as he told me years later). "If we honor our father and mother, You promised that it would go well with us. I have always done that, so why has this happened? How will we feed our children?" I can still see him walking back, hunched over in despair. The next morning a farmer, C.W. Toews, drove onto the yard with ten hundred-pound bags of flour. "Brother Rempel, I heard of your misfortune and thought this flour would help you."

After Canada entered WWII in 1939, the market began to recover, and the price of grain, pork and milk began to nudge upward, as did the cost of farming. A letter from the Canada Board of Colonization, June 9, 1941, shows that a renegotiated mortgage was larger than the original in 1928. Although Nicolai's medical work kept him busy, it brought little income. Because he was not a licensed "doctor," he could not set a fee. Whatever the patients volunteered to drop into the small metal container at the door as they left, that was it, and it was little enough since most people were in similar straits. But the produce from the farm, vegetables, eggs and meat, kept the family in food, and wheat ground to flour by the local miller, put bread on the table. Ministers in the Mennonite churches received no salary then.

When in 1944 our farm was sold and we were preparing to move to Chilliwack, British Columbia, petitions were circulated asking my father not to leave. The mayor of Three Hills wrote, "I have learned recently that you have sold your farm and intend leaving this district. I regret very much that you have made this decision… Mr. Rempel, our district really needs a man of your ability, and I would like you to give the matter very serious thought before you definitely decide to leave us." *C.J. Davidson.*

The president of the Board Of Trade wrote, "…I regret indeed that you have made the decision [to leave] and wish you would reconsider this matter. I might point out that you have made a considerable number of friends where you are now; you have gained a reputation as a bone specialist, which is worth considerable [to the community]" *L. H. Arnold.*

Although not named in those petitions, it was Tina who made Nicolai's public success possible, sacrificing unstintingly for him and her family. The list of things she did for him and her children is endless. Many years later, after our parents were long gone, my brother John assessed our family dynamic in these words: "Dad was not a good farmer, perhaps because he was too busy serving the Lord and his church. He would travel to conferences and other fledgling churches to preach and might be gone for two or three days. The family suffered, especially Mother, she took care of the home front [as she had during WWI] humming some hymn softly while she toiled on, never complaining. I regret to this day that we didn't love our mother more." In the late 1930s Nicolai was gone some months doing a residency at the Thiessen Osteopathic Clinic in Nebraska. That is the only time I saw my mother overwhelmed by the task of keeping the home and the farm going. She stood in her garden weeping quietly.

Our move in May 1944, to a fourteen-acre dairy farm in the beautiful Fraser Valley in British Columbia was dramatic and disruptive. In Chilliwack, my brother John and sister Irma helped on the farm until they found other employment. Our father began to set up his medical practice immediately and soon enjoyed a full schedule of patients. He also became engaged in establishing the East Chilliwack Mennonite Brethren church where he became the lead minister. This church, too, like other Mennonite churches established in British Columbia in the 1930s and 1940s consisted mainly of recent migrants from the prairie provinces, part of whose identity was still the socially-gated community, a spillover from Russia, that had been destroyed with the revolution. But the adhesive that had held the Mennonites together for twenty-two generations was now failing.

My two younger brothers, Nicky and Bernard, and I were sent off to school several days after our arrival in Chilliwack. I found myself quite bewildered among the hundreds of students milling around in long hallways of the high school as I tried to find my classrooms. I was a transplant, a migrant. Just a week before, my two brothers and I were still innocent Mennonite boys in bib overalls attending a one-room, eight-grade school with a total of seventeen students. Now in this big high school I heard derisive comments about "Mennonites yellow draft dodgers" and other uncomplimentary names. The fact that my two brothers were serving in the army in Europe, both having married English women, did not quiet caustic remarks. This scoffing at the Mennonites made me feel quite out of place, and I needed place, an identity. So I tried to the hide the markers that fingered me as a Mennonite, seeking acceptance by the "Englische" students. And I succeeded, somewhat! This was the plight of many young people in the Mennonite communities in western Canada.

In 1917 in Moscow, Nicolai had joined 700 other medics who raised their voices, warning their elders back in the colonies who were entrenched in their "old Mennonite ways" that they should adapt to the great political and social changes that were transpiring in Russia, to join the revolution. These men, the medics, sent representatives to the Minister of Justice asking for assurance that they, the Mennonites, were Russian citizens with equal rights of all citizens. This was a struggle for identity. There had been voices in some quarters accusing them of being Prussians "spying for the Kaiser."[155] However, there seems to be something ironic

---

[155] See Nicolai's letters April 15 and May 6, 1917

about this last minute attempt by the Mennonites to establish a Russian identity. How had it been possible for these people to retain their religion, their Dutch roots, the German language, and their Mennonite culture for six generations in that "foreign land" Russia (Ukraine), whose language and social norms they never truly embraced. Nicolai's letters never mention Russians among his close associates. Although he was most sympathetic toward the wounded Russians and cared for them with compassion, as did the other Mennonite medics, it appears that he had no close association with any of the Russians, including the Russian members of the staff on Royal Red Cross Evacuation train No. 160. It was only when the Mennonites came under loud attack in the newspapers as Prussian sympathizers and a call went out for the redistribution of their land that they stepped forward, proclaimed their loyalty to Russia and requested full citizenship. Had they been lulled into complacent slumber enjoying promised privileges assured them in the *Privilegium* those many decades?

In Canada, Nicolai and Tina tried desperately to retain their Russian Mennonite heritage and pass it on to their offspring. In Alberta, they had sent their Russian-born children to Bible School instead of high school, hoping that they would become certified Mennonite Brethren. Certification took hold with the three daughters, Alice, Hilda and Selma, but their two sons, Bill and Herman, very soon fled the field, deserted, remaining sequestered from their tearful, prayerful parents for some weeks. I once heard a theologian caution parents against trying to create their children in an image of their own fantasy. "Children are the most important guests you will ever have in your home. You are there as their guide, not their creator." One could say the same about a church that forces its members into molds of its perception of Godliness.

Salman Rushdie says that an immigrant suffers a triple disruption, *He loses his place, he enters into an alien language, and he finds himself surrounded by beings whose social behavior and code is very unlike…his own. And this is what makes migrants such important figures: Because roots, language, and social norms have been the three most important parts of what it means to be human. The migrant, denied all three, is obligated to find new ways of being human.*[156]

This was the plight of Nicolai and Tina's children on their arrival in Canada, and that to some extent was my plight, a migrant from the Alberta prairies to the beautiful Fraser Valley that on my arrival was in full blush with cherry blossoms—and I was in blush with shame of my Mennonite heritage. Until the February Revolution, 1917, when Kaiser Nicholas II was forced to abdicate, these letters touch mainly on the complex issues faced by a Mennonite couple who are separated by the Great War. The family held together during the civil war with its brutal anarchy, retaining their Mennonite identity. When they arrived in Canada, they tried to reestablish the "Mennonite" way of life they had enjoyed in Russia until the Great War. But in the new country, much to Nicolai and Tina's disappointment, their children shed much of that identity and by the third generation of their offspring, croissants had replaced the zwieback and hymns sung in four-part

---

[156] Günter Grass, "Introduction," in *On Writing and Politics* (New York: Harcourt, Brace Jovanovich, 1986, p. xi.

harmony were now hot gospel songs projected on the big screen, supported by electric guitars and drums.

William Faulkner points out that the great problem of 20th century is our loss of identity. The century has instilled in us the phantom belief that we are what we do, i.e., *our jobs,* what we *own*, and what *others think of us*. We can be robbed of those at any moment, and who are we then?

The letters of Nicolai and Tina Rempel, however, suggest an alternate path to identity: commitment to family, serving others, working for peace, and believing in a power higher than ourselves to help us love our neighbor. That is the legacy they leave their descendants.

Children and Grandchildren of Katharina and Nicolai Rempel

Alice (1910-2001) wed 1935 to Henry Unger (1909-1977)
 Children: Werner (D), Henry (D), Theodor, Waldemar, Ernst (D)

Hilda (1911-2001) wed 1933 to Nick Langemann: (1913-1991)
 Children: Rita, Ralph, Sigrid and Helen (D)

Selma (1913-2014) wed 1937 to Henry Fleming: (1906-1989)
 Children: Florence, Dorothy, Victoria, Marie Anne, and Terence

William (1917-2000) wed 1944 to Joyce Fillingham (1922-2005)
 Children: Gary, Barbara, Stuart and Gillian

Irma (1919-1923)

Herman (1921-2003) wed 1944 to Mary Kane (Divorced 1945)
 Children: Peter
Second marriage 1948 to Irene Stepsky (1925—)
 Children: Irene, Robert and JoAnn

Eduard (1924-1925)

Irma (1925-1980) wed 1951 to Frank Willms: (1926-2009)
 Children: Charles, Diane and Paul

John (1927-2001) wed 1953 to Ruth Gruenhagen (1931—)
 Children: Joanne, Kenneth (D) and Allen

Teodor (1929-) wed 1953 to Doris Loewen (1932—)
 Children: David, Marcus, Timothy and Nicholas

Nicholas (1930-1950)

Bernard (1932-) wed 1955 to Teresa Ruston (1926—)
 Children: Rhonda, Robyn and Donald

Preußische Haus-Bibel,
das ist:
die gantze

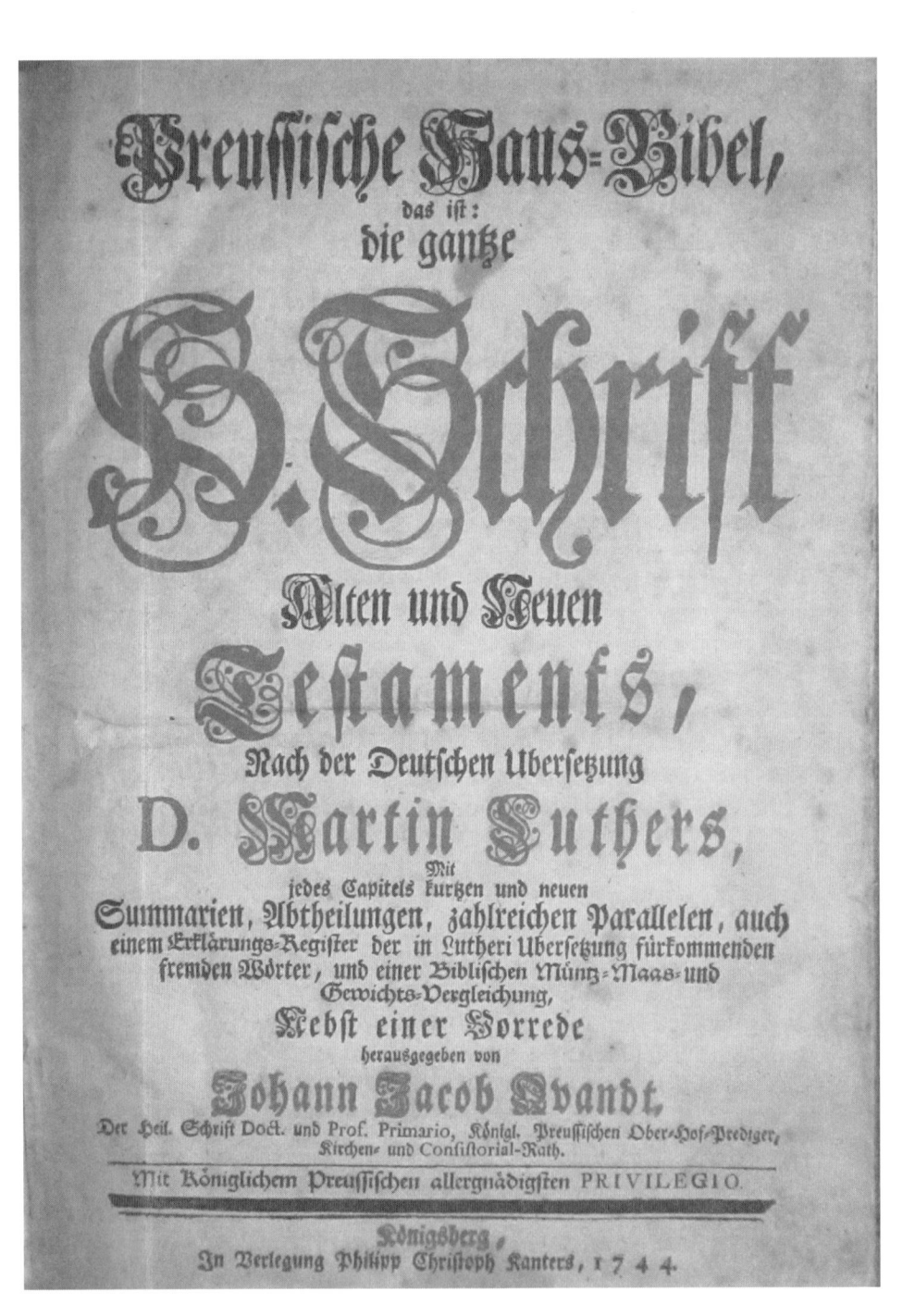

H. Schrifft

Alten und Neuen
Testaments,
Nach der Deutschen Ubersetzung
D. Martin Luthers,
Mit
jedes Capitels kurtzen und neuen
Summarien, Abtheilungen, zahlreichen Parallelen, auch
einem Erklärungs-Register der in Lutheri Ubersetzung fürkommenden
fremden Wörter, und einer Biblischen Müntz-Maas- und
Gewichts-Vergleichung,
Nebst einer Vorrede
herausgegeben von
Johann Jacob Qvandt,
Der Heil. Schrifft Doct. und Prof. Primario, Königl. Preussischen Ober-Hof-Prediger,
Kirchen- und Consistorial-Rath.

Mit Königlichem Preussischen allergnädigsten PRIVILEGIO.

Königsberg,
In Verlegung Philipp Christoph Kanters, 1 7 4 4.

The Family Heritage Bible 1744

Entries Made in the Bible

First Entry made by Sara Woelk March 8, 1807

This beautiful Bible Book belongs to me, Sara Woelk, nee Janzen. That is my joy that I can cling to my God: Psalms 73:28

―――――0―――――

Second Entry made by Abram Sudermann on March 10, 1821

The Bible entry above was written by the hand of our blessed, departed mother, Sara Woelk, who died in the year 1821 on the 10th of August, at Kaldova [Prussia] and was interred (begraben) at the Heubodenschen Cemetery on this date. (She) was born in the year 1750 on the 25th of August at Neukirch in the great Werder at Marienburg. [Vistula Delta] The above handwritten entry reads thus: "1807 the 8th of March. This beautiful Bible Book belongs to me, Sara Woelk, nee Janzen. It is my joy that I can cling to my God: Psalms 73:28"

That year and day (1807, the 8th of March) was for my dear mother[-in-law] a very difficult time in that her almost new house was torn down by the [our] enemy [Napoleon] in order to raise on that site a barricade (Schanzen) as a defense against their enemy [We Prussians]—In this her rather dire situation, she sought comfort in her beautiful Bible book and found it. And on that above-mentioned occasion, wrote those few but comforting words.

I, her son-in-law, [Abram Sudermann] had the fortune of knowing this loving, pious mother-in-law [Sara Woelk] from 1816 to her blessed end and to have her live with me on the property that I had taken over from her through purchase.

―――――0―――――

Third Entry made by Anna Lange on the 30th of August 1865

Abram Sudermann in Kaldova born in Elsing on the 29th of July 1790.

In the year 1865, on the 30th of August, my dear father, Abram Sudermann, who made the above entry, died in firm faith in his savior and redeemer Jesus Christ, and on the 10th of January, my dear mother Elizabeth Sudermann, [nee Woelk] the youngest daughter of the above mentioned dear grandmother [Sara Woelk] died gently and peacefully in the Lord. May the faithful shepherd and bishop of our souls keep His promise and make it come true for us so that no power can tear us out of His Hand and grant us a blessed reunion (Wiedersehen) with our dear parents before His throne.

I, Anna Lange, nee Sudermann, have inherited this beautiful Bible book from my dear parents. Your Word is a lamp to my feet and a light on my path.

―――――0―――――

Fourth Entry by Sara Rempel nee Lange on June the 10th, 1924, Nicolai's mother

1924, the 10th of June, the second day of Holy Pentecost, (new calendar)

My dear children, Katharina [nee Rempel] and Johannes (Harder)! When you open this Bible, my wish is that it will always grant you lasting comfort and true peace, strength of faith the can move mountains, the mountains of worries, of pain and sorrow. Yes, that it may all of the days of your life be a comfort, a support. That this my precious word of God may always be a light on your path….May the Lord shield you with His protective hand on your dangerous journey. May He be with you on all of your paths when you have reached your destination. [The young couple was immigrating to Canada] The Lord bless you and keep you. May His face shine upon you and grant you His peace in time and in eternity.   Your deeply loving mother, Sara Rempel [nee Lange]

The first entry in this Bible was made on March 8, 1807, by Nicolai's great-great grandmother, Sara Woelk, in Kaldova, Prussia (now Poland) on the day Napoleon's troops marched onto her yard, tore down her almost new house and built barricades on the site. The piety expressed in the first entry in **Family Heritage Bible** by great grandmother Woelk reached forward into the letters of Nicolai and Tina.

BIBLIOGRAPHY

Baedeker, Karl, *Russia A Handbook for Travelers* (New York: Random House, 1971, A Facismile of original 1914 edition).

Dyck, Cornelius J., *An Introduction to Mennonite History*. Third Edition. (Scottsdale, PA: Herald Press, 1993).

Grass, Gunter, *On Writing and Politics* (New York: Harcourt, Brace and Jovanovich, 1986)

Friesen, Abraham, *In Defense of Privilege: Russian Mennonites and the State Before and During World War I* (Winnipeg: Kindred Productions, 2006).

Friesen, Rudy, *Building on the Past: Mennonite Architecture, Landscape and Settlements in Russia/Ukraine* (Winnipeg: Raduga Publications, 2004).

Hofer, D.M., *Die Hungersnot in Russland* (Chicago: K.M.B. Publishing House, 1924).

Loewen, Harry, ed., *Shepherds, Servants and Prophets: Leadership Among the Russian Mennonites, ca. 1880-1960* (Kitchener, ON: Pandora Press, 2003).

Loewen, Harry and Nolt, Steven, *Through Fire and Water: An Overview of Mennonite History* (Scottdale, PA: Herald Press, 2003).

Katkov, George, *Russia 1917: The February Revolution* (New York: Harper and Row, 1967).

Katkov, George, Russia 1917: *The Kornilov Affair. Kerensky and the Break-up of the Russian Army* (London: Longman, 1980).

Peters, Victor, *Nester Machno: The Life of an Anarchist* (Winnipeg: Echo Books, 1970).

Pipes, Richard, *A Concise History of the Russian Revolution* (New York: Random House, 1996).

Quiring, Walter and Bartel, Helen, *Als Ihre Zeit zu Ende War* (Saskatoon: Modern Press, 1964).

Rempel, David G. with Cornelia Rempel Carlson, *A Mennonite Family in Tsarist Russia and the Soviet Union, 1789-1923* (Toronto: University of Toronto Press, 2002).

Regehr, T.D., *A Generation of Vigilance: The Lives and Work of Johannes and Tina Harder* (Winnipeg: Canadian Mennonite University Press, 2009).

Rempel, Henry, *KjennJie Noch Plaudietsch?: A Mennonite Low German Dictionary* (Altona, MN: Friesen Printers, 1984).

Rodzianko, M.V. "Krushenie Imperii," *Arkhiv Russkoi Revoliutsii*, volume XVII (Berlin: 1926). Translated by J.S. Curtiss in *The Russian Revolutions of 1917* (New York: Van Norstrand, 1957), pp. 82-85.

Toews, John B., *Czars, Soviets & Mennonites* (Newton, KS: Faith and Life Press, 1982).

Toews, John B. Translator and Editor, *Mennonites in the Ukraine Amid Civil War and Anarchy, 1917-1920* (Fresno: Center for Mennonite Brethren Studies, 2013).

Toews, Paul, ed., *Bridging Troubled Waters: Mennonite Brethren at Mid-Century* (Winnipeg: Kindred Productions, 1995).

Urry, James, *Mennonites Politics and Peoplehood: Europe - Russia - Canada, 1525-1980* (Winnipeg: University of Manitoba Press, 2006).

SKETCHES AND PAINTING

Sketches by Doris Rempel

Painting by Canon Tolon, *Untitled* (polyptych) 1996, Oilstick on mylar, mounted on canvas, 49 x 36 inches.